The Columbia Guide to
American Indians of the Southeast

The Columbia Guides to American Indian History and Culture

The Columbia Guide to
American Indians of the Southeast

Theda Perdue
and
Michael D. Green

COLUMBIA   UNIVERSITY   PRESS   NEW   YORK

COLUMBIA UNIVERSITY PRESS
Publishers Since 1893
New York   Chichester, West Sussex

Copyright © 2001 Columbia University Press

Library of Congress Cataloging-in-Publication Data

Perdue, Theda, 1949–
    The Columbia guide to American Indians of the Southeast /
Theda Perdue and Michael D. Green.
        p. cm. — (The Columbia guides to American Indian history and culture)
    Includes bibliographical references and index.
    ISBN 0-231-11570-9 (alk. paper)
    1. Indians of North America—Southern States—History. 2. Indians of North America—
Southern States—Social life and customs. I. Green, Michael D., 1941– . II. Title. III. Series.
    E78.S65 P45 2001
    975′.00497—dc21

                                                                                    2001035338

c   10 9 8 7 6 5 4 3 2

Credits

All maps have been prepared by Christopher L. Brest.

Figures 1, 3: Georgia Department of Natural Resources, Historic Preservation Division.

2: Courtesy of the Research Laboratories of Archaeology, University of North Carolina, Chapel Hill.

4: Cahokia Mounds State Historic Site.

5, 6, 7, 8, 9: From Jacques Le Moyne de Morgues, *Brevis narratio eorum quae in Florida Americae provincia Gallis acciderunt, secunda in illam nauigatione, duce Renato de Laudoniere classis praefecto: anno MDLXIII* (Francoforti ad Moenum: Týpis Ioanis Wecheli, sumtibus vero Theodori de brý, venales reperiutur in officina Sigismundi Feirabedii, 1591). Copy in the North Carolina Collection, Wilson Library, University of North Carolina, Chapel Hill.

10, 11, 12, 13, 14, 16, 20: Copyright © The British Museum.

15: Courtesy of the Research Laboratories of Archaeology, University of North Carolina, Chapel Hill.

17: National Anthropological Archives, Smithsonian Institution. Neg. no. 1129-b-1.

18: Greenville County Museum of Art, Greenville, S.C. Gift of the Museum Association, Inc.

19: New Orleans Museum of Art. Gift of William E. Groves.

21, 22: From Thomas L. M'Kenney and James Hall, *History of the Indian Tribes of North America*, 2 vols. (Philadelphia: F. W. Greenough, 1838–44). Copy in the Rare Book Collection, The University of North Carolina, Chapel Hill.

23, 24: Smithsonian American Art Museum. Gift of Mrs. Joseph Harrison Jr.

25: The Georgia Cherokee descendants of Rachel Martin Davis (photo courtesy of the Atlanta History Center).

26: Mississippi Department of Archives and History.

27, 28, 30, 31: The Archives Division, Oklahoma Historical Society.

29: *Harper's Weekly*, 30 March 1872. From a copy in the Rare Books Collection, Wilson Library, University of North Carolina, Chapel Hill.

32: National Anthropological Archives, Smithsonian Institution. Neg. no. 1044-A.

33: National Anthropological Archives, Smithsonian Institution. Neg. no. 44,353A.

34: Courtesy of Wilma Mankiller.

35: Photo by Danny Bell.

Contents

Acknowledgments

The authors would like to thank those who helped bring this project to completion. Three history graduate students at the University of North Carolina, Joe Anoatubby, Karl Davis, and Rose Stremlau provided research assistance, and their names appear on the sections on which they worked. David Baird, Harry Kersey, and Vincas Steponaitis critiqued chapters in manuscript, Patricia Wickman made suggestions relating to the Florida Seminoles, and John Finger read the entire narrative. A number of tribes and state Indian agencies provided useful information. Danny Bell performed numerous tasks associated with getting a manuscript ready for the process of publication. Summer grants from the Institute for Research in the Social Sciences and the Center for the Study of the American South underwrote research. Although all projects such as this one are collaborative in a number of ways, the authors accept responsibility for any errors.

Introduction

The Native peoples of the Southeastern United States have regionally unique cultures and histories. By the time of European contact, the cultivation of corn, squash, and beans enabled them to establish chiefdoms with a hierarchical social structure, complex ritual life, and monumental architecture in the form of temple mounds. The European invasion dramatically altered this culture through disease, economic dependency, and the erosion of political autonomy. When the Europeans who claimed the South as their own found that wealth lay in the soil, Native people became obstacles to the exploitation of the land. By the mid-nineteenth century the large Indian tribes had been forced west of the Mississippi where they faced new challenges, and the remnant groups that remained in the South struggled to sustain themselves and their ethnic identity. Despite intense pressure, they succeeded. In Oklahoma and the Southeast Native peoples adapted ancient cultural traditions to new circumstances, demonstrating remarkable creativity and persistence. Instead of disappearing, Native Southerners are increasing in number, and, across the region, their influence is being felt. This book tells their story. To make it as useful and accessible to readers as possible, we have divided it into four parts, which are connected conceptually to each other but may be used independently.

In part 1 we present a broad overview of the cultures and histories of Southeastern Indian people. We begin chapter 1, "Writing About Native Southerners," with a discussion of some of the approaches that scholars have used to try to make sense of the Native American past. In subsequent chapters we draw on work from many disciplines to describe the experiences of Native people. The chapters are both chronological and thematic, and they try to construct a narrative based on common experiences and, at the same time, to convey a sense of the enormous diversity in Native America.

In chapter 2, "Native Southerners," we examine the period before European contact. We rely heavily on the oral traditions of Native people and on archaeological evidence. A distinct culture began to emerge among Native people in the Southeast about 8000 B.C. They learned how to exploit the region's rich environment and developed a way of life based on seasonal migrations. By 3000 B.C. agriculture had emerged, and over the next four millennia farming permitted the development of complex cultural traditions. In particular, the Mississippian tradition, which reached its height in the centuries just before the arrival of Europeans, relied on intensive agriculture to support its hierarchical chiefdoms, elaborate ceremonial cycle, and construction of enormous temple mounds.

When Europeans arrived in the Southeast in the sixteenth century, they encountered mostly Mississippian peoples. Chapter 3, "The European Invasion," deals with early European exploration and its impact on Southeastern Indians. Hernando de Soto commanded the most extensive expedition through the Southeast in the sixteenth century, and the chronicles of his expedition paint a dramatic picture of Mississippian life. De Soto and other invaders, however, disrupted that way of life by destabilizing polities and introducing diseases to which Native people had no immunity. Epidemic disease had a particularly profound effect on the Native Southeast, and by the seventeenth century, when the French and English began to expand into the region, Mississippian chiefdoms had largely disappeared.

Chapter 4, "Native Peoples and European Empires," explores the ways in which Spain, France, and England attempted to incorporate Native people into their empires and the response of Native peoples to this attempt. Spain colonized Florida to provide protection to treasure fleets from Mexico, but the Spaniards also undertook the conversion of Native people. A chain of missions across North Florida disrupted Native societies as priests demanded that mission residents not only follow a new religion but also adopt new patterns of work, new family relationships, and new lines of authority. But the missions also provided some protection in an increasingly unstable world. In the early eighteenth century British colonists and their Indian allies destroyed the missions, and the surviving priests and converts relocated to St. Augustine. For over half a century following this invasion, the British primarily engaged the French in the contest for the continent. Native people in the Southeast generally tried to remain neutral, but the French, in particular, offered Indians powerful inducements in the form of gifts to ally with them. Native people took French presents, but they used these tokens to engage in play-off diplomacy with Britain and Spain. Ultimately, Britain won the contest among European powers, ending this successful strategy. When Britain subsequently lost the American Revolution, Native people found themselves confronted with an incessant demand for their lands and little concept of how to deal with the avarice.

Following the American Revolution, the United States was in no position to force land from Native people, and so it adopted the British practice of acquiring lands through treaties. This practice recognized the sovereignty of Native people, that is, their right to make decisions for themselves. Chapter 5, "'Civilization' and Removal," focuses on the development of a federal Indian policy that encouraged Native people to agree to land cessions. Central to the effort was the inculcation of the values of "civilization," particularly the concept of private property and the advantages of personal wealth. Ultimately, the five large Indian nations in the Southeast, the Cherokees, Chickasaws, Choctaws, Creeks, and Seminoles, did cede their land and move west of the Mississippi to Indian territory in a forced migration euphemistically called "removal."

Chapter 6, "Native Southerners in the West," examines the history of the Southern Indians who went west and established new homes, governments, schools, and ways of life in what is today the state of Oklahoma. Drawn into the American Civil War on the side of the Confederacy, the Five Tribes signed Reconstruction treaties that eroded their sovereignty and opened their lands to railroads and economic development. Political and economic pressure led to the allotment of tribal land to individuals in the 1890s, the formal dissolution of tribal governments, and the admission of Oklahoma to the Union in 1907 as a state in which Indians are a minority.

Chapter 7, "Those Who Remained," looks at the Native people who did not go west in the 1830s. As the cotton kingdom expanded and racial slavery became more entrenched during this period, the South increasingly regarded itself as a society composed of free whites and enslaved blacks. All free people of color, the category into which Indians fell, were anomalous, but Indians, who lived in their own communities, maintained distinct traditions, and had no history of bondage, were particularly so. After the Civil War, the dichotomy shifted to white/black, with Native people often categorized as "black," or, in the parlance of the time, "colored." The history of

Indians who remained in the South is largely that of their struggle to retain their ethnic identity and the rights—civil, land, and treaty rights—inherent in that ethnicity. Some tribes have managed to do so through federal recognition and the retention of reservations while others have achieved state recognition and/or social acceptance as Indians.

Part 2 of this book, "People, Places, and Events, A to Z" provides an alphabetical listing, which is cross-referenced in bold type, to some of the individuals who have played important roles in the history of Native Southerners. The listing also includes places that have important cultural and/or historic meaning, the major treaties that Southern Indians have negotiated, and the federal Indian policies and chief legislative acts that have affected the lives of Southern Indians.

Part 3 is a chronology of the major events in the history of Native Southerners. The timeline also includes events, such as wars or federal legislation, that had an impact on all Native people. Most entries also appear in parts 1 and 2, and we encourage readers to think about these events in the broader context that can be found in part 1.

Part 4 lists a number of resources to which readers can turn to learn more about Southern Indians. We have included the addresses of state Indian commissions or offices as well as those of state and federally recognized tribes. Other tribes that have had contact with the Bureau of Indian Affairs but have no formal recognition from either the states or the BIA have simply been listed. We urge readers embarking on serious research projects to consult the section on bibliographies and finding aids. Our own bibliography is by no means comprehensive, but we have compiled these titles for those who want to go beyond the resources we have included here. We have not listed manuscript holdings in this bibliography, largely because they are numerous, scattered, specific to particular projects, and of limited value to most readers of this volume, but we have listed many published primary sources. Most of these are widely available in public libraries or through interlibrary loan, and they will provide endless term paper topics and sufficient documentation for many scholarly projects. Although ethnohistorians use oral tradition and archaeology, we established distinct categories for these because their methodologies and disciplinary conventions distinguish these books from those in most of the subsequent categories. In the section on general works, which includes works that deal with more than one tribe, and in the sections on particular tribes, we have drawn books from a number of disciplines, but especially from history and anthropology. Virtually all are based on documentary evidence, develop a narrative line, and forego technical language or jargon. For "Selected Fiction" we chose works by South-eastern Indian authors or by non-Indians who write about Southeastern Indians. We realize that this only scratches the surface, but literature is not the focus of this book. The same could be said for the remaining categories— we provide an introduction to film, museums, and internet resources rather than a comprehensive listing. Internet resources present a unique challenge since they change often as sites are updated or abandoned and new sites come online. Nevertheless, we offer a place for readers to begin, and we wish them well as they explore their own avenues of interest.

Readers, after all, are the reason books are written, and we hope that this volume will be interesting to readers who know little about the Indians of the Southeast as well as useful to those who are specialists. At its core Native American history is tribal history because each people has its own cultural traditions and historical experiences. This work makes no effort to alter that essential character, but it does seek to weave the disparate threads of tribal histories into a common cloth. In the process, we hope to give readers a view of Native people not only as members of sovereign tribes but also as Southerners and as Americans.

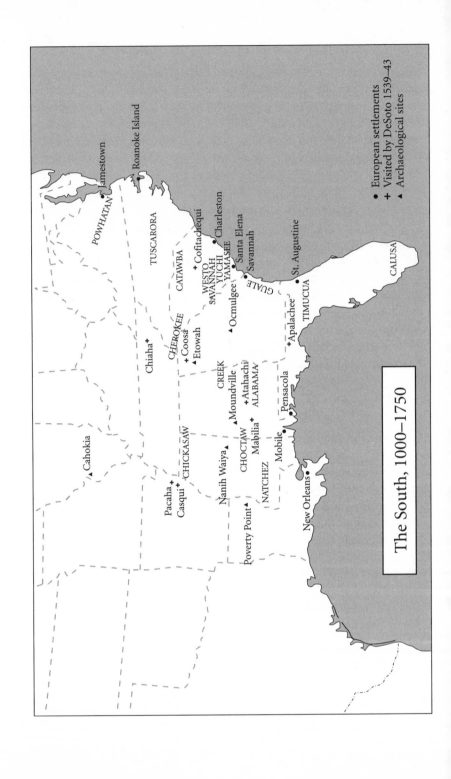

The South, 1000–1750

Jamestown
Roanoke Island
POWHATAN
TUSCARORA
CATAWBA
Coftachequi +
Charleston
WESTO
SAVANNAH
YUCHI
YAMASEE
Santa Elena
Savannah
GUALE
St. Augustine
CALUSA
TIMUCUA
Apalachee +
Chiaha +
CHEROKEE
Coosa +
Etowah ▲
CREEK
Ocmulgee ▲
Moundville ▲
Atahachi +
ALABAMA
Pensacola
Cahokia ▲
CHICKASAW
Casqui +
Pacha +
Nanih Waiya ▲
CHOCTAW
Mabila +
Mobile
NATCHEZ
Poverty Point ▲
New Orleans

• European settlements
+ Visited by DeSoto 1539–43
▲ Archaeological sites

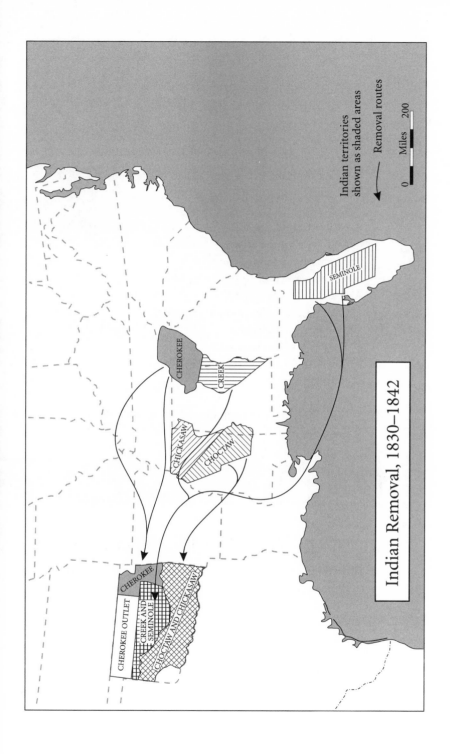

Indian Removal, 1830–1842

Indian territories shown as shaded areas

Removal routes

0   200
Miles

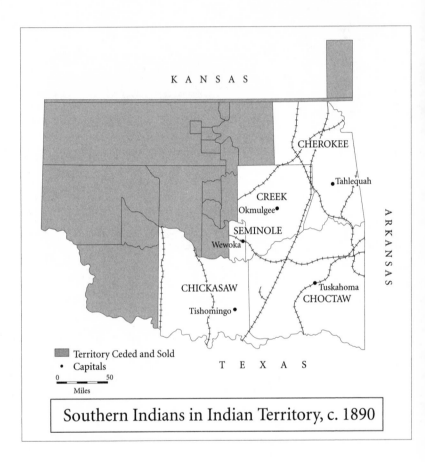

KANSAS

CHEROKEE

•Tahlequah

ARKANSAS

CREEK
Okmulgee•

SEMINOLE
Wewoka•

CHICKASAW

Tishomingo •

Tuskahoma•
CHOCTAW

■ Territory Ceded and Sold
• Capitals

0 ____ 50
Miles

T E X A S

Southern Indians in Indian Territory, c. 1890

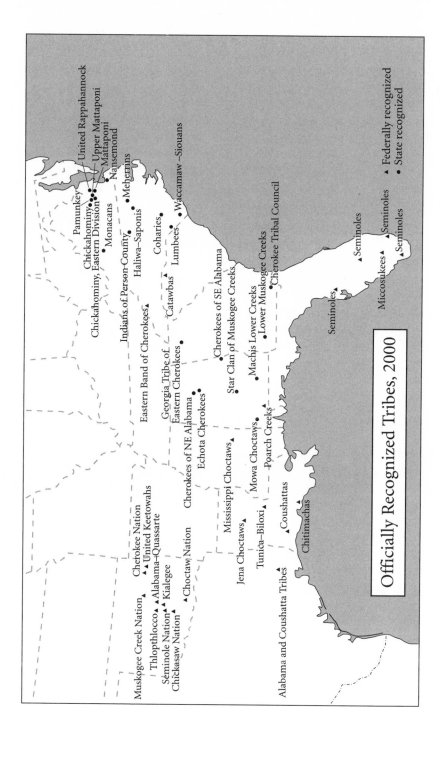

Officially Recognized Tribes, 2000

▲ Federally recognized
• State recognized

United Rappahannock
Upper Mattaponi
Mattaponi
Pamunkey
Chickahominy
Chickahominy, Eastern Division
Nansemond
Monacans
Meherrins
Indians of Person County
Haliwa–Saponis
Coharies
Waccamaw–Siouans
Lumbees
Catawbas
Eastern Band of Cherokees
Cherokees of SE Alabama
Cherokee Tribal Council
Georgia Tribe of
Eastern Cherokees
Star Clan of Muskogee Creeks
Machis Lower Creeks
Lower Muskogee Creeks
Cherokees of NE Alabama
Echota Cherokees
Mississippi Choctaws
Mowa Choctaws
Poarch Creeks
Seminoles
Miccosukees
Seminoles
Seminoles
Seminoles
Jena Choctaws
Tunica–Biloxi
Coushattas
Chitimachas
Alabama and Coushatta Tribes
Cherokee Nation
United Keetowahs
Alabama–Quassarte
Kialegee
Choctaw Nation
Muskogee Creek Nation
Thlopthlocco
Seminole Nation
Chickasaw Nation

The Columbia Guide to
American Indians of the Southeast

Part I

History and Culture

1 Writing About Native Southerners

The Native peoples of the Southeast share common cultural features and a rich history. Long before the arrival of Europeans, they began to cultivate corn, beans, squash, and other crops. Agriculture enabled their societies to live in relatively permanent villages, develop a social/political/religious hierarchy, construct an elaborate ceremonial complex, and support a large population. The European invasion disrupted this way of life, but Native Southerners displayed remarkable adaptability. They drew on their precontact cultural traditions to sustain their villages, beliefs, and social systems, but they also entered into commercial and diplomatic relations with Europeans that produced substantial change. Native people became entangled in a world economy and European imperial schemes, both of which compromised their sovereignty. By the end of the eighteenth century they had become incorporated into the territorial boundary claimed by the United States, a rapidly expanding nation that saw its aboriginal population as an impediment rather than a constituent part. Some Native people became a marginalized third race in an increasingly biracial region; others managed to retain sovereignty, but most lost their tribal domains. A majority were removed west of the Mississippi to what is today eastern Oklahoma where they reestablished their nations, only to lose them once again at the end of the nineteenth century. The twentieth-century resurgence of Native people in Oklahoma and in the Southeast is a testament to the enduring power of culture, the strength of ethnic identity, and the ironic twists of history.

The geographic boundaries of the Native Southeast tend to be rather fluid. Anthropologists delineate a Southeastern Culture Area, but, as Charles Hudson has noted, "Any boundaries drawn are inevitably somewhat arbitrary because all of the aboriginal people east of the Rocky Mountains and north of the Gulf of Mexico to the boreal forest of Canada shared many cultural features." Nevertheless, Hudson maintained that "a rather distinctive set of physiographic, biotic, and climatic features . . . underlay the distinctiveness of the Southeastern way of life."[1] In particular, the Southeast gets more than forty inches of rainfall in general each year and has a growing season of more than 180 days. That is, the Southeast can support agricultural societies, and farming forms the basis of this particular culture area (see **agriculture**).

Historians do not quibble with this anthropological definition of the Southeast, but they focus on the ways in which a distinctive Anglo-American culture in the South shaped the lives of the region's Native people. In the process, they broaden the definition of Southeastern Indians. Plantation agriculture made the lands of Southeastern Indians particularly desirable, and racial slavery made the oppression of all nonwhites acceptable. Therefore, historians consider the Native people who lived in the slave states of the antebellum period to be Southeastern. They include in this definition peoples to the north and west of the culture area boundary, such as those in Virginia, who in the twentieth century struggled to maintain their identity and rights as Indians against efforts of segregationists to reclassify them as "Negro." Historical events such as removal also have expanded the boundaries of the Native Southeast to include eastern Oklahoma. In this case the line simply followed peoples whom both anthropologists and historians consider to be Southeastern (see **removal**).

In writing about the Native peoples of the Southeast, scholars of all disciplines encounter a number of interpretative problems. The archaeological, ethnographic, and historical record is never as complete as scholars would like, and, consequently, no discipline or combination of disciplines can ever reveal all we would like to know about Native people. Because the evidence uncovered is fragmentary, scholars must try to make sense of it. In the process, they have developed ways to use that evidence to construct comprehensible narratives of Native life. Not all scholars emphasize the same evidence or interpret that evidence in identical ways. Consequently, they construct different narratives. The sections below focus on some of the problems scholars encounter with evidence and the ways in which they have used that evidence to interpret Native culture and history.

Archaeology

The evidence for the ancient past of Native peoples comes from archaeology. Archaeologists are particularly interested in the physical characteristics of human beings and in their material culture. Skeletal remains have helped scholars chart the migrations of peoples, their nutrition and diseases, and even some cultural practices. Physical evidence, for example, reveals the cranial deformation of infants on cradle boards; other evidence points to the existence of scalping in North America before the arrival of Europeans. Archaeology can identify sites of dwellings through soil discoloration caused by postholes and hearths, and it can plot change over time by sequencing pottery and projectile points. Similarities and differences in construction techniques and decorative motifs can delineate friends and enemies, and disparities in grave goods can reveal hierarchies. Burial practices can also hint at religious beliefs. Nevertheless, archaeology is limited in what it can tell us about Native people. Excavations do not reveal the languages people spoke, the laws they followed, the intricacies of their religions, the relations between men and women, the structures of families, and many other things that we would like to know (see **Archaic tradition; Mississippian tradition; Paleo-Indian tradition; Woodland tradition**).

As early as the eighteenth century Europeans had developed an interest in the physical remains of ancient civilizations in North America. Thomas Jefferson, among others, acquired Indian artifacts. The systematic excavation of Native sites in the Southeast, however, stems from the late nineteenth century. Archaeological discoveries of the city of Troy and Egyptian tombs sparked interest in ancient America, and a debate raged over who built the earthworks that dotted the eastern third of the United States. Some people insisted that the mounds must have been constructed by a superior race of "moundbuilders" whom the Indians extirpated, while others maintained that the ancestors of Native Americans had, in fact, built them. Partisans of competing schools of thought rushed to excavate many mounds, in the process destroying them for future generations.

Some mounds yielded extensive caches of artifacts, many of which were exquisitely wrought, and the finds attracted the attention of collectors. The disposable income of the American upper class had never been greater, and the wealthy often competed with each other in establishing collections of Native artifacts. Furthermore, the middle class had more leisure time, and museums emerged to provide entertainment and enlightenment for those not rich enough to amass their own collections. For example, the Valentine Museum in Richmond scoured the South in search of items to line its shelves, and a company in eastern Oklahoma commercially "mined" the spectacular Spiro Mound for artifacts (see **art; Southeastern Ceremonial Complex**). By the time archaeology had become an academic discipline with established procedures, much of the South's distant past had been looted.

Modern archaeologists do not excavate a site merely for its artifacts. Archaeologists seek to reveal a society through its physical remains. Consequently, they are interested in cornfields and dwellings as well as temples and mounds and in utilitarian stone hoes and knives as well as shell gorgets and ceremonial celts. Using these artifacts to reconstruct Native society is possible only when a site is relatively undisturbed. Professional archaeologists map and measure carefully so that they know the context in which an artifact is discovered. Unsystematic digging disrupts the sequence of artifacts—the oldest items in an undisturbed site are deepest—and the identification of the purpose of each area of the site. If the oldest artifacts in a site have been interspersed with the most recent ones, an archaeologist might assume that two peoples lived together at the site rather than sequentially, and a mixture of domestic and ceremonial items in the same area might well prevent accurate identification of the artifacts or the place.

The early exploitation of Native sites and artifacts as well as the cultural resurgence of Native people in the twentieth century has led to a debate between Native Americans and archaeologists over the propriety of excavations. Most sensitive are physical remains, which Native people complain have been ripped from the earth, analyzed, stored, and sometimes even exhibited. While many Native people distinguish between the desecration of graves by amateur pot hunters and professional excavations, others demand the suspension of all archaeological research. Devon A. Mihesuah, a Choctaw historian, has questioned what actually can be learned from skeletons: "In dialogues with social scientists, Indians plead for convincing evidence that having the remains of their ancestors scrutinized, then stored for decades in basements and vaults of universities and museums, in addition to being separated from the grave goods with which they were buried, contributes to the well-being of Indian people."[2] In response to the demands of Native people, in 1990 Congress passed the Native American Graves Protection and Repatriation Act, which provides for the return of human remains and funerary objects to the tribe with which affiliation can be proved. Many archaeologists support this act and work with Native people to meet its provisions. Archaeologists also have become sensitive to the concerns of Native people and often seek their input before initiating projects.

Documentary Evidence

While the evidence that archaeology yields, whether in skeletal remains or artifacts, was created by Native people, the documentary record is more likely to have been produced by non-Natives. Native Southerners used pictographs and other symbols to communicate, but they did not have written languages until long after Europeans arrived (see **Algonkian languages; Caddoan languages; Iroquoian languages; Muskogean languages; Siouan languages**). Therefore, Europeans generated the early documentary record of Native peoples. Official records, such as legislative journals, diplomatic correspondence, trade regulations, and minutes of treaty conferences, provide much of the written evidence for Native peoples after the arrival of Europeans. Perhaps more useful, however, are the works of natural historians, who described Native people with the same care they gave flora and fauna, and travelers, who often made astute observations about the Native people they encountered and conscientiously recorded their interactions with them.

Whether official or private, all these sources share certain problems. First, their authors saw Native people through their own cultural lens and often misinterpreted what they saw. When Native people at treaty conferences referred to the English king or the president of the United States as their "father," Anglo-Americans believed that it signaled Indian subservience since fathers dominated patriarchal European households. Native people in the Southeast, however, were matrilineal, and the term *father* connoted respect, not power (see **kinship**). Furthermore, exchanging gifts held a central place in Native diplomacy as a demonstration of respect and good will. When Native people demanded gifts from Europeans at treaty conferences, however, official records interpreted their behavior as the result of greed or impoverishment and the gifts as bribes.

Europeans also tended to draw analogies between Native customs and their own practices and beliefs. They created Native royalties in societies where none existed and misunderstood the nature of political hierarchy in societies where it did exist. The "Suns," whom French colonists in Louisiana described as a Natchez upper class much like their own aristocracy, were elites, but the similarity of eighteenth-century France to this Mississippian society stopped there (see **government**). European powers created "Medal Chiefs," to whom they awarded silver emblems of authority and from whom they expected the exercise of power in their interest. When Europeans found differences between their own societies and those of Native people, they usually disparaged Native practices or simply ignored them. Some observers dismissed the Cherokees, whose chiefs had no coercive power, as living in a state of anarchy and made no effort to understand the councils by which the Cherokees really governed themselves. When Europeans discovered that Southeastern Indians had no structures reserved solely for religious rituals and no deities they could clearly identify, they assumed that they had no religion at all (see **religion**).

Finally, Europeans were not privy to much of Native life. Native people closed certain ceremonies and council deliberations to Europeans. Native hunters and warriors were usually loath to have Europeans accompany them, because non-Natives did not know the rules or rituals that ensured success and a wrong move could jeopardize the entire venture (see **hunting**). Those who documented Native life before the nineteenth century were virtually all men, and they had no access to most aspects of women's lives. Therefore, we know little about Native women, the organization of domestic life, practices regarding menstruation and childbirth, or the ceremonies specific to women, including those associated with growing corn.

By the time Native people began to generate their own written records in the nineteenth century, their cultures had changed dramatically (see **Sequoyah**). Or, at least, that is what most authors of these documents wanted readers to believe. Engaged in a struggle to retain their lands in the Southeast, Native people used written language to press their case. Most Native people, however, did not immediately internalize literacy. That is, people did not necessarily find it satisfying to create personal records, such as journals and private letters, just because they had the skill to do so. Therefore, the written Native record was that of a mission-educated, highly acculturated elite. There are some exceptions—Cherokee religious leaders recorded sacred formulas in the Cherokee language—but the documentary records of Native people, like those of other Americans, disproportionately represent the elite.

Ethnographic Research

Ethnography is the study of culture. Ethnographers pursue their research through participant observation in which they live with the people whom they are studying, learn their language, participate in their activities, and record their experiences. Ethnographers then explore the structure of the society by analyzing their findings topically. Their categories of analysis include belief system, social organization, subsistence, and political organization (see **agriculture; fishing; gathering; government; hunting; kinship;**

religion). The emphasis of ethnography is on living peoples, and the view of society that emerges from ethnographic research tends to be frozen in time. There is little sense of the ways in which the culture has changed. Nevertheless, ethnography can have important implications for the study of a people's past. Cultures change very slowly, and scholars often use ethnographic research to trace particular practices and beliefs back in time, a process that anthropologist William Fenton has called "upstreaming."[3] This approach must be used with care because cultures, however slowly, do change, and there is no way to standardize the rate and extent of change.

Systematic ethnographic research among Southeastern Indians began in the late nineteenth century at the very time that all Native Americans seemed to be vanishing. The Native population in the United States reached its nadir in 1890, and philanthropists and policy makers focused their attentions on assimilating surviving Indians into the dominant culture. Museums, universities, and organizations such as the Bureau of American Ethnology rushed to record basic information about Native cultures before Indians and their ways of life disappeared. Ethnography flourished until World War II and formed the basis of cultural anthropology.

The people who conducted the fieldwork were overwhelmingly non-Indian, and the quality of their research varied dramatically. Understandably suspicious of researchers, many Indians were less than forthright about their beliefs and practices, and some took delight in spinning yarns for gullible ethnographers. Other Indians, however, shared ethnographers' concerns for the loss of their cultural traditions and gladly shared information about their people with researchers. Swimmer, an important religious leader among the Cherokees, for example, turned over to ethnographer James Mooney the sacred formulas that he had carefully recorded in the **Sequoyah** syllabary, and George Washington Grayson, a Creek, revealed to John Swanton the intricacies of Creek social organization.

Oral Traditions

Ethnographers often collected the oral traditions of Native people, but the acceptance of these traditions by other scholars has come slowly. Academics trained in a written literary tradition grounded in empiricism have had great difficulty with orally transmitted Indian myths in which animals speak and human beings possess extraordinary powers. Native historical narratives do not clearly locate events in the past, follow a linear chronology, or empirically link cause and effect. Using oral traditions for purposes for which they were never intended raises ethical as well as intellectual problems. While debates continue on how literally scholars should accept these traditions, most historians and archaeologists as well as cultural anthropologists regard oral tradition as an essential tool in understanding how Native peoples organized their thoughts and interpreted their lives. Ethnographers tapped deeply into creation myths and explanations of how the world came to be the way it is (see **religion**). In the 1930s employees of the Works Progress Administration added to these records by interviewing thousands of elderly Indians, particularly in Oklahoma, about their lives. More recent projects have added to this oral record of Native Southerners. Questions, however, still remain. How accurate are the memories of the people interviewed? To what extent have external influences, such as Christianity, shaped modern renditions of myths? How do we deal with oral traditions that contradict in fundamental ways the documentary and archaeological record?

Interpreting Native American History and Culture

Scholars use the research methods outlined above to uncover information about Native American history and culture, but then they must make sense of what they have found. The sheer volume of information compels them to be selective and to focus on specific aspects of Native life. Since not all information is of equal value to a particular subject, scholars must choose what to incorporate and what to leave out. Just as the data is subjective because it reflects the biases of the people who created it, the interests and concerns of the scholar shape the interpretation of the evidence. That does not mean that scholars intentionally distort data to make a point, but two scholars reading the same evidence may well reach entirely different conclusions about what it means. While individual perspectives account for some of the differences in interpretation, more generalized historical change also explains shifts in scholarly interpretation.

For many years scholars regarded Native peoples as an appropriate subject of study primarily for anthropologists and archaeologists. Because Indians did not leave written records and seemed to live in largely static societies, historians gave them very short shrift. Native people appeared in historical works only when their actions impinged on the lives of Euro-Americans. Consequently, Native American history existed largely as the history of Indian relations with Euro-Americans. Early works of this genre depicted Native people as savages who stood in the way of progress. More recently, historians of Indian-white relations have tended to focus on the victimization of Native peoples or the paternalism of Euro-Americans in their dealing with Indians.

The classic account of the victimization of Southeastern Indians is Angie Debo's *And Still the Waters Run: The Betrayal of the Five Civilized Tribes*, a chilling account of the early twentieth-century frauds perpetrated on Southern Indians in Oklahoma after the allotment of their tribal domain (see **allotment**). "The orgy of exploitation that resulted," Debo wrote, "is almost beyond belief." She held the government as well as individuals responsible for the impoverishment of thousands of people and the dissolution of their tribes: "The policy of the United States in liquidating the institutions of the Five Tribes was a gigantic blunder that ended a hopeful experiment in Indian development, destroyed a unique civilization, and degraded thousands of individuals."[4] In Debo's work and that of other scholars who focused on the wrongs done to Native people, the villains as well as the victims are obvious.

For the major twentieth-century scholar of Indian-white relations, Francis Paul Prucha, the roles are not so clear. Prucha maintained that "cries for extermination of the Indians occasionally sounded by aggressive frontiersmen and exasperated frontier commanders were rejected by United States officials responsible for Indian affairs." Instead, these officials implemented a policy based on paternalism, which Prucha defined as "a determination to do what was best for the Indians according to white norms, which translated into protection, subsistence of the destitute, punishment of the unruly, and eventually taking the Indians by the hand and leading them along the path to white civilization and Christianity."[5] Prucha regarded the **removal** of Indians from the Southeast to Oklahoma in the 1830s as a pragmatic and even humane action on the part of Andrew Jackson, who recognized that the United States could not protect the Indians where they were from land-hungry cotton planters.[6]

Most scholars no longer portray Indians as primarily victims and the United States government as either diabolical or paternalistic. Indeed, the focus of Native American history has moved away from Indian-white relations. The impetus for this intellectual shift came partly from the **Indian Claims Commission** established after World War II to resolve tribal claims against the United States. In researching the validity of the claims, historians and anthropologists began to uncover histories far more complex than narrowly construed studies of Indian-white relations permitted. Each Native people had its own discrete culture and history, influenced but not controlled by government policy. This academic awareness coincided with demands of Native people for a more Indian-centered history that takes culture into account. The result was the emergence of a new interdisciplinary methodology designed specifically to study the past of Native Americans.

Ethnohistory

The new methodology, ethnohistory, developed out of history and anthropology. Practitioners of ethnohistory ask anthropological questions of historical sources, and they focus their attention on the ways in which cultures change over time. In the process, ethnohistorians also borrow from other disciplines, such as linguistics and folklore, in order to identify and understand the cultural information they find in historical sources. By combining such a variety of disciplines, ethnohistory is able to address the weaknesses inherent in a single disciplinary perspective. Ethnographic research, for example, has helped us understand what Indians meant when they used the term *father* and expected gifts at treaty conferences.

One of the most significant results of ethnohistory is that it attributes agency to Native peoples. No longer are Indians merely the victims or beneficiaries of United States policy, as they generally are in works that focus on Indian-white relations, but instead they are active participants in their own histories. One result of an emphasis on agency is that Indians become more complicated historical figures who have complex motives. They make decisions for a whole range of reasons, some altruistic and some self-serving, and their decisions have consequences that sometimes benefit and at other times harm their people. Agency moves us away from one-dimensional and stereotypical Indians. At the same time, ethnohistorians acknowledge that Indians were victims of Euro-American expansion and oppression while also recognizing that victimization is only one part of the Native American experience.

Unlike ethnohistorians, scholars of Indian-white relations view Native history as a corollary to Euro-American history. Prucha, for example, considered the **Creek War** of 1813–1814 in the context of the War of 1812 between the United States and Great Britain. Many Native peoples, he suggested, took advantage of a British alliance during the war to redress their grievances against the Americans. Although a major cultural revitalization was in progress among Native peoples, Prucha attributed resistance north of the Ohio to the determination of Tecumseh and the Shawnee Prophet "to stop the westward advance of whites." Tecumseh took his message to the Creeks, and "with promises that Spanish and British aid would support the Indians he won over the young warriors, or Red Sticks."[7] The Creeks appear to be the naive pawns of imperial rivalries. Their history is meaningful only in its relationship to Euro-American history: white Americans pushed west and Indians resisted by forming alliances with the United States's enemies.

Ethnohistorians understand the Creek conflict differently, although they do not necessarily agree with each other on the primary causes. One way to examine the conflict is to focus on factionalism, which, Robert F. Berkhofer has suggested, provides an opportunity to write "Indian history from the Indian point of view."[8] As part of his broader study of Creek government, Michael D. Green examined political factions in the Creek Nation on the eve of civil war, particularly the split between the Upper and Lower Creeks. Upper Creeks resented the cozy relationship that Lower Creek leaders had with United States officials, the "salaries, medals, honors, and countless other emoluments" that this friendship brought them, and the concessions that chiefs from the Lower Towns seemed far too willing to make. When prophets called for cultural revitalization, "their popularity in many towns was a measure of the depth of popular frustration with the headmen." At the heart of the civil war, therefore, was political factionalism exacerbated by corruption, land cession, and white encroachments and fanned by a prophetic message.[9]

Joel Martin shifted the focus from political factionalism to the prophets and their revitalization movement. The Creeks, he wrote, "found their very existence profoundly threatened, and to meet extraordinary economic, political, and cultural crises, they responded with bold and extraordinary spiritual creativity."[10] Just as Green rested his argument on Berkhofer's theory, Martin turned to the work of anthropologist Anthony F. C. Wallace. Wallace defined a revitalization movement as "a deliberate, organized, conscious effort by members of a society to construct a more satisfying culture." Certainly, the Red Stick movement among the Creeks that precipitated civil war qualifies as a revitalization movement. Prophets regarded Creek culture as morally and socially bankrupt and preached a return to a more traditional way of life. Their revitalization movement also qualifies as what Wallace calls "nativistic," because it was characterized by "the elimination of alien persons, customs, materials, and/or materiel" from the society and its members. Furthermore, Martin regarded the Creek prophets as millenarians because, in Wallace's words, they envisioned "an apocalyptic world transformation engineered by the supernatural."[11]

Both Green and Martin used theoretical constructs as well as research in traditional documentary sources to place the Creeks at the center of events and explain the war in Creek terms. In their work a British alliance and the War of 1812 were secondary to profound cleavages that existed within Creek society, which explain the war that left 15 percent of the Creeks dead. The Creeks in these accounts are human beings with ambitions, grievances, strongly held beliefs, and deep emotions. At the same time, these ethnohistorians did not ignore the ways in which the United States exploited divisions within Creek society to acquire twenty million acres of land in Georgia and Alabama immediately after the war and to deport the entire Creek Nation west of the Mississippi two decades later.

Scholars have used dependency theory, developed primarily by political scientists, to understand the process by which Native peoples lost their autonomy. Richard White, a pioneer in the application of dependency theory to Native American history, pointed out that "there is no single symptom of dependency, but rather a syndrome of social, political, and economic characteristics, which deny some countries the ability either to expand or to be self-sustaining."[12] In White's analysis of Choctaw **trade**, he identifies an elastic demand for alcohol, in contrast to the inelastic demand for durable goods such as metal tools, as key to understanding Choctaw dependency. Kathryn E. Holland Braund identifies another commodity as crucial to the asymmetrical relationship between European traders and Creek hunters: "Creek producers depended on outsiders for guns and ammunition—their means of production and the basis of their power."[13] Both agree, however, that dependency is a central theme in the eighteenth-century history of Southeastern Indians.

An older theoretical concept that ethnohistorians have borrowed from social scientists is acculturation, which they use to examine the adoption of European beliefs and practices by Native people. The Social Science Research Council has pointed out that acculturation did not involve the wholesale acceptance of a foreign culture by a society. Instead, "the patterns and values of the receiving culture seem to function as selective screens in a manner that results in the enthusiastic acceptance of some elements, the firm rejection of other elements." Furthermore, acculturation provided for the agency of Native peoples in the process of culture change: "the elements which are transmitted undergo transformations in the receiving cultural systems."[14]

Before the advent of ethnohistory, scholars regarded the adoption of Euro-American cultural practices as a shift from "savagery" to "civilization." Henry Thompson Malone, for example, described eighteenth-century Cherokees as "primitive forest children" and then turned his attention to nineteenth-century "Indians moving impressively toward the white man's way of life."[15] Grace Steele Woodward chronicled the emergence of the "primitive" Cherokees "from dark savagery into the sunlight of civilization."[16] This language implies that Indians found their own culture so deficient that they gratefully accepted a superior one, or that the power of the dominant culture, militarily and intellectually, was so overwhelming that it squelched any effort at cultural preservation.

Using the concept of acculturation permits a far less ethnocentric view of culture change and sanctions considerable flexibility on the part of Native people in their adaptation to the Euro-American presence. William McLoughlin, for example, attributed the success of the Baptist missionaries Evan and John Jones among the Cherokees to "a syncretic form of Christianity among their converts that allowed the old and new religions to coexist in ways comfortable to the Cherokees." The Joneses believed that the Bible was silent on many issues important to the Cherokees—"their medical system, their harvest dances, their ball plays, their hospitality ethic, their view of women's rights, and their commitment to hold their land in common"—and so they did not interfere.[17] Cherokees did not mindlessly desert their own religion for Christianity, and the Joneses' approach permitted them to be both Christians and Cherokees (see **religion**). Similarly, Theda Perdue has demonstrated that in the early nineteenth-century Cherokee Nation "a dual system of jurisprudence existed in which some people, perhaps most, applied customary methods of social regulation to a traditional code of behavior and others followed the laws of the republic" (see **government**).[18] The Cherokees' law code, based on those of Anglo-Americans, coexisted with traditional practice, a contradiction that Cherokees embraced in order to accommodate divergent cultural orientations in their community. McLoughlin and Perdue presented a very different way of understanding culture change than earlier scholars; in their view the process of culture change was neither uniform nor complete. While they did not ignore the disparity of power that encouraged culture change, they focused on the creativity of Native people in coping with the demands of the dominant society.

Perdue has used gender as a category of analysis to examine cultural persistence and change among the Cherokees. She has drawn on the work of a number of feminist scholars, including Joan Wallach Scott, who defined gender as "the social organization of sexual difference."[19] Gender is socially constructed and relational, and it changes over time. The ways in which gender relations change has long interested scholars, who generally have seen a decline in the status of Native women following contact with Europeans.[20] Perdue did not totally reject the declension model, but she demonstrated that decline resulted in large part from Native people's loss of power vis-à-vis Anglo-Americans rather than the growing oppression of Native women by Native men who had been co-opted by a market economy. Perdue also argued that a gender analysis of Cherokee society in the eighteenth and early nineteenth centuries revealed far more cultural persistence than histories focusing on men had allowed: "Women did not completely acquiesce to a new order shaped by a European presence in their country and European attitudes toward women. They found ways to retain traditional prerogatives, preserve corporate values, and maintain the fundamental structures of Cherokee society on which their status rested."[21]

As scholars have become more concerned with agency, they have had to explain why Native people made the choices that they did. Bruce Trigger, a Canadian anthropologist, suggested that interpretations of Native behavior fall into two camps, which he called "rational" and "romantic."[22] Scholars who seek rational explanations for Native behavior assume that all human beings, regardless of their cultures, react to situations in similar ways. Those inclined to romantic interpretations emphasize cultural differences that can produce varied responses and adaptations to change. Two recent works on Southeastern Indians provide examples of these contrasting approaches.

Claudio Saunt placed his study of Creeks in the eighteenth and early nineteenth centuries in the context of the Atlantic world and contended that "unexpected parallels exist between the experiences of diverse groups of Native and nonnative Americans." The expanding Atlantic economy subjected Creek society as well as the non-Native South to enormous strain, and Saunt found that "the rhetoric of Creek proponents of the new order mirrored that of South Carolina regulators." When divisions emerged within Creek society, some Creeks differentiated between "the 'idle' and the 'industrious,' words familiar to London dock workers in the late eighteenth century." Not only did Creeks react to economic inequality and a corresponding concentration of political power in the same way that other Americans did, but the forces that disrupted Creek life in this period, Saunt maintained, were those "that propelled the American Revolution" as well.[23] In this rational interpretation Creek history is part of a global history and Creek responses are universal (see **government**; **trade**).

James Taylor Carson, on the other hand, described Choctaws in terms of the fundamental structures of the Mississippian culture that flourished before European contact. These structures were "chiefly political organization, matrilineal kinship, a gendered division of labor, and a complex cosmological system based on the sanctity of the sacred circle and the rules and rites necessary to protect it from foreign invasion" (see **government**; **kinship**; **religion**). Although European contact brought enormous change to the Choctaws, Carson insisted that, well into the nineteenth century, these structures remained largely intact. And despite the fact that the market revolution of the early nineteenth century brought significant change by replacing traditional reciprocity with "notions of sale, profit, and surplus production," the crucial component of the Choctaw economy, a gendered division of labor, endured. When Greenwood **Leflore** proclaimed new laws in 1828, he did so in the "sanctifying shadow" of **Nanih Waiya**, a **Mississippian** mound from which the Choctaws believed they had emerged, in order "to buttress his claims to authority and power."[24] Although Carson acknowledged the changes precipitated by Europeans, he insisted that "when the Choctaws left Mississippi they carried with them a culture that bore a remarkable yet superficial resemblance to that of their Anglo-American antagonists. . . . For all these appearances, they remained at heart Choctaw." Carson's argument, resting on his understanding of Choctaw culture, fits Trigger's conception of a romantic interpretation.

Ethnohistorians are likely to continue arguing over whether an economic self-interest shared by other inhabitants of the Atlantic world or a moral economy deeply rooted in the ancient past motivated Southeastern Indians in the late eighteenth and early nineteenth centuries. In some ways the debate signals the maturation of ethnohistory as a methodology. No longer focused merely on *how* scholars should write about the Native American past, ethnohistorians are advancing conflicting interpretations that impart some of the complexity that practitioners think is the essence of the subject.

Notes

1. Charles Hudson, *The Southeastern Indians* (Knoxville: University of Tennessee Press, 1976), 10–11.

2. Devon A. Mihesuah, "American Indians, Anthropologists, Pothunters, and Repatriation," *American Indian Quarterly* 20 (1996).

3. William N. Fenton, *American Indian and White Relations to 1830: Needs and Opportunities for Study* (Chapel Hill: University of North Carolina Press, 1957), 21–22.

4. Angie Debo, *And Still the Waters Run: The Betrayal of the Five Civilized Tribes* (Princeton: Princeton University Press, 1940), x–xi.

5. Francis Paul Prucha, *The Great Father: The United States Government and the American Indians* (Lincoln: University of Nebraska Press, 1984), xxviii.

6. Francis Paul Prucha, "Andrew Jackson's Indian Policy: A Reassessment," *Journal of American History* 56 (1969): 527–39.

7. Prucha, *The Great Father*, 77, 79.

8. Robert F. Berkhofer Jr., "The Political Context of a New Indian History," *Pacific Historical Review* 40 (1971): 357–82.

9. Michael D. Green, *The Politics of Indian Removal: Creek Government and Society in Crisis* (Lincoln: University of Nebraska Press, 1982), 40–41.

10. Joel Martin, *Sacred Revolt: The Muskogees' Struggle for a New World* (Boston: Beacon, 1991), 133.

11. Anthony F. C. Wallace, "Revitalization Movements: Some Theoretical Considerations for Their Comparative Study," *American Anthropologist* 58 (1956): 265, 267.

12. Richard White, *Roots of Dependency: Subsistence, Enviroment, and Social Change Among the Choctaws, Pawnees, and Navajos* (Lincoln: University of Nebraska Press, 1983), xvii.

13. Kathryn E. Holland Braund, *Deerskins and Duffels: The Creek Indian Trade with Anglo-America, 1685–1815* (Lincoln: University of Nebraska Press, 1993), 137–38.

14. "Acculturation, an Explanatory Formulation," *American Anthropologist* 56 (1954): 985–86.

15. Henry Thompson Malone, *Cherokees of the Old South: A People in Transition* (Athens: University of Georgia Press, 1956), chapter 1, 184.

16. Grace Steele Woodward, *The Cherokees* (Norman: University of Oklahoma Press, 1963), 3.

17. William G. McLoughlin, *Champions of the Cherokees: Evan and John B. Jones* (Princeton: Princeton University Press, 1990), 6.

18. Theda Perdue, *Cherokee Women: Gender and Culture Change, 1700–1835* (Lincoln: University of Nebraska Press, 1998), 151.

19. Joan Wallach Scott, *Gender and the Politics of History* (New York: Columbia University Press, 1988), 2.

20. Mona Etienne and Eleanor Leacock, eds., *Women and Colonization: Anthropological Perspectives* (New York: Praeger, 1980).

21. Perdue, *Cherokee Women*, 63.

22. Bruce G. Trigger, "Early Native American Responses to European Contact: Romantic Versus Rationalistic Interpretations," *Journal of American History* 77 (1991): 1195–1215

23. Claudio Saunt, *A New Order of Things: Property, Power, and the Transformation of the Creek Indians, 1733–1816* (Cambridge: Cambridge University Press, 1999), 7.

24. James Taylor Carson, *Searching for the Bright Path: The Mississippi Choctaws from Prehistory to Removal* (Lincoln: University of Nebraska Press, 1999), 11–12, 85, 102.

2 Native Southerners

The first sentence of Charles Hudson's landmark ethnography of Southeastern Indians reads, "The native people of the American South—the Southeastern Indians—possessed the richest culture of any of the native people north of Mexico."[1] When Hudson wrote that line, he was thinking of the people of the Mississippian societies who lived in the South when the first European explorers entered the region and began to write their descriptions of Southeastern Indians. The accounts of those sixteenth-century Spanish explorers—Hernando de Soto and others—drew word pictures of societies marked by levels of social, political, economic, and spiritual complexity that we still understand imperfectly. But we do know that this Mississippian world was the product of thousands of years of history. The evidence for most of this history lies in the ground, not in the libraries, and the scholarship is the work of archaeologists, not historians, but the patterns of life over the millennia are clear enough to help us appreciate that change is normal, that people have always been adaptable, and that in the process of time Southern Indians made their own histories.

Origins

Southern Indians have stories for explaining their origins. Some, like the Yuchis, tell about the world when it was covered with water. The animals needed land on which to rest and eat and conferred on how to find some. After several animals failed, a crawfish dived to the bottom and brought up some mud in its claws, which was the beginning of dry land. The people who came to live on the land emerged from their ancient homes within the earth. The Alabamas relate how their ancestors crawled to the surface through a groundhog's burrow. The Choctaws explain how they, preceded by the Creeks, Cherokees, and Chickasaws, emerged from the sacred **Nanih Waiya** mound in western Mississippi. The Creeks, on the other hand, say that they migrated to the Southeast from somewhere in the distant west (see **religion**).[2]

Scientists have a different explanation. Many thousands of years ago in the Pleistocene epoch temperatures were much lower than now. Water froze into massive ice sheets that ultimately forced sea levels to fall. On two occasions, between 75,000 and 45,000 years ago and between 25,000 and 14,000 years ago, the level of the oceans was so low that North America and Siberia were connected by land, the so-called Bering Land Bridge. Scholars believe that Pleistocene mammals, including mammoths, horses, ground sloths, musk oxen, and other animals, grazed their way across the land bridge from Asia and human hunters followed (see **hunting**). Based on their understanding of human population movements in Asia, most scholars believe that this migration occurred during the more recent exposure of the land bridge. Thus, sometime during the period from 25,000 to 14,000 years ago, humans came to America. Students of this phenomenon have suggested many scenarios for what happened next, none of which can be proven. Some believe people worked their way down the eastern slopes of the Rocky Mountains, others think they followed the Pacific coast. One scholar thinks they pressed south in a sort of human tidal wave, reaching the tip of South America in a relatively brief time, but most imagine a long process of migrating small groups. At any rate, people ultimately made their way into the Southeast.

Because the massive northern ice sheets affected the climate of the South, it was much cooler than it is now and densely forested. But beginning about fourteen thousand years ago, world temperatures rose. As the ice sheets melted, water formed lakes, rivers, and marshes, the plants and animals that could adapt to warmer, more humid conditions thrived, and the face of the South gradually changed. By about ten thousand years ago the deciduous forests had crowded out the spruce and pine forests and the giant Pleistocene mammals were extinct. As temperatures continued to rise, the wet humid environment became drier, ultimately reaching a point, about five thousand years ago, when the climate of the South became much as it is today.

Archaeologists who study eastern North America periodize human history before the arrival of Europeans into three broad cultural sequences. The first, **Paleo-Indian**, extended to about 8000 B.C. and concluded with the extinction of Pleistocene animals. The second, **Archaic**, ran to about 700 B.C., when it phased into the third, or **Woodland**, period. Distinctive cultural changes mark each sequence, even as within each period change and adaptation to new challenges and opportunities were continuous. Many factors drove culture change, including environmental shifts, but perhaps one of the most significant was population growth.

Paleo-Indians

The Paleo-Indians were hunters who probably lived in small family groups (see **Paleo-Indian tradition**). Their numbers remained very low, they used large areas, they rarely stayed in one place very long, and they left behind very little for archaeologists to study. The absence of any kind of evidence about house construction plus the necessity to move about in search of game suggests that Paleo-Indians lived in caves or rock shelters or erected temporary houses out of brush (see **housing**). We know they were in the South, however, because they left behind hundreds of distinctive Clovis-style spear points, which have been dated to the time of Paleo-Indians. And about 12,800 years ago one unfortunate man fell more than eighty feet into Little Salt Spring in Florida. Unable to climb out, he swam to an exposed ledge and later died, presumably of starvation. Following his accident, the spring filled to the top, inundating his skeleton. When divers recently discovered the ledge, they found the oldest known Southerner.[3]

Paleo-Indians hunted with short, heavy thrusting spears tipped with Clovis points, which were large and heavy, making them unwieldy for throwing but quite adequate for killing large animals. Hunters preferred to ambush their quarry in marshes or at water holes. It was safer that way. But, thinking that killing and butchering such large animals required several men and some planning, scholars have speculated that Paleo-Indian bands had some form of political organization, at least for the hunt.

Southern Paleo-Indians also developed a smaller, lighter spear point called Dalton, which made hunting small game possible. Large numbers of Dalton points have been found in association with deer bones, indicating that Paleo-Indians had begun to expand their list of preferred game animals. This adaptation smoothed the transition from Paleo-Indian to Archaic by easing the process of learning how to live without Pleistocene animals. Logic also suggests that Paleo-Indians had probably learned to gather wild plants and nuts.

Archaic

During the period from 8000 B.C. to about the dawn of the Christian era, the climate of North America stabilized, creating the large number of local and regional environments we recognize today. The forests and plants, the animals that lived on them, and the people who subsisted on both began to assume characteristics that look familiar. The South became a definable place and Native Southerners developed traits that suited their needs in the region.

For the first four thousand years of the Archaic period, change was mainly evolutionary. People had long since stopped making Clovis points and in their place had developed a range of designs that fit the game, the region, the available raw stone materials, and the artistic tastes of the group. These changes in points are cultural markers for archaeologists. The most important thing the new points tell us is that variations in regional cultures became pronounced. Uniformity gave way to diversity in point design and, by inference, in culture. Hunters used their array of points to kill many species of small animals and birds, but deer and turkeys were by far the most important. They also fished the streams, gathered shellfish, and expanded their dependence on plants, nuts, and berries (see **fishing**). Populations grew as well, which set into motion all sorts of cultural changes.

Increased population suggests that the amount of territory available for the use of each band of Archaic Southerners probably shrank. Such shrinkage led to a more intimate acquaintance with the territory and permitted the development of an enhanced knowledge of its resources. This in turn introduced people to new foods, new **hunting** and fishing sites, and new sources of useful stone for tools. The reduced size of a band's territory also meant that people returned to favored sites, usually seasonally, changing the nature of their movement from a random search to an informed commute from one known resource to another. All this enhanced knowledge and experience permitted greater efficiency in the exploitation of natural resources.

During the second half of the Archaic period, from 4000 B.C. until about 700 B.C., greater changes occurred in the cultures of Native Southerners. Four important developments mark this period: horticulture, increased sedentism, pottery, and long-distance exchange of goods. Each development is connected with the other, each permitted new things to happen, and together they transformed the ancient South.

Women, generally understood to have been the gatherers of plants in ancient as well as modern times, almost certainly invented horticulture. As they gathered plants, they likely cleared the space around the plants they wanted, thereby removing weedy competitors and enabling the plants they preferred to thrive. If seeds dropped as the women carried them back to camp and sprouted in places they had never grown before, women learned the relation between seeds and plants. Planting and weeding lessons learned, women began to domesticate seed plants such as sunflowers and chenopodium. By 2440 B.C., Native Tennesseans were also growing bottle gourds and squash. The squash were valued as food; the gourds, as their name suggests, often became bottles (see **agriculture**).

The evidence for increased sedentism is apparent in the enormous shell middens that appear on the banks of rivers and along the coast (see **fishing**). Some of these piles of discarded shells extend for hundreds of feet and are twenty and more feet deep, suggesting that people gathered and ate shellfish at such places for long periods of time. Post molds are associated with these midden sites, indicating that the people built houses nearby. They also dug storage pits where they cached food and goods for extended periods. Taken together, these bits of evidence indicate that people lived in such places for at least part of every year for many years.

Beginning about 3000 B.C. people in the Appalachians carved simple bowls out of steatite, a soft stone (see **art**). Where there was no suitable stone, as along the coast, people made bowls from clay. The bowls were crude, tempered with fibers, heavy and clumsy, but they provided people with the means to boil food directly on a fire. This was so much easier than cooking in skin bags with heated stones that the technology spread. The earliest such pots were made on coastal South Carolina and Georgia about 2500 B.C. By 2100 B.C. Native Floridians were making pots, and by 1000 B.C. Appalachian people had switched from stone to pottery bowls. Along with the evidence of horticulture and shell middens, pottery also suggests increased sedentism.

The fourth change in the second half of the Archaic period, long distance exchange, is indicated by the presence in sites of goods made from materials that were locally unavailable (see **trade**; **Poverty Point**). Favored exchange items found in Southern sites include seashells, Great Lakes copper, slate, and colorful stones. Craftsmen either used these materials to make jewelry, points, and other things, or Native Southerners imported finished goods.

Archaeologist Vincas Steponaitis has suggested a hypothesis to explain these Late Archaic changes that is linked to population growth and the related shrinkage of band territories. As their movement became restricted, people had to expand their subsistence base by experimenting with new food sources. This led to horticulture and a greater reliance on shellfish, both of which intensified the process of increasing sedentism. People also needed to develop ways to store surplus food for periods of shortage. Storage pits, pots, and bottle gourds all offered solutions to that problem. Finally, bands came into increasing contact with one another. Friendly relations were cemented by gift exchanges that moved goods ever further from their points of origin. At the same time, exchanging gifts created opportunities for social and political relationships between bands, which forged alliances. The evidence of exchange networks indicates that Native Southerners had become active participants in a world larger than their own. Even as their world grew larger, however, it also had become smaller. As bands became ever more closely identified with a territory, they probably began to think of it as theirs, developing a range of emotional and religious ties to the place that explained and affirmed their dependence on it.[4]

Woodland

The third cultural sequence, **Woodland,** began about 700 b.c. Many Native Southerners continued in this cultural tradition until well after the European invasion that began in the sixteenth century. Others, however, transformed Woodland life into a specialized cultural complex that scholars call Mississippian. Thus in the South two distinct ways of life marked Native societies at the time of European contact.

In some ways Woodland cultures represent a continuation of changes that had begun in the Archaic period. Sedentism, for example, became even more the norm. By about a.d. 400, people occupied many villages year around. Sedentism is important because it roots people in place. As they make their communities permanent, invest their labor in them, and get born, live, and die in them, people develop attachments that make the place their own. They name themselves the people who live in that place. Their worldview is linked to that place because it is at the center of their world. For archaeologists, sedentism is important because sedentary people leave a lot more behind than nomadic people do. The careful study of sedentary communities permits a more profound understanding of the people, their institutions, their ways of life.

This trend toward increasing sedentism is connected to the increasing dependence of Native Southerners on horticulture (see **agriculture**). By at least A.D. 300, Southern women had added corn to their list of garden crops. Corn was an import from the Southwest. Easily adapted to local conditions, corn slowly increased in importance, but for many centuries it remained, along with domesticated native crops, important largely to supplement the **gathering** of wild plants and nuts. Men continued to hunt deer, turkeys, and waterfowl, catch fish, and gather shellfish, but meat declined in importance relative to plants in peoples' diets (see **fishing; hunting**). Native Southerners were never vegetarians, but they ate far less meat than do modern Americans.

One feature of Woodland culture that had few Archaic antecedents was elaborate and complex mortuary rituals (see **religion**). People celebrated death and burial publicly, they constructed mounds in which to inter the deceased, and they buried the body with large quantities of valuable and rare imported goods. Two things are especially important about this. Only a few individuals received fancy burials in mounds with piles of shell beads and jewelry, copper gorgets, and carved and polished stonework (see **art**). Most people were simply buried in the ground. Scholars interpret this as evidence of social ranking and assume that those who received special treatment were leaders of some kind. We can only guess, however, about how they came to command such respect. One hint lies in the grave goods. Items were valued because they were rare. The ability of leaders to accumulate rare things suggests that they controlled exchange relations with other groups. The goods that passed between leaders thus became status markers, identifying those with power as well as affirming their leadership. Control of exotic foreign goods was not the only way to achieve high status positions in Southern Woodland societies, of course. But the presence of such grave goods demonstrates that foreign exchange networks continued to be important and that control over those networks was an important element in the emergence of social ranking (see **government**).

Remarkably, this pattern of elaborate mortuary ritual, burial mounds, and exotic grave goods lasted only a few centuries—by about 600 or 700 it was gone. With its demise went most evidence of social ranking, chiefly power, and foreign exchange. In the absence of explanatory evidence, scholars have speculated that the common folk perhaps rejected the costs of tolerating and maintaining such excess. The basic pattern of Woodland life remained for many centuries and characterized the people who lived in coastal North and South Carolina. Women gathered and cultivated plants, men hunted, people lived in villages, and societies remained generally egalitarian.

Some Woodland peoples even developed the centralized, hierarchical societies that scholars call **chiefdoms** (see **government**). In northern Florida

Timucuan people created chiefdom societies that grew corn, beans, and squash, but good land was scarce and Timucuan communities tended to be small and scattered. Probably for that reason they did not build mounds or other kinds of ceremonial earthworks, and thus their beliefs were no doubt different from the Mississippian peoples who lived in **chiefdoms**.[5] Further south in Florida lived the Calusas. They did not farm at all, but rather lived on fish, shellfish, and various land animals and plants (see **fishing**). Their numbers are not known, but the natural environment was so rich they could concentrate large populations in permanent villages without having to farm. Even without agriculture, the Calusas organized a chiefdom under the leadership of powerful paramount chiefs who collected tribute from dozens of tribes throughout southern Florida.[6] The Powhatans of Virginia, another Woodland people, also developed a chiefdom, but many scholars think it was a response to the arrival of Europeans rather than a development from ancient needs.

The power of these Woodland chiefdoms, however, pales in comparison to that of the Mississippian societies that Hudson found so impressive. By the time Europeans arrived, Woodland peoples in the South were merely remnants of a waning tradition, and Mississippian chiefdoms had dominated Southern history for about seven hundred years.

Mississippian

Scholarly investigations of Mississippian societies over the past half-century have not only deepened our understanding of these remarkable people, they have broadened our sense of what those cultures were (see **Mississippian tradition**). Initially, academic definitions of Mississippian focused on three particular aspects of their physical culture. Shell-tempered pottery, for example, became recognized as a Mississippian characteristic. Tempering clay with pulverized shells increased the strength of pots, permitting the creation of finer, thinner walled containers and encouraging Mississippian potters to experiment with new shapes. Instead of the circular houses most Indians built, the houses of Mississippian people were square, made out of poles set upright into trenches (see **housing**). But most spectacular of all, they constructed mounds. Mississippian mounds are pyramidal in shape with a flat top. A ramp or stairs ascend one side, and on top they erected buildings for ceremonies or as residences for chiefs. Some mounds were huge. The largest known, Monk's Mound at Cahokia, which is near St. Louis, was one hundred feet high and covered sixteen acres of ground. Most were not so large, but there are thousands of them scattered throughout the South, from Spiro in Oklahoma to Town Creek in North Carolina. Most are in the Mississippi valley south of Cahokia, and to the east of that river in Mississippi, Alabama, and Georgia (see **Cahokia; Etowah; Ocmulgee; Moundville**).

As archaeological investigation has become more sophisticated, scholars have expanded their definition of Mississippian societies by adding to these material traits less obvious but more important cultural characteristics. For example, cleared-field corn **agriculture** has come to be recognized as particularly Mississippian. Aware of corn for several centuries, Southern women grew it in their gardens along with many other vegetables and used what they grew to supplement what they and their husbands gathered and hunted. Gardening was important, but it was not central to the subsistence of Southern Indians. This system changed, however. Beginning around 800 in some places, by 1200 Native people nearly everywhere except in southern Florida depended on corn for perhaps 50 percent of their diet. Like so many other changes, this one seems to have been precipitated by population growth. Increased numbers put so much pressure on the natural food supply that the people had to do things differently. Deciding to move toward cleared-field agriculture was not easy. With only stone tools and fire, clearing forest land for cornfields was an extremely difficult and expensive investment in time and labor. Cultivating large fields was also difficult, but locating Mississippian communities in river valleys made it easier. The rich alluvial bottom land was soft and could be tilled easily by Native women using digging sticks or hoes made by tying flint or the shoulder blades of deer to wooden handles. Once Native people had made the shift, food production increased dramatically, which encouraged the population to continue to increase.

Innovation continued. Southern women learned about beans around 1000. They were a perfect supplement to corn because they return to the soil the nitrogen that the corn consumes, they can climb up the corn stalks as on a trellis, and when eaten together they produce a tasty dish, succotash, which is much more nutritious than corn alone. Along with squash, which Indian women had been growing for centuries, corn and beans became the staples of Native America. **Gathering** wild plants, nuts, and berries, **hunting,** and **fishing** continued to be important sources of food, but they quickly assumed a secondary role to agriculture.

Another marker of Mississippian culture is a ranked social order based on birth rather than achievement and a hierarchical political system headed by a chief (see **government**). Agriculture is not necessary to the development of sociopolitical ranking, as the history of the Calusas makes clear, but among the Mississippians both political and social order seem to have depended on the production of bumper crops of corn. Intensive agriculture not only fed the people, it also provided a surplus large enough to purchase goods and services from elsewhere. In other words, agriculture made Mississippian culture possible.

The problem of Mississippian origins is both basic and not well understood.[7] Scholars have given up trying to develop a single scenario that fits all Mississippian groups. Rather, they have begun to work backward through the histories of specific groups in hopes of finding the trigger mechanisms that precipitated change. The problem, however, is simply stated. Why did people abandon basically egalitarian Woodland ideas in favor of subjecting themselves to authoritarian rule by a hereditary chief and his elite relatives and friends? In the absence of answers, scholars must try to figure out what had to exist in order to produce a ranked hierarchical form of social and political organization. Two obvious preconditions are population and surplus. The community had to have enough people and sufficient production to be able to tolerate inequality in the possession of goods. In the interior Southeast only agriculture could support the sedentism necessary to generate large enough populations and surpluses.

Several possible explanations for Mississippian emergence connect agriculture to hierarchy. One points to excessive strains on subsistence economy that threatened starvation. Another possible explanation is the danger of invasion and conquest by some foreign enemy. Finally, a belief that a particular lineage and an individual within that lineage possessed special spiritual power apparently fostered a new religion and encouraged charismatic leadership. There is evidence of all of these scenarios in Mississippian history. The problem is that we do not know how they fit into the sequence of events that led to Mississippian culture. The time of Mississippian emergence is generally thought to have been between 800 and 1000, the period when people adopted intensive cleared-field corn agriculture. As a result, most scholars conclude that a food crisis at least contributed to the development of Mississippian chiefdoms. All these scenarios have one factor in common, the need in moments of crisis for planning, direction, administration, and leadership (see **redistribution**). Someone had to take charge. The political term scholars have applied to Mississippian societies is **chiefdom**, suggesting that chiefs rule in much the same ways that kings rule kingdoms.

The availability of food surpluses seems to be connected to another feature of Mississippian life, the exchange of goods with neighboring chiefdoms (see **trade**). Gift exchanges mean two important things. On the one hand, people get goods they cannot produce, which, by virtue of their rarity, are valuable and socially important. And in the exchange of gifts with foreigners people also gain goodwill, friendship, and allies. Chiefs controlled the diplomatic relations with foreign chiefs that produced these benefits. Even as they protected their borders by surrounding their communities with friendly foreigners, they distributed exotic goods to their relatives and friends and cemented their political support. These were important contributions to the well-being of the community. At the same time, the possession and display of this wealth reaffirmed the high status of those who received the largess of the chief. Limited to his relatives, such generosity underscored the prestige of the chiefly lineage.

Chiefs lived on the tops of mounds. Socially and politically over all other members of the community, they were physically above them as well. But the mounds were also important for ceremonial purposes. Archaeologists cannot tell us much about what the ceremonies were like, but the evidence suggests that the people regarded their leaders as holy, in possession of special spiritual power and able to use that power to assure that things went right for the people. The **Southeastern Ceremonial Complex**, an artistic tradition associated with Mississippian chiefdoms, is replete with references to the special relationship between chiefs and the sun, widely regarded as the most powerful and sacred force in peoples' lives and essential to **agriculture** (see **art**). If the religion of Mississippian people taught that the chief was associated with the sun, then it would be clear to them that the chief had access to ultimate power and that thanks to his care and oversight they would survive and succeed.[8] Some believe that a purpose of the mounds in Mississippian towns was to lift the chief closer to the sun. Scholars also think that religious belief caused Mississippian people to build the mounds. Chiefly leadership was probably necessary to organize the construction labor, but, in the absence of any implication that the laborers were unwilling to work, religious motivation was almost certainly behind the digging, carrying, dumping, and spreading of tens of millions of cubic yards of dirt using only the technology of stone hoes and baskets.

Chiefs did not depend on sacred power alone. The other motif most common among the artifacts of the Southeastern Ceremonial Complex relates to **warfare**. War was a constant in Mississippian life. People seem to have feared invasion, because they encircled many of their communities with moats, palisades, and other defensive constructions. The carved shells, engraved copper gorgets, and other art objects suggest that Mississippians glorified warriors, thereby encouraging young men to defend their communities from attack as well as fight for the greater glory of the chief .

Chiefdoms grew. Scholars rank chiefdoms as simple, meaning one mound center or capital with surrounding farmsteads and fields, complex, meaning a chief with a mound center or capital controlling another chief and his chiefdom, and paramount, meaning a chief controlling complex as well as simple chiefdoms. Complex and paramount chiefdoms probably came into being through conquest. Paramount chiefs did not directly rule the chiefdoms they conquered. Rather, subordinate chiefs paid tribute to their overlords, thereby magnifying and reaffirming the spiritual and temporal power of the paramount. In return, the paramount defended his subordinates from the aggressions of others. The principle of reciprocity, which underlay all relations in the Mississippian world, thus governed the relations between and within chiefdoms (see **government**).[9]

Chiefdoms tended to be extremely unstable. Mississippian history is so marked by stories of rise and fall that archaeologist David Anderson has described their trajectories as "cycling."[10] Foreign invasion and conquest is partly to blame, but the primary cause of the collapse of Mississippian chiefdoms was probably internal and had to do with problems of succession. Because status was important in Mississippian societies, lineages competed for rank. And because the chief held the highest status, his lineage was supreme (see **kinship**). The result was that competing lineages took advantage of the death of a chief to put forward one of their own, often causing the institution to collapse. People could not be certain that the upstart lineage controlled the spiritual power necessary to assure future survival. Or several lineages vying for power would so deeply fragment society that there could be no agreement. Or, in the face of a leadership vacuum, a foreign neighbor might step in. Or people would simply leave. Mississippian demographic history demonstrates that whole regions would become denuded of their residents, sometimes for very long periods of time.

Scholars probably know more about the history of **Moundville**, a chiefdom on the Black Warrior River in west Central Alabama, than any other Mississippian society. Thanks to the careful work of dozens of archaeologists over the past thirty years, Vincas Steponaitis and Vernon James Knight have suggested a pattern of development, change, and collapse that extends from 900 to 1650.[11] Moundville was unusual in that its history does not conform to the picture of cycling described by Anderson. Rather, its chiefs dominated the region for 350 years. Archaeologist Paul D. Welch interpreted the unusual stability of Moundville in terms of the relationship between economic centralization and religion. His explanation is useful because it connects the religious, economic, and political elements of the Mississippian culture and argues that survival depended on the successful manipulation of those elements. He also described what all Mississippian chiefs tried to accomplish: "Leaders are supported by an ideology that attributes to them the ability to invoke or enlist abnormal (supernatural) powers. Prestige goods are material components of the ideology. As such they are visible, tangible emblems of the chief's supernatural power . . . . Chiefly monopoly of these goods would have been potent symbols of the quality and character of the chief, no doubt even a source of pride within the community. This may be why Moundville was so prominent for so long."[12]

When the Europeans arrived in North America, they entered into a dynamic world as full of history as it was of people. Over thousands of years Native Americans had moved into all parts of the continent and made it their own. They had developed cultures that made sense in the context of their environments and their needs, and they changed their cultures as their environments and needs changed. Europeans introduced new kinds of changes. The challenges for Native people came in their efforts to figure out how to respond to them.

Notes

1. Charles Hudson, *The Southeastern Indians* (Knoxville: University of Tennessee Press, 1976), 3.

2. George E. Lankford, ed., *Native American Legends: Southeastern Legends— Tales from the Natchez, Caddo, Biloxi, Chickasaw, and Other Nations* (Little Rock: August House, 1987), 107–17.

3. Brian M. Fagan, *Ancient North America: The Archaeology of a Continent* (New York: Thames and Hudson, 1991), 111–12.

4. Vincas Steponaitis, "Prehistoric Archaeology in the Southeastern United States, 1970–1985," *Annual Review of Anthropology* 15 (1986), 374–75.

5. Jerald T. Milanich, *The Timucua* (Cambridge, Mass.: Blackwell, 1996).

6. Randolph J. Widmer, *The Evolution of the Calusa: A Nonagricultural Chiefdom on the Southwest Florida Coast* (Tuscaloosa: University of Alabama Press, 1988).

7. Bruce D. Smith, ed., *The Mississippian Emergence* (Washington: Smithsonian Institution Press, 1990).

8. Patricia Galloway, ed., *The Southeastern Ceremonial Complex: Artifacts and Analysis* (Lincoln: University of Nebraska Press, 1989).

9. This summary of Mississippian history has drawn on the following works: Steponaitis, "Prehistoric Archaeology," 387–93; John F. Scarry, ed., *Political Structure*

and Change in the Prehistoric Southeastern United States (Gainesville: University Press of Florida, 1996); Randolph J. Widmer, "The Structure of Southeastern Chiefdoms," in *The Forgotten Centuries: Indians and Europeans in the American South, 1521–1704,* ed. Charles Hudson and Carmen Chaves Tesser (Athens: University of Georgia Press, 1994), 125–55.

10. David G. Anderson, *The Savannah River Chiefdoms: Political Change in the Late Prehistoric Southeast* (Tuscaloosa: University of Alabama Press, 1994).

11. Vernon James Knight Jr. and Vincas P. Steponaitis, "A New History of Moundville," in *Archaeology of the Moundville Chiefdom,* ed. Vernon James Knight Jr. and Vincas P. Steponaitis (Washington: Smithsonian Institution Press, 1998), 1–25.

12. Paul D. Welch, "Control Over Goods and the Political Stability of the Moundville Chiefdom," in *Political Structure and Change,* ed. Scarry, 91.

3 The European Invasion

The European invasion of the South formally began with the arrival of Ponce de Leon on the peninsula he named Florida in 1513. While shipwrecked sailors may well have preceded him, De Leon's expedition, which was partly exploratory but mostly a slave raid, initiated a century of repeated attempts by the Spanish to discover wealth in the Southeast (see **slavery**). Early Spanish interest in Indians was limited to their usefulness as laborers, hostages, porters, sexual partners, purveyors of food, interpreters, and guides. Nevertheless, Spanish chroniclers who accompanied the *conquistadores* have provided us with the first written accounts of the Native people of the Southeast. Particularly when used in conjunction with archaeological excavations, this documentary record reveals a world that had largely disappeared by the time the English and French colonized North America.

The *Conquistadores*

At the time Ponce de Leon made his foray into Florida, Spanish settlement did not extend beyond the Caribbean, but the Spaniards' need for labor to work island sugar plantations attracted them to other regions. The discovery of the wealthy and populous Aztec empire in 1519 suggested possibilities other than sugar production and slave raiding for acquiring fortunes in the Americas. Two years later, De Leon's attempt to colonize Florida ended in disaster when Indians attacked the colonists. In 1526 Lucas Vásquez de Allyón attempted to plant a colony on what would become the Georgia coast, but it too failed, largely because of starvation and illness, which claimed the lives of 350 of the 500 colonists. These casualties did not approach those suffered by Panfilo de Narváez, whose expedition in 1528 suffered Indian attacks, storms, and a host of difficulties so severe that only 4 out of 400 members of the expedition survived, and it took them nine years to reach Mexico. This series of colonizing disasters might have dampened enthusiasm for exploring the Southeast had it not been for Francisco Pizarro's discovery and conquest in the early 1530s of the fabulously wealthy Inca empire of South America. The success of this expedition whetted the ambitions of one of its participants, Hernando de Soto, who sailed for Florida in 1539 with approximately six hundred men to seek riches and establish a profitable colony.

De Soto's journey across the Southeast reveals a great deal about the Native people of the region. Although they were organized politically into chiefdoms, Southeastern Indians had neither the empires nor the wealth of the Aztecs and Incas. They possessed copper and freshwater pearls, but the value of these paled in comparison to the gold and silver of Native empires to the South. What most of the Southeastern **chiefdoms** did have was copious quantities of corn, which De Soto seized, and a substantial population, many of whom he enslaved to carry the expedition's plunder (see **agriculture**). Southeastern Indians lived in permanent villages whose location shaped De Soto's route as he moved from one to another seeking food, shelter, and riches. De Soto became so accustomed to the bounty of these towns that disease and famine in particular regions and unpopulated buffer zones that separated chiefdoms presented major logistical problems for the expedition. Even as he seized their food and enslaved their people, De Soto left a compelling testament to the prosperity and power of the Native Southeast.

De Soto landed at Tampa Bay in May 1539 and established a base camp. The land in the vicinity, however, was relatively barren and incapable of supporting an army the size of De Soto's. Furthermore, the local people remembered well the cruelty of Narváez, whose soldiers had cut off the chief's nose while his dogs had devoured the man's wife, and embarked on a harassing campaign. By July De Soto had decided to seek better provisions, more hospitable conditions, and great wealth elsewhere. Leaving part of his force at the base camp, he moved east and then north with more than three hundred others. They killed or captured many of the Native people they encountered, seized their stores of food, and destroyed their villages. One chief described the Spaniards in a message he sent to captive Indians: "They are demons, not sons of the Sun and moon, for they go about killing and robbing. They do not bring their own women, but prefer to possess the wives and daughters of others. They are not content to colonize a particular piece of land because they take such pleasure in being vagabonds, living upon the labor of others. They are thieves and murderers."[1]

By fall De Soto had reached the province of Apalachee in north Florida, the first **Mississippian** chiefdom he had encountered. The people of Apalachee had a reputation among their neighbors for ferocity, a lesson learned by a young Spaniard whose sexual assault on an Apalachee woman ended when his victim forcefully seized his genitals and refused to let go until other soldiers came to his rescue. The military might of Apalachee, like other Mississippian chiefdoms, rested on its ability to produce enormous quantities of food. The promise of food had been one factor that lured the Spaniards to Apalachee, and De Soto's men were not disappointed. According to anthropologist Charles Hudson, "They passed through fields of corn and vegetables as far as the eye could see, with many houses scattered about."[2] The Apalachee constructed fences and barricades to obstruct the progress of the horses and harrassed the army from behind cover, but eventually De Soto reached the principal town of Anhayca, which the Indians had fled. He made the town his winter camp. Food stores were so plentiful that the expedition spent five months there without traveling more than five miles for additional provisions.[3] But De Soto did not find gold, silver, or jewels, and so in the spring he moved further into the interior of the Southeast.

In what is today South Carolina, De Soto encountered the Lady of Cofitachequi, whom he considered to be the ruler of a large chiefdom that reached from the mountains to the coast. She lived in a ceremonial center in a large house atop a high mound, which denoted her power and prestige as well as that of her lineage. When De Soto arrived on the other side of the river from another of her major towns, servants carried the Lady of Cofitachequi down to the river on a litter draped with a white cloth. She boarded a dugout canoe, sat on cushions beneath an awning, and crossed the river along with her principal men to meet De Soto. Her subjects provided a seat on which she sat, and they remained absolutely quiet while she spoke. She told De Soto about her chiefdom, and she presented him with gifts including several strings of freshwater pearls.

De Soto rewarded her hospitality by desecrating temples, which were located on mounds, and robbing Cofitachequi's dead of the pearls with which they had been adorned. At the mortuary temple of the ruling lineage, he found lifelike wooden statues (the men were armed for war), pearls, shell gorgets, feathered headdresses and mantles, painted deerskins, and valuable pelts. Apparently appalled by the Spaniards behavior, the Lady of Cofitachequi fled, and a warrior who was related to her committed suicide rather than reveal her whereabouts. When she reappeared, De Soto placed her under guard and made plans to move on. The supply of corn in Cofitachequi was running low, possibly because of recent drought, epidemic, or political instability, and the chiefdom's inhabitants had told De Soto that a "great lord" lived twelve days away in Chiaha. De Soto further humiliated the Lady of Cofitachequi by forcing her to accompany him on foot. A little more than two weeks after the expedition left Cofitachequi, the Lady and one of her attendants went into the woods to relieve themselves and escaped, taking a basket of pearls with them. They joined several Indian and African slaves who had also escaped, and the last De Soto heard of the Lady of Cofitachequi she had taken one of them for her husband.[4]

De Soto pressed on through other chiefdoms and into the territory of the paramount chiefdom of Coosa, which lay in eastern Tennessee, northwestern Georgia, and northeastern Alabama. To ensure the submission of this powerful people, he took the chief and his sister hostage. Once the expedition reached the boundary of Coosa, De Soto released only the chief and kept the woman as his slave. He then entered the domain of Tascaluza, another paramount chief who was Coosa's rival.

Tascaluza apparently had been preparing for the expedition's arrival. He sent his son and other emissaries ostensibly to greet the Spaniards but in reality to spy on them. When the Spaniards met Tascaluza at Atahatchi, near present-day Montgomery, they found him waiting in front of his house, which was built atop a mound. He wore a long feathered cloak and a cloth turban and seated himself on two cushions under a sunshade made of a painted deerskin and held by one of his retainers. Although Southeastern Indian men in general were taller than the Spaniards, Tascaluza and his son were particularly large, towering more than a foot above the men in De Soto's expedition. As was his custom, De Soto took Tascaluza hostage and demanded porters and women. Tascaluza provided the porters and promised that the women would be available at another town named Mabila. The expedition set out for Mabila with Tascaluza, feet just inches above the ground, riding De Soto's strongest packhorse.

Based on the accounts of De Soto's chroniclers, Hudson has described Mabila as "a small, strongly stockaded village situated in a cleared field." The Indians had bound poles crosswise to upright posts and plastered the

whole over with mud to form the pallisade, and at intervals they had built
bastions and openings for archers. They also had cleared ground surrounding the village not only of buildings and shrubbery but even of weeds. The
population of the village was unusual — mostly young men with a few young
women but no children or elderly people. The chief of Mabila greeted De
Soto as he approached the village, presented him with gifts, and invited him
to proceed through the gate in the pallisade. De Soto and a few other Spaniards went inside where beautiful young women entertained them with dancing. Then Tascaluza entered one of the houses and refused to come out,
precipitating a series of events that culminated with the attack of 5,000 Indians hidden in the houses of Mabila. All the Spaniards inside the palisade
were injured or killed. Although he was wounded, De Soto escaped and
directed a counterattack. Ultimately Mabila fell to the Spaniards who had
managed not only to use their horses and armor to great advantage but also
to scale the palisade and torch the thatch-roofed houses inside. Twenty-two
Spaniards died and 148 suffered wounds. These casualties, however, were
negligible compared to those of the Natives at Mabila. Estimates place the
toll at 3,000 (see **warfare**).[5]

The force amassed against De Soto at Mabila may represent a cooperative
effort of several chiefdoms, including Coosa, that put aside their differences
to combat this new foe. More commonly, De Soto encountered chiefs who
sought to use Spanish military might to defeat neighboring chiefdoms. Upon
reaching the Mississippi, he became drawn into one of these conflicts. The
Mississippi presented a real challenge, and De Soto ordered the construction
of crafts to ferry the expedition across the mighty river. Every day for nearly
a month a fleet of two hundred to three hundred dugout canoes manned
by seven thousand Indians harried the Spaniards and forced them to construct defensive foxholes. Oarsmen expertly maneuvered the canoes in the
rapid current in compliance with the orders of a chief who sat under a
canopy, and a line of archers, many protected by shields, stood in the middle
of each canoe from stem to stern. They told De Soto that they came from
the paramount chief Pacaha, who ultimately ordered them to let De Soto
cross.

Once he reached the west bank of the river, De Soto learned that Pacaha
had an enemy, Casqui, and he decided to visit Casqui before going to Pacaha, home of the ferocious canoes. The towns of Casqui and Pacaha were
located in what is today eastern Arkansas. The rich alluvial soil supported
enormous fields of corn interspersed with pecan, mulberry, and persimmon
trees, and towns were often visible from each other. Casqui warmly wel-

comed De Soto, whom he hoped to enlist in his war against Pacaha. Believing that De Soto possessed great spiritual power, he asked for a religious symbol to which he could pray. De Soto obliged with the construction and erection of a great cross on top of the mound in Casqui's principal town, an act that seemed to confirm the Spaniard's power when a heavy rain on the very day the cross was consecrated ended a long drought.

Casqui and some of his warriors accompanied De Soto's expedition to the main town of Pacaha, but most of the people and their chief had fled, taking with them much of their movable wealth. The discovery of a number of Casqui's people, enslaved by Pacaha and maimed to keep them from fleeing, infuriated the warriors, and they plundered the town, sacking Pacaha's house and temple and destroying the bones of his ancestors. Casqui provided canoes to transport the army to the island in the Mississippi where Pacaha and his people had taken refuge. The refugees had placed a large quantity of clothing and other goods on rafts, one of which broke free and drifted down river. Casqui's warriors went after it, but when they retrieved it they did not return the goods to De Soto. Increasingly irrational after the battle at Mabila, De Soto repudiated his alliance with Casqui, ordered a raid on his former friends, and opened negotiations with Pacaha. Ultimately, the three parties came to an uneasy truce, and De Soto departed.[6]

De Soto spent the next year exploring west of the river, but he never found the gold and silver he sought. By May 1542 he had returned to the Mississippi River south of Casqui and Pacaha, where he died. His men tried to reach Mexico overland, but ultimately they made their way back to the Mississippi where they constructed boats. By drifting, rowing, and sailing, approximately 350 of them arrived in Mexico in September 1543, nearly 4½ years after their expedition had begun.

De Soto's failure to find riches or establish a colony only momentarily slowed European colonization attempts in the Southeast. Before the end of the sixteenth century Tristán de Luna y Arellano and Juan Pardo would penetrate the interior and visit the chiefdom of Coosa. In 1565 Pedro Menéndez de Avilés founded colonies at St. Augustine and Santa Elena, now Parris Island, and crushed a French Huguenot colony established in the previous year near the mouth of the St. John's River. Soon Jesuit and then Franciscan priests began to missionize the Guale Indians along the south Atlantic coast. St. Augustine survived a raid by Sir Francis Drake in 1587 to ultimately claim the title of oldest continuously occupied European settlement in the United States. But the Spanish abandoned Santa Elena that year after two Indian rebellions, the threat of a raid by Drake, and rumors of a nearby English colony, actually located on Roanoke Island on the North Carolina coast. The century closed with Europeans more determined than ever to dramatically change the region. Unknown to them, the process was already well underway.

Depopulation

The major factor of change in the Native Southeast was a massive decline in population. We may never know the scope of depopulation because arriving at aboriginal population figures is very difficult. In the early twentieth century James Mooney made a systematic attempt, based on historical sources, to determine the Native population north of Mexico in 1600, nearly a century after contact with Europeans. Mooney found 52,200 Indians in the south Atlantic states and 114,400 in the Gulf states. More recently, Douglas Ubelaker of the Smithsonian has revised these figures. Using Mooney's regional designations, Ubelaker concluded that 92,916 Indians lived in the south Atlantic states and 473,616 in the Gulf states at the time of European contact. Although some scholars have accepted Ubelaker's figures as relatively accurate, most regard them as too low, and some such as Henry Dobyns have directly challenged them. Based on a calculation of the population that a particular environment and technology can support, Dobyns has suggested that the shores of the Gulf of Mexico supported 1,100,000 people, the Atlantic coast from Florida to Massachusetts had 2,211,000 people, 5,250,000 lived in the valleys of the Mississippi and its tributaries, and the peninsula of Florida alone was home to 697,000 in 1492.[7] Many scholars consider Dobyns's methodology based on the carrying capacity of the environment to be flawed and his population estimate to be far too high. Hudson, using the much lower depopulation rate of 6.47 to 1, which scholars have established for the main towns of Coosa, and totals for the entire Southeast in 1685, has arrived at a precontact population of 1,294,000.[8] Hudson's work, however, has also placed a face on population counts. His descriptions of five thsouand warriors battling De Soto at Mabila or seven thousand Indians maneuvering Mississippi River currents in a fleet of two hundred to three hundred war canoes make the point better than abstract numbers: a large population lived in the Southeast when Europeans arrived.

That population, however, declined dramatically. Dobyns has estimated that the Timucuan-speaking population shrank from 722,000 prior to 1519 to just 36,750 in 1618, and his more generalized assessment indicates a decline of 95 percent.[9] Peter Wood, who charted populations after 1685, estimated that Southeastern Indians numbered 199,400 at his baseline, long after the first epidemics had struck, and 55,900 in 1790, a depopulation rate of 72 percent. In North and South Carolina east of the mountains, only 600 people remained out of 20,000 for a decline of 97 percent.[10] Russell Thornton has estimated that between 1492 and 1900 the Native population north of Mexico decreased 93 percent.[11]

The military victories of the *conquistadores* took their toll, but **disease** accounts for most of this population loss. Native Americans had little resistance to the pathogens of Europe. Epidemic diseases such as smallpox and bubonic plague, which killed large numbers of people in Europe as well, had devastating effects, but less deadly maladies such as measles produced horrendous casualties among Indians. Dobyns estimated that a documented outbreak of measles in Florida in 1596 claimed a quarter of the Native population.[12] Mumps, scarlet fever, diptheria, typhus, typhoid fever, and influenza as well as the tropical diseases, malaria and yellow fever, came to America with Europeans. People who recovered from one of these diseases usually acquired some immunity from that particular disease, but few had time to recover fully before a different disease struck. On average, Dobyns estimated, an epidemic swept North America every 4 ½ years. An account from the Roanoke colony in the 1580s vividly describes the impact of disease on neighboring Indians: "The people began to die very fast, and many in short space; in some towns about twentie, in some fourtie, in some sixtie, & in one six score, which in truth was very manie in respect of their numbers."[13]

These diseases took a heavy toll because Native Americans had little immunity to them. The Americas and its peoples had long been separated from the rest of the world. The arctic through which Paleo-Indians traveled on their migrations from Asia may have acted as a germ filter, killing most pathogens. In the centuries after the land bridge disappeared, Europe became urbanized, particularly in the late Middle Ages when people crowded into walled cities with little thought to sanitation. While Native people lived in towns, some as large as European cities, their density did not approach those of European cities in the period just before contact. Over the centuries Europeans, unlike Native Americans, domesticated a variety of animals whose diseases can be transmitted to humans. People living in European cities did not leave their livestock on the farm, and so animal wastes combined with the garbage generated by humans to create deplorable living conditions and breeding grounds for disease. Europeans died in large numbers from epidemic disease—the Black Death of the mid-fourteenth century killed perhaps one third of them—but this death rate does not approach those suffered by Native people.

The lack of experience with European diseases probably increased the death toll, although Europeans had few treatments that worked either. The epidemic suffered by the Indians at Roanoke was "so strange, that they neither knew what it was, nor how to cure it; the like by report of the oldest men in the countrey never happened before."[14] When smallpox struck in the 1730s the Cherokees explained its cause to trader James Adair as "the adulterous intercourse of their young married people, who in the past year, had in a most notorious manner, violated their ancient laws of marriage in every thicket, and broke down and polluted many of their honest neighbors bean plots, by their heinous crimes, which would cost a great deal of trouble to purify again."[15] Because the Cherokees, like other Southeastern Indians, attributed disease to spiritual causes, they sought to purify themselves through sweat baths and plunges in icy rivers. Those who survived the treatment often took their own lives because they could not bear the scars that reminded them of their impurity: "Some shot themselves, others cut their throats, some stabbed themselves with knives, and others with sharp-pointed canes; many threw themselves with sullen madness into the fire."[16] The inability of their priests to cure these new diseases probably created a crisis of confidence in their religious leaders. The Cherokees have an oral tradition that they rose up and destroyed their priests because the holy men had violated sexual rules. Given the connection made by the Cherokees, they might simply have assumed that only the most serious violations could cause an epidemic of massive proportions and took measures accordingly.

Priests, however, may have been disproportionately victims of disease. Native Southerners, like many people who rely on oral tradition, revered age and the lifetime accumulation of knowledge that age represented. Priests were likely to be elderly people whose long lives had enabled them to learn elaborate ceremonies, healing herbs and rituals, oral traditions, and religious teachings as well as acquire heightened spiritual purity. But their advanced age made priests more likely to die of epidemic disease. Therefore, many Native communities lost their spiritual leaders and the repositories of knowledge these leaders had become. In this way, disease destroyed their past. Disease also claimed their future. Particularly susceptible to the dehydration that accompanies high fevers, children also died disproportionately. For every child who succumbed, the population lost not only an individual but also the children that person would have had if he or she had lived to adulthood.

With such massive population loss Native people were no longer able to sustain the world De Soto saw. Specific Mississippian chiefdoms had collapsed periodically before the Spanish entrada for reasons that are not fully understood and new ones had emerged, but the arrival of the Spanish marked the end of an entire cultural tradition. The elites who combined spiritual and military power to govern extensive chiefdoms largely disappeared, and chiefdoms dissolved into confederacies of loosely linked towns (see **government**). The Indians abandoned many towns and relocated others, and when the population was not sufficient to sustain a society, they created new peoples by merging disparate groups. Mound building came to a halt, as did the fabrication of elaborate pottery, wooden statues, and shell gorgets. By the time European traders pushed into the interior Southeast in the eighteenth century, Native people truly lived in a new world.

A New World in the Southeast

One of the most frustrating things about the new world that emerged in the Southeast during the sixteenth and seventeenth centuries is that the profound changes wrought by disease and invasion obscure links between the peoples De Soto encountered and the Indian tribes of the eighteenth century. Archaeological excavations have provided some clues, but many mysteries remain. We do not know, for example, the location of Mabila, where the great battle took place. Even more problematic, we do not know precisely which of the peoples De Soto met became the Choctaws, Creeks, Cherokees, and other historic tribes. Native people only rarely proved helpful in making these links. Eighteenth-century inhabitants of mound sites often had little notion of who built them: the Cherokees near the **Etowah** site in North Georgia, for example, were as perplexed by the great mounds in their midst as the Europeans who inquired about them. The names of towns De Soto passed through constitute linguistic evidence, but since some of the chiefdoms seem to have been polyglot, languages are not a clear indicator of whose ancestors lived where (see **Algonkian languages**; **Caddoan languages**; **Iroquoian languages**; **Muskogean languages**; **Siouan languages**). Furthermore, as Patricia Galloway has demonstrated for the Choctaws, some peoples were amalgams of several chiefdoms that collapsed and combined.[17] Consequently, there is a discontinuity in the past of Native Southerners that scholars like Hudson and Galloway are only beginning to reconcile. As ethnohistorians reconstruct the culture histories of Native peo-

ples, however, they have been able to discern cultural practices that probably
have their roots in **Mississippian.**

Perhaps the eighteenth-century people who most closely resembled Mississippian chiefdoms were the Natchez who lived on the lower Mississippi. The Natchez distinguished between their elite ruling class and commoners, and they gave extraordinary deference to the Great Sun, who was their ruler, and to his family, the Suns. When the people encountered the Great Sun or even came in sight of his temple, they performed a ceremonial greeting. They gave him enormous quantities of food, and head warriors cultivated a sacred field of corn for him. Other Suns had special prerogatives: they never ate with commoners or permitted their food dishes to be touched by them. When a Sun died a number of people, including spouse and servants, were ritually killed. The Great Sun, however, also had obligations, in particular, the generous redistribution of food to his people, and while people treated him deferentially he also had a council that advised him. The Great Sun's position descended matrilineally to his sister's son rather than to his own, but individuals obtained other elite positions in Natchez society through merit rather than birth. Therefore, while the power of the Great Sun exceeded that of chiefs in other Southeastern societies, other aspects of Natchez society such as redistribution, councils, matrilineality, and leadership based on merit were widespread in the eighteenth century (see **government; kinship**).

One of the ways that scholars have tried to establish connections between the Mississippian world and the Native peoples who appear in the documentary record is through their religious beliefs. In *The Southeastern Indians*, Hudson linked the myths anthropologist James Mooney collected among the eastern Cherokees at the end of the nineteenth century with Mississippian artifacts, especially shell gorgets incised with religious symbols, to describe "the categories and beliefs of the Southern Indians [which] represented the world as they believe it existed, and this included both the natural and the supernatural, the normal and the abnormal, and the sacred and the profane." Hudson insisted on beginning his massive analysis of culture with the belief system: "The social arrangements, customary practices, and rituals of the Southeastern Indians make sense only when viewed against the ideological background of their belief system" (see **religion**).[18]

Southeastern Indians conceived of a three-level cosmos consisting of the Upper World, the Under World, and This World. The Upper World was the domain of past time and predictability, and fire was its earthly representative. The Under World controlled the future and change, and water was associated with it. This World, the domain of human beings, mediated between the two. People not only had to balance the Upper and Lower Worlds, they had also to keep the two separate. Consequently, Indians never put out fire with water; they used the soil of This World instead. Maintaining the purity of discreet categories, preventing or repairing the pollution of those categories, and balancing opposites formed the core of Southeastern Indian religious belief and practice.

Native Southerners did not envision a hierarchical world, like Europeans did, in which man had dominion over the rest of creation. Indeed, people occupied a rather precarious position. In one of the myths collected by Mooney, the animals decided to go to war against human beings because men indiscriminately hunted and killed them. After several botched attempts to get revenge, they decided to send diseases to afflict man whenever he killed one of them without showing proper respect. Plants, however, took pity on people and offered a remedy for each disease. Therefore, plants balanced animals. Human beings came to rely on plants for cures, but they also took pains not to offend the animals and offered prayers and sacrifices when they had to kill one.

This system of opposites that balanced one another extended to the relations between men and women, hunting and farming, summer and winter (see **agriculture**; **hunting**). In winter men hunted deer and other animals, including bears and turkeys. In summer women cultivated fields of corn, beans, squash, and other vegetables. Women did not know the ceremonies that men conducted when they killed game, and men were not privy to the songs and rituals associated with agriculture. Feminist anthropologists have described these distinct realms as arenas of power because radically separate tasks and rites meant that neither men nor women had control over the other's economic activities. Women supervised their own work and controlled the product of their labor just as did men.[19]

Since agriculture formed the basis of Southeastern Indian societies, their primary religious ritual, the **Green Corn Ceremony**, commemorated the crop. Held when the corn first became edible, the Green Corn Ceremony celebrated both the crop and the communitarian ethic that shaped their lives. The community spent days preparing for the event by cleaning public buildings and private houses, spreading a new layer of soil over the plaza, extinguishing the sacred fire that burned constantly, and destroying any surplus from the year before. Men fasted in advance of the consecration of the corn; we are not sure what women did because our sources are from European men who did not have access to their preparations. At the central event elderly women presented the new crop. Priests then rekindled the sacred fire whose embers lit fires in each household and reminded people of their obligations to the community. Individuals received absolution for wrongs they had committed (except murder), and estranged spouses became free to take new partners. Finally, the people performed sacred dances, ritually bathed in the river, and feasted on the green corn, their community cleansed of physical, spiritual, and social pollution (see **music and dance**).

Like agriculture, the **kinship** system that organized domestic and public life also may have come from Mississippian. Scholars think that the kin ties that bound elite Mississippian families together were those traced through women. Therefore, nephews inherited positions from maternal uncles, not fathers, and sisters assumed an exalted position in men's lives that Europeans associated with wives. This helps explain why the chief of Coosa became distraught over De Soto's refusal to release his sister, whose children would have been his heirs. As Hudson phrased it, "The chief of Coosa would sooner have parted with his wife than his sister."[20] The matrilineal kinship system was well intact in the eighteenth century and remains so in some Southeastern Indian communities at the beginning of the twenty-first.

People were born into the clans and lineages of their mothers, and they retained those affiliations throughout their lives. A clan was a very large kin group, often numbering into the thousands, that descended from an ancient mythical ancestor. Clans usually took the names of animals, but sometimes they had names, such as Wind and Long Hair, that strike us today as odd. Lineages descended from a known woman, and the members often lived together in multigeneration households. Women were the permanent residents of these matrilocal households, and their husbands lived with them. Brothers resided with their own wives, but they frequently visited their own lineages—those of their mothers and sisters—and contributed to their support. When marriages dissolved, husbands simply left their wives and children, who were not blood relatives, and returned to the houses of their mothers and sisters.

Matrilineal kinship did far more in Southeastern Indian society than order domestic relations. With lineages scattered throughout the towns of a particular tribe, clans served to link those towns together and form the basis of a political entity. A person traveling through his or her tribe's territory could expect to find a warm welcome in households of clan kin, even if members of a household had never met that person before. Clans also performed many of the functions we associate with governments, and the mutual obligations of clan members helped create a polity (see **government**;

kinship). Clans sought retribution for crimes committed against their members, and they exacted blood vengeance for the deaths of relatives. If the individual responsible could not be found, another clan member suffered instead. Relatives refused protection to the person responsible for murder, and they refrained from further retaliation once a death had been avenged. Therefore, acts of vengeance did not degenerate into feuds, because everyone understood that a death required that the imbalance between clans be rectified.

The same principle of retaliation applied to foreign tribes, with one important exception: retaliation went on, back and forth, indefinitely. When Cherokees killed a Creek, Creeks retaliated in order to redress the imbalance. But Cherokees had acted originally in order to establish equilibrium, and so, from their perspective, this new death upset things once again. As a result, Southeastern Indians were constantly at war, but wars usually consisted of little more than raids by small groups of young men related to the latest victim. These raids required elaborate ritual preparation: men secluded themselves in the townhouse, fasted, purged themselves, and abstained from sex. Participation was strictly voluntary, and anyone who had misgivings stayed home rather than jeopardize the entire venture. When the war party achieved its goal, it returned home. The warriors marked their victory publicly with ritual dancing and stories of war exploits and privately with seclusion from the rest of society until they had been ritually purified. Sometimes war parties brought captives home from their raids and turned them over to women. Clans adopted some of these captives, but women made others atone for the deaths of relatives through torture. Among Southeastern Indians only Cherokee women actually went to war, but women, like men, had a responsibility to avenge the deaths of relatives. Torture gave women an opportunity to exact vengeance and fulfill a sacred obligation (see **warfare**).

Southeastern Indians dealt with rivalries or disputes that did not demand blood vengeance by playing ball. Sometimes towns played each other and occasionally tribes took to the field. Far more than a sport, the ballgame was regarded as the "younger brother of war," and young men prepared for a match with rituals similar to those they performed before going to war. In order to win they needed spiritual rather than physical power, and they looked to medicine men to prepare them for a game. A medicine man might scratch players to purify them or give them pieces of wood that had been struck by lightening to carry in their pockets. The game itself, the forerunner of modern lacrosse, was an exacting and often violent event in which two teams armed with ballsticks, a kind of racket, sought to get a small deerskin ball across opposing goal lines. In the 1830s the artist George Catlin described a ballgame between six hundred and one thousand Choctaws "denuded, and painted various colors, running and leaping into the air, in all the most extravagant and varied forms, in the desperate struggle for the ball."[21]

Among the Creeks and perhaps other Southeastern peoples as well, clans organized political leadership, with some providing war leaders and others peace chiefs. In the Creek war organization a town's war chief was called *tastanagi thlako*, secondary war leaders were the *tastanagalgi*, following them were the *imathla thlako* and *imathla labotke*, and finally there was the *tasikayalgi*, or private. In the civil government a head chief, or *miko*, presided over a council composed of professional peace advocates, or *henihalgi*, and distinguished elder statesmen, *isti atcagagi*. Creeks had other titles as well, and these titles became so much a part of men's identity that Creek leaders usually appear in the historical record only as a title attached to a town, as much a reflection of how they viewed themselves as how Europeans regarded them (see **government**).

Despite the hierarchical nature of Creeks political organization, they, like other Southeastern Indians, governed themselves by consensus. Chiefs earned their positions by their accomplishments rather than inheriting rank by birth. Councils met for days, weeks, and sometimes months to discuss important issues and forge a consensus. In most Southeastern societies in the eighteenth century, men did most of the speaking in council, although women occasionally voiced their opinions, especially on land cessions. Cherokee women, and perhaps women in other tribes, held separate councils, and, even if they did not have formal meetings, women no doubt made their views known to clan kin who sat in council (see **government**).

These were the governments that Europeans negotiated with in the eighteenth century. Chiefs, even among the Creeks, never had as much power as Europeans thought they did—or as their Mississippian progenitors had enjoyed. Through seemingly endless debate, councils reached consensus on major issues, and chiefs carried out these decisions. Although often persuasive in debate, chiefs did not rule; they led. The decision-making process reinforced the corporate ethic that characterized Southeastern societies in the eighteenth century. The practice of **redistribution**, inherited perhaps from Mississippian, extended the ethic to economic activities. Chiefs collected corn and other goods into a public granary from which those in need were supplied. From the perspective of individualistic, acquisitive Europeans, perhaps no practice better illustrated how different they were from Native Southerners.

Notes

1. The information on the de Soto expedition is a summary of material in Charles Hudson, *Knights of Spain, Warriors of the Sun: Hernando de Soto and the South's Ancient Chiefdoms* (Athens: University of Georgia Press, 1997). Quote is from 109–10.

2. Ibid., 119.

3. Ibid., 127.

4. Ibid., 172–92.

5. Ibid., 228–49.

6. Ibid., 284–309.

7. For a summary of the problems involved in calculating population and depopulation, see Russell Thornton, *American Indian Holocaust and Survival: A Population History Since 1492* (Norman: University of Oklahoma Press, 1987), especially chapters 2 and 3. Dobyns's fascinating and controversial book is *Their Number Become Thinned: Native American Population Dynamics in Eastern North America* (Knoxville: University of Tennessee Press, 1983). See 41–42 for estimates.

8. Hudson, *Knights*, 425.

9. Dobyns, *Their Number*, 34–44, 294.

10. Peter H. Wood, "The Changing Population of the Colonial South: An Overview by Race and Region, 1685–1790," in *Powhatan's Mantle: Indians in the Colonial Southeast*, ed. Peter H. Wood, Gregory A. Waselkov, and M. Thomas Hatley (Lincoln: University of Nebraska Press, 1989), 38–39.

11. Thornton, *American Indian Holocaust*, 42.

12. Dobyns, *Their Number*, 285.

13. From Thomas Hariot, *A Briefe and True Report of the New Found Land of Virginia*. Quoted in Thornton, *American Indian Holocaust*, 66–67.

14. From Hariot, *A Briefe*. Quoted in Thornton, *American Indian Holocaust*, 67.

15. James Adair, *Adair's History of the American Indians*, ed. Samuel Cole Williams (1775; reprint, Johnson City, Tenn.: Watauga, 1930), 244–45.

16. Ibid.

17. Patricia Galloway, *Choctaw Genesis, 1500–1700* (Lincoln: University of Nebraska Press, 1995).

18. Hudson, *The Southeastern Indians* (Knoxville: University of Tennesse Press, 1976), 120.

19. See Laura F. Klein and Lillian F. Ackerman, eds., *Women and Power in Native North America* (Norman: University of Oklahoma Press, 1995).

20. Hudson, *Knights*, 228.

21. George Catlin, *Letters and Notes on the Manners, Customs, and Conditions of the North American Indians*, 2 vols. (1844; reprint, New York: Dover, 1973), 2:123.

4 Native Peoples and Colonial Empires

When Christopher Columbus sailed into the Caribbean Sea in 1492 under the flag of Spain, he began the process by which Europe laid claim to America. That claim extended not only to the land and its resources but also to the Native people who for thousands of years had lived on the land and used it as their own. Columbus and other Spaniards followed that initial voyage to establish colonial settlements in the islands, explore neighboring lands and, beginning in 1519, invade and conquer the Native empires of the mainland. Spain's success sparked competition, and soon England and France entered the race for colonial empires. Each European nation brought to America a culture and history as distinct as those of the Native peoples they encountered. Consequently, interactions between Natives and newcomers were both varied and complex.

Spain

By 1565, when Pedro Menéndez de Avilés arrived in Florida to establish yet another colony for his king, almost seventy-five years of colonial experience and Spanish law guided his actions. Indians and their place in Spanish American society were centrally located in that body of law and experience. The Papal Donation of 1493 stipulated that in return for the pope's recognition of Spain's claims to America, the Spanish crown had to see to the Christianization of the non-Christian Native Americans. This put the Spanish monarchs under heavy moral, if not legal, obligation to become, in effect,

Spain's first missionaries. In 1512, following the virtual annihilation of the Indians of Spain's island colonies, the crown promulgated the Laws of Burgos. These laws forbade the enslavement of Indians and established the *encomienda*, an alternative system for exploiting Native labor. Each Spanish colonist who received an *encomienda* grant was required to compensate his Indian laborers with good food and housing, protection, and instruction in Christianity. In 1542, following the conquest of the Aztecs and Incas, the New Laws of the Indies established the future status for conquered Native people. As soon as they could be prepared for the responsibilities of citizenship, they should be integrated into Spanish American society as full citizens. To accomplish that task, the king ordered the Catholic Church to expand its mission activity to educate Native people in the mysteries of Christianity and Spanish culture.

Almost immediately following the announcement of the New Laws of the Indies, the Spanish became embroiled in the Chichimec Wars in northern Mexico. Lasting from the 1540s to the 1580s, these wars were little more than slave raids launched for the purpose of gathering workers for the silver mines at Zacatecas and San Luis Potosí. The Spanish, who had gained control of the Aztecs and Incas relatively easily by cutting off the political heads of their empires and substituting their own, found the Chichimecs, hunting and gathering people, virtually impossible to defeat, let alone control. This lesson, and the vast expense of the wars, led the Spanish crown to issue, in 1573, the Pacification Ordinance. According to this law, military conquest of Native societies was forbidden. Henceforth, priests would spearhead Spanish expansion and would win through love and devotion the loyalty of Native people to the Spanish Empire. In the process, of course, they would also create a peasant class of controllable, Hispanicized Indian laborers who would do the work of Spanish America.

Colonists in America could often evade laws enacted in Spain, and the history of Spanish imperialism looks different from what the laws might suggest. On the other hand, the Spanish imperial bureaucracy grew rapidly in America, and its charge was to see that the laws were obeyed. When Menéndez signed his contract with the king to colonize Florida, he promised to obey the laws of the crown. Accordingly, when he arrived in 1565 to settle Florida he had in his company three Jesuit priests whose task was to begin the missionization of Native Floridians.

Menéndez established Santa Elena (briefly his capital) on Parris Island, South Carolina, Saint Augustine on the Saint John's River, and a half dozen other outposts on the Florida coast. All were located adjacent to Native communities and none but Saint Augustine and Santa Elena lasted more than a year or two. Native resistance to a Spanish presence close by was partly responsible for closing the posts, but Menéndez also ran short of money and was thus not reluctant to retrench. The Jesuits found ministering to the Indians difficult, and by the early 1570s they had fled the colony. Franciscan priests arrived in 1573 to take their place, and by the 1590s they had launched a major missionary offensive.

Franciscans established missions first on the Georgia coast among the Guale Indians. Guales lived by a mixed economy that took them from fishing sites to hunting grounds to corn fields in seasonal migration. With no permanent villages Guales were difficult for the Franciscans to deal with. The priests wanted to build churches, gather Indian neophytes around them in orderly villages, and instruct them on a daily basis. They tried to force the Guales to live lives that conformed to Spanish standards of morality and propriety. In 1597 the Guales responded to a particularly offensive attempt by a priest to punish a man with several wives for the crime of polygyny by killing all but one of the missionaries and burning the churches. While this particular episode triggered a reaction, the revolt actually resulted from many years of oppressive demands imposed on the Guales by the Spanish for labor and provisions. As archaeologist David Hurst Thomas noted, the Guale revolt "shook La Florida to its core."[1] The king even contemplated abandoning the colony. Nevertheless, the Franciscans returned to Guale in 1605 and reopened their missions. Diseases killed off large numbers of Guale people in the mission villages and many of those who survived fled into the interior. The priests closed mission stations one after another and consolidated the people, which drove away others who were not committed to the mission life. Finally, in 1683, the last of the Guale missions closed, and the few Native converts remaining relocated to Saint Augustine.

In 1587 another group of Franciscans established missions among the Timucuas. Extending along northern Florida from the Atlantic coast to well into the interior, the Timucuan chiefdoms occupied settled villages and seemed much easier for the priests to convert. The tactic of ruling through established leaders also worked better there than among the Guales. Timucuan chiefs, anxious to preserve their authority in such unsettled times, accepted gifts from the priests and assumed responsibility for the actions of their people. Such behavior was in line with assumptions about chiefly power and its relation to foreign goods. The chiefs collected food for the priests and arranged for corn and other products to be carried to Saint Augustine. The chiefs also organized labor groups to build mission churches, work on roads, and construct fortifications at Saint Augustine. The mission system depended on the continuation of the leadership of the chiefs, validated their authority, and attracted them into the Christian fold. Their conversions could be counted on to entice others to live and work in the missions. The social and economic disruptions caused by epidemic disease probably played a more important role in bringing Native people into the missions, however. The priests provided food, shelter, order, and security.

The Apalachees, west of the Timucuas, received missionaries in 1633. Their numbers were dramatically higher than the Timucuas, which encouraged the priests, but equally important was their agricultural productivity, which had drawn De Soto to their villages a century earlier. Saint Augustine became increasingly dependent on foodstuffs, especially corn, produced by Native women, and the Apalachee fields beckoned. The problem was distance, which made transporting Apalachee produce difficult and expensive. As in Timucua, the key to controlling the Apalachee people was the enthusiastic cooperation of the chiefs. Apalachee had been a Mississippian chiefdom, its chiefs had enjoyed substantial power, and in the demographic and political collapse that followed De Soto, the chiefs were scrambling to retain their authority. The costs were high, however. As the populations of both Guale and Timucua continued to fall, the Spanish increased their demands for Apalachee labor. Hostility over labor levies exploded in 1647 in a brief revolt in which Apalachees killed three of the eight missionaries stationed among them, destroyed seven mission stations, and brought a temporary halt to all mission activity. A second revolt occurred in 1656, at Timucua, which also jeopardized Florida's missionary machine.

From the beginning, Spain's missionary goals had been as much political and economic as religious. Conversion to Christianity was always important, of course, but both Spanish law and the colonists expected that Hispanicized Indians would be the labor force of Spanish America. In Florida, which was initially established as an outpost to protect the shipping lanes used by the treasure fleets, poverty, low populations, and bad living conditions had always been the lot of the Spanish troops and officials who were stationed there. Unable or unwilling to produce its own food or do its own construction labor, the colony depended on the missions to supply the goods and workers it needed. This expectation, in line with Spanish policy throughout its empire, cost Native Floridians a great deal. They were subjected to demands for tribute payment in the form of food and labor, they were punished if they failed to meet their quotas, and they were required to conform to the moral expectations of the priests. Furthermore, the missions incubated disease. Attractive in bad times, the missions were loathsome in good, and Native people fled them as readily as they joined them. Clearly, Native Floridians viewed the missions as refuges available when needed, but not permanent homes.

Beginning in the 1680s and culminating in the first years of the eighteenth century, the Florida Indians and the missions felt the additional pressures of invading interior Indians armed with guns and looking for captives they could sell to the English in the Charles Town slave markets (see **slavery**). Creek and Yamasee warriors for the most part, they swept down the Guale coast, into northern Florida, struck the Timucua missions, and then razed Apalachee. These invasions cost the lives of many Florida Indians, and perhaps as many as ten to twenty thousand ended up as captives for sale. Some also joined the invaders and retreated north and west with them, hoping to escape the misery of mission life. Others fled south to the security of the peninsula's interior. By 1708 there were no Spanish missions left standing except at St. Augustine, and the only mission Indians remaining in Florida lived in a cluster of barrios on the outskirts of the city.[2] By the mid-eighteenth century, however, many of those who had fled returned to their homeland, and along with those who remained they began to reestablish an independent Native community in Florida that the English would call the Seminoles.

England

When the English arrived to establish colonies in North America, the closest they had to experience with invasion, conquest, and colonization was their bloody occupation of Ireland. Indeed, Humphrey Gilbert, Walter Raleigh, and other English activists for colonizing America had served in Ireland. Their enthusiasm about America was largely economic. In addition to the gold and silver they hoped to discover, they looked to Native Americans as suppliers of valuable American commodities and purchasers of English manufactured goods. The English, unlike the Spanish, had no interest in Native human or property rights. The patent Queen Elizabeth issued Walter Raleigh in 1584 authorized him to discover, claim, and occupy whatever "remote heathen and barbarous lands, countries and territories not actually possessed of any Christian prince and inhabited by Christian people" he might find. Drafted to avoid challenging Spanish claims, the patent failed to follow the Spanish pattern of defining relations with the Indians. Rather, it contained no reference to them, leaving them to the uncertain mercies of the colonists.[3]

In 1584 Raleigh sent scouts to America to locate a site for his colony. They landed on the coast of North Carolina, liked what they saw, and in 1585 Raleigh sent colonists to build a settlement on Roanoke Island. Having attacked and beheaded Wingina, the chief of the Roanoke Indians, the settlers began to fear for their lives, and when the opportunity arrived to hitch a ride home on Sir Francis Drake's pirate ship, the colonists took it. In 1587 Raleigh sent yet another group of colonists, this time including women and children, in hopes of establishing a permanent agricultural settlement. They, too, settled on Roanoke. The next spring, John White, one of the leaders of the settlement, sailed to England for supplies. Because of war with Spain, he was unable to return to Roanoke until 1590, by which time the colony had disappeared.

White may have failed as a colony builder, but as an artist his contribution to our understanding of Native Southerners has been unsurpassed. He explored the Outer Banks and mainland coast of North Carolina, painting portraits of men, women, children, chiefs, and religious leaders. His paintings of people doing ordinary things like cooking, eating, hoeing, and fishing are invaluable. And when he painted whole towns he made it possible for us to see what Native houses looked like and how they organized their living space. The written record of Native cultures as early as the sixteenth century is very incomplete, but thanks to White's drawings we have an idea of who those people were that no document could convey.

The English learned important lessons about colony founding from Raleigh's experience with Roanoke, chief among them being that greater care had to be given to infant settlements. Roanoke could not survive without timely resupply and reinforcement. Roanoke's predicament also revealed another flaw—creating a colony required more resources than one man, even a very rich one, could provide. When the Spanish threat passed and English merchants renewed their interest in colonization, they invested in joint stock companies to finance them.

The Virginia Company, responsible for the development of Virginia, received its charter in 1606. Armed with royal authorization to exploit the riches of Virginia, the company intended to plant a trading post, acquire furs and other valuables from the Indians, sell them manufactured goods and textiles, search for gold and silver, and begin the development of industries, such as the production of naval stores and the manufacture of shingles. Investors also contemplated agricultural development, such as wheat production. These and other enterprises would be profitable and would advance the glory and power of England. Different from Raleigh's patent, however, the Virginia Company charter required that the colonists must treat the Indians with kindness so that they could be brought to "civilization."

Jamestown, the Virginia Company's outpost near the mouth of the James River, was planted in 1607 on the lands of the **Powhatan** chiefdom, a polity that included some thirty tribes. Powhatan's policy toward the English colony seems to have been shaped by his experience as a paramount chief—Jamestown would become another tribe within his jurisdiction. To that end he agreed to trade relations with the English, tested their military strength, and then captured their war chief, John Smith, for the purpose of incorporating Jamestown into the chiefdom. The ceremony of incorporation, which lasted more than a month, culminated with **Pocahontas** protecting Smith from her father's war club. As anthropologist Frederick Gleach pointed out, it was all "a ritual of redefinition, establishing the forms of the relationship between the colony and the Powhatans."[4] Through Pocahontas's ritual act, the Powhatans transformed Smith from an enemy into a kinsman. But neither Smith nor the other English colonists understood the ordeal that way, just as all scholars do not agree with Gleach's interpretation of the event, and the English failed to uphold their end of the arrangement. As a result, relations between Jamestown and the Powhatans were never as cooperative as Powhatan expected nor as profitable as the English hoped.

Jamestown remained a trading post for the first decade of its existence. But it never amounted to much. The Powhatans did not produce anything of particular value to the English market. The pelts of their warm-water beavers could not compete with the luxuriant fur produced by northern, cold-water beavers, and the demand for deerskins had not yet developed. The result was that the Virginia Company showed no profits to justify its investments. Not until tobacco. Tobacco transformed Virginia. Until the English recognized the profitability of growing tobacco, the colony grew slowly and posed little threat to Powhatan society. But beginning about 1618, when tobacco profits became apparent, Virginia grew rapidly. The expansion of Virginia up the rivers that flow into Chesapeake Bay put English colonists into direct territorial competition with the Powhatans because Virginians looked to Powhatan corn fields as spaces already cleared for tobacco. Encroachment followed encroachment. At the same time, the Virginia Company encouraged more aggressive measures to assure that Powhatans be converted to English culture and Christianity. There were no missions, but the company authorized the establishment of a school where Indian children would receive the necessary training. In 1622 Powhatan warriors, led by Native leaders with an "undying enmity for the invaders who dared to dispossess their people while lecturing to them," attacked and killed an estimated one-fourth of the Virginians.[5] Another fourth probably died within a year from sniping and hunger. The attack, which nearly destroyed the English colony, led to ten long years of warfare in which Virginians and Powhatans struggled for control of Virginia. A dozen years after the uneasy peace, war broke out again, only to end in 1646 in utter Powhatan defeat (see **Powhatan Wars**). "The Powhatans were now clearly subjects of the English," wrote anthropologist Helen Rountree, "obliged to pay an annual tribute in beaver skins."[6] Continued English expansion further reduced the Powhatan land base, even as continued conflict and disease reduced the population of the Powhatan people. By the end of the seventeenth century they were no longer in a position to interfere with the growth of England's Virginia.

Maryland in 1634, Carolina in 1670, and Georgia in 1733 followed in Virginia's wake as England pressed ever southward in North America. Each of these colonies has its own unique history, shaped in large part by the unique cultures of the Native people who inhabited them. But the Virginia experience demonstrates historical patterns that the other colonies shared.

Except for Maryland, which immediately embraced Virginia's tobacco culture, the Southern colonies found trade with the Indians in their hinterlands extremely important, just as the early residents of Jamestown had hoped. By the end of the seventeenth century deerskins commanded a huge market in England. As a result, influential groups in Carolina and Georgia, after its founding in 1733, as well as Virginia looked to Native hunters as their valued partners in a very lucrative business (see **hunting**).

Nevertheless, in all the southern colonies plantation agriculture came to dominate economic life. Tobacco in Virginia and Maryland and rice in Carolina and Georgia represented the avenues to prosperity for most English colonists. Crops are the fruits of the land, and as the English populations grew the demand for more land became ever greater. Thus, in the colonial South, two agricultural peoples collided in their effort to control a single resource. When land conveniently available for cultivation became scarce, colonists looked to the Indians for more. If the Native farmers proved reluctant to surrender to colonial demands, colonists tried to take it. Struggles for land often turned violent, as in Virginia during the first half of the seventeenth century. Such competition convinced the English that Indians and their claims to their lands were impediments to colonial progress. Quite simply, Indians were in the way. Few colonial Southerners could imagine a place in their societies for Indians.

All the English colonies professed an interest in converting Native Southerners to Christianity and English culture, but none developed an organized mission effort to accomplish these goals. Although some colonists claimed to believe that Indians would convert themselves upon seeing the superiority of Anglo-American society, most argued that it was pointless to convert Indians because civilized Indians could have no place in American society. The Spanish developed a mission system because they had a place for Indians in their American society, as workers. The English either did their own work or imported African slaves (see **slavery**). Except for the Indians they enslaved in their wars or accepted in trade, the English had little interest in Indian laborers. As a result, the English represent a perception of Indians sharply different from the Spanish. While the Spanish hoped to educate Indians in preparation for their incorporation into Spanish-American society as a laboring class, the English, thinking of Indians as competitors, chose to exclude them from Anglo-American society.

Many English colonists, however, did not exclude Native people economically. Indeed, Southern Indians were directly involved as trade partners, and from the mid- seventeenth to the end of the eighteenth century, few if any experience had a greater impact on their histories and cultures. While tobacco agriculture supplanted trade as the economic centerpiece of Virginia, **trade** remained important. After the final defeat of the Powhatans in 1646, backcountry Virginians began an effort to explore the West, largely for the purpose of establishing commercial relations with Western tribes. By the 1670s Virginia traders leading packhorse trains of up to one hundred horses laden with guns and powder, cloth, iron tools, brass kettles, and other goods made their way to the Catawbas, Cherokees, and other Western Indians. The Appalachian Mountains blocked the Virginia traders in the West, however, and in the competition for trade with Western tribes they lost out to Carolina. By the end of the seventeenth century Charles Town had become the center of the Southern Indian trade.

Most of the manufactured goods traders brought to Indian country did not represent new technologies. Rather, they provided Indians with new goods and tools that made old technologies more efficient. Knives, hatchets, and hoes made of iron, for example, were extremely popular. Shaped like similar tools made of stone and used in the same ways, they remained sharp longer, were harder to break, and they did not have to be laboriously chipped out of unshaped stones. Woolen cloth could be sewn into clothes more easily than animal skins, was warmer, and when drenched was much more comfortable. A Native woman could drop a brass kettle full of stew and be thankful it did not shatter the way a clay pot would have. These and other goods replaced items of Native manufacture with similar imported things that in many ways were easier to use and more durable.

Guns, powder, and liquor were in a separate category. By the eighteenth century European industry produced light, cheap, relatively durable, and deadly guns that transformed the balance of power in intertribal relations. Native Southerners used guns primarily for **warfare**, not **hunting**, and groups with guns enjoyed an immediate advantage over groups without them. The Creek and Yamassee warriors who raided the Spanish missions carried guns, the Guale, Timucua, and Apalachee victims of the raids did not have them, and the Creeks and Yamassees defeated their enemies relatively easily. Such lopsided victories would end only when tribes without guns acquired them.

Scholars debate the role of liquor in the eighteenth-century Native South. The political leaders of all the English colonies served Native diplomats drinks during talks in colonial capitals and often gave out kegs of liquor as gifts. English diplomats carried liquor with them when they visited Native capitals. Traders also brought liquor into Indian country. The evidence suggests that until the 1760s traders generally used it for gifts, however, and did not offer it to hunters in exchange for their furs. Alcohol, therefore, seems to have been available to Native Southerners relatively rarely and in rather limited quantities. They developed a taste for it, appreciated receiving it when offered, and got drunk on it if enough was available. But they by no means surrendered themselves to it. After the 1760s the amount of liquor in Indian country seems to have increased dramatically, and alcohol abuse may have become a serious social problem.[7]

Virginia and Carolina traders offered their goods in exchange for animal skins and war captives that they could sell as slaves. Colonial and especially European tastes determined which skins were attractive. Except when the market was flooded, beaver pelts were always valuable because their fur was important in the manufacture of felt hats, which all Europeans, it seems, wished to wear. In the South raccoons were more common and more valuable than beaver, and large numbers of them were killed and skinned for the market. By far the most important animal in the South, however, was deer. Colonial and English men wore deerskin trousers and boots; both men and women loved deerskin gloves. Southern Indians sold the skins of tens of thousands of deer annually.

The skills of hunting and warfare were similar, and Native men were good at both. Since the ancient past, warriors had brought home prisoners captured in war. Usually, the women tortured the captives to death, but sometimes they would adopt one instead (see **Ward, Nancy**). On rare occasions a captive would be neither killed nor adopted, but simply kept to help with the work of the community. Though it was rare, slavery was not unknown in the Native South, and while English traders mostly dealt in furs and skins, they also purchased captives. Native slaves, however, often caught English diseases, sickened, and died in slavery. And because they were frequently held near their own country, Indian slaves could escape and incite their relatives to attack. As a result, English colonists preferred slaves from Africa and usually sold captive Indians to dealers who shipped them to the sugar islands of the Caribbean. Carolinians learned about enslaving Indians from the Virginians, and they too usually sold them to the islands. They kept many, however. A Carolina census in 1708 listed 1,400 Indian slaves in a total slave population of 4,300 (see **slavery**).

The high value of captives persuaded Native warriors to capture their enemies and hold them for sale rather than kill them. Commercial slave raiding by Native warriors had probably begun by the mid-seventeenth century. The Westos, refugees from the Great Lakes country, were in the Virginia backcountry by the 1660s trading captives to Virginia traders for guns. Well armed, they terrorized many of the coastal and piedmont tribes of Virginia and Carolina looking for more captives to sell. In 1680 the Savannahs, armed with guns from Carolina, wiped out the Westos in a war that sent many of the former slave raiders into slavery. The Yamassees, who lived on the Carolina-Georgia coast, were active slave raiders, as were the Creeks who lived in the interior. The Chickasaws, who lived in northern Mississippi, were also major suppliers of captives for the slave markets.

War, which had always been the glorious occupation of Indian men, received encouragement by English traders and sometimes even colonial governments. The **Tuscarora War**, fought in 1711–13 between Carolina and the Tuscaroras of northeast North Carolina, was a slave war in the sense that the colonial government paid its soldiers in Indian captives. Mostly, however, Native warriors captured the slaves from other tribes. Scholars have no idea how many Southern tribes the slave trade destroyed, nor can we estimate how many Indian people were captured and enslaved. Historian J. Leitch Wright estimated that during the heyday of slave raiding, from the 1680s to the 1730s, the number was several tens of thousands.[8] Within Native societies the practice of selling rather than adopting or torturing captives undermined the importance of clans and the status of women. Clans no longer had a source for replenishing their numbers and women lost their opportunity to fulfill the obligation to kin killed by the enemy.

Traders from Carolina and Georgia followed the practice of the Virginians by using pack trains to carry their merchandise in and out of Indian country. This meant that the trade occurred in Native communities, under the watchful eyes of the chiefs. An important source of power for **Mississippian** chiefs had been controlling the importation and distribution of valuable foreign goods. Southern chiefs, after the collapse of the Mississippian culture, continued this practice. They welcomed the traders, negotiated the rates of exchange, and controlled the trade by imposing the rules of **kinship** on the process. Kinship governed the trade because people who were not kin were under no obligation to one another and were, in fact, either actual or potential enemies. Trade, or an exchange of gifts, only occurred between kin because gifts were the symbols of goodwill, and so the establishment of a kin relationship, ceremonially by adoption or through marriage, had to precede exchanges. In Mississippian times chiefs of neighboring chiefdoms seem to have married into one another's families. When an English trader arrived on the scene, the chief of the village usually arranged a marriage with one of his clan relatives, presumably one of his nieces. The trader thereby became incorporated into the social system of the village and became subject to the rules of kinship. He would assume responsibilities for his new family, be generous with his gifts, and treat people fairly and honestly.

Traders recognized that such marriages benefited them as well (see **Musgrove, Mary**). Wives explained culture, assured customers, provided security, grew corn, taught the language, and often became loving companions. As historian Joel Martin suggests, such traders "connected themselves to the existing culture instead of proscribing or attacking it."[9] If the trader conformed, he could be certain of the goodwill of his Indian family and friends and likely to prosper. But sometimes the traders did not fully understand what marriage meant, or perhaps they understood but decided it would be more profitable to ignore the rules of kinship. In such cases the chief would have to order the unruly trader expelled or killed for violating the rules. The most spectacular example of Native Southerners disciplining traders who refused to follow the rules was the **Yamassee War** of 1715. That conflict, which involved virtually every Southern Native nation except the Cherokees, cost the lives of nearly all the Carolina traders and almost destroyed the colony. For most of the eighteenth century, until tribal autonomy had been eroded so much that their enforcement power was gone, Native rules governed the exchanges that took place in their towns.

The trade impacted many areas of Native life. Men, always the hunters, devoted increasing amounts of time **hunting** deer for the skins traders demanded. Rituals associated with hunting waned, and when no terrible disease befell backsliders, the entire belief system was compromised (see **religion**). Having killed and skinned the animal, the hunter owned the hide, made the trade, and owned the goods his labor had provided. A good hunter could kill many deer and buy many goods with his skins. As his possessions accumulated, his prestige and influence in his village rose. Men who were not of the proper lineages for leadership could use their wealth and power to challenge the positions of their chiefs. Thus the trade could undermine established social and political patterns and jeopardize the communitarian ethic of society.

The relations between men and women also may have been affected. If women depended on their men to supply them with tools they formerly had made, that made them dependent and perhaps their status declined. Kathryn Braund argued that Creek women regularly accompanied their male relatives on their hunts. Present at the kill, they had to skin the deer and prepare and transport the hides their men sold. By increasing the time in the woods and the number of deer killed, Creek men imposed a significant increase in the workload of their women.[10] Theda Perdue, on the other hand, suggested that the lives of Cherokee women were not quite so adversely affected. Cherokee women did not normally accompany the men on hunting expeditions and Cherokees did not do much processing to the skins they sold; therefore, women did not become "the laboring class of the deerskin trade."[11] Clearly, however, becoming commercial hunters kept men out of their villages for long periods of time, which no doubt reshaped the social dynamic of the communities.

One problem Native Southerners faced in the trade was growing dependence on the goods they purchased. Indians did not forget how to make their own tools, weapons, and clothes, but they grew to be so used to having manufactured items that they became afraid of life without them. And in a world where enemies had guns and powder, no nation could afford to give up access to them. Dependence on the goods meant dependence on the traders, which in turn meant that the tribes became vulnerable to the demands of the colonial governments. By the 1760s a favorite tactic of colonial governments was to threaten to withhold trade if the tribes did not do as they demanded. Sometimes the tribes remained firm and their economies collapsed, causing suffering and hardship. When the tribes caved in to colonial demands, it often meant giving up land. In 1773, for example, the Creeks and Cherokees granted 2.5 million acres of land to Georgia to pay the debts they owed their traders. As several Creek chiefs argued about whether they should agree to it, one pointed out that until the Indians "could make guns, ammunition etc." they had no choice but comply.[12] By the end of the eighteenth century the Southern tribes owned much less land than they had a generation earlier.

English traders, through the very nature of the trade, were the most active and accomplished explorers of early North America. Often with Native companions and guides, the Carolinians went virtually everywhere in their incessant search for customers. Before the end of the seventeenth century they were on the banks of the Mississippi River establishing relations with the Chickasaws. Small in number, Chickasaw warriors armed with English guns became some of the most active slave raiders in the Carolina trade orbit, preying mostly on Choctaws but also on other regional tribes. Growing wealthy and powerful in the trade, the Chickasaws exerted enough control over their portion of the Mississippi valley that they could dictate who could use the river. This position as Carolina's westernmost trade ally developed at the very time that France attempted to take control of the river for itself.

France

Like the Spanish but unlike the English, the French entered the South with a long experience with Native Americans. For perhaps two centuries the French had interacted with Native people in the St. Lawrence River valley of Canada, in the Great Lakes country, and beyond. Like their European counterparts, they had been attracted to America for economic reasons. At first it was fish, but by the beginning of the seventeenth century they entered into Canadian Indian trade networks in order to acquire beaver pelts. The demands of the trade shaped French assumptions and expectations about Native people. From the beginning the economy of French Canada rested on the fur trade alliances that French traders established with the Indians. As suppliers of furs, Native Canadians were integral to the system and no Frenchman could ignore their interests. Never bashful about asserting their demands, Native Canadians shaped the relationship in ways that conformed to their cultural expectations. French traders had no choice but to comply.

The needs of the trade also influenced the role of the Jesuit priests, actively involved in a missionary effort significantly different from that of the Spanish. The Jesuits had no immediate plans to turn Native Canadians into Frenchified men and women whom they could integrate into Franco-American society as a peasant labor force. Rather, they understood that the role of Indians in French Canada was as trade partners and allies. Their value lay in their autonomy and their continued work as suppliers of furs. As a result, the Jesuits developed the idea that Indians could be Christian and still be Indians, or at least still do the things that Indians must do in order to keep the economy healthy.

By the end of the seventeenth century the French began to look beyond Canada. Locked in a struggle with England for control of America, they developed a policy to encircle the English and block their penetration into the country west of the Appalachian Mountains. Explorations across the mountains by Virginians in the 1660s and the establishment of the Carolina-Chickasaw trade alliance in the 1690s dramatized to the French the full extent of the English threat. French officials looked to the Mississippi River as their western axis. It linked Canada to the Gulf of Mexico, provided an alternative transportation route for furs and manufactured goods, and completed the circle. In 1699, after thirty years of exploration and diplomacy in the Mississippi valley, they built a post on the coast of the Gulf of Mexico at Biloxi Bay. In 1702 they were permanently established at Mobile, and in 1718 they founded New Orleans. The French colony of Louisiana came into being.

Louisiana had economic pretensions that were never realized. Hoping to become a plantation colony on the English model, Louisiana was unable to attract enough French settlers to make it work. Consequently, it remained essentially a strategic settlement designed to develop and maintain an alliance system with the Southern tribes that could block further English expansion. The Choctaws, living in central and southern Mississippi and numbering at least seventeen thousand people in 1690, welcomed French help against Chickasaw slave raiders.[13] The Choctaws were the largest Native group in the area, and the French quickly embraced them, making the French-Choctaw alliance the centerpiece of the French strategic plan in the South. Over the next several decades French trade and diplomacy extended into the interior South, connecting other tribes to the network the French hoped would cement their position in the region.

Resistance to French plans came from several fronts. In 1729, after the French constructed Fort Rosalie adjacent to the main Natchez town on the

Mississippi, the Natchez attacked and burned the fort and killed a number of French settlers and soldiers (see **Natchez Revolt**). Counterinvasions by French troops and allied Choctaw warriors successfully destroyed the Natchez chiefdom in 1731 and scattered surviving Natchez people into surrounding tribes. More serious opposition to French pretensions came from the Chickasaws. That tribe, allied with and armed by Carolina and reinforced by several hundred Natchez refugees, "waged a guerrilla resistance to French colonization, attacking the annual convoys between New Orleans and Illinois and marauding outposts along the Mississippi."[14] Invasions by French troops and Choctaw warriors beginning in 1736 tried repeatedly over the next several years to crush the Chickasaws, but to no avail. But constant warfare took its toll. Exhausted by the wars, several villages of Choctaws opened relations with the English in hopes of making peace and replenishing their supplies of trade goods.

This policy of the Choctaws to establish relations with the English as well as the French replicated the policy of other Southern tribes to play the contending imperial powers against each other. By engaging in diplomatic negotiations with all sides, receiving gifts from competing imperial officials, and developing trade relations with all comers, several tribes successfully enhanced their own power, wealth, and prestige while simultaneously avoiding costly entanglements that did not serve their purposes. Brims, chief of Coweta and one of the most prominent Creek leaders, was a master at the art of play-off diplomacy. In 1715 a French diplomat described his technique: "No one has ever been able to make him take sides with one of the three European nations who know him, he alleging that he wishes to see every one, to be neutral, and not to espouse any of the quarrels which the French, English, and Spaniards have with one another." In hopes of breaking down his neutrality, envoys gave "very great presents to [Brims] to regain his friendship . . . which makes him very rich."[15] Like the Choctaws, Brims and the Creek leaders who followed him demonstrated that their relations with European colonies rested on tribal needs and interests, not on those of the Europeans. As long as contending powers sought their alliance, the tribes could manipulate the relationships in ways that benefited them.

Imperial Wars

The European struggle to master the continent began in 1689 with a series of wars that continued in various guises until the War of 1812. During the first four of these wars, the primary contenders were the English and the French, who were sometimes allied with the Spanish. The armies fought mostly in the North, and, until the final war, called the Seven Years War or the French and Indian War (1756–1763), they pitted British troops against French soldiers and their Indian allies in conflicts fought in New England and New York. Southern tribes knew what was going on up north because both English and French officers tried to recruit warriors for their armies. Some Cherokee warriors responded to English requests because French-allied Choctaws as well as Indians from the North had attacked their towns. In 1758, after the English built Fort Loudoun and Fort Prince George to defend Cherokee towns from enemy Indians, the warriors set out to fight French and Shawnee enemies in Ohio. After several weeks of severe winter weather, the Cherokees gave it up and headed home. Starving, they killed some cattle in western Virginia that belonged to local farmers. The farmers, claiming that they thought the Cherokees were enemy Shawnees, attacked the party, killed several, and sold their scalps to collect Virginia's scalp bounty. The relatives of the slain warriors took revenge by raiding English settlements. The English took hostage 22 Cherokee headmen who had gone to Charleston to try to arrange a truce and demanded the surrender of those who had killed colonists in exchange for the chiefs (see **Attakullakulla; Cherokee War; Oconostota; Ward, Nancy**).

The English next mounted three invasions of the Cherokee country. The first, composed of South Carolinians and a few Chickasaws and Catawbas and led by the South Carolina governor, got only as far as Fort Prince George in upcountry South Carolina (see **Hagler**). When smallpox struck, the force disbanded and the governor returned to Charleston, leaving the captive headmen with the garrison. A Cherokee force threatened Fort Prince George. When they killed an English officer, the garrison panicked, and the soldiers slaughtered the 22 hostages. The Cherokees then put Fort Loudoun, in what is today eastern Tennessee, under siege, and in 1760 a troop of 1,200 British regulars accompanied by perhaps an equal number of South Carolinians and Native allies set out to rescue the garrison and subdue the Cherokees. They got as far as Echoe in western North Carolina before the Cherokees struck, killing 20, wounding 70, and forcing a nighttime retreat. Fort Loudoun surrendered. The Cherokees killed 32 soldiers and took the rest captive. A Frenchman who was present reported that the warriors who killed the commanding officer stuffed dirt in his mouth and said, "Dog, since you are so hungry for land, eat your fill." The Cherokee victory, however, was short-lived. In 1761 another force invaded and met little resistance. The

English commander reported the damage his soldiers had inflicted: "Fifteen towns and all the plantations in the country have been burnt—about 1,400 acres of corn, beans, pease, etc. destroyed; about 5,000 people, including men, women and children drove into the woods and mountains to starve." Disease, battle casualties, exposure, and starvation may well have claimed the lives of half the Cherokee people.[16]

While the Europeans worried about the autonomy of the Southern tribes and worked to control their policies, the tribes found little of interest in fighting the wars of empire. Except for the Cherokees, the Southern tribes did not participate in the French and Indian War, and in fact the invasions in 1759–61 had much more to do with the fear and hatred the Carolina settlers felt for the Cherokees than it did with larger imperial policy. Settler encroachment into the Cherokee Nation had seriously tainted relations between the two groups, and ill will had been building for some time. Neither side had much tolerance for the other, and in many ways the Southern frontier was little more than an explosion waiting to happen.[17]

This Cherokee experience also illustrates an important idea about Native American history: tribes made decisions and adopted policies that served their best interests, not the interests of the European groups that courted them. The Cherokees were allied to the English as long as the alliance served Cherokee needs. When the alliance no longer worked to their satisfaction, the Cherokees adopted a different policy.

The French and Indian War ended with a complete English victory. The French relinquished their colonies in Canada and Louisiana, the Spanish lost Florida, and the English claimed everything east of the Mississippi River. Spain acquired Louisiana, but in its weakened condition offered little challenge to the English or help to the Indians. French and Spanish defeat cost Southern tribes the play-off policy they had perfected over the previous several decades. Native leaders recognized their predicament immediately. Tribal power, the preservation of autonomy, and the protection of land from expansionist colonies had been possible, in large measure, because the Europeans had been primarily concerned with watching one another. This had created a situation that Native leaders could exploit. Never uncertain about their long-term goals, European competition had given them both the time and the distance they needed to fashion policies that could work. Whenever the demands of one of the Europeans threatened to interfere, Native leaders could simply look to another for aid. Loosing France and Spain denied the chiefs the all-important alternatives to the English. Thus the period after 1763 was one of both new problems and old problems magnified. Trade regulation, for example, virtually ended. Southern colonial legislatures lifted restrictions, and hundreds of men, fired by the dream of quick profits, flocked to the interior free of a French threat. The huge numbers of traders made it nearly impossible for chiefs to impose and enforce the rules of kinship on the system. The result was wild competition and a massive increase in the amount of liquor brought to Indian country. Rum and whiskey became important trade items and caused significant social problems. At the same time, English traders entered the Choctaw Nation where the French had been dominant and flooded that country with liquor as well.[18]

The royal government in England attempted to head off the violent conflict that threatened between colonists and Indians after the removal of the French menace. The Royal Proclamation of 1763 drew a line down the peaks of the Appalachian Mountains that was supposed to separate Native from colonial settlements and established a more efficient system for managing relations between England and the tribes. Neither policy worked well because the colonies were generally able to subvert them. Colonial agitation for independence from England began almost as soon as the French and Indian War ended. Like the earlier conflict, the American Revolution was a struggle for control of North America, and, except for the Cherokees, Southern Indians played a limited role in it as well.

Southern tribes listened as the representatives of both Royal and Rebel forces appealed to them for alliance and military support, but they made their decisions on the basis of local conditions. They always needed trade goods, and one way for non-Indians to cement an alliance was to provide them. At the same time, the tribes all had resident traders who were married into the community, and kinship obligations could influence political decisions. Young men needing war honors could force the councils to make decisions, or they might act on their own regardless of a council decision. Women could cajole men into avenging the deaths of relatives or they could dissuade war parties for fear of endangering the lives of captives whom the enemy had taken. And old, highly respected men could agree with everyone, receive the presents proffered by both sides, and take no action at all. The result was that neither side, Royal or Rebel, could predict what a tribe might do. And a tribe might do several things simultaneously. All that was certain was that Native Southerners made decisions based on their perceptions of tribal interest, which could of course change as new conditions demanded.

In the Revolution, for example, the Catawbas fought with their neighbors on the American side. The Catawbas owned a 144,000-acre reserve in western South Carolina, but non-Indian planters and farmers leased much of their land. Having experienced a devastating smallpox epidemic in 1759 that reduced their numbers to no more than one thousand people, they lived on only a small portion of their holdings. Because of their small numbers and their proximity to whites, Catawbas were particularly vulnerable to local political interests. Consequently, they not only joined the Patriot cause, they also changed the title of their leader from "king" to "general," impressing Carolina leaders with their republicanism and providing some security for themselves. The other Southern nations, less vulnerable to the political dictation of surrounding settlers, made their decisions about the war largely independent of settler expectations.

In 1776 armies from the two Carolinas and Virginia once again invaded the Cherokee Nation, laying much of it to waste. Revolutionary politics justified the action, but, as before, the ongoing pattern of settler encroachment and Cherokee resistance was the real cause of the war. Hundreds of homeless and hungry Cherokees fled into the neighboring Creek Nation. The Creeks took them in and learned from their experience to stay out of the conflict. Except for small actions by groups of ambitious young men, the Creeks played little role in the Revolution. Creek and Choctaw warriors briefly cooperated with British forces in the unsuccessful defense of Pensacola, and Choctaws harassed a minor American invasion down the Mississippi River, but generally they too remained neutral. Except for the Cherokees, whose lands were devastated twice in 15 years, the wars that rocked America in the eighteenth century had little impact on Native Southerners.

The peace, on the other hand, transformed the life of every Native person in America, North as well as South. Confronted with enormous change, the Southern tribes in the late eighteenth century were not without options. They had significant military power, their leaders were skilled politicians and diplomats, and Florida's return to Spain held out the possibility of a renewal of the play-off system in Southern international affairs that had for decades empowered the Southern Native nations. Peace, however, ended the period when English colonists were subject to the king and bound to follow his policies. Independence removed royal restraint and put the settlers in power. From that point on, the tribes had to contend with the power of the United States.

Notes

1. David Hurst Thomas, "The Spanish Missions of La Florida: An Overview," in *Archaeological and Historical Perspectives on the Spanish Borderlands East*, vol. 2 of *Columbian Consequences*, ed. David Hurst Thomas (Washington: Smithsonian Institution Press, 1990), 375.

2. Jerald T. Milanich, "Franciscan Missions and Native Peoples in Spanish Florida," in *The Forgotten Centuries: Indians and Europeans in the American South, 1521–1704*, ed. Charles Hudson and Carmen Chaves Tesser (Athens: University of Georgia Press, 1994), 276–303; John H. Hann, *A History of the Timucua Indians and Missions* (Gainesville: University Press of Florida, 1996); John H. Hann, *Apalachee: The Land Between the Rivers* (Gainesville: University Press of Florida, 1988).

3. David Beers Quinn, *Set Fair for Roanoke: Voyages and Colonies, 1584–1606* (Chapel Hill: University of North Carolina Press, 1985), 9.

4. Frederic W. Gleach, *Powhatan's World and Colonial Virginia: A Conflict of Cultures* (Lincoln: University of Nebraska Press, 1997), 114–15.

5. Helen C. Rountree, "The Powhatans and the English: A Case of Multiple Conflicting Agendas," in *Powhatan Foreign Relations, 1500–1722*, ed. Helen C. Rountree (Charlottesville: University of Virginia Press, 1993), 194.

6. Ibid.

7. Peter C. Mancall, *Deadly Medicine: Indians and Alcohol in Early America* (Ithaca: Cornell University Press, 1995), has a somewhat different view of Indians and alcohol in the colonial period.

8. J. Leitch Wright Jr., *The Only Land They Knew: The Tragic Story of the American Indians in the Old South* (New York: Free Press, 1981), 148.

9. Joel W. Martin, "Southeastern Indians and the English Trade in Skins and Slaves," in *Forgotten Centuries*, ed. Hudson and Tesser, 311.

10. Kathryn E. Holland Braund, "Guardians of Tradition and Handmaidens to Change: Women's Roles in Creek Economic and Social Life During the Eighteenth Century," *American Indian Quarterly* 14 (1990): 239–58.

11. Theda Perdue, *Cherokee Women: Gender and Culture Change, 1700–1835* (Lincoln: University of Nebraska Press, 1998), 71.

12. Kathryn E. Holland Braund, *Deerskins and Duffels: Creek Indian Trade with Anglo-America, 1685–1815* (Lincoln: University of Nebraska Press, 1993), 150–51.

13. Daniel H. Usner Jr., *American Indians in the Lower Mississippi Valley: Social and Economic Histories* (Lincoln: University of Nebraska Press, 1998), 35, estimates the 1700 Choctaw population at 17,500 minimum.

14. Daniel H. Usner Jr., *Indians, Settlers, and Slaves in a Frontier Exchange Economy: The Lower Mississippi Valley before 1783* (Chapel Hill: University of Nebraska Press, 1992), 82.

15. Quoted in Michael D. Green, *The Politics of Indian Removal: Creek Government and Society in Crisis* (Lincoln: University of Nebraska Press, 1982), 22.

16. Tom Hatley, *The Dividing Paths: Cherokees and South Carolinians Through the Era of the Revolution* (New York: Oxford University Press, 1993), 119–66. Quotes are from 133 and 156.

17. Ibid.

18. Richard White, *The Roots of Dependency: Subsistence, Environment, and Social Change Among the Choctaws, Pawnees, and Navajos* (Lincoln: University of Nebraska Press, 1983), 69–96.

5   "Civilization" and Removal

The American Revolution was a disaster for Southern Indians, but the full implication of the Revolution—independence for the English colonies—became clear only in the future. The guiding political assumptions of the revolutionary movement, that independence brought sovereignty for the new nation and that the political order was to be based on the principles of democratic republicanism, meant that the will of the people, expressed through their votes, would become public policy. With no externally imposed restraint, such as that of the Royal government, to balance popular interests, Southern Indians faced the threat of intensified demands for their land and resources. In the competition for control in the South, the independence of the United States implied a significant increase in the power of the settlers.

The 1783 Treaty of Paris, in which Britain recognized American independence, conveyed title of all the land claimed by the king between the Great Lakes and Florida east of the Mississippi River to the United States. Without reference to the Indians living upon it, this vast territory, held by Great Britain by right of discovery, passed to the United States by right of conquest. It was up to the United States, as victor and new owner, to develop definitions of the rights of the Indians to the land and shape policies to guide future relations.

Conquered Nations

Until 1789 and the establishment of constitutional government, the terms of the Articles of Confederation governed the infant United States. The articles provided that Congress had the "sole and exclusive right of . . . managing all affairs with the Indians," but only with those tribes "not members of any of the states." In 1784 Virginia surrendered its claim to the land north of the Ohio River, but to the south Virginia retained Kentucky, North Carolina held Tennessee, and Georgia laid claim to the portions of Alabama and Mississippi north of the 31st parallel, the boundary between the United States and Spanish Florida. These claims seemed to suggest that in the South the United States had no authority regarding the Indians. That, in any case, was the interpretation of the Southern states. Virginia had already begun to settle Kentucky and had treaties, largely spurious, with the Cherokees legalizing that occupation. The North Carolina legislature simply confiscated Indian rights to Tennessee. In 1783 Georgia dictated a treaty to a handful of Creek chiefs who surrendered three million acres as indemnity for damage pro-British Creek warriors had supposedly done to the state during the war.

The assumption underlying these actions was that the tribes, allied with the enemy Great Britain, had lost the war just as England had. The price of defeat was the loss of all claims to the land. Congress shared this assumption and crafted an Indian policy for the Northwest that rested on the same idea. Congress acted on this policy by demanding lands from northern Indians and supported the parallel efforts of Southern states to do the same. Nevertheless, Congress was anxious to achieve peace with all the neighboring tribes. Exercising its ambiguous authority in the South, despite protests from the states, in 1785 it authorized the negotiation of peace treaties with the Southern tribes. The first negotiation, with the Creeks, failed to take place when only a handful of headmen showed up to talk. Georgia commissioners were not reluctant to negotiate with an unrepresentative group, however, and concluded a treaty that affirmed the 1783 cession and added to it. Meetings with Cherokee, Choctaw, and Chickasaw delegates at Hopewell, South Carolina, during the winter of 1785–86 resulted in treaties (see **Hopewell treaties; Piomingo**). They opened formal relations between each tribe and the United States, established peace, discussed future trade relations, and recognized boundaries. Little land changed hands. These treaties affirmed British colonial practice of negotiating formal diplomatic arrangements with the tribes. By implication, they also conveyed recognition of tribal sovereignty that established an important precedent.

The Creeks, under the leadership of Alexander **McGillivray**, pursued a separate policy. Son of a Scottish trader and a Creek woman of the Wind clan, McGillivray had served during the Revolution as an official in the British Indian service. After the war his connections and experience gave him an important leadership position in the Creek Nation. Literate and well read, he understood the Anglo world and recognized that the boundary provisions of the Treaty of Paris threatened both the territory and independence of the Southern tribes. He also believed that American claims to the lands occupied by the tribes were without legal basis. England "never possessed either by session purchase or by right of Conquest" the lands of the Southern tribes, McGillivray wrote. Neither had the tribes done "any act to forfeit our Independence and natural Rights to the Said King of Great Brittain that could invest him with the power of giving our property away." England could not grant what it did not own.[1] As McGillivray orchestrated the Creek response to the treaty, he articulated a clear definition of tribal sovereignty. The Creeks were "a free Nation," he explained, with the right to protect "that inheritance which belonged to our ancestors and hath descended from them to us Since the beginning of time."[2]

Georgia was the focus of McGillivray's attention. The treaty of cession it had dictated to Hoboithle Miko, Eneah Miko, and a handful of Creek chiefs in 1783 not only cost the Creek Nation a large block of territory with no compensation, it required the Creeks to admit that they owed Georgia an indemnity for acts committed during the Revolutionary War. McGillivray rejected the cession, arguing that it was concluded with an unrepresentative group of chiefs, that it was achieved under threat, and that the Creek council did not approve of such an act. His solution to the problem posed by Georgia lay, in part, in the redevelopment of the old Creek technique of play-off diplomacy. Spain's return to Florida in 1783 provided the opportunity, and the Spanish recognized that a Creek alliance could help stall American expansion. Talks in Pensacola in 1784 produced a treaty that committed the Spanish to support Creek land claims, supply a satisfactory trade, and provide military aid. In hopes of forging an alliance of Southern tribes under his leadership, McGillivray encouraged the Chickasaws and Choctaws to conclude similar treaties with the Spanish.[3]

When Georgia attempted to occupy the contested ground, McGillivray sent warriors, armed with Spanish weapons, to throw the settlers out. He found allies among a mixed group recently located at the junction of Chickamauga Creek and the Tennessee River (modern Chattanooga). Made up of people from many tribes including Creeks, the Chickamaugans were mostly Cherokees who refused to recognize the Treaty of **Hopewell**. Together they worked to evict settlers from the Cumberland River valley as well.[4] The settlements on the Tennessee River, frustrated by the policies of North Carolina, formed the breakaway state of Franklin, under the leadership of the indomitable John Sevier, to resist Cherokee claims to the region.

Thus during the mid-1780s the Southern frontier was marked by war. The Indians were successful, in part, because the government of the Articles of Confederation had no money, no taxing authority, no army, and little unity of purpose. The Constitution changed all that, creating unity where there had been division, providing for money where there had been none, and power. The "distracted" American republic, which McGillivray had predicted in 1784 would self-destruct, had found a way by 1789 to maximize its position and present itself to Native Southerners as a force to be reckoned with.[5]

"Civilization"

President George Washington and his secretary of war, Henry Knox, crafted an Indian policy that some scholars have labeled "expansion with honor."[6] Their idea was to assure the continued growth of American settlements through the purchase of lands from the Indians. These purchases were to be carefully timed to coincide with the expected retreat of Native people from the frontier, the purchase arrangements would be negotiated peacefully in treaties that assumed the sovereign independence of each tribe, and boundaries would be run and enforced to separate Indian from American territory. Believing that Indians were intellectually capable of changing their ways of life and assuming that they would recognize the superiority of Anglo-American culture and prefer it to their own, Washington and Knox also devised a **"civilization"** policy to achieve the cultural transformation of Native people. This, they believed, was the ultimate compensation they could offer Indians in return for their land. Thus they committed the federal government to provide the tribes with livestock, agricultural implements, and instruction on their use. Such a program, Washington and Knox believed, would make everybody happy, keep peace on the frontier, and assure that eventually Native Americans would be assimilated into American society as fully equal members.

This policy was first articulated in the 1790 **Treaty of New York** between the United States and the Creeks and followed in 1791 in the Treaty of Holston with the Cherokees. To execute these treaties, Congress enacted in 1790 the first of a series of **Indian Trade and Intercourse Acts** designed to define the specifics of Indian policy. The laws put into effect the obligations contained in the treaties, established rules to regulate trade, prohibited unauthorized persons from entering tribal lands, and generally outlined the pattern of relations between the federal government and the tribes. In 1796 Congress supplemented the laws regulating trade by establishing a system of government trading posts, called factories, to be located throughout Indian country. The president hoped these posts would enhance the effort to assure a fair trade as well as forge economic ties binding the tribes to the United States. These and other laws, along with the treaties negotiated with the Southern nations during the 1790s and into the nineteenth century, reveal both the expectations and the weaknesses of early federal Indian policy.[7]

Government expectations that Native people would naturally retreat from the boundaries separating them from American settlements, thereby freeing land that they would eagerly sell, proved unfounded. The assumption rested on the contention that Southern Indians were nomadic hunters who would follow the game away from American settlements. Men were hunters, to be sure, and during the eighteenth century they had greatly expanded their hunting activities to satisfy the market demand for deerskins (see **hunting**). But this was only one side of the economy of Southern Indians. While men hunted, women farmed. The subsistence economy of Southern Indians was fundamentally agricultural, and they built their villages in the midst of their fields. But Americans found it difficult to take seriously the agricultural economy of women and thus they persisted in thinking that the tribes had no real investment in the land.

Cessions of land brought American settlers closer to Native villages, but, instead of drifting off, the Indians stiffened their resolve to preserve what remained of their territories. The "civilization" program actually tended to make men more attached to the land than they would have been if they had remained hunters. Thus contacts and the possibility for conflict greatly increased over time. And the competition for land occurred throughout the South. Tennessee entered the Union in 1796 and Congress created Mississippi Territory in 1798. Gradually encircling the Southern tribes, American population growth and increasing Western political power impacted Choctaws and Chickasaws as well as Cherokees and Creeks. A year rarely went by without some negotiation about land somewhere in the South.

Knox and Washington devised the "civilization" program in part because they believed it was the honorable thing to do. Convinced that "savage" Indians could not survive in close proximity to "civilized" Americans, they concluded that there were only two future alternatives for Native people. They would either remain "uncivilized," die out, and become extinct, or, preferably, they would become "civilized," thrive, and enter American society. They had a second motive, however, for encouraging "civilization." If

Indians became like Americans, they would need less land and would want more money. Thus they would be happy to sell what the settlers wanted.

"Civilizing" the Southern Indians meant comprehensive culture change. Gender roles would have to be reversed. Men would become the farmers and heads of household; women would become homemakers subject to male authority. Men would use draft animals and plows to grow crops for sale at market. Wheat, cotton, and other "civilized" crops would supplant corn, an "uncivilized" crop with little market value. Women, in addition to caring for children, cooking, and keeping house, would turn the cotton into woven cloth for clothing their families. Adults would wear leather shoes, American-style clothes, keep time with clocks, and furnish their log or clapboard houses with chairs and tables, beds, and a rug for the floor (see **clothing; housing**). The children would attend school, learn to speak, read, and write English, study arithmetic, and listen to history lessons that taught them George Washington was the father of their country. And the entire family would attend a Protestant church on Sunday (see **religion**).[8]

Remarkably, many of these changes occurred, at least among some Southern Indians. Baptist, Methodist, Moravian, and Presbyterian mission societies established schools among the tribes taught by ministers who often worked as hard at conversion as they did at education. Beginning in 1798 among the Cherokees and 1799 among the Chickasaws, missionaries gained permission to establish schools, and by the 1820s they operated dozens of mission schools among the Southern Indians. Most Native people did not become Christian, but some did, and many added Christian values to their traditional religious beliefs (see **religion**). Many more profited from the secular education the missionaries provided. Men became increasingly comfortable with English, the language of diplomacy and the marketplace. Women also attended school, where, in addition to academic subjects, they discovered the mysteries of spinning, weaving, and other domestic skills. Many found such work economically rewarding. More important, from the missionaries' perspective, they learned how to be the chaste subservient wives of "civilized" Native men.

Some men even became farmers. Most, however, did not. Such a reversal of gender roles was not only too radical, it violated the spiritual order of things. Men's sacred knowledge acquainted them with the world of animals, while only women knew the prayers and songs that made the crops grow. But hunting deer for the skin trade was becoming unprofitable as both deer populations and the European market for their skins were in decline. Stock raising, not the cultivation of crops, became the economic alternative to which most men turned. Cattle, hogs, and horses took the place of deer in Southern forests. Native men branded them, turned them loose, and at market time hunted them down in much the same way they had once hunted deer. The horse market was so hot that young men, no longer able to win honors at war, sometimes used their skills to steal, smuggle, and sell horses in neighboring American settlements. Among the Cherokees, a sort of "ring" developed in which one gang of young men stole horses in Tennessee for sale in Georgia while another took horses in Georgia that they sold in Tennessee. Young Choctaws did the same on the lower Mississippi.

Men also acquired African American slaves (see **slavery**). The model of "civilization" in the South was plantations, staple crops, and slaves. With slaves Native men could meet the government's demands for "civilization" while preserving the cosmic order. Benjamin Hawkins, federal Indian agent for the South from 1796 to 1816, lived among the Creeks and ran a model plantation staffed by several dozen slaves. He experimented with various crops, made and repaired tools, and offered instructions in the efficient management of a slave labor force. When he made periodic tours of the Creek Nation, he commented in his journal on whether or not his Creek hosts used their slaves to the most profitable advantage, and he usually complained that they did not.[9]

Federal agents appointed to administer the "civilization" policy and missionary teachers and preachers were in part responsible for the economic and social changes that began to occur in the Southern tribes in the 1790s, but they were not the most important agents of change. Since the late seventeenth century Scottish, English, Irish, and French traders had lived in the towns of Southern Indians, and most had married Native women of prominent clans. These marriages produced children who, according to the rules of matrilineal kinship, belonged to the clans of their mothers, which meant that Native people considered them members of the tribe. At the same time, the sons often fell under the influence of their fathers (see **kinship**). Thus they grew to adulthood shaped by two cultures, speaking two languages, and able to participate knowledgeably in both Native and Euro-American worlds. By the end of the eighteenth century all the Southern tribes had numbers of these bicultural people. Members of prominent clans and possessing valued skills, they often filled positions of influence or leadership in tribal affairs.

The roles of these men in Southern Indian society are most visible in economic and political affairs. They often joined their fathers in trade, they accepted market values as important, and they sought educational opportunities for their children. The entrepreneurial class in Southern Indian communities was not exclusively composed of the children of traders — many Native people without trader fathers shared their economic interests — but they were likely to be in the forefront of those interested in business and profits. They were among the first to own slaves, they often developed plantations and planted cotton for market, and when the federal government opened the Natchez Trace and the Federal Road through their countries they built and operated ferries and taverns to serve travelers. They constructed nice houses furnished according to the American style, dressed in suits, and put clocks on their mantels and locks on their doors. In other words, they lived differently from their Indian relatives. They set a style. They became a planter and merchant elite. But, most important, they could and did explain their actions in the language of their Indian relatives, many of whom embraced some, if not all, of the new ways they saw. Some young men of exclusively Native ancestry followed the same path to success as the sons of traders. They too invested in slaves, ferries, and other enterprises and began to compete for wealth in the same way they once had competed for war honors. Therefore, any correlation between ancestry, wealth, and acculturation was far from absolute. To the federal government this new way of life meant that the Southern Indians were becoming "civilized." Agents, missionaries, and non-Indian neighbors pointed to the changes they saw in the Southern tribes and were impressed.[10]

The Creek War and the Crisis in Indian Affairs

Native Southerners generally accepted these changes as part of a normal process. Some embraced many or all of them, many embraced none, but only in the Creek Nation did the struggle between change and continuity become violent. There, the civil war of 1811–14 was destructive, bloody, and debilitating (see **Creek War**). Some scholars argue that the conflict was over "power and property." They point to the emergence of wealth and the efforts of the elite to use their political positions to protect their possessions.[11] Others give it a religious interpretation, arguing that many Creeks believed they were at a cultural crossroads. They could choose to "become more and more like Anglo-Americans" or they could embrace "conscious and critical resistance . . . informed by spiritual interpretation."[12]

Religious prophets became war leaders. Burning and plundering the plantations and livestock herds of "civilized" Creeks, the Redsticks, as the followers of the prophets were called, attacked the communities of those who did not follow them. Their rampages led the headmen to appeal to the United States for help, and by 1813, following the destruction of Fort Mims, a United States army commanded by Tennessean Andrew Jackson had arrived. Aided by allied Choctaw, Chickasaw and Cherokee warriors as well as Creek opponents of the prophets, Jackson's invasion crushed the Redsticks (see **Mushulatubbee**). In the **Treaty of Fort Jackson**, negotiated in August 1814 at a site near where Montgomery, Alabama, is now, Jackson extorted twenty million acres of land from the Creeks. Justified as necessary to pay the costs of the war, he carefully designed the cession to divide Southern Indian country into three blocks of land surrounded by American settlements. This, Jackson knew, would absolutely preclude any chance that the Southern tribes could unite against their common expansionist American antagonist (see **Big Warrior**).

The Creeks lost about one-fourth of their population in the war. Many were killed, but perhaps 1,500 Redstick survivors managed to flee. Most went to Florida, where they joined their cultural cousins, the Seminoles. At home, Creek country was a wreck. Towns, plantations, and farms destroyed, herds wiped out, ferries and taverns burned, the Creek Nation had been pillaged from one end to the other for the first time in memory. Recovery was a long, difficult thing that was not made easier by the new attitude in Washington about Indians and their future in the United States.

Andrew Jackson's invasion of the Creek Nation and defeat of the Redsticks put an end to Creek military power. In the same period American troops smashed the multitribal alliance system that Tecumseh had assembled in the North. Thus in 1815, as the United States returned to peace after the War of 1812, it could look to Indian country and see not power but weakness, devastation, and defeat. Andrew Jackson, who understood the implications of American victory better than most, constructed an Indian policy based on the idea of Indian weakness and American strength. The United States, he argued, should change its policy of considering the tribes to be sovereign nations and should end its practice of negotiating treaties with them. Instead, Congress should understand that the Indians were subject to federal law, with rights to the land that were subordinate to the sovereignty of the United States. Indian policy should reflect the fact that the "arm of government" was capable of enforcing whatever Congress legislated, including the confiscation of tribal land for the use of American settlers.[13] John C. Calhoun, secretary of war from 1817 to 1825, agreed. In a report to the House of Representatives in 1818 he announced that "the neighboring tribes are becoming daily less warlike, and more helpless and dependent on us." No longer able to pose a significant military threat, "the time seems to have arrived," he concluded, that "our views of their interest, and not their own, ought to govern them."[14]

These challenges to the idea of Native tribal sovereignty and the treaty system reflected more than the shifting balance of power in the West. Jackson's treaty with the Creeks opened twenty million acres, much of it prime cotton land. The best was in eastern Mississippi Territory, reorganized in 1817 as Alabama Territory and admitted to the Union as a state two years later. Between 1815 and 1820 tens of thousands of Carolinians and Georgians, infected by "Alabama Fever," rushed into the region, attracted by rich land and high cotton prices. The cotton boom crashed in the Panic of 1819, bankrupting many of the newly settled planters. Recovery took most of the 1820s, cotton prices never reached pre-Panic levels, and prosperity depended on opening more land quickly. But the only land available belonged to the Southern tribes. Negotiating treaties with them to purchase it was slow, tedious, expensive, and uncertain because the tribes, as sovereigns, could always refuse to sell. Jackson's idea of simply confiscating the country in the name of national security would simplify and hasten the acquisition of land. Congress refused to agree, however, and reaffirmed the system of recognizing and respecting the sovereign rights and powers of the Southern tribes.

Between 1816 and 1821, federal commissioners negotiated nine treaties with the Southern tribes. The Creeks surrendered a large tract in central Georgia between the Ocmulgee and Flint Rivers, the Chickasaws sold western Kentucky, western Tennessee, and a parcel in northern Alabama, the Choctaws gave up large blocks of land in western Mississippi and western Alabama, and the Cherokees ceded a number of small parcels in northern Alabama and Georgia, east Tennessee, and western North Carolina. Much of this was valuable cotton land. But none of the tribes agreed to sell everything the United States asked for, and few of the cessions would have been concluded at all if the government had not used high-pressure tactics, threats, intimidation, and bribery. The days of "expansion with honor" were over. In the period after the War of 1812, as the populations of Georgia, Alabama, Mississippi, and Tennessee soared, few politicians worried about justice for the Southern Indians. Rather, they became increasingly convinced that the tribes were little more than troublesome obstacles blocking the way of the economic progress and prosperity of their constituents.

Washington policy makers, burdened by ideas of tribal sovereignty and the treaty system Congress refused to abolish, found themselves facing what one administrator called a "crisis in Indian Affairs." While President James Monroe announced that the removal of Eastern Indians to the country west of the Mississippi River was the "great object" of his administration, tribal leaders countered that they were opposed to removal, had sold all the land they could spare, and expected the United States to honor its commitments made in previous treaties to respect and protect their lands.[15]

Tribal Sovereignty and Political Centralization

Tribal leaders also agreed that the 1820s was a period of crisis. State pressures to sell more land, settlers squatting illegally across their boundaries, and federal commissioners hounding them for treaties convinced some headmen that their traditional political systems lacked the means for protecting their nations. Before the War of 1812 none of the Southern tribes had centralized governmental organizations (see **government**). All had national councils that received foreign diplomats, provided for the negotiation of treaties, and discussed matters of national concern, but the men who attended them possessed little authority to enforce laws within their villages; local autonomy was the rule. The laws of the nations were customs and history, their police and courts were the clans, and while both the Cherokees and the Creeks had experimented with more direct forms, none of the tribes was set up to do political battle with the Americans. Evidence of the problem was everywhere. Against the will of the people, chiefs accepted bribes and sold land no one wanted to give up. Throughout the South, tribal councils struggled with the problems of controlling the leaders in their midst.

The leadership for the movement to centralize authority and make it accountable tended to come from that group in each of the tribes that had reacted to the collapse of the deerskin trade by becoming planters, ranchers, and merchants. Since the beginning of the nineteenth century the numbers of these market-oriented entrepreneurs had increased. Appreciative of an English-language education, they had supported the establishment of schools in their nations. Economically aggressive, publicly assertive, literate, and interested, they were often chosen by their more traditional peers to serve in government. And, when given the opportunity, they tended to look after their own economic interests. As accumulators of wealth, private property was important to them, and they led in the development of laws to protect what they owned.

At various times in the early nineteenth century the national councils of all the Southern nations enacted laws to protect private property rights. Furthermore, they wrote these laws into legal codes and appointed national police forces to enforce them. This seemingly innocuous innovation is extremely significant. National laws and a national police force redefined the nation and its government. **Government**, not the clans, became responsible for the maintenance of public order (see **kinship**) The nation, not the towns, became the arbiter of the public good, and law challenged custom and history as the definer of proper behavior. These changes indicate that in each of the Southern tribes a national idea was developing. In addition, leaders sitting in national councils soon recognized that if a national government could protect private property it could be used to protect public property as well. Once national laws and national police came into being, they could be put to a whole range of public purposes.

After the failure of Alexander **McGillivray** to establish a centralist government among the Creeks in the late eighteenth century, the Cherokees led the way. As early as 1808 the Cherokee National Council drafted a law against theft and created a police force to enforce it. But the Cherokees quickly moved beyond the protection of private property to develop mechanisms to defend the common property of the nation as well. In 1817 they drafted Articles of Government that created a Standing Committee charged with conducting the affairs of the nation when the National Council was not in its annual session. The purpose of this move was to prevent an individual claiming to be a chief from conducting negotiations for the nation. In 1819 the National Council affirmed a law that prohibited the sale of land to the United States. Any leader who did so would suffer death. Within a decade, and united in the belief that "a strong central government would be best able to protect the land that all Cherokees held in common," they drafted a national constitution that dramatically increased the power of the principal chief. The constitution called for a two-house legislature, a national court system, and an elected principal chief. Most important, however, the framers wrote into its preamble a description of the nation's boundaries and proclaimed that within those limits the Cherokee Nation was sovereign. Following a national vote for ratification, the constitutional government took office in 1828 (see **government**).[16]

The institutional changes in Cherokee government paralleled or perhaps reflected the emergence of Cherokee nationalism. The Cherokees increasingly identified more strongly with the nation than with clans or towns. In 1810 Cherokee clans agreed to limit the practice of blood vengeance, and ultimately murder became a crime against the nation rather than the clan. In 1820 the National Council established electoral districts and apportioned representation among them, replacing the traditional practice of town, clan, or at-large representation. Since the National Council originated with the need to conduct diplomacy, the business of men, women played little role in it, and the elimination of clans and towns from the political system largely removed their influence. Women's councils petitioned the National Council to reject land cessions in 1817, 1818, and 1831, and the National Council protected the rights of married women to separate property and of people to choose matrilineal descent patterns, but they had no formal role in the new government.

Cherokee nationalism found a number of expressions that led to the assumption that the Cherokees were the most "civilized" of all Native Americans. **Sequoyah**, who was not literate in any language, developed a system for writing Cherokee in the early 1820s. Having seen Anglo-Americans exchange messages on paper, he became convinced that writing was a skill, not magic. He worked for years to perfect a system of symbols for Cherokee syllables. When he succeeded, the syllabary caught on rapidly with Cherokees teaching each other to read and write. By 1835 nearly a quarter of all Cherokees were literate in their own language and slightly more than half of the households had members who read Cherokee. Another 18 percent of households had English readers, making Cherokee literacy comparable if not higher than that of their white neighbors. Literacy led to the inauguration of a bilingual newspaper, the *Cherokee Phoenix*, in 1828, which not only informed Cherokees about the actions of their government, local events, and world news but also educated the American public, many of whom subscribed, about the Cherokees.

While the Cherokees adopted a constitution that followed the American model, the Choctaw constitution of 1826 was very different. The Choctaw Nation was divided into three districts, southern, northeastern, and northwestern. Each was autonomous, having its separate council and chiefs. When the Choctaw planter and merchant elite, led by Greenwood LeFlore, presented their constitution, they did not change the ancient pattern of district governance, and when the national council met to alter traditional Choctaw customs, it did so in the shadow of Nanih Waiya mound. The Choctaws, however, did make modifications in the structure of their national government. They established a national executive committee composed of the three district chiefs and authorized the committee, in conjunction with a national council, to draft and execute laws to protect property, encourage schools, and enforce temperance (see **Folsom, David**). Like the Cherokees, the Choctaws hoped that formal legal institutions might protect them from the threat of removal.[17]

Neither the Chickasaws nor the Creeks followed the constitutional example. In the 1820s, according to sociologist Duane Champagne, "The
Chickasaw national council continued to be based on representatives from
local iksas [kin groups], chiefs from four major districts, and several hereditary warrior and civil chiefs." The Chickasaw king, Ishtehotopa, and second
chief and head warrior, **Tishomingo**, came to power through traditional
avenues—inheritance and merit—and while they rejected many aspects of
Anglo-American culture, Ishtehotopa owned a ferry and Tishomingo operated a prosperous farm. The highly acculturated planter elite, largely members of the extended Colbert family (see **Colbert, Levi**), served in various
positions in the government, but they followed traditional protocol and did
not push for structural innovation until 1829, when they successfully
achieved a written law code protecting private property and establishing a
national police force. Traditional Chickasaws were willing to innovate,
within limits, to accommodate the planters, but they also took steps to prevent treachery and protect the common domain from individual greed. In
1826 the national council prohibited any Chickasaw from receiving a private
reservation, a customary tactic used by the federal government to gain land
cessions.[18]

The Creeks shared the Chickasaws' disinterest in constitutions, but they,
too, were by no means reluctant to innovate governmental forms in the protection of their lands. In the late 1790s, with the encouragement of their agent,
Benjamin Hawkins, the Creeks reorganized their national council, announced laws against theft, and created a special police force to enforce them.
The police were called "lawmenders," men appointed to fix laws that were
broken. In 1818 the Creek council reduced to writing its legal code, including
a law forbidding the unauthorized sale of land. Like the similar Cherokee law,
upon which it may have been patterned, this act prescribed death as the
penalty for its violation. In 1824, as Georgia's demands for the acquisition of
all Creek land in the state became nearly hysterical, Secretary of War Calhoun
appointed two Georgians to open negotiations for a cession. The Creek council rejected their offers and sent them off, but William **McIntosh**, one of the
most prominent of Creek leaders, followed them and arranged to make the
sale happen in return for a large bribe. Resuming talks in his tavern, McIntosh
and the commissioners, along with a handful of other Creek men who were
also to be paid, agreed to the treaty. Signed February 12, 1825, the **Treaty of
Indian Springs** ceded all the Creek land in Georgia and about two-thirds of
their holdings in Alabama. In return, the United States agreed to locate land
in the West and pay the expenses of removal. Ignoring protests that it was an

illegal instrument, the Senate ratified the treaty March 7. The stunned and outraged Creek Council met, agreed that McIntosh had violated the law, and ordered his execution. On the night of April 30, a specially appointed posse of lawmenders surrounded McIntosh's plantation, executed him, and on May 1 caught and executed two of his cronies.

Georgia governor George M. Troup and the state legislature protested the execution of McIntosh and threatened to invade the nation. President John Quincy Adams recognized the execution as the legal act of a sovereign nation and warned Georgia to desist. Tempers flared and for a while there was talk of war between Georgia and the federal government. But the Adams government cooled things with a second legal negotiation in which the Creeks, worried that Georgia might invade, agreed to sell the land Georgia claimed and received a block of country in the West (see **Big Warrior**). Thus, in the end, Georgia got the land it wanted and forced out the Creeks who lived on it.

The significance of the council decision to enforce its law by executing one of its most prominent leaders was not lost on anyone. The broken law rested on the idea that the land within its boundaries belonged to the Creek Nation and only its national government had the right to decide what to do with it. The law thus represented an expression of Creek national identity, defined a Creek national domain, and, in effect, declared that its violation was an act of treason. In executing McIntosh, the council also demonstrated that it had the will and the power to enforce its decisions. Without drafting a constitution the Creek council asserted the sovereignty of the Creek Nation in a most unmistakable way. The execution of McIntosh also rippled throughout Southern Indian country. The Choctaw and Chickasaw councils contained men who were as susceptible to bribery as McIntosh. His fate gave them pause, however, and strengthened the resolve of the councils to resist further land cessions.[19]

Removal

President Thomas Jefferson had begun to think about the **removal** of Eastern Indians to the region west of the Mississippi in 1803, at the time he was arranging for the purchase of Louisiana. He recommended the plan to delegations of Native leaders when they visited him in Washington, and in 1810 a group of Cherokees agreed to relocate in the West. Another Cherokee land cession and western migration occurred in 1817–19. The 1820 Treaty of Doak's Stand with the Choctaws provided that in exchange for a cession of some five million acres carved from their nation the United States would grant them thirteen million acres in the West (see **Mushulatubee; Pushmataha**). Thus when President Monroe proclaimed in 1817 that Indian removal was the goal of his administration, he had reason to hope for success. On a small and limited scale it had already begun. The uniform rejection of removal during the 1820s by all but small groups of Southern Indians, however, indicated otherwise.

To most Southerners in the 1820s, Indian removal solved two problems. The first was largely economic. Much of the Indian-owned land in the South was extraordinarily fertile and capable of producing enormous crops of cotton. As the South struggled to recover from the Panic of 1819, Indian land seemed to promise recovery from the worst depression yet experienced by the United States.

The second problem was racial. The "civilization" program Washington and Knox had devised in the 1790s assumed that Indians could successfully learn to become like white Americans. Once they did so, they would be assimilated into American society on a fully equal footing. But by the 1820s thinking about Indians had changed. In part, Americans were frustrated because most Indians had no interest in changing their cultures. While Native people were usually quite ready to adopt aspects of American culture, their approach tended to be selective. But Americans often interpreted Native selectivity as evidence that Indians lacked the ability to change. This attitude fit with the hardening views of whites about blacks. As the plantation system became ever more dominant in the South, white Southerners became increasingly insistent that African Americans were racially unfit for any position other than enslavement. Society became more rigidly polarized along racial lines and Indians—persons who were not white—fell into the subordinate category occupied by black slaves. Indians who became "civilized" could never be integrated into free white Southern society on an equal footing. Senator John Forsyth of Georgia spoke for most Southerners when he characterized Indians as "a race not admitted to be equal to the rest of the community . . . not yet entitled, and probably never will be entitled, to equal civil and political rights."[20] Race had replaced culture as the distinguishing characteristic of Native people and had branded them as unredeemably inferior. The practical problem this redefinition entailed was clear. If the Indians sold all their land, which the states demanded, what would happen to the people? Removal answered this question by expelling the people to some distant place.

When tribal councils rejected removal and strengthened their governmental institutions in order to more effectively exercise their sovereign rights to refuse to sell out and leave the country, the "crisis in Indian affairs" simply became worse. And McIntosh's execution so frightened others of like mind that federal and state officials despaired of their ability to use bribery and corruption to achieve their ends. If removal was the solution to the "crisis," the problem became to convince tribal leaders to agree to it, commit their people to it in treaties, and peacefully leave.

The Southern states discovered the means to induce Southern Indians to flee. Citing the principle of state sovereignty, a sentiment gaining support in the South, state legislatures began to challenge the federal claim based on the Constitution to exclusive jurisdiction over Indian affairs and denied the supremacy of treaty guarantees of tribal lands. The Alabama general assembly began to move in that direction in 1824. In 1827 the legislature extended the civil and criminal jurisdiction of Autauga County into a portion of the Creek Nation, but with the proviso that no Indian would enjoy "any political or civil rights" under state law. Laws enacted in 1828 and 1829 expanded Alabama's legal authority into all the Creek Nation, and in 1832 prohibited the functioning of the Creek national government.[21] In 1826 and 1827 the Georgia general assembly approved nonbinding resolutions threatening to invade and confiscate Cherokee land if the Indians refused to sell. When the Cherokees drafted their constitution in 1827, declaring their nation sovereign and demonstrating that they had no intention to sell out and move west, the ire of Georgians reached new heights. The state responded with legislation enacted in 1828, 1829, and 1830 that extended Georgia's civil and criminal jurisdiction into the Cherokee Nation, declared the Cherokee national government illegal, imposed penalties on any Cherokee politician who attempted to serve in a governmental capacity, and appointed a special police force to enforce Georgia law in Cherokee country. Mississippi and Tennessee likewise extended state jurisdiction into the countries of the Choctaws, Chickasaws, and Cherokees.[22]

State politicians made no effort to hide the intent of their actions. As the Alabama House of Representatives announced in its debate on the 1829 act, "The great object of the proposed measure must be to bring about [Creek] removal." As soon as the Creeks "see and feel some palpable act of legislation under the authority of the state," the lawmakers asserted, their fear of it "will induce them speedily to remove."[23] The policy of the states was obvious.

They would use their legislative power to make life for the Indians so miserable they would be happy to escape by agreeing to move west.

The effects of these laws were both complex and devastating. When the states banned the operation of tribal governments and made public service by Indians a crime, they denied the sovereignty of the Native nations. Robbed of their power to govern themselves, even to meet publicly to discuss common problems, the tribes were politically shattered. When the states subjected Indians as individuals to state civil and criminal jurisdiction, they made them accountable to a bewildering array of laws the people could neither read nor understand. Furthermore, the states denied Indians the right to testify in court on their own behalf. This opened the way to a wide range of swindles. One common scam was for a white man to forge a promissory note made out to him and signed by an Indian. The note would allege that in payment for a loan made by the white man, the Indian would pledge certain listed property. The property was usually easily portable, such as livestock or slaves. Armed with the spurious note, the swindler would get a court order foreclosing on the pledged property. Accompanied by the sheriff, the crook would descend on the Indian's farm or ranch, take the listed goods, and the victim could do nothing to protect himself. Such legalized theft was widespread and commonplace. Others not so slick simply looted Indian homes. As long as only Indians witnessed the crime, they were safe. Those who were victimized quickly understood the full meaning of the Alabama House of Representatives when it explained that the purpose of extending jurisdiction into Indian country was to drive the Indians out. Many white sharks made fortunes, while many Indians lost everything they owned.

Tribal leaders appealed to the federal government for protection from the states. Despite treaty provisions that obligated the United States to defend the tribes from encroachment and state interference in their domestic affairs, both Presidents John Quincy Adams and Andrew Jackson refused. In fact, Jackson actively defended the states. His view was that the Indians now had two clear choices: they could remain where they were under the authority of the states or they could leave.

During the spring of 1830 Congress debated Jackson's removal bill (see **Indian Removal Act**). Recommended in December 1829 in his first annual address to Congress, Jackson represented his removal plan as necessary both for state economic development and the survival of the Indians, who would surely suffer under state law. Georgians led the pro-removal forces in Congress but Jackson made passage a matter of Democratic party loyalty, and the final votes in both houses generally followed party lines. The narrow 102 to 97 passage in the House of Representatives demonstrates that the nation was deeply divided on the issue. Jackson signed the removal act into law on May 28, 1830.

The removal act authorized the president to enter into negotiations with all the Eastern tribes. If the tribes agreed, removal treaties would stipulate an exchange of their land in the East for equal or greater amounts in the West. The United States would pay the moving costs of the people, provide support during their first year of residence in the West, and compensate individuals for the value of improvements left behind. The language of the act, in conformity with the principle of tribal sovereignty, stressed that removal was voluntary. Only those tribes that agreed to the exchange of land and signed treaties to that effect were to be removed. This pretense of voluntarism underscored the importance of the legislative harassment by the states. While neither the federal nor state governments could force the tribes to sign removal treaties, hostile and discriminatory state legislation could make life miserable for thousands of Indian people and drive them to the conclusion that their only hope was flight. That, in fact, is what happened.[24]

Secretary of War John Eaton negotiated the first removal treaty with the Choctaws. Gathered on the banks of Dancing Rabbit Creek in September 1830, Choctaw leaders listened to Eaton. The three division chiefs privately indicated a willingness to remove, but the public meeting with the United States commissioners produced another result. The chiefs and captains faced the commissioners with seven women sitting between them. Only a single Choctaw spoke in favor of removal, and to him one of the women replied angrily, "I could cut you open with this knife. You have two hearts." As the farmers and the heads of matrilineages, women traditionally had controlled the land, and they now made their feelings known about its sale. No one else dared oppose them publicly. Two days later after most of the seven to eight thousand in attendance had departed, a rump council met. In a rage, Eaton told them that if they did not agree to remove the president would declare war on them and send in the army. Fearful that this might happen, the Choctaws agreed to sell their land in Mississippi and remove to their Western country (see **Folsom, David; Mushulatubbee; Pitchlynn, Peter; Treaty of Dancing Rabbit Creek**).[25] Removal was to occur in three waves of about seven thousand people each, one a year from 1831 through 1833, but families could stay in Mississippi if they wished. By registering with their agent, they would receive land and citizenship in the state. But the agent refused to register most who asked, destroyed the registrations of many he signed up, and in every way blocked the efforts of those Choctaws who wished to remain. In the end only sixty-nine families received allotments of land in Mississippi under the treaty.

Choctaw removal began in 1831, late in the fall after the corn had been harvested. Government agents moved the people overland to Vicksburg and Memphis, where they loaded them on steamboats and carried them via the Mississippi, Arkansas, and Ouachita Rivers as far as water levels permitted. Then they walked. The winter was unusually cold and snowy, the people lacked warm clothes, the transport agents failed to supply enough food, and the news of the hardships and suffering terrified the Choctaws waiting their turn to remove. The weather during the 1832 trek was somewhat less harsh, but cholera struck the migrants and killed many. After two horrifying migrations, when it came time to round up the last third of the Choctaws, only about 900 people agreed to go. Fourteen thousand Choctaws left Mississippi, 2,500 people died in the move. About 6,000 remained in the East, some of whom moved themselves west over the next several years.

As soon as he left the Choctaws, Secretary Eaton ordered the Chickasaws to send a delegation to his home in Tennessee to discuss removal. The Chickasaws agreed in principle but succeeded in inserting an article into the treaty that declared it would be null and void if a party of land rangers could not find a suitable homeland for the nation in the West. They could not. But neither Mississippi nor the United States was willing to accept failure, and pressures and threats led to a second round of talks in 1832 (see **Colbert, Levi**). This treaty, signed at Pontotoc, again committed the Chickasaws to remove. But removal would be delayed until the entire nation was surveyed and each adult received a tract of land, which, upon removal, would be sold with the allottee pocketing the money. The United States would sell unallotted land and deposit the proceeds into a tribal fund (see **Treaty of Pontotoc**). The problem of finding land remained, however. Some thought of purchasing a tract from the Choctaws, but they refused to sell. Land rangers continued to report their inability to find an acceptable homeland, and harassment from Mississippians, both in and outside of court, made many Chickasaws frantic to escape. In 1837, in an act of desperation, the Chickasaws worked out a deal with the Choctaws in which the latter, in return for a payment of $530,000, permitted the former to move in with them. The measure of Chickasaw desperation is in the arrangement. In addition to the payment, the Chickasaws were forced to surrender their national identity (see **Treaty of Doaksville**). Not until 1855, for an additional payment of $150,000, were the Chickasaws able to purchase land from the Choctaws and recreate their nation.

Despite the efforts of Mississippians to swindle Chickasaw allottees of their allotments, many succeeded in hanging on to them until removal time. More remarkable, they often got good prices for the allotments when they sold them. With investment capital they purchased movable goods, such as livestock and slaves, that they took with them west (see **slavery**). Removal was traumatic for the Chickasaws as it was for all Southern Indians, but in some ways it turned out to be less devastating for many of them, perhaps because they largely retained control of their own affairs.

Some Seminole leaders signed a removal treaty in 1832 as well. The Seminoles had cultural and historic ties to the Creeks, but they were a distinct people politically. Slave raids and Anglo-American invasions in the early eighteenth century led many Indians in north Florida to move into Creek country. By mid-century, however, Native people, probably the refugees and their descendants, had begun to move back into this region and take up rich hunting, grazing, and farm lands. They congregated in two areas, in the heart of the old Apalachee country where Tallahassee is now and on the Alachua Prairie near present Gainesville. Distance from the center of Creek population and an ancient tradition of independence enhanced the autonomy of their towns. In the 1780s they were so far removed from Creek affairs that Alexander McGillivray, bent on developing a centralist government in the Creek Nation, had to admit he did not know who the leaders of the Seminoles were. The name Seminole first appears in the English record in the 1760s, either an English rendition of the attempt by Muskogee speakers to pronounce the Spanish word *cimarron*, meaning people or animals who refuse to be controlled, or, as ethnohistorian Patricia Wickman has suggested, an Anglicization of a Muskogee word meaning "free people."[26] When refugee Redsticks fled to the Seminoles in 1814, substantially increasing their population, the political distance between Seminoles and Creeks widened.

The Seminoles also generally permitted black slaves who fled from their Carolina and Georgia owners to settle near them and augment their fighting force. Blacks entered Seminole country as autonomous allies and as slaves, and by the early nineteenth century their presence in Seminole territory drew the attention of irate Americans who saw Florida as a haven for racially dangerous malcontents (see **slavery**). An American invasion in 1816–18, the First Seminole War, was little more than a slave raid, but it convinced Spain to sell Florida to the United States (see **Seminole Wars**). This led to the first treaty between the Seminoles and the United States. Signed in 1823, it restricted Seminoles to a reservation in the interior of the peninsula where much of the land was so swampy that people could not eke out a living. This did not ease the pressure Americans put on the tribe to remove. As in most tribes, the Seminoles split on the question. Some believed the time had arrived to get out and save what they could; others argued they should resist. The **Treaty of Payne's Landing**, signed in 1832, provided for their removal on one condition: like the Chickasaws, the Seminoles insisted on sending land scouts into the West to see if a suitable homeland could be found. Seven men, escorted by their agent, made the tour. While in the West, their agent forced the men to sign a paper asserting that the land was good and committing the nation to move. They had no authority to make such a decision, but, even worse, the land they supposedly agreed to belonged to the Creek Nation.

The Seminole people denounced the document as fraudulent, but the federal government insisted on its validity and gave the Seminoles until January 1,1836, to get out of Florida. In December 1835, warriors led by **Osceola** killed Charley Emathla, one of the treaty chiefs, executed their United States agent, and then wiped out a column of the United States army. The Second Seminole War was on (see **Seminole Wars**). The war lasted until 1842. It cost the United States $30 to $40 million and 1,500 lives. No one knows how many Seminoles died. But in the end some 4,000 Seminoles and their African-Amerian allies were transported to the West. An estimated 500 Seminoles remained in Florida under the leadership of **Arpeika**, or Sam Jones. Despite their protests, the government assigned the Seminoles to lands already allocated to the Creeks. In 1856, after several years of conflict between the two groups, the United States paid the Creek Nation one million dollars for a tract of land so the Seminoles could reconstitute their nation in the West.

The Creek treaty of 1832 was not a removal treaty (see **Treaty of Washington**). The Creeks already had land in the West, granted in the 1826 treaty in exchange for the land they surrendered to Georgia. During the late 1820s and into the early 1830s some three thousand Creeks moved there. Some were followers of the executed William McIntosh but many simply believed that the days of their nation in the East were numbered. Most Creeks, however, agreed with **Opothle Yoholo**, the speaker of the National Council, when he said that leaving their homeland for a strange and distant place in the West was unthinkable. The result was a treaty that attempted to satisfy everyone, Alabamians and Creeks alike. Opothle Yoholo hammered out the details in Washington with President Jackson's new secretary of war, Lewis Cass. The plan was to survey the entire nation, then allot parcels to individuals who would cluster their allotments into town groups, thus creating a pattern in which Creek towns would survive like islands in a sea of white Alabamians. The land not allotted passed to the United States. The Creeks received various payments and settlements totaling nearly $125,000 plus an annuity for twenty years that totaled $210,000.

If Opothle Yoholo and the Creeks believed they could remain in Alabama on their allotments, Cass and the government expected them to move west. To encourage that decision, the treaty provided that the allottees could sell their allotments at any time. It also promised to pay the costs of removal for any Creeks who decided to go. Alabamians launched the usual swindles, and many Creeks lost their allotments. Squatters poured into the cession in violation of the treaty and added physical violence and grave robbing to the nefarious repertoire of crimes committed against Southern Indians. But in the end it was the Seminole War that caused the Creeks to be evicted. The army feared, with some cause, that the Creeks might enter the war in alliance with the Seminoles. If that happened, a conflict that was isolated in Florida would spread into Georgia and Alabama. Citing national security concerns, in the fall of 1836 the army simply began to round up Creek people, dragging them from their homes, and put them on the road. Given no time to gather their belongings or sell their allotments, the Creeks marched west with virtually nothing. Through the winter and into the spring of 1837, overland and by riverboat, freezing, starving, and drowning, about fifteen thousand people were "drove off like dogs" to the West.[27]

The Cherokees were the last to sign a removal treaty. Concluded in December 1835 at the national capital of New Echota, the treaty ended a legal battle that had begun several years earlier, when Georgia first extended its jurisdiction and declared that the Cherokee Nation was illegal.

Early in 1830 a Cherokee man named Tassel fought with another Cherokee man and killed him. Georgia police arrested Tassel, charged him with murder, and hauled him to a nearby county court for trial. Cherokee chief John **Ross** hired an attorney to defend Tassel. The lawyer argued that the Georgia court lacked jurisdiction in this case because the act of the Georgia legislature to extend state criminal jurisdiction into the Cherokee Nation, where the crime took place, was unconstitutional. The court ruled against that argument, tried Tassel, found him guilty, and sentenced him to hang. Ross then contracted with William Wirt, a prominent Baltimore attorney and former U.S. attorney general, to appeal the ruling of the state court to the United States Supreme Court. In early 1831 Wirt argued the case, **Cherokee Nation v. Georgia**. He claimed that the sovereignty of the

Cherokee Nation and the many protections and guarantees written into the treaties between the Cherokee Nation and the United States precluded any legal authority of Georgia to extend its jurisdiction into the Cherokee Nation or interfere with Cherokee internal affairs. Chief Justice John Marshall was sympathetic to the Cherokee argument but denied the right of the Cherokee Nation to sue Georgia. Referring to it as a "domestic dependent nation," Marshall left open the door for a suit brought by a United States citizen against the state. By that time Georgia had already executed Tassel.

Shortly thereafter, Georgia police arrested two missionaries, citizens of the United States, who had refused to swear an oath of allegiance to the state of Georgia. They were tried and found guilty of the crime and sentenced to four years hard labor at the state prison. Wirt managed the appeal of one of the missionaries, Samuel Worcester, in the 1832 Supreme Court case *Worcester v. Georgia*. He repeated the argument used in the Cherokee Nation case, and this time Justice Marshall ruled on the merits. Marshall developed two lines of argument. The Cherokee Nation, he ruled, had been a sovereign nation since before the birth of the United States, and, while it had surrendered elements of that sovereignty at various times in return for certain benefits, the nation retained all attributes of sovereignty not expressly given up. That included the sovereign right to govern its own internal affairs. Marshall also noted that the United States, in its treaty relations with the Cherokee Nation, had recognized and affirmed Cherokee sovereignty and pledged to protect it from external threat. These treaties, under the federal Constitution, were equal to federal law and superior to state law. Thus, Marshall ruled, Georgia's interference in the internal affairs of the Cherokee Nation by extending its civil and criminal jurisdiction was unconstitutional, the extension legislation was null and void, and Georgia should end all unlawful attempts to impose its law onto the Cherokees. Citing state sovereign rights and counting on the support of President Jackson, Georgia ignored Marshall's ruling. The decision has become a cornerstone in federal Indian law, but in 1832 it was a pyrrhic victory for the Cherokees.

Georgia did not desist, Cherokee property owners continued to be harassed, and after the momentary jubilation over the Court's decision, a pall of gloom settled over the nation. Principal Chief John Ross spent most of the next several years in Washington trying to work out a solution, but, at home, conditions simply got worse. The Georgia legislature had provided for a survey of Cherokee land in preparation for a lottery, the established method by which the state distributed public land to its citizens. In 1832 the lottery wheels began to turn. Although Georgia law gave some protection to land that Cherokees actually occupied, the process for halting an eviction by a lottery winner was so complicated and expensive that few Cherokees availed themselves of it. As a result, holders of winning tickets swarmed into the Cherokee Nation.

Elias **Boudinot**, editor of the *Cherokee Phoenix*, his cousin, John **Ridge**, and Ridge's father, Major **Ridge**, despaired of the Cherokees being permitted to remain in their homeland. Despite the nearly universal support the people gave Ross and his efforts to hang on, they began to advocate a removal treaty. The Cherokee government forced Boudinot's resignation as editor and impeached the Ridges from their seats in the National Council. Boudinot and the Ridges, along with a small number of other people dubbed the Treaty Party, persisted in their conviction that, painful as it was, removal had become inevitable. Life in the East had become unbearable, and popular suffering and social collapse had reached crisis proportions. Rather than continue to follow Ross and the national government, they agreed to open private talks with government agents with the view of escaping to the West. These talks produced the **Treaty of New Echota**.

The Cherokees already owned land in the West, granted early in the nineteenth century to encourage voluntary removal, and so this was not an exchange treaty. Rather, for a sum of $5 million dollars plus various other awards, compensations, and judgments, the Treaty Party agreed to sell all the nation's land in the East and to remove, at government expense, within two years of the time the treaty was ratified. Treaty Party members knew that by agreeing to the treaty they defied public opinion and government policy, that they were an unofficial and unrepresentative group of private individuals with no legal authorization to commit the nation to anything, and that in signing the document they were in violation of Cherokee law. Major Ridge reportedly said, as he made his mark on the treaty, "I have signed my death warrant."[28] The Senate, aware that the treaty was fraudulent and unmoved by considerable opposition, particularly in the Northeast, quickly ratified it. Thus the nation was bound by its terms unless Ross could get them changed.

Ross failed. In the spring of 1838 Georgia and federal troops began to gather up Cherokee people in preparation for the trek west. Military units plucked people out of their homes and farms, often denying them time to pack a bag, and hauled them off, sometimes leaving uneaten supper on the table. The troops built holding camps throughout the nation to house the people until enough were gathered to make up a removal party. Many Cherokees languished throughout the summer in these stockades, suffering from exposure, bad water, and inadequate food. Much of the death toll attributed to the "Trail of Tears" occurred in these camps before the actual march. Three detachments of about one thousand each headed west during the summer, but extremely hot weather and food shortages caused excessive suffering and General Winfield Scott, in charge of the operation, agreed to delay the rest until fall. He also agreed to permit the Cherokee government to manage the removal. The first of thirteen detachments organized by Cherokee officials headed west on August 23. The final detachment arrived in the Western nation in March 1839. No one knows the cost in lives, but many think that perhaps four thousand out of a total of about sixteen thousand Cherokees died.[29]

In 1840 the Office of Indian Affairs, by then a formally established bureau of the War Department, computed that in the previous ten years more than 100,000 Eastern Indians had been removed to the West. Between 60 and 70 percent of them had come from the South. Removal did not empty the South of Indians, but it certainly robbed the region of the political, economic, and social dynamic the Five Tribes had contributed to its history. For the next 150 years, the history of the Five Tribes has occurred primarily in the country that came to be called Indian Territory, since 1907, the state of Oklahoma.

Notes

1. Alexander McGillivray to Arturo O'Neill, July 10, 1785, in *McGillivray of the Creeks*, ed. John W. Caughey (Norman: University of Oklahoma Press, 1938), 91–92.

2. Ibid.

3. David J. Weber, *The Spanish Frontier in North America* (New Haven: Yale University Press, 1992), 282–84.

4. Michael D. Green, "Alexander McGillivray," in *American Indian Leaders: Studies in Diversity*, ed. R. David Edmunds (Lincoln: University of Nebraska Press, 1980), 41–63.

5. Ibid. See also *McGillivray*, ed. Caughey, 23.

6. Robert F. Berkhofer Jr., *The White Man's Indian: Images of the American Indian from Columbus to the Present* (New York: Vintage, 1978), 134.

7. See Francis Paul Prucha, *American Indian Policy in the Formative Years: The Indian Trade and Intercourse Acts, 1790–1834* (Cambridge: Harvard University Press, 1962); and Reginald Horsman, *Expansion and American Indian Policy, 1783–1812* (East Lansing: Michigan State University Press, 1967).

8. See William G. McLoughlin, *Cherokees and Missionaries, 1789–1839* (New Haven: Yale University Press, 1984).

9. Benjamin Hawkins, *Letters, Journals, and Writings of Benjamin Hawkins*, ed. C. L. Grant, 2 vols. (Savannah: Beehive Press, 1980), 24.

10. James Taylor Carson, *Searching for a Bright Path: The Mississippi Choctaws from Prehistory to Removal* (Lincoln: University of Nebraska Press, 1999), 70–75.

11. Claudio Saunt, *A New Order of Things: Property, Power, and the Transformation of the Creek Indians, 1733–1816* (Cambridge: Cambridge University Press, 1999), 250.

12. Joel W. Martin, *Sacred Revolt: The Muskogees' Struggle for a New World* (Boston: Beacon Press, 1991), 141–42.

13. Andrew Jackson to President James Monroe, March 4, 1817, in *Correspondence of Andrew Jackson*, ed. John A. Bassett (Washington: Carnegie Institute, 1926–35), 2:277–82.

14. John C. Calhoun to the House of Representatives, December 5, 1818, *American State Papers, Indian Affairs* 2:183.

15. President James Monroe, First Annual Message to Congress, December 2, 1817, in *Messages and Papers of the Presidents*, comp. James D. Richardson (New York: Bureau of National Literature, 1897), 2:585.

16. V. Richard Persico, "Early Nineteenth–Century Cherokee Political Organization," in *The Cherokee Indian Nation: A Troubled History*, ed. Duane H. King (Knoxville: University of Tennessee Press, 1979), 92–109.

17. Carson, *Searching*, 99–102.

18. Duane Champagne, *Social Order and Political Change: Constitutional Governments Among the Cherokee, the Choctaw, the Chickasaw, and the Creek* (Stanford: Stanford University Press, 1992), 158–60.

19. Michael D. Green, *The Politics of Indian Removal: Creek Government and Society in Crisis* (Lincoln: University of Nebraska Press, 1982), 69–125.

20. Quoted in *The Cherokee Removal: A Brief History with Documents*, ed. Theda Perdue and Michael D. Green (Boston: Bedford, 1995), 15.

21. Green, *Politics of Indian Removal*, 145–47.

22. Perdue and Green, *Cherokee Removal*, 58–68.

23. Quoted in Green, *Politics of Indian Removal*, 147.

24. Ronald N. Satz, *American Indian Policy in the Jacksonian Era* (Lincoln: University of Nebraska Press, 1975).

25. Quoted in Carson, *Searching*, 121–22.

26. Patricia Riles Wickman, *The Tree That Bends: Discourse, Power, and the Survival of the Maskoki People* (Tuscaloosa: University of Alabama Press, 1999), 217.

27. From a letter of the Creeks of Kashita Town, in Holatte Cvpvkke (C. B. Clark), "'Drove Off Like Dogs': Creek Removal," in *Indians of the Lower South: Past and Present*, ed. John K. Mahon (Pensacola, Fla.: Gulf Coast History and Humanities Conference, 1975), 118–24.

28. Quoted in *Cherokee Tragedy: The Story of the Ridge Family and of the Decimation of a People,* ed. Thurman Willkins (New York: Macmillan, 1970), 278.

29. Grant Foreman, *Indian Removal: The Emigration of the Five Civilized Tribes of Indians* (Norman: University of Oklahoma Press, 1932), contains the details on the history of removal.

6   Native Southerners in the West

When the Five Tribes arrived in what is today eastern Oklahoma, they found a land that bore some similarities to that they had left behind, but they also noted many differences. Forests covered much of the land, which the Canadian, Arkansas, and Red Rivers and their tributaries drained. Tall grass prairies interspersed the forests, and the rivers tended to be shallow braided streams flowing through wide, sandy beds. In the northeast, where the Cherokees settled, the southern edge of the Ozark Plateau known as the Cookson Hills provided topographical relief, just as the ridges of the Ouachita and Arbuckle Mountains did to the south in Choctaw and Chickasaw territory. The best farmland lay in the Red River valley that divided the Chickasaw and Choctaw nations from Texas, but less fertile land offered opportunities. The prairies made superb grazing land for cattle, and salt springs abounded in river valleys. Southern Indians recognized the potential for exploiting these resources almost immediately, and, after the Civil War, they found that their land held other treasures—coal, timber, asphalt, and oil. Those resources helped set the stage for yet another struggle over land and sovereignty.

Before the arrival of the Southern Indians, the land between Kansas and Texas had been a cultural crossroads where southern farmers interacted with plains hunters. The Caddos had lived there in ancient times, but by the time the Five Tribes arrived the Quapaw and Osage peoples lived in the eastern part of the territory. They had much in common culturally with the Five Tribes from the deep South, but the Apache, Kiowa, and Comanche peoples to the west influenced their cultures as well. The Osages and Quapaws farmed corn, beans, and squash and lived in permanent villages, but they also hunted buffalo on the plains and traded with their western neighbors. These tribes knew some of the peoples who replaced them. Cherokees had begun to settle west of the Mississippi, perhaps as early as 1775 on the St. Francis River in Arkansas, and their numbers grew in the migrations of 1810 and 1817–19. The Osages and Cherokees had long been enemies, and well into the nineteenth century Cherokee war parties from the east crossed the Mississippi to join their western relatives in fighting the Osages. In 1828 the Cherokees exchanged their lands in Arkansas for territory further west and relocated in what is today northeastern Oklahoma, pushing their old enemies into Kansas. Choctaws and Chickasaws also traveled west of the Mississippi to hunt and trade, and in 1820 the Choctaws obtained territory in the West. Two Creek towns, Alabama and Coushatta, moved further south into Louisiana and then Texas, and while they did not relocate in Oklahoma or "Indian Territory," their story is part of this westward migration and intercultural contact between the Southeast and the southern plains.

In 1818 the Quapaws relinquished their territory south of the Arkansas River, and the Osage ceded their lands in Arkansas and Oklahoma in treaties of 1818 and 1825, clearing the way for **removal** of the Southern Indians west of the Mississippi. The Apaches, Kiowas, and Comanches still lived and hunted on land to the west, and Southern Indians regarded their presence as a threat to property and person as well as to their own reputation. Consequently, the Five Tribes distinguished themselves from the "wild Indians" to the west by embracing the term "civilized tribes," an ethnocentric term scholars no longer use.

Settling in the West

When the Five Tribes arrived in their new homelands, they confronted a host of problems. The trauma of removal and the suffering en route had taken their toll. Virtually every family in all tribes had lost kin. Thin blankets, rancid meat, weevil-infested flour and meal, insufficient and/or unsafe conveyances, polluted drinking water as well as inclement weather claimed thousands of lives and weakened those who survived. Few people received adequate compensation for their claims, and treaty allowances for subsistence were inadequate. Therefore, many people had little with which to begin life anew.

Equally daunting were the tensions that existed, particularly among the Creeks and Cherokees, between those who had favored removal and those who had opposed it. Creeks tended to separate into two communities. Most

Creeks who favored removal migrated west in the late 1820s and early 1830s and carved out farms and plantations in the Arkansas River valley. The followers of **Opothle Yoholo**, who had opposed removal, arrived in the West in 1836–37 and settled along the Canadian River, 50 miles away from their opponents. Reconstituting tribal towns and their redistributive economy, these Creeks maintained traditional values of generosity and community. The two Creek divisions governed themselves separately until 1840, when they established a National Council that met annually at a halfway point between them. An attempt to create constitutional **government** in 1859 failed because it mandated districts as the electoral units rather than towns, and the Canadian Creeks refused to accept this modification to traditional practice. The rejection of the constitution reflected a wide gulf between the two groups.

Among the Cherokees, civil war erupted in the west. The small unauthorized group that signed the removal treaty departed for the west before the major exodus of 1838–39 that has come to be known as the Trail of Tears. Having violated national law, they feared for their lives. When they arrived they allied themselves with the Old Settlers, those Cherokees who already lived in the West, in the hopes of preventing Principal Chief John **Ross** and his followers, who comprised a majority, from reasserting control. Upon his arrival with the main body of Cherokees, Ross called a council to resolve differences between the three groups. Before an agreement could be reached, unknown Cherokees killed three leaders of the Treaty Party, Major **Ridge**, John **Ridge**, and Elias **Boudinot**. They had committed the capital offense of selling land, and they suffered the prescribed penalty. Armed guards surrounded Stand **Watie**, Boudinot's brother, on whom fell the mantle of leadership of the Treaty Party. Fearing reprisals, supporters of Ross gave the principal chief their protection. Hoping to stave off armed conflict, several leaders of the Old Settlers agreed in 1840 to an Act of Union and an 1839 constitution, much like the one written in the East, that recognized majority rule and thereby confirmed Ross's leadership. Their efforts, however, did not prevent civil war. Intermittent violence wracked the Cherokee Nation until 1846, when Ross, Watie, and other leaders signed a treaty pardoning all involved and uniting the nation. The desire for revenge on the part of many Cherokees who had lost relatives during the conflict smoldered (see **Ridge, John Rollin**).

The Seminoles, who had been captured and deported militarily from Florida, faced a problem unique to them. The other four nations had brought with them African American slaves whose legal status was virtually the same as slaves in the antebellum white South—they were chattel property that could be bought, sold, mortgaged, bequeathed, stolen, and redeemed (see **slavery**). Among the Seminoles, however, most African Americans lived in autonomous villages and had fought alongside Indians in the armed struggle against removal. Many of these African Americans had been slaves who had run away or been stolen from their Anglo-American or Creek owners. The Creeks not only believed that many of these people or their forbears had belonged to them, they had paid the claims of white owners for others following the Creek War. Therefore, the Creeks argued that they had a legitimate right to the African Americans among the Seminoles. The Seminole removal treaty that united them with the Creeks provided the Creeks with an opportunity to recover their property. Fearing this outcome, many Seminoles refused to leave the vicinity of Fort Gibson in the Cherokee Nation, but the Cherokees protested that the Seminole blacks had a bad influence on their own bondsmen. The Seminoles who actually settled in the Creek Nation were also unhappy because they had little power in this nation dominated by people who in the Creek War had been their enemies. Some African and Indian Seminoles followed Coacoochee, or Wild Cat, first to Texas and then to Mexico in search of independence and safety. In 1845 the Creeks agreed to permit the Seminoles to establish their own towns, and in 1856 the Seminoles established a separate nation to the west of the Creeks.

The Chickasaws had a similar problem in that they, too, originally had no separate nation in the West. Unable to find suitable land, they paid the Choctaws for the right to live in their western territory (see **Treaty of Doaksville**). Exhausted from removal, devastated by a smallpox epidemic in 1838, and fearful of attack by the Apaches, Kiowas, and Comanches, most Chickasaws refused to leave the five widely separated emigrant camps in which they lived. Distance prevented the reorganization of a formal government, and the Choctaw constitution of 1838, which gave the Chickasaws one fourth of the seats on a national council, threatened to make them a permanent minority in the Choctaw Nation. The construction of Fort Washita and Fort Arbuckle alleviated fears of the plains tribes, and by 1853 approximately 90 percent of the Chickasaws had moved into their separate district. In 1855 the Chickasaws paid the Choctaws $150,000 for this land, and in 1856 they established their own separate constitutional government (see **Colbert, Daugherty Winchester**).

Even though they were first, and suffered enormously in the removal ordeal, nation building in the West may have been easiest for the Choctaws.

Their new homeland, bounded by the Red River on the south and the Arkansas and Canadian Rivers on the north, was the most fertile country in Indian Territory. And, with easy Red River access to distant markets, Choctaw planters and merchants soon emerged as an important economic elite. Robert Jones, the Choctaw planter prince, worked five hundred slaves on his five plantations in the Red River bottoms and shipped his produce to New Orleans markets on his own steamboats. Perhaps motivated by their economic interests, the planters sought and found widespread popular support for American-style education. Before the end of the 1840s the Choctaws had the most comprehensive public education system in the territory and had become the model the Creeks, Chickasaws, and Seminoles sought to emulate. Choctaw leaders did not abandon their old political institutions, however. Until 1860 they retained their structure of three semiautonomous districts. Enshrined in the constitution of 1834, this system confounded those who believed the nation should follow the American constitutional model.

Despite the difficulties they faced, the Five Tribes recovered remarkably in the period before the Civil War. The people cleared farms and built houses while their nations established governments. In some ways they tried to replicate life in the East. But the pace of change quickened in Indian Territory. Following the Choctaw lead, by the mid-1840s the Chickasaws negotiated an agreement with the Methodist mission board to open schools. The Cherokees began once again to publish their newspaper, renamed the *Cherokee Advocate*, in 1844 and added the motto "Our Rights—Our Country—Our Race." They established a system of public schools, and in 1851 they opened two "seminaries," one for men and one for women, to provide higher education. The desire for education led the Canadian River Creeks to temper their stand on Christianity. They had demanded in 1836 that missionaries be expelled from the nation, and although several Christian congregations existed on the Arkansas, they succeeded in obtaining the prohibition. In 1841, however, the National Council agreed to permit the Presbyterians to establish a boarding school, and two years later it lifted the ban on preaching. The Presbyterians also built a mission for the Seminoles. The number of Christians among all the Southern Indians began to grow.

Civil War and Reconstruction

The number of slaves also grew. By 1860 more than eight thousand slaves lived in the Southern Indian nations. Slaves accounted for 14 percent of the total population, although only 2.3 percent of the citizens of these nations owned slaves. In addition to farming, slaves operated salines, herded cattle, worked on steamboats and ferries, performed domestic chores, and held other kinds of jobs. As in the white South, the wealth that slaves produced helped their masters dominate the political and economic life of their respective nations. Many Indians, however, particularly among the Cherokees, Creeks, and Seminoles, had serious misgivings about **slavery**. This attitude rose less from a belief in racial equality than from resentment of the power commanded by the slaveholding elite and a desire to preserve traditional culture.

When the **Civil War** broke out in the United States, the Southern Indians faced a serious dilemma. Cherokee Chief John **Ross** described the situation: "Our locality and institutions ally us to the South, while to the North we are indebted for a defence of our rights in the past, and that enlarged benevolence to which we owe chiefly our progress in civilization."[1] Support for the Confederacy was nearly unanimous among the Choctaws and Chickasaws, but the other nations were seriously divided. Nonslaveholding traditionalists and even some slaveholders like Cherokee Chief John Ross and the Creek leader **Opothle Yoholo** preferred neutrality, which meant that existing treaties with the United States remained in effect. The United States, however, withdrew its troops from Indian Territory, and the Confederacy increased pressure on the Five Tribes to negotiate alliances. In July 1861 the Creeks, Chickasaws, Choctaws, and Seminoles signed **Confederate treaties** that guaranteed their security and continuation of annuities. The Cherokee Nation held out until Stand **Watie** began actively raising troops for the Confederacy (see **Colbert, Daugherty Winchester**). Rather than see his nation divided, Ross negotiated a Confederate treaty in October and called for a national force to act as a home guard.

Opothle Yoholo, however, refused to put aside his convictions for the sake of national unity. Creeks who opposed a Confederate alliance began to gather at his plantation, and in November Opothle Yoholo decided to lead them to Kansas where they would come under the protection of Union troops. Several thousand men, women, and children joined the flight. The Confederate command ordered the refugees stopped, but, when directed to attack Creek traditionalists, Cherokees under the command of John Drew defected and joined the fleeing Creeks (see **Downing, Lewis**). The remaining Cherokees under Watie's leadership along with other Confederates engaged Opothle Yoholo's people in three battles in which the refugees lost their livestock and provisions. Frozen, starving, and exhausted, nearly six thousand refugees finally managed to reach Kansas. Housed in tents, they continued to suffer. In March 1863 their leader Opothle Yoholo died of exposure and old age.

In 1862 federal troops briefly invaded the Cherokee Nation and captured or rescued, depending on interpretation, Chief Ross, who spent the remainder of the war in Washington and Philadelphia. Watie stepped into the political breach, declared himself principal chief, and began to exact retribution from his rivals. The situation in Indian Territory deteriorated quickly. Many Seminoles, Cherokees, and even a few Chickasaws joined the Creeks in Kansas where able-bodied men joined the Union army while women and children eagerly anticipated the day they could return home.

In the Cherokee and Creek Nations there would be little to which to return. Confederates and Unionists, who had little opportunity to meet in battle, waged war against each other's property. A Creek woman recalled the devastation inflicted: "Raiding parties from both sides scoured the country, burning houses and cabins, driving off horses and cattle, and in fact destroying and demolishing everything they could find."[2] Slaves became victims of Union sympathizers because they were the property of Confederates. A ten-year-old Cherokee slave remembered that "the Indians was always talking about getting their horses and cattle killed and their slaves harmed. I was too little to know how bad it was until one morning my own mammy went somewhere down the road to git some stuff to dye cloth and she didn't come back."[3] She was found stabbed and shot to death. Most Indian men in the two nations were serving in one army or the other, and their families were vulnerable to raiding parties. A Union woman alone with five children in the Cherokee Nation wrote in her journal: "Today we hear that Watie's men declared their intention to come back and *rob* every woman whose husband has gone to the Federals, and every woman who has Northern principles." A few days later Watie's men came to her house, "took many valuable things, and overhauled every closet, trunk, box & drawer they could find."[4] Because of the danger of remaining at home, Creeks and Cherokees fled if they could, Unionists to Kansas and Confederates to the Choctaw and Chickasaw nations or into Texas.

Even though General Robert E. Lee surrendered his army on April 9, 1865, the war in Indian Territory continued into the summer. Finally, in June, Brigadier General Stand Watie became the last Confederate general to surrender, and in July the Chickasaws became the last of the Five Tribes to abandon the Confederate cause. The Cherokees and Creeks, who had lost many soldiers in service to the Union, expected the United States to recognize the loyalty of the majority of their citizens. Loyalists and Confederates sent delegations to a peace conference at Fort Smith, where the treaty commissioners announced that the nations had forfeited all rights under previous treaties and must come to Washington to negotiate new treaties.

The treaties that the United States demanded had several common features: they united rather than divided the factions within each nation, freed slaves and established their status with each nation, compensated loyalists, and provided for railroad rights of way. The treaties also required all the tribes but the Cherokees to cede to the United States all their lands west of the 98th meridian (see **Reconstruction treaties**). The government intended to locate Plains tribes on reservations there. The Seminoles surrendered their entire territory and accepted a smaller tract at the junction of the Canadian River and its north fork, across which they granted a railroad right of way. The Chickasaws and Choctaws negotiated jointly because their treaty required them to cede the Leased District, a tract of land west of the Chickasaw Nation that they held jointly and leased to the United States, for which they obtained $300,000 (see **Pitchlynn, Peter**). They also agreed to one east-west and one north-south right of way for railroads. The Creeks lost the western half of their domain, some of which the Seminoles bought for their new nation, and granted railroad rights of way. The Cherokee treaty proved the most difficult because the southern Cherokees sought division of the nation, but ultimately the nationalists prevailed by agreeing to permit the former Confederates to settle in the Canadian District. The Cherokees also gave up rights of way for railroads.

The Cherokees, Creeks and Seminoles granted both freedom and citizenship rights to their former slaves. This meant that the freed people had the right not only to vote and enjoy equal protection under the law but also to cultivate unused tracts of land. The treaty with the Choctaws and Chickasaws, however, did not extend such rights to their former slaves. Instead, the United States held the $300,000 the two nations received for the sale of the Leased District for two years during which time they were supposed to pass laws providing citizenship rights and forty acres of land to each former slave. Freed people who left the nations were to receive $100 each from the fund. If the time period expired and the former slaves neither received citizenship nor left the nations, they would be considered intruders, which presumably meant that the United States was obligated to remove them. Neither nation passed the requisite legislation within the two years. Two decades later, the Choctaws finally agreed to adopt their freed people, but the Chickasaws, claiming that former slaves and their descendants outnumbered Indians in their nation, never complied (see **Colbert, Daugherty Winchester**).

Economic Development

The economic redevelopment of much of Indian Territory after the Civil War was not much different from the challenges new immigrants had faced following their removal from the East. For most Native people, it meant starting from scratch. The Cherokee and Creek Nations were desolate. Refugees began to return in 1865 to find their homes destroyed, their fields grown up in weeds, and their livestock gone. A grasshopper plague in 1866 and 1867 wiped out the newly planted crops and only by 1868 were the people able to harvest enough to feed themselves adequately. The Seminoles had a different problem. Forced to give up their country, they had to resettle in a new place. Only the Choctaws and Chickasaws avoided such trauma, but their country had been sorely taxed by the hordes of wartime refugees, and, with most of their young men in Confederate service, neither tribe had weathered the war unscathed. Thus the first problem of economic development after the war was recovery. By the end of the 1860s, however, the natural bounty of the land was evident. Indian farmers had surpluses for sale, ranchers found markets in Kansas for their stock, and people were able to think that the prewar prosperity might return.[5]

Some, of course, looked for more than subsistence. While most Indian citizens of the Five Tribes had little contact with the market, the economic distinctions that had marked their societies since before removal intensified. Entrepreneurship attracted a growing number, and the opportunities for ambitious men on the make in Indian Territory seemed boundless. Many forces promised economic opportunity, but none were as important as the railroads.

Under the terms of the 1866 treaties all the tribes promised to permit railroad construction within their boundaries (see **Reconstruction treaties**). The Missouri, Kansas, and Texas Railroad, nicknamed the Katy, was the first line to enter Indian Territory. Heading south out of Kansas, it crossed the border into the Cherokee Nation in 1870, veered southwest into the Creek Nation, crossed the Canadian River near North Fork Town, proceeded southwest through the Choctaw Nation, and crossed the southeastern extremity of the Chickasaw Nation on its way to the Red River and Texas. Averaging about 1½ miles a day, the line reached the Red in January 1873. The Atlantic and Pacific, soon to become the St. Louis and San Francisco

Railroad, or Frisco, entered the Cherokee Nation from the east in 1871, met the Katy, and stopped. Within the next 20 years the Frisco built another line from Fort Smith, Arkansas, southwest across the Choctaw Nation to the Red, the Chicago, Rock Island, and Pacific laid track south from Kansas and along with the Colorado and Santa Fe extended across the Chickasaw Nation, also heading to the Red River and Texas. The Choctaw, Oklahoma, and Gulf Railroad built west from Arkansas across the Choctaw and Seminole Nations and several short lines, including the Pittsburg and Gulf Railroad, connected the others.

All this railroad construction had a revolutionary impact on the Five Tribes. Building the roads required the railroads to import thousands of laborers. Temporary towns located at the rapidly moving ends of the lines housed and fed the trackmen, served their needs for liquor, women, and other recreation, and disrupted the lives of the Native citizens. The railroad companies imported their rails but depended on local suppliers for ties. Cedar, which grew in huge forests in eastern Indian Territory, seemed ideal. At 2,700 ties per mile, the railroads gobbled up the forests. Tribal governments tried to assure that citizens provided the ties. Both the Choctaw and Chickasaw governments, for example, enacted legislation that limited the exploitation of tribal resources to citizens. For the payment of a license fee Native businessmen organized lumber companies and sold thousands of board feet of timber to the railroad companies. Tribal governments profited as well by collecting royalties on the lumber. But timber poaching by noncitizens was widespread as well. With no judicial jurisdiction over Americans, the tribal courts could do nothing to enforce laws that regulated timber cutting. Only a sympathetic agent willing to challenge the power of the railroads could bring lawbreakers to justice. But miscreants had to be tried in the federal district court in Arkansas, difficult to get to from Indian Territory.

Timber poaching was just the beginning, and it was not limited to railroad suppliers. Furniture and gunstock makers from as far away as Germany learned about the beautiful walnut that grew in Indian Territory, and stealing that timber also became a lucrative business. In addition, railroad companies needed enormous amounts of stone for roadbeds and construction, coal to fuel their locomotives, and water. All these abounded in Indian Territory, and tribal governments found that controlling the exploitation of these commodities was equally difficult.

No matter what non-Indian scoundrels did to steal the resources of Indian Territory, none could lay their hands on the land. Owned in common by the tribes, the legal access for non-Indians was to marry a Native citizen, which many did, or to figure a way to be adopted into a tribe. But the railroads wanted stations and towns along their routes. The tribes laid out towns, either as tribal enterprises or by granting licenses to individual citizens. The non-Indians who flocked there leased lots on which they built businesses and homes. These railroad towns, such as Muskogee, Eufaula, Atoka, McAlester, Ardmore, and others, grew into substantial communities. In 1890 the Chickasaw Nation alone contained eight railroad towns with populations of more than 1,000. Some Indians moved into them and opened their own stores and shops, but the towns remained essentially non-Indian in population and aspiration. Inhabited by noncitizen foreigners, the towns were anomalies. Their residents could not vote in tribal elections, and without the power to incorporate or tax themselves they had no urban services such as police or schools. As a result, by the end of the nineteenth century they had become nests of agitation against tribal sovereignty.

Despite the desire of railroad companies to build into Indian Territory, their lines were not as profitable as they might have been. Part of the problem was that they could not cash in on the land grants Congress and the **reconstruction treaties** had conveyed to them. As long as the tribes held the land in common, private ownership by foreign corporations was impossible. The companies tried to solve this problem by lobbying in Congress to dissolve tribal ownership in the territory. The other problem was caused by tribal culture. Most Indians were not oriented toward the market: they had little to sell and no interest in buying. But railroads make their money by hauling freight. Long distance shipments between Kansas and Arkansas and Texas provided some income, but until large numbers of farmers and ranchers producing for the market inhabited Indian Territory, there was little to ship. One railroad executive complained that operating a line through Indian Territory was like running his trains through a tunnel several hundred miles long. Thus the railroads had two economic reasons to agitate for the end of tribal sovereignty and the opening of tribal lands to American settlers.[6]

While some Indians welcomed the arrival of the railroads and developed businesses to profit from them, others looked to the land for economic opportunity. Common ownership meant that any citizen could claim and use any land that no one else was using. Some Chickasaw and Choctaw entrepreneurs, with access to rich Red River valley lands, developed commercial farms of several thousand acres. They worked these giant enterprises by either leasing out parcels to renters or by sharecropping. Former slaves supplied some of the labor, but farm operators also recruited laborers and their families from neighboring states. To both regulate and profit from such foreign immigration, the tribal governments levied a fee on each foreign worker imported into their nations. Ranging from $.25 to $5 per year, the employer either paid or evaded the tax. These farms produced whatever the market demanded, but cotton was especially profitable. Ardmore, a railroad town in the Chickasaw Nation, became one of the largest inland cotton marketing and shipping centers in North America.[7]

Ranching was an even bigger business. Texas was full of cattle. Cowboys drove herds north through Indian Territory, headed for railroad towns in Kansas. But cattle fresh off the trail were gaunt and skinny and not worth very much. If the drovers could fatten their steers on Indian grass on the way, they could command better prices. In 1882 the Cherokee Nation entered into a contract with the Cherokee Strip Livestock Association to lease an enormous grassland in the Cherokee Outlet, land to the west of their nation the Cherokees owned but did not inhabit. The proceeds largely supported the Cherokee government until the United States, regarding the land as "surplus" and intent on **allotment**, pressured the Cherokees into ceding it for $1.40 an acre, not much more than the cattlemen offered for their lease. Tribes also awarded huge blocks of grassland to individual tribal citizens who fenced them as pastures. Texas ranchers leased the land from the Indian holders, paid a tax of $.25 per head to the tribal government, and fattened their cattle at leisure. Native ranchers did the same, although usually on a smaller scale. For example, George Washington Grayson, a Creek merchant in Eufaula, developed a ranching operation with cattle traded to him for goods. By 1890 nearly one-third of Creek tribal land was fenced and under the control of 61 Creek individuals.[8]

Politics and Government

Supervising and regulating this vast array of novel economic activities preoccupied tribal governments. The issues were clear: tribal autonomy, service to citizens, responding to popular concerns, and the maintenance of satisfactory diplomatic relations with the United States. Solutions were not so clear. But even within the context of tribally unique cultures and historical experiences, some patterns of similarity can be found.

No railroad entered the Seminole Nation until the mid 1890s, making that tribe an exception to the history of rapid and complex social and economic change that marked the last half of the nineteenth century in Indian Territory. Spared the influx of foreign corporations and people and with a population of only about two thousand, the Seminoles were the only tribe to govern themselves without a written constitution or code of law. Instead, their tribal council consisted of town leaders chosen in traditional kin-based ways. The council selected a principal chief, the citizens ratified the choice. John Chupco, an important leader since before the Civil War, became principal chief in 1866. The tribe's second chief, John Jumper, served until 1877, when he retired from office to devote full time to the Baptist ministry. He assumed the leadership role in 1881 when Chupco died. In 1885 Jumper retired a second time, to be replaced by his son-in-law, John F. **Brown**. Brown, a Baptist minister and partner in the million-dollar Wewoka Trading Company, remained chief until the end of the century. Such extraordinary political stability in this volatile period is a measure, in part, of the isolation of the Seminole Nation.[9]

The Cherokees, Chickasaws, and Choctaws all had written constitutions that predated the Civil War. They had already had the debates about constitutionalism and had generally agreed that an American form of governmental organization seemed appropriate to their circumstances. Thus for them it was not necessary to forge new political institutions in order to cope with the challenges of the times. All three also shared the problem of reunification following the Civil War, although neither the Choctaws nor the Chickasaws had been as deeply divided in their loyalties as the Cherokees. Nevertheless, early postwar political controversies sometimes reflected a continuation of the Union versus Confederate rivalry (see **Downing, Lewis**).

Perhaps the most important institutional innovation in the governments of the Choctaw, Cherokee, and Chickasaw nations after the Civil War was the development of political parties. Each tribe used distinctive names for their parties, but the Choctaw nomenclature of National and Progressive best fits the philosophies of division in each of the nations. Nationalist parties tended to attract members with little or no formal education, who either did not speak English or who were neither comfortable with nor literate in it, who supported themselves with a traditional subsistence pattern of small-scale farming and hunting, and who had little or no contact with the market. Progressives, on the other hand, were likely to be educated and either comfortably bilingual or English speakers. They also were generally deeply invested in the emerging market economy as large-scale farmers, ranchers, merchants, and professionals. Intermarried or adopted non-Indians were particularly likely to support progressive candidates.

Elections in all three nations were hotly contested, but the record indicates that governmental policy did not change much no matter which party was victorious. Both parties supported the development of educational systems in their nations based on the American model. The tribes invested proportionately enormous sums in the establishment and support of dozens of local grammar schools and regional boarding high schools taught mostly by Native teachers and administered by tribal school boards. The tribal governments also encouraged many mission groups with cash subsidies to reopen their highly regarded boarding manual labor schools. In addition, the tribes funded scholarship programs that identified the best and brightest to be sent to colleges in the "States." Tribal governments supported orphanages to care for hundreds of children whose parents had been killed in the Civil War, and, after accepting their former slaves as citizens, the tribes built separate schools and orphanages for their children. They also maintained elaborate judicial systems, with local, district, and supreme courts and police squads to preserve the peace.

The challenge of tribal governments, whether under progressive or nationalist leadership, was to fund these and other public programs. The 1866 treaties reinstated the regular annuity payments by the United States for land sales made in the East, but those sums were pitifully inadequate. Governments therefore depended for income on royalty payments for the exploitation of timber, coal, and other resources, on license fees on pastures and head taxes on Texas cattle, on the income from leasing lots in railroad towns, and on the permit fees for imported foreign labor. The result was that, beneath the partisan rhetoric, neither party had much room to maneuver. Nor was there much popular pressure to challenge things. Subsistence farmers needed little land and apparently did not resent their fellow citizens who engrossed thousands of acres for commercial farm and ranch operations. All worried about the massive influx of foreigners, but laborers imported on permits did not represent the main problem. Rather, Indian Territory was inundated by unauthorized immigrants who flocked to the towns, squatted on tribal land, and complained loudly about the injustice of their foreign status. The United States promised in the 1866 treaties to eject intruders, and during the 1870s federal officials made periodic efforts to do so. By 1880, however, the government gave up all pretense of helping the tribes defend their borders against illegal aliens. Despite repeated efforts to convince the United States to remove them, the intruder problem simply got worse. Compounding the problem, tribal police and courts lacked jurisdiction over Americans. Most of the intruders were not violent criminals, but some were, and when stories of their crimes appeared on the front pages, they made the tribes look like outlaw heaven. With little money and less help from the United States, the tribal governments struggled mightily to preserve their sovereign independence and serve the needs of their citizens.

The story of the Creeks was somewhat different. While they had drafted a constitution in 1859, the Civil War had rendered it moot. Thus, their 1867 constitution was their inauguration of American style governmental institutions. The constitution provided for a two house legislature, elected principal and second chiefs, and a judicial system. Samuel Checote, a Methodist minister and former colonel in the Confederate Army, won the first election for chief. Early in Checote's first term a party division emerged that resembled the progressive versus nationalist division in the other tribes. But in addition to these two parties there was a third political force, representing a significant proportion of the Creek people, that rejected constitutionalism and insisted on returning to the old council system. This third group often ran candidates for national office on a ticket of dismantling the government, but they also frequently challenged the legitimacy of constitutional government by other means. Four times in the 40 years after 1867 they mounted insurrections against the system, only to be squashed by the tribal militia. The result, however, was that the Creek government never reached a degree of institutional stability that permitted it to effectively counter the outside forces of change.[10]

Territorialization and Allotment

Whether or not the tribal governments were stable or effective mattered little in the late nineteenth century. Federal policy aimed at their destruction and, in the struggle for survival, the Five Tribes had little chance to counter the power of the United States. Intruders, railroads, and the interference of federal courts shaped the process, but Congress and the Johnson administration made their plans clear in the 1866 treaties.

Every treaty included a long and elaborate formula for the establishment of a territorial government in Indian Territory modeled on the system by which frontier states entered the Union. The plan called for an intertribal legislative council proportionately representative of the Five Tribes, a governor appointed by the secretary of the interior, and a series of territorial courts. The legislature would enact laws for the common interests of the tribes but would not interfere with their internal affairs. Once organized, the territory would send a delegate to Congress.

Coming together to discuss common problems was normal practice in Indian Territory. Since the mid-1840s the Five Tribes, often hosting delegations from the Southern Plains tribes, met periodically to resolve differences, plan strategies, and agree on policies for dealing with the United States. The problem with the scheme written into the treaties was that the intertribal council would be under the control of federal officials. Consequently, the tribes were reluctant to act. But Congressional debates on bills to mandate a territorial government convinced Creek Chief Checote that the tribes should take control of the movement and thus blunt the threat from the outside. In 1870 he invited the tribes to send delegates to Okmulgee, the Creek national capital, to develop a plan of action. In the first of a series of seven annual Okmulgee Councils, the delegates drafted a territorial constitution, submitted it to Congress for approval, and prepared to hold plebiscites in their respective nations. In debates on what to call their territory, Choctaw Chief Allen Wright suggested it be named "home of the red man," or, in Choctaw, Oklahoma. The Chickasaw electorate defeated the constitution because proportional representation would put their small nation at a disadvantage. Congress rejected it because it provided for an Indian-controlled territorial government, complete with a popularly elected territorial governor. Washington policy, of course, was to diminish the autonomy of the tribes, not enhance it. Reflecting that perspective, in 1874 Congress abolished the separate tribal agencies and collapsed all their business into one, the Union Agency, established at the railroad town of Muskogee, Creek Nation.[11]

In 1871 both Congress and the Supreme Court redefined the relations between the federal government and the tribes. Congress passed a bill proclaiming that the United States would no longer recognize the tribes as sovereign nations to be dealt with by treaty. It would honor the treaties in place, however. During the same year, the Supreme Court ruled in the **Cherokee Tobacco Case** that Congressional law superceded the treaties. Supreme Court decisions handed down in 1886 and 1903 reaffirmed and extended the doctrine that Congress had total power over Indians, regardless of the guarantees of tribal sovereignty and internal autonomy written into the treaties (see **Boudinot, Elias Cornelius**). Thus Congress was under no constitutional obligation to fulfill treaty commitments made with the tribes. Congressmen recognized the opportunity immediately. In a debate in 1872 on one of many territorial bills presented to the House of Representatives, Texas Democrat John Conner argued that Congress both could and should abolish "these miserable Indian nationalities, for they are a burlesque on government."[12] Over the next twenty years such attitudes gained support and power as Christian reformers, railroad companies, and homestead interests sharpened their attacks on Native cultures, tribal autonomy, and common landholding. The Five Tribes of Indian Territory were by no means the only targets of the movement to destroy tribal society and allot tribal lands in severalty, but when those programs hit them in the 1890s they struck with particular force.

After years of discussion in Congress and the press, the allotment policy took shape in the 1887 Dawes Severalty Act (see **allotment**). Henry Dawes, senator from Massachusetts, was a leading Christian reformer who dedicated himself to the goals of Indian culture change and assimilation into American society. Misunderstanding the essential conservatism of culture, he was convinced that past failures to accomplish the transformation of Native people were due to the inherent strength of tribal communities organized on the basis of kinship and rooted in commonly held land. Thus, he reasoned, culture change could never occur as long as tribal society remained intact. Allotment was his solution. Tribal lands should be surveyed, tribal populations should be counted, and each tribal citizen should receive a parcel of land for a farm. The land not distributed should be sold to American settlers. Railroad companies and homesteaders, uninterested in Indian reform, found Dawes's allotment policy extremely attractive. If Congress dissolved the tribal title to land, the railroads in Indian Territory would be able to acquire and sell the land grants they had been promised in the 1866 treaties, and the sale of "surplus" tribal land would open millions of fertile acres for settlement. Non-Indian homesteaders would be more likely than most Indians to produce for the market and engage the services of the railroads, further enhancing profits.

Theodore Roosevelt once compared Dawes's allotment policy to a rock crusher. Into this "mighty pulverizing engine" Congress dumped intact tribes and out of the spout came individuals to be scattered across the landscape like gravel.[13] The boulder of solidarity destroyed, the separate pebbles could easily be manipulated.

The 1887 Dawes Act exempted the Five Tribes of Indian Territory, but only temporarily. In 1893 Congress appointed a special commission, chaired by Dawes, to open an office in Indian Territory and begin negotiating allotment agreements with the Five Tribes. Rebuffed by the tribal governments, the **Dawes Commission** launched a smear campaign designed to defame the Five Tribes and crush their resistance with public outrage. Ignoring the concentrations of wealth and power in the United States, Dawes waxed indignant about the ways entrepreneurial Indians used large tracts of land for farming and ranching businesses. Population estimates also figured prominently. Of some 178,000 people in Indian Territory in 1890, 109,000 were noncitizens. Ignoring the fact that they were aliens living in foreign countries, the commissioners depicted them as innocents deprived of civil and economic rights, educational opportunities, and protection for life and property by corrupt tribal governments. The health, welfare, and safety of fellow Americans demanded that Indian Territory be dismembered.[14]

Their misrepresentation of conditions in Indian Territory persuaded many. In 1895 Congress empowered the **Dawes Commission** to begin to survey tribal lands and the next year it ordered the commissioners to start the enumeration of tribal citizens for allotment rolls, thus handing to a federal commission the power to determine tribal citizenship. The **Curtis Act** of 1898 completed the process. Frustrated at the unwillingness of the tribes to negotiate allotment agreements, Congress simply mandated allotment and the termination of tribal governments. The terms specified in the Curtis Act could be modified by tribal negotiation, however, and between 1897 and 1902 each of the tribes concluded allotment agreements that attempted to secure some additional benefits for their people. Despite that, Congress's timetable required that allotment be completed and tribal governments dissolved by 1906.[15]

Virtually no Native people in Indian Territory desired allotment, but many argued in the 1890s that it was inevitable (see **Boudiniot, Elias Cornelius; Brown, John F.; McCurtain, Green**). They advocated entering into negotiations in the hope of controlling the disposition of their resources rather than leaving their fate to Congress and government bureaucrats. Active resistance developed in both the Cherokee and Creek nations. Redbird **Smith**, a Cherokee holy man, organized a movement of religious revitalization, the Nighthawk Keetoowahs. The Keetoowahs rejected American culture, refused to be listed on the allotment rolls, and resisted all efforts to assign them allotments. **Chitto Harjo**, a conservative Creek leader who had earlier opposed Creek constitutionalism, established a traditional council government at Hickory Ground that rejected allotment. Most Creeks did not follow his lead, but many respected his dedication to the old ways. Like the Cherokee followers of Redbird Smith, many Creeks found solace in their stomp grounds (see **music and dance**). Fearing that Chitto Harjo's opposition could interrupt and perhaps even perhaps derail Creek allotment, federal officials arrested and jailed him.[16]

Congress also allotted the lands to the west of Indian Territory that the tribes had surrendered in the 1866 treaties. In 1890 this region was organized as Oklahoma Territory. As the allotment of Indian Territory neared completion, Congress began to make plans for linking the two territories into a single state. Pleasant Porter, chief of the Creeks, reflected the widespread opposition in Indian Territory to that idea. In 1905 he called a convention to draft a constitution for a separate state, to be called Sequoyah. Congress rejected that plan, joined the two territories, and in 1907 admitted them to the Union as the state of Oklahoma. At a huge celebration to commemorate statehood, boosters staged a ceremony in which they joined in marriage an Indian "princess" dressed in buckskins representing Indian Territory to an American man outfitted in boots, chaps, and a ten-gallon hat who personified Oklahoma Territory. Many Indians did not share the excitement. As one Cherokee woman recalled thirty years after the event, "It broke my heart. I went to bed and cried all night long. It seemed more than I could bear that the Cherokee Nation, my country and my people's country, was no more" (see **Posey, Alexander**).[17]

Twentieth Century

Reflecting the racial thinking of turn-of-the-century Americans, the tribal rolls carefully categorized the racial composition of each tribal citizen. Scientific racism was at its height, and most Americans believed that ancestry determined behavior. The **Dawes Commission** assumed that "full bloods," Indians with no apparent non-Indian ancestry, were the most culturally traditional, the most ignorant, the least likely to understand American society, and the most vulnerable. Those identified as "three quarters or more" Indian were somewhat more sophisticated, and so on, in clusters based on blood quantum that listed "one half to three quarters," "one half," "less than one half," black, and white. According to this scale the less Indian blood one possessed, the more successful one was likely to be in a nontribal world.

Allotments were classified in two types, a protected "homestead" of 40 acres and a "surplus." The size of the surplus depended on the size of the allotment, which ranged from an average of 310 acres for Choctaws and Chickasaws to 110 acres for Cherokees. Allottees received both the homestead and the surplus with restricted title, meaning that the tracts could not be sold or taxed for a stipulated period. Surplus lands, however, could be leased. When the **Dawes Commission** handed over the rolls to the Union Agency, they contained the names of 101,526 men, women, and children recognized as tribal citizens qualified to receive an allotment. A total of 37,187 people were identified with a blood quantum of one half or more. Another 23,405 were blacks, former slaves of Five Tribes planters and their children (see **slavery**). The balance, 40,934, were under one-half Indian by blood.[18]

Selecting an allotment could be confusing. Each nation had one land office, a number of officers who spoke no Native languages, lists of qualified citizens, and maps laid out in ranges and townships, sections, half sections, and quarter sections. The allottee had to find his home place on the map. This was his homestead. The location of the surplus could be anywhere. Grafters, posing as helpers, hung around the land offices and offered their services to confused allottees. In return for their help they asked to lease the surplus. Allottees often agreed, especially if they had been helped to select their surplus at a distance from their homestead. For $15 or $20 and perhaps a vague promise of more later, the allottee signed the lease. The lease agreement often contained a clause that named the grafter as heir as well. Inherited allotments had no restrictions. The grafter packaged the leases together and leased them to someone else at profit. By 1902 grafters controlled more than one million acres. While this was profitable, purchasing the land was preferable. Unless Congress changed the restrictions, however, gaining title to the land was impossible. Oil provided the incentive to make Congress move.

The histories of the Five Tribes allottees and oil are intimately connected. As early as 1872 the Chickasaw Oil and Gas Company began drilling on land used by Chickasaw and Choctaw families. In 1891 the Cherokee government authorized 36 of its citizens to form the Cherokee Oil and Gas Company. In 1895 the Creek Nation incorporated the Creek Oil and Gas Company. These early efforts produced some oil, but transportation to markets was difficult and the companies were not particularly successful. But in 1905 drillers on the allotment of Ida Glenn, a Creek woman, hit an enormous underground lake of oil. Oil companies organized overnight, geologists and drillers hunted everywhere, oil derricks sprang up like weeds, and land that might have oil beneath it became spectacularly valuable. Two years before statehood, Oklahoma was on the way to becoming one of the world's richest oil producers.

In eastern Oklahoma, former Indian Territory, allottees owned more than 90 percent of the land, including that rich in oil. With so much at stake Congress responded in 1904 by lifting the restrictions on the allotments of blacks. At one minute past midnight, April 21, 1904, black allottees could sell their land. Within an hour grafters had purchased more than one million acres, much of it for unconscionable prices. Congress next freed from restrictions the surplus lands belonging to allottees of less than half blood. In 1906 Congress lifted the restrictions on the homesteads of those considered to be less than half Indian and on the surplus of those with blood quantums of one half to three quarters. The law extended restrictions on the allotments of full bloods to 1931, later to 1956, and then for the life of the original allottee. But Congress also established competency commissions for each tribe, which were empowered, upon application, to lift the restrictions on anyone's allotment. The law of 1906 put eight million acres on the market. By this time grafters were so skilled at swindling Indians that most of the land changed hands.

Many of the allottees whose restrictions were lifted were minor children. There were sixty thousand of them, and the combined agricultural and oil value assigned to their allotments in 1908 was nearly $200 million. The law assigned them to the Oklahoma county courts as incompetents, charging the courts to appoint guardians to manage their affairs. This simply institutionalized the system that had emerged informally. Attorneys and county probate judges engineered the process by which allotted Indians of the Five Tribes were despoiled. Grafters became professional guardians, responsible for looking after the interests of dozens, perhaps hundreds, of children. Kate Barnard, Oklahoma's commissioner of charities, found three Creek children living in a hollow tree and eating garbage while their guardian grew fat on their oil royalties.[19] Another astonishing case involved Jackson Barnett, a Creek full blood who could not sell his oil-rich restricted allotment if he wished. In 1920 Annie Lowe hauled the 78-year-old man to Kansas, got him drunk, and married him. Despite her best efforts, she could not spend all his money. When he died in 1934 he left an estate valued at more than $4 million. These and other stories hit the national press and titillated the public, but they failed to convey the full extent of the swindles. By 1924 the grafters had successfully stolen 90 percent of the land from which the restrictions had been lifted. Of the more than 101,000 original allottees, the Union Agency managed the restricted allotments of only 18,000 people.[20]

Not all of the land was allotted. Town lots were sold at auction, the proceeds held in trust by the government for tribal members. The government also leased Choctaw and Chickasaw coal and timberlands with the royalties accruing to tribal use. As a result, even though the **Curtis Act** of 1898 had disbanded tribal governments as of 1906, some form of tribal authority was necessary to represent tribal interests in the management of tribal funds and property (see **Brown, John F.**). Beginning in 1906, the president of the United States appointed tribal chiefs. Expected to be figureheads who did little except sign official papers, the chiefs assumed leadership roles as well (see **McIntosh, Waldo Emerson "Dode"**). In association with informal tribal councils, which in most tribes continued to meet, the chiefs worked to recover claims against the government, lobby in Congress for favorable legislation, and generally provide a focal point for public relations. The appointed chiefs were usually highly acculturated businessmen, but in 1922, just two years after the women's suffrage amendment to the United States Constitution, President Warren Harding appointed Alice Brown **Davis** chief of the Seminoles. She served until her death in 1935.[21]

While no allotted Native people in the United States suffered swindles as comprehensive as those imposed on the citizens of the Five Tribes, allotment everywhere produced terrible results. Beginning in the 1920s national organizations like the Society of American Indians and the American Indian Defense Association called public attention to the widespread poverty, wretched health, and social collapse that permeated Indian country. Congressional investigations documented conditions, reform groups lobbied for relief, and John Collier emerged as the leading force demanding change in federal Indian policy. In 1933 President Franklin Roosevelt appointed Collier commissioner of Indian affairs. Collier immediately launched a program to end allotment, reorganize tribal governments, recover lost land, revitalize Native cultures, and fund various economic development efforts. The **Indian Reorganization Act**, passed by Congress in 1934, contained most of the elements of his reformist agenda (see **Bronson, Ruth Muskrat**). Senator Elmer Thomas of Oklahoma opposed Collier's reforms and succeeded in amending the law so that it would not apply in his state. Oklahoma Indians, he argued, no longer had reservations, had no wish to reestablish them, and opposed any plan by Washington bureaucrats to impose them.

Thomas discovered, however, that among the Five Tribes there was substantial interest in some features of Collier's bill. Responding to his constituents, in 1936 Thomas supervised the passage of the **Oklahoma Indian Welfare Act**. Bowing to pressure from county bar associations, Thomas removed an early provision that would have taken guardianship responsibilities away from county courts and local attorneys and placed them in the Interior Department. The bill did, however, authorize the secretary of the interior to purchase land for landless Indians and permitted Indian groups to draft constitutions and incorporate for purposes of managing tribal funds and directing economic development. The law also established a loan fund to make investment money available to individual Indians or to corporate groups. While falling far short of meeting the needs of Oklahoma Indians, most of whom suffered from grinding poverty, Thomas's legislation provided means for beginning recovery.[22]

Slowly, tribes organized. Either dusting off nineteenth-century constitutions or writing new ones, drafting articles of incorporation, and negotiating loans for investment purposes, tribal governments began to plan for the future. Within the Creek Nation, the tradition of town autonomy resulted in the incorporation, in 1939 and 1940, of three tribal towns as separate and distinct political entities. In 1946 the United Keetoowah Band of Cherokees received recognition under the same legislation.

Since World War II, change has continued. In the 1950s many Southern Indians moved from rural Oklahoma to urban centers, sometimes as far away as California, under the auspices of a federal **relocation** policy. More likely to find poverty than prosperity, most migrants longed to return home. By the 1960s the federal War on Poverty and growing Indian activism brought new economic and political opportunities to Oklahoma's Native people. In 1970 Congress authorized the tribes to resume the popular election of their leaders, bringing an end to the system of presidentially appointed chiefs (see **self-determination**). Limited to chiefs, this law left the legal status of tribal councils unclear. In 1976 the case of *Harjo* v. *Kleppe* determined that the **Curtis Act** of 1898 had not destroyed the right of the Five Tribes to govern themselves with legislatures and courts. This had an invigorating effect on the tribes. By the end of the decade, tribal self-government was reborn (see **James, Overton; Swimmer, Ross**). Tribal governments have sued the United States before the **Indian Claims Commission** and won millions of dollars in judgments for lands sold below value. And in suits against Oklahoma the tribes won their claim to the bed of the Arkansas River, rich in oil, gas, and gravel concessions that are worth millions in royalty money. Often with the support of tribal scholarships, young men and women in increasing numbers continue the tradition of seeking education and entering the worlds of business, the professions, and the arts (see **Hogan, Linda; Harjo, Joy; Tiger, Jerome**). With their support and leadership tribal governments manage housing complexes and retirement homes, hospitals and clinics, farms and ranches, museums and cultural centers, and a wide range of business enterprises (see **Anoatubby, Bill; Mankiller, Wilma**). And in the 1990s they have exercised their sovereign right to open gaming establishments that promise to fund additional tribal enterprises.

In many ways the Five Tribes are very different from the other Native nations of the United States. While many of the citizens of each of the tribes live in the counties Oklahoma carved out of their nations, there are no reservation boundaries drawn on a map. Each of the tribes holds land in trust, but the parcels are relatively small and scattered, and most were purchased in recent decades. Virtually no one remains alive who was listed on the allotment rolls, but, because the restrictions on the allotments of full bloods were extended to coincide with the life of the allottee, many descendants of those people still live on their farms. As always, culture both changes and remains intact. Most citizens of the Five Tribes are nominally Christian, however, large numbers of them also participate actively in the ancient ceremonies celebrated at the many stomp grounds (see **religion**). Many people continue to speak their tribal languages, and those who cannot may study them in tribal language programs. Most citizens of the Five Tribes have moved to the cities and towns of Oklahoma or elsewhere and live not so differently from other Americans. But, by their citizenship in those tribes, they are distinct. And for all of them, from the farmer in McIntosh County to the professor at UCLA, that citizenship defines them and commits them to protect the essential sovereignty of their tribes.

Notes

1. John Ross, Annual Message, October 4, 1860, in *The Papers of John Ross*, 2 vols., ed. Gary E. Moulton (Norman: University of Oklahoma Press, 1985), 2:450.

2. Indian Pioneer Papers, Oklahoma Historical Society, quoted in *Nations Remembered: An Oral History of the Five Civilized Tribes, 1865–1907*, ed. Theda Perdue (Westport, Conn.: Greenwood, 1980), 9.

3. George P. Rawick, ed., *The American Slave: A Composite Autobiography*, 19 vols. (Westport, Conn.: Greenwood, 1972), 7:257–59.

4. Hannah Hicks, "The Diary of Hannah Hicks," *American Scene* 13 (1972): 10.

5. M. Thomas Bailey, *Reconstruction in Indian Territory: A Story of Avarice, Discrimination, and Opportunism* (Port Washington, N.Y.: Kennikat, 1972).

6. H. Craig Miner, *The Corporation and the Indian: Tribal Sovereignty and Industrial Civilization in Indian Territory, 1856–1907* (Columbia: University of Missouri Press, 1976).

7. Grant Foreman, *A History of Oklahoma* (Norman: University of Oklahoma Press, 1942), 334–35.

8. Mary Jane Warde, *George Washington Grayson and the Creek Nation, 1843–1920* (Norman: University of Oklahoma Press, 1999), 97–99.

9. Edwin C. McReynolds, *The Seminoles* (Norman: University of Oklahoma Press, 1957), 331–33.

10. Duane Champagne, *Social Order and Political Change: Constitutional Governments among the Cherokee, the Choctaw, the Chickasaw, and the Creek* (Stanford: Stanford University Press, 1992), 208–40.

11. Angie Debo, *The Rise and Fall of the Choctaw Republic* (Norman: University of Oklahoma Press, 1934), 214–18.

12. Jeffrey Burton, *Indian Territory and the United States, 1866–1906: Courts, Government, and the Movement for Oklahoma Statehood* (Norman: University of Oklahoma Press, 1995), 36.

13. Roosevelt used the phrase, which he stole from an Indian reformer, in his Message to Congress, December 3, 1901. Quoted in Francis Paul Prucha, *The Great Father: The United States Government and the American Indians*, 2 vols. (Lincoln: University of Nebraska Press, 1984), 2:671.

14. Angie Debo, *And Still the Waters Run: The Betrayal of the Five Civilized Tribes* (Princeton: Princeton University Press, 1940), 23–27.

15. Angie Debo, *A History of the Indians of the United States* (Norman: University of Oklahoma Press, 1970), 299–315.

16. Janey B. Hendrix, *Redbird Smith and the Nighthawk Keetoowahs* (Park Hill, Okla.: Cross-Cultural Education Center, 1983); Warde, *Grayson and the Creek Nation*, 194–95.

17. Quoted in Rennard Strickland, *The Indians in Oklahoma* (Norman: University of Oklahoma Press, 1908), 54.

18. Foreman, *Oklahoma*, 305.

19. Debo, *And Still the Waters Run*, 185.

20. See Debo, *And Still the Waters Run*, for the details of this astonishing story.

21. Paula Waldowski, "Alice Brown Davis: A Leader of Her People," *Chronicles of Oklahoma*, 58 (Winter 1980–81), 455–63.

22. Peter M. Wright, "John Collier and the Oklahoma Indian Welfare Act of 1936," *Chronicles of Oklahoma*, 50 (Autumn 1972), 347–71.

7   Those Who Remained

Removal in the 1830s did not eliminate Native people from the southeastern United States, and so not all Southern Indians live today in Oklahoma. Remnants from the five removed nations remained in the vicinity of their homelands, and four of these peoples have managed to reconstitute nations. Furthermore, the United States government never tried to relocate thousands of other Indian people who owned their land individually, occupied marginal areas, or resided on land set aside for them by the states. Many of these Indian communities have retained their tribal identities, and some enjoy state and even federal recognition. Retaining an Indian identity in the Southeast after 1835, however, became increasingly difficult. White landowners and black slaves typified the antebellum South, leaving little room for Native people, most of whom were landless but free. Historian James Merrell's description of the Catawbas applies to Southern Indians more generally: "[They] had become an anomaly. Neither useful nor dangerous, neither black nor white, they did not fit into the South's expanding biracial society."[1] Native people fought classification as "colored," a battle that intensified after the Civil War. Communities that retained elements of traditional Native culture fared somewhat better than those that did not, but most Southern Indians struggled against racism and discrimination. Recognition as Indians, creation of a land base, control of institutions such as schools and churches, and economic development became major concerns of Native Southerners in the twentieth century. Specific goals have varied from group to group, as has success, but the result has been growing visibility for those who remained in the Southeast.

Remnants

A variety of circumstances permitted some Cherokees, Chickasaws, Choctaws, Creeks, and Seminoles to remain in the Southeast when the United States government forced their nations west of the Mississippi (see **removal**). A few managed to obtain individual title to land and became absorbed into the white population. Greenwood Leflore, the Choctaw chief, provides the best example. Accepting the generous allotment of land provided him in the Treaty of Dancing Rabbit Creek, Leflore became a wealthy planter and successful politician. By the Civil War he had acquired 15,000 acres and 400 slaves, and he had served three terms in the Mississippi legislature where he protested his pretentious colleague's liberal use of Latin in their speeches by delivering an hour-long address in Choctaw. Adept in dealing with Anglo-American culture, some of these individuals and their children retained the names of their Indian forebears and usually the memory of their descent from Indians, but decades later they no longer regarded themselves primarily as Indians. Among the Creeks, Choctaws, Cherokees, and Seminoles, however, Native communities, whose members spoke their own languages and preserved their cultural traditions, also survived in the Southeast and ultimately created new tribes.

Ironically, removal treaties paved the way for Choctaws, Creeks, and Cherokees to remain in the Southeast. Article 14 of the Choctaw treaty of 1830, reflecting the Jackson administration's contention that removal was "voluntary," provided that Choctaws who wished to remain in Mississippi could register with the United States agent and receive an allotment of land. Policy makers expected that only highly acculturated Choctaws would avail themselves of the provision, but after the final detachment left for the West in 1833, 6,000 Choctaws remained in Mississippi. They attempted to comply with Article 14, but the agent either refused to register them or destroyed their documentation. Only 69 Choctaw heads of household ended up on the agent's list. Others believed they were entitled to stay and refused to remove. In 1838, 1,349 heads of household appealed to a federal commission to receive allotments in Mississippi, but when the commission reconvened in 1842 not enough Choctaw land remained to provide homesteads for those who still wished to stay. A federal program to redeem the claims with scrip, the machinations of land speculators, and constant pressure from Mississippi politicians encouraged thousands of Choctaws to move west.

One group of five families got only as far as Jena, Louisiana, where they settled and retained their identity as Choctaw. By 1860 only about a thousand Choctaws were left in Mississippi. Those who remained confronted the greed and racism of their white neighbors. In 1849 a group of Choctaws described their experiences: "We have had our habitations torn down and burned; our fences destroyed, cattle turned up into our fields and we ourselves have been scourged, manacled, fettered and otherwise personally abused."[2]

Largely landless, the Choctaws withdrew into the swamps and sandhills of Neshoba and surrounding counties and eked out a living on public lands that no one else wanted. In the 1870s a demand for agricultural labor drew many of them into sharecropping for white landowners, an arrangement that resulted in debt peonage for most. The allotment of the Choctaw Nation in the late nineteenth and early twentieth centuries attracted some Mississippi Choctaws to Oklahoma and focused federal attention on those who remained in Mississippi. Following World War I, the United States established an agency at Philadelphia, Mississippi, began to acquire land for the Choctaws, built a hospital, and opened schools. Today the descendants of the Choctaws who managed to avoid removal are known as the Mississippi Band of Choctaw Indians. Since 1969, when the Choctaws created the Chata Development Corporation, the Mississippi Choctaws have become a major economic force in Mississippi by attracting many manufacturing firms, which employ both Indians and non-Indians, to their industrial park (see **Martin, Phillip**).

Two treaties provided the means by which a few Creeks remained in the East. The 1814 Treaty of Fort Jackson, negotiated after the Creek War (1813–14), permitted Creeks who had allied with the United States to receive one-mile-square "reservations," or individual allotments, within land that the Creek Nation ceded. If the "reservee" or his descendants vacated the tract, it reverted to the United States. This meant that title to these reservations remained with the United States. Since the Creek removal treaty of 1832 stipulated that all Creeks receive allotments and provided that they could "go or stay, as they please," the Creeks briefly became individual landowners and citizens of Alabama.[3] When white depredations and Creek resistance precipitated wholesale removal in 1836, a few Creeks managed to stay in the East, but over the next two decades most of them joined their people in the West. Four of those who remained in Alabama, including Lynn McGhee, had been entitled to reservations under the Treaty of Fort Jackson, and in 1836 Congress granted them tracts of land.

Alabama Creeks were subject to the same frauds and pressures as the Choctaws in Mississippi, but McGhee and his descendants managed to hold onto their reservation, and an Indian community, known today as the Poarch Band of Creek Indians, coalesced around their holdings in southwestern Alabama. Although counties taxed Indian land throughout the nineteenth century, the cutting of timber in 1904 led the United States to enjoin counties from further taxation since title ultimately rested with the United States and federal land is exempt from state taxes. In 1924 the United States conveyed title to individuals, and the Creek land base dwindled further since it could now be taxed, mortgaged, foreclosed upon, subdivided, and sold. Following World War II, however, the Poarch Creeks enjoyed a resurgence, and, under the leadership of Calvin **McGhee**, they organized themselves as the Creek Nation East of the Mississippi. A federal court case permitted them to share in a land settlement awarded the Creeks in Oklahoma in 1962, which paid only $112.13 per capita, but the settlement affirmed their status as Creek Indians. With integration the Indian elementary school at Poarch closed, but the tribe secured title to the land and converted the building to a community center. This commonly held land became central to the tribe's quest for federal recognition, which they achieved in 1984, thereby securing after nearly 150 years an official Creek community in Alabama.

The Eastern Band of Cherokee Indians, who live today in western North Carolina, emerged from treaties between the Cherokee Nation and the United States in 1817 and 1819. The treaties provided for individual 640-acre reservations for Cherokees living within the ceded territory. At least 49 heads of household, under the leadership of Yonaguska, took advantage of this provision and became citizens of the state of North Carolina. When the Cherokee Nation, of which these people were no longer citizens, entered into a removal treaty with the United States in 1835, 60 heads of household, representing 333 individuals, secured permission to remain in North Carolina, and the state legislature passed an act to protect them from fraud. Another group of Cherokees, led by Euchella, obtained permission to remain as a reward for executing Tsali and two other Cherokee men who killed two soldiers rounding up Cherokees in preparation for removal. Because these Cherokees lived in the Smoky Mountains, land considered worthless by whites, and employed a skillful and honest agent, William Holland Thomas, they avoided many of the hardships suffered by Creeks and Choctaws. Nevertheless, as historian John Finger has written, "They faced the monumental task of preserving both themselves and their cultural identity."[4] Thomas tried to protect Cherokee landholdings in 1845 by incorporating them as the Cherokee Company under a law that permitted incorporation strictly for the purpose of producing silk and sugar. The Cherokees did neither, of course, and so the corporation failed, but the idea resurfaced not only in Cherokee history but also, by the 1930s, in United States policy.

After the **Civil War**, however, Thomas's health failed, leaving his financial affairs in disarray and the title to various tracts of land he had purchased for the Cherokees in doubt. Mediators finally resolved the land issues in the 1870s, and the Cherokees cleared their titles and acquired additional acreage. The United States Congress recognized the Eastern Band of Cherokees as a distinct tribe in 1868, but, because they had become state citizens in 1819, their status remained ambiguous. In 1889 the Eastern Band again incorporated under state law: tribal members in essence became shareholders, the council became the board of directors, and the chief became chairman of the board. In an era in which the United States Supreme Court was rapidly expanding the rights of corporations, this move provided considerable protection to the Eastern Band (see **Smith, Nimrod Jarrett**). The Cherokees continue to govern themselves under an amended version of the corporate charter. The tribe's assets also acquired federal protection when an appellate court ruled that the Cherokees were not citizens but wards of the federal government. This ruling, however, served to disfranchise Cherokees, who officially regained their voting rights in 1930 but were unable to exercise them until after World War II.

The mountainous terrain that made the Cherokees' land undesirable to nineteenth-century farmers attracted middle-class tourists in the twentieth century. In the 1930s the federal government opened the Great Smoky Mountains National Park on the edge of the Eastern Cherokee reservation, and North Carolina constructed modern highways into the community. The Cherokees avoided being landscaped into the park and having the limited access Blue Ridge Parkway run through the middle of their major town, but many of them welcomed the opportunity for economic development that came with these nearby projects. The Cherokees' agent organized a craft guild to encourage and market traditional Cherokee handicrafts such as baskets and pottery. An outdoor pageant, "Spirit of the Smokies," enjoyed brief success, but its popularity was far surpassed by the drama, "Unto These Hills," that opened in 1950. Property holders along the new highways began to lease their land to white entrepreneurs who built motels, restaurants, gift shops, and tourist attractions. Businessmen advertised their establishments with Cherokees wearing Plains Indian garb, standing next to tin tipis and totem poles, and posing for pictures with tourists. While providing an income for many Cherokees, "chiefing," as local people call it, encouraged white stereotypes of Indians. Economic development also exacerbated long-standing divisions within the community that Eastern Cherokees continue to confront.

Treaty provisions played no role in the persistence of the final remnant group, the Seminoles. Historian Harry Kersey has described the Seminoles as "masters of tactic and terrain."[5] They managed to outmaneuver and outlast the United States army in the Second Seminole War (1835–42) and withdrew into the Everglades of south Florida. In 1855 Billy **Bowlegs** launched the Third Seminole War (see **Seminole Wars**) by retaliating against army patrols and surveyors who had reportedly pillaged his camp. After three years Bowlegs and 160 of his followers agreed to go west, leaving behind scattered Seminoles who subsisted on hunting, fishing, and gathering in the everglades and farming small plots on hammocks, slightly elevated terrain within the swamps. They continued to recognize traditional leaders and clan affiliation; kin ties and the annual observance of the Green Corn Ceremony continued to unite them.

The Seminoles had little contact with non-Indians for two decades after the conclusion of the Third Seminole War. During the last quarter of the nineteenth century, however, the Seminoles entered the international market economy by selling plumes from tropical birds for women's hats, the pelts of fur-bearing animals for collars, and alligator hides for various leather goods. Oblivious to the realities of Seminole life but aware of the encroachment of white settlements, a philanthropic organization, the Women's National Indian Association, bought four hundred acres of land for the Seminoles in 1891 and established a mission. Prodded by local groups and hoping to encourage Seminole "civilization," the state of Florida and the United States began to acquire land for the Seminoles. The United States appointed an agent and opened a school, store, and sawmill. Although "civilization" had limited success, additional acreage was acquired over the years and these tracts became Big Cypress Reservation in 1911. World War I and changing fashion destroyed the Seminole trading economy, land drainage projects altered their ecosystem, and a growing non-Indian population intruded on their traditional lands. Ironically, an influx of tourists following the war enabled some Seminoles to replace incomes lost by these changes. Setting up camp at Musa Isle or Coppinger's Tropical Gardens, they maintained a fictitious routine under the tourists' eyes, pausing occasionally to wrestle alligators or stage an "Indian wedding," an entirely fake event that appealed to the tourists' romantic sensibilities. In 1926 the federal government opened the reservation now known as Hollywood near Ft. Lauderdale, and during the Depression state and federal governments acquired land north of Lake Okeechobee that became Brighton Reservation. As their situation worsened in the 1930s, Seminoles began to move onto the reservations and gradually began to take advantage of the services provided there. Between 1957 and 1962, the Seminole people split into two tribes, the Seminole Tribe of Florida and the Miccosukee Tribe of Indians, but citizens of both sovereign nations are the descendants of those Seminoles who avoided removal from their homeland (see **Jumper, Betty Mae**). In the 1980s the Seminoles acquired a tract of land at Immokalee and a small parcel in Tampa. The Miccosukees, who are heavily dependent on tourism, have "special use" lands in Everglades National Park and a reservation between the two highways that cut across Florida.

Although we know little about them, other communities of Indians from removed nations remained in the South. Some managed to retain a social as well as ethnic identity as Indian, and they have organized in recent decades as Indian tribes, seeking recognition from the federal or state governments with limited success. Other descendants of removed tribes simply retain a sentimental attachment to their ancestors while they primarily identity themselves as non-Indians. Descent from a member of a particular tribe alone does not constitute a valid claim for enrollment in that tribe. The Mississippi Band of Choctaws, Poarch Creeks, Eastern Band of Cherokees, Seminole Tribe, Miccosukee Tribe, and Jena Band of Choctaws control their tribal roles, and a candidate for enrollment must meet criteria, often including blood quantum, that each tribe establishes for itself.

Nations Not Removed

The large Indian tribes that were forced from their homelands by the United States owned millions of acres of some of the best land in the South. Since wealth in the antebellum period rested on agriculture, these tribes fell victim to the region's insatiable appetite for arable land. Other Native peoples, fewer in number and occupying marginal lands, avoided removal by adopting a range of strategies that make them almost as invisible to the modern historian as they did to nineteenth-century white Southerners.

The origins of some of these communities are clear. The Pamunkeys and Mattaponis of Virginia, for example, descend from the **Powhatan** Confederacy that dominated eastern Virginia at the time Jamestown was founded. Although non-Indians have intermarried with them and they are much reduced in number, these tribes still live in the vicinity of their ancestors. Others have more muddled beginnings. European diseases decimated Native populations, and warfare, trade, and white settlers dislocated them. When a community could no longer sustain itself socially or economically, its members banded with other groups. The Houmas of Louisiana probably incorporated members of the Bayogoula, Acolapissa, Chitimacha, Washa, and Chawasha as well as other tribes. Enoes, Occaneechis, Waterees, Keyauwees, Cheraws, and others joined the Catawbas of upcountry South Carolina. The Lumbees of North Carolina, whose particularly obscure origins have led some to claim descent from the "Croatan" Indians and survivors of Raleigh's Lost Colony, probably descend from Cheraws, or Sauras, a tribal name often found in eighteenth-century records but used by no modern tribe (although some Lumbees advocate its adoption). The Cheraws demonstrate the difficulty of precisely locating Indian tribes over time. The Cheraws lived in southwestern Virginia at the beginning of the eighteenth century but soon moved to the Pee Dee River in South Carolina. They then seem to have split into two groups, with one remaining on the Pee Dee and the other moving in with the Catawbas. According to historian James Merrell, a group of them moved to Drowning Creek in southeastern North Carolina, where Lumbees currently live, and, "tired of attacks by enemy Indians and aggressive settlers," tried to disappear.[6]

Some tribes had communal land bases officially recognized in the colonial period, but a reservation did not protect every tribe from white encroachments and dispossession. The Spanish government recognized the Tunicas' right to land on the Avoyelles Prairie in the late eighteenth century, and when the United States acquired the Louisiana territory in 1803 President Thomas Jefferson promised that Indian titles would be respected. Nevertheless, federal commissioners refused to acknowledge the Tunicas' title, and in 1844 a prominent white man seized their land and killed their chief. A local lawyer took up the Indians' cause and worked out an arrangement that permitted the Tunicas to retain their village site, but they lost much of the hunting and fishing territory on which they depended for subsistence. The 130 acres they retained, however, gave them a tangible corporate identity, helped them achieve federal recognition in 1981, and received federal protection as trust land.

The Chitimachas received a Spanish land title in 1767; they sued for United States recognition of that title in the 1830s. They won a 1,062-acre reservation, but the title to much of the land vested in individuals who gradually lost their tracts, usually for their inability to pay taxes. In 1903 a court divided the remaining 505 acres among individuals who had to sell more than half of it to pay attorney fees. A group of Chitimacha women appealed to a wealthy white woman, Sarah Avery McIlhenney, to save their land, which she purchased and then turned over to the federal government to hold in trust for the Chitimachas. They gained formal federal recognition in 1917.

The Alabama and Coushatta peoples also acquired land titles under Spanish rule. These tribes had been part of the Creek Confederacy, but in the 1760s they moved west from their villages on the Alabama River to establish new homes, first on the Mississippi River in what is today Louisiana and then, by the early nineteenth century, in east Texas. They came under Mexican rule in 1821, and in 1835 their territory became part of the Republic of Texas, which sought to establish reservations for them. Whites, however, already occupied the land granted the Alabamas and Coushattas. In 1854, after Texas had become a state, they received other grants. The Alabamas were able to occupy their tract of land in Polk County, but once again the Coushattas found their grant taken. Many of the Coushattas returned to Louisiana, while others joined the Alabamas. After World War I, Congress appropriated funds for education and land acquisition, and federal oversight promised protection.

Reservations recognized solely by state law often proved vulnerable. At the time of the Revolution, the Gingaskins owned in common a reservation of 690 acres, and the Nottaways held a 3,900-acre reservation. The state of Virginia acknowledged both reservations. In 1813, however, the legislature allotted the Gingaskins' reservation, but most individuals held onto their land for nearly two decades. In the racial hysteria that followed Nat Turner's slave revolt of 1831, the Gingaskins' white neighbors pressured them to sell, and within a month nearly all their land had passed into white hands. Legislation enacted in 1823 permitted the Nottoways to sell their individual shares of the tribe's reservation. According to anthropologist Helen Rountree, "The last plot was lost to Indian-descended ownership only in 1953."[7] Nevertheless, two other Virginia tribes, the Pamunkey and the Mattaponi, still own lands granted them before the American Revolution, and they retain elements of sovereignty not extended to tribes who received state reservations after the founding of the United States.

The Catawbas of South Carolina received a reservation of 144,000 acres from the British in 1763 (see **Hagler**). As the white population expanded, the Catawbas began leasing most of their land, and many of them moved to North Carolina to live with or near the Cherokees. In 1840 the Catawbas ceded their land to South Carolina on the assumption that they would obtain a new territory near the Cherokees and permanently leave the state, but the land purchase in North Carolina never materialized. Most Catawbas left the Cherokees, and about half returned to South Carolina. The state gave back 630 acres of their reservation, appointed an administrator for the tribe, and began paying a small annuity. In 1944 South Carolina purchased 3,432.8 acres for the Catawbas "for patriotic service their forefathers had rendered and the financial obligations likewise due them because of the unscrupulous methods employed by white citizens in business transactions with them especially in acquiring title to most of their land."[8] The Catawbas received no further compensation for their land until 1993, when the United States Congress passed legislation that paid the Catawbas $50 million, restored their federal recognition, which had been terminated (discussed later in this chapter), and settled the Catawba land claims that had thrown property titles of thousands of acres in doubt.

Native people who held individual title had at least as difficult a time holding onto their land as those who held land communally. Just as whites defrauded Indians of their allotments in the removal era and at the end of the nineteenth century, unscrupulous people took advantage of the powerlessness of Native landowners. In the late nineteenth century, in particular, intense racism tainted the judicial process, and nonwhites throughout the South had little recourse when victimized by whites. "Tied mule" incidents proliferated. In these frauds a white farmer staked out his mule on his Indian (or African American) neighbor's land. He then summoned the sheriff and charged that the Indian had stolen the mule. In order to defend himself against criminal charges or settle the case outside of court, the Indian surrendered his land. White law enforcement officials and judges often colluded with the perpetrator to take Indian land.

Official dispossession also occurred. According to anthropologist Ruth Underhill, the Houmas of southern Louisiana, whose situation she examined in 1938, "have been robbed of their property but by entirely legal procedure, hard to upset in court."[9] The Houmas rarely married according to the custom of whites or the laws of Louisiana. The state, therefore, considered children of traditional Native unions to be illegitimate, and according to law they could not inherit their fathers' property even if there was a will. Consequently, most Houma land passed out of Houma hands.

In eastern North Carolina, the Waccamaws lost much of their land in the 1920s when the state decided to survey "vacant" land, that is, land for which no recorded deed existed. Waccamaw residence on the land, of course, predated recorded deeds, but according to state officials they did not have legal title to it. The surveyor who located the Waccamaw land was also in the employ of a timber company, and so he declared their property "vacant" and promptly arranged for the state to sell it off for logging. North Carolina received the money for the land sales, the surveyor got a commission, and the Indians were forced off the land they had occupied for years.

Indians who lost their land in the late nineteenth- and early twentieth-century South had little alternative to sharecropping, and many sank into debt and peonage. A 1935 survey of conditions among the Lumbee Indians of Robeson County, North Carolina personalized sharecropping conditions. Leonard Bullard lived with his wife and two children in a 24-foot-square house whose roof, although it was new, leaked. He cultivated eight acres of cotton, fifteen acres of corn, and a quarter-acre vegetable garden. His landlord, on whose land he had lived for twenty years, got all the cotton seed and one half the lint as well as two-thirds of the corn, and Bullard cleared about $80. He earned an additional $20 per year harvesting tobacco for others, and he had four pigs and twenty chickens as well as a mule. Out of his annual income of $100, Bullard had to pay for clothing, tools, housewares, and medical care as well as any food that the family did not raise.[10] If he could not meet his expenses, he had to borrow from the landlord, reducing his income and binding himself to the same landlord for the following year. Many people never managed to extract themselves from this cycle of debt.

The great Depression of the 1930s made the situation of some sharecroppers even worse. One of the key features of the Agricultural Adjustment Act was the removal of agricultural land from production. Economists believed that a surplus in farm commodities had led to a boom/bust cycle, and they thought that reducing the surplus would help stabilize crop prices. Removing land from cultivation, however, displaced thousands of sharecroppers, some of them Indian, and efforts to relieve their distress often fell short. Nevertheless, Indians tried to take advantage of New Deal Programs. Loans from the Farm Security Administration, for example, enabled seventy-five Lumbee farmers to purchase land and fifteen other families to organize the Red Banks Mutual Organization, a cooperative that endured until 1968. More generally, however, the Depression was time of deepening poverty and growing uncertainty.

Race

The greatest challenge faced by the Native people who remained in the South after removal was racism that distinguished only between black and white. The dominant white society often refused to acknowledge any distinction among "people of color" and placed African Americans and Native Americans in the same category. This biracial obsession denied the distinct cultures, histories, and problems of Native people. In the antebellum period the institution of slavery controlled the activity of most nonwhites, but, following the Civil War and the return of the conservative regimes in the South, whites kept African Americans and Native Americans subservient through legislation, intimidation, and overt acts of violence.

The Lumbees waged a particularly dramatic struggle against white domination. A series of laws in the 1820s and the North Carolina Constitution of 1835 classified Indians as "free people of color" and stripped them of their civil rights. Nevertheless, the state attempted to benefit from the labor of "free people of color" in the **Civil War** by conscripting young men to build fortifications on Cape Fear to protect the major Confederate port of Wilmington. The Lumbees resisted and began to hide in the swamps to avoid conscription. The Home Guard began to harass the Lumbees, ransacking homes, stealing property, and killing the father and brother of Henry Berry **Lowry**. The killings triggered the Lowry War waged by Lumbees as well as sympathetic blacks and whites against the Confederacy, conservative Democrats, and wealthy whites in Robeson County. The Lowry gang enjoyed widespread support. A local white lawyer testified: "Besides the terror that Lowry and his gang inspire, there is a little sympathy, too. I think that among his class and color there is a little pride that we have been unable to take them; that he and his men can conquer and whip all who go after them."[11] An elderly African American woman told a newspaper reporter that sympathy for Henry Berry Lowry extended far beyond the Native community: "He's only a payin' 'em back! It's better days for de brack people now. Massta, he's de king o' dis country."[12] The war dragged on until 1872, when Lowry disappeared and what was left of his company disbanded. One of the tangible legacies of the Lowry War was official acknowledgment that the Lumbees were Indians. The racial ideology of the time simply could not countenance the notion that "people of color" had waged a decade long war against whites. Instead, North Carolinians preferred to regard the conflict as an Indian War and its protagonists as Native. The Lumbees continued their tradition of resisting oppression well into the twentieth century. In 1958 they routed the Ku Klux Klan, which had tried to hold a rally in a Lumbee community.[13]

The acknowledgment that Lumbees were Indians brought with it the state's creation of a separate Lumbee school system in North Carolina and the founding of a normal school to train Native teachers (see **Dial, Adolph**). Other Native communities throughout the South struggled, usually without state aid, to provide education for their children. The federal government generally operated schools on the reservations it administered, but for most nonreservation Indians in the segregated South the only public schools available were those designated "colored." Indians resisted attending these schools for a variety of reasons. Some Indians had adopted the racial attitudes of white Southerners and did not want to associate with African Americans. Even those who were not racist, however, recognized the inequities of segregation: "colored" schools received far less funding than white schools and, therefore, offered an inferior education. Most important, Native people regarded a biracial school system as a denial of their ethnicity as Indians. Many simply refused to be reclassified.

The most common solution to the school problem in the late nineteenth and early twentieth centuries was private subscription schools. Parents, who often were desperately poor, pooled their limited resources, constructed a building or arranged to use a church, and hired a teacher for their children. In 1891 the Waccamaws organized a school committee and built a one-room schoolhouse. Families paid $40 a year to hire a teacher. Because they were so poor, the Waccamaws could not always raise the necessary funds, and the school operated sporadically until the 1930s, when county officials offered to pay the teachers if the Waccamaws built a new school. The Indians constructed a building with materials salvaged from a razed white school and, by the early 1940s, 200 Native students were enrolled in the first through eighth grades. Much to the Waccamaws' dismay, the county classified their school as "white" in their official reports.

Although the Waccamaws were justifiably proud of their school, the facility left much to be desired. An article published in *The American Indian* in 1950 gave the following description of the school:

> The present school is inadequate. It is poorly constructed, drafty, overcrowded, lacking in books and desks, and portions of it have never been ceiled on the inside. Bare studs in the room add to the general dismal appearance. There are no cloak rooms; no entry halls. Access

to certain rooms are only through another. No playground or playground equipment. Three of the rooms have an ordinary tin wood
heater. The fourth is provided with no heat at all. Its construction as
well as lack of exits, create an extremely dangerous fire hazard. There
is no fire fighting equipment or extinguishers. The only source of water
is a hand pumped well which required priming.[14]

Many Indian schools, insufficiently funded by impoverished parents and
racist state legislatures, had similar deficiencies.

States ultimately took over many subscription and church schools. In
1885 a local church opened the Sardis Indian School for Pee Dee Indians
living in Dillon County, South Carolina. When a state supreme court ruling
mandated separate schools for children who were neither black nor white —
in this case, "mulatto" children — the state assumed operation of the Sardis
Indian School as well as subscription schools at Four Holes and Creeltown
in Colleton County. The Catawbas had built their own school building in
1897–98, and white mission societies usually provided the teachers, but
South Carolina began paying the teacher's salary in the early twentieth century. The state also opened additional schools in Indian communities, sometimes designating them, like the Waccamaw school in North Carolina, as
"white." Other states provided at least elementary schools for Indian students. In 1939 Escambia County, Alabama created a consolidated Indian
school on land owned by an Episcopal mission in the Poarch Creek community, and in 1944 two Louisiana parishes established a separate school
system for Houmas.

Religion helped some Southern Indians distinguish themselves from their
white and black neighbors. While most Native people who converted to
Christianity became Methodists, Baptists, Presbyterians, or Pentecostals, a
few communities adopted religions that are fairly exotic in the rural South.
In 1883 Catholics established a mission to the Mississippi Choctaws, and
the following year they opened a church and school. In a period in which
many Choctaws depended on sharecropping to survive, the Catholic mission
gained support by purchasing more than two thousand acres of land and
making it available in forty-acre tracts to Choctaw families. Catholic priests
and nuns learned Choctaw and taught children how to read and write in
their own language as well as English. Even more significantly, William
Ketcham, a priest who headed the Board of Catholic Indian Missions and
served on the federal Commission of Indian Affairs, was largely responsible
for securing congressional appropriations for the Mississippi Choctaws after

World War I. Even Protestant Choctaws appreciated the role the Catholic Church played in their federal recognition.

For the Catawbas, Mormonism served to separate them from non-Indian Carolinians. Mormon elders baptized their first Catawba converts in 1883, and within several years most Catawbas had converted, despite the hostility of local whites to Mormonism. Mormons placed special emphasis on the conversion of Native people, whom they believe to be descended from Israelites, God's chosen people. According to Charles Hudson, the Catawbas' "identification with the church was a source of alternative values. At a time when they were becoming physically and culturally like whites, it both set them apart from whites, mestizos and Negroes and made them feel that they were in some sense a chosen people."[15] Being Mormon also reinforced the Catawbas' contention that they were not black.

White racists in the late nineteenth and early twentieth centuries regarded Southern Indians as subversive of the caste system. Refusing to accept the notion that many Native people survived in the South, they insisted that individuals claiming to be Indians were merely African Americans establishing a racial way station to "passing" as whites. Virginia went to the greatest extreme in attempting to thwart this challenge to white racial purity. The state tacitly recognized the existence of its Indian population for two decades after the passage of segregation laws at the turn of the twentieth century. In World War I draft boards declined to call Indians, who were not considered citizens, and the local county exempted businesses on the Mattaponi reservation from taxes. In the 1920s tribes began to hold powwows and organize themselves formally. The Rappahannocks secured a corporate charter, and the Chickahominy began to press for state recognition. Nevertheless, many Virginia Indians lived in fear. An anthropologist conducting fieldwork among the Rappahannock reported, "Some even asked if they were in danger of being killed by white people."[16]

Although whites did not normally attack Indians physically, the state did begin to take measures to eradicate Native identity in the 1920s. Virginia had permitted Indians to use many of the same facilities as whites. Pamunkeys rode in "white only" railway cars, for example, and the University of Virginia hospital admitted Indians to white wards. The physician who headed the state's Bureau of Vital Statistics, however, was convinced that Virginians who claimed to be Indians were really African Americans, and he embarked on a campaign to reclassify them as "colored." He convinced the United States Census Bureau to qualify classifications of people as "Indian" in Virginia, and he attached a warning to birth certificates that although the infant might be identified as "Indian," the child should be treated as "colored." He circulated a list of common Indian surnames to county officials, teachers, and health workers and urged them to prevent these people from using white facilities. Finally, the Racial Integrity Law that he inspired insisted that any time a person filled out a form requiring race, the designation had to conform with that in the Bureau of Vital Statistics, which for Indians was "colored." Only the civil rights movement substantially changed things for Virginia Indians.

Segregation imposed a range of indignities on both African Americans and Native Americans, but many Indians found a biracial system's refusal to acknowledge their identity particularly offensive. In 1981 a Coharie man in North Carolina recounted incidents of discrimination for a reporter from the *Winston-Salem Sentinel*:

> There [w]as a period of time here when the Indians were just classified as blacks . . . . I'd go down [to] the courthouse, for example, and the white man would come in and chase me out . . . . And you'd pee upside the wall before you'd go to the black bathrooms. I remember one Indian veteran came home from Vietnam and he and his wife went to get a hot dog at one of these [white only] restaurants and the owner tried to run him out and called a cop. The Indian fellow gathered up a crowd to stop it, but the cop shoved him out . . . . These things have become a part of the past now. But it's only changed during the '70s.[17]

Most Native people, like this man, resisted reclassification in every way they could.

Native people welcomed the end of segregation and the daily humiliation that it imposed, but Indians mourned the loss of their schools, especially in retrospect. Schools were a unifying force in Native communities, particularly those that had no common land base. Some communities such as the Poarch Creeks managed to obtain title to their former school buildings and turn them into community centers, but the closing of Indian schools represented a profound loss. While Native churches continued to exist, they did not cut across communities in the same way as schools. The closing of schools may very well have given rise to increased interest in establishing tribal organizations, councils, and commissions in the 1970s. The end of legal segregation also meant better economic opportunities, a real plus for Indians, but this gain also had its down side as young people began to leave rural Indian communities for employment in urban areas. Although most of these emigrants maintained close ties to home, they no longer participated in day-to-day community life.

The participation of Indians in the civil rights movement that ended legal segregation varied depending on their circumstances. Many Native people hesitated to join with African Americans and regarded treaty rights as a more appropriate issue for them than civil rights. Nevertheless, there are incidents of cooperation. The Southern Christian Leadership Conference headed by Dr. Martin Luther King, for example, funded Lumbee voter registration drives in the 1960s. Like African Americans, Native people had often been denied the right to vote, and years of intimidation made many wary of political activism. Therefore, Southern Indians also had different responses to the American Indian Movement founded in the 1970s to press for Native rights. While Lumbees were engaged in AIM's takeover of the Bureau of Indian Affairs in Washington, for example, the Eastern Band of Cherokees evicted AIM organizers from their reservation. Opposite responses of Indians within the same state point to the profound differences that exist between Native Southerners.

Recognition

One of the things that distinguish Indian tribes in the South from one another is federal recognition, which establishes a government-to-government relationship between the tribes and the United States. Some tribes enjoy federal recognition, others have state recognition, and still others are merely self-designated groups claiming to be Indian tribes. Tribes that do not have federal recognition usually consider achieving it to be a primary goal. Tribes acquire federal recognition in three ways: the first is based on history, the second comes through Congressional action, and the third is acknowledgment by the Bureau of Indian Affairs. Recognition brings the services of the BIA and sovereignty over trust land, but for many Native people in the South the real advantage lies in official admission that they are indeed Indians.

The Chitamachas, Coushattas, Alabama-Coushattas, Eastern Band of Cherokees, Mississippi Choctaws, Florida Seminoles, Miccosukees, and Catawbas established official government-to-government relationships with the United States before 1970. Their federal recognition rested on a history of treaties, Congressional appropriations, military jurisdiction, land grants, agreements with the Bureau of Indian Affairs, and/or appointment of agents. Ironically, most of these tribes came under the direct supervision of the Bureau of Indian Affairs, had the guardianship of the United States over them affirmed, or placed their land in trust with the federal government in the late nineteenth and early twentieth centuries, the very time that Oklahoma Indian lands were being allotted.

Most Southeastern tribes strengthened their ties to the United States during the Indian New Deal of the 1930s. The **Indian Reorganization Act** (or Wheeler-Howard Act) passed in 1934 encouraged Native people to write formal constitutions. Several Southeastern tribes, including the Mississippi Choctaws, Alabama-Coushattas, Florida Seminoles, and Miccosukees, ultimately did so, but the model encouraged by the IRA did not always conform to the traditions or meet the needs of Southern Indians. The Alabama-Coushatta constitution, for example, established a blood quantum requirement for membership that, according to historian Jonathan B. Hook, "undermined the traditional concept of inclusion through participation in the community." Furthermore, it shifted power from the *mikko*, or chief, to an elected council, and reduced the *mikko*'s role to an advisory one. White agents and missionaries became the point of contact between the tribe and the federal government, and, as Hook points out, "The council was essentially irrelevant in dealing with the federal government in the 1930s and 1940s because there was limited contact between the two entities."[18]

The purpose of the IRA was to halt allotment, strengthen Indian communities, and protect Native landholdings, but **termination**, the subsequent federal policy implemented in the 1950s, threatened these very things by severing the relationship between the United States and an Indian tribe. According to the legislation, tribes had to agree to termination, and those tribes initially targeted were ones that supposedly had become highly acculturated. Despite the fact that many Seminoles did not even speak English, their tribe was slated for early termination. The Seminoles successfully fought against termination, and in 1957 the tribe enacted an IRA constitution. The debate over termination and the constitution, however, widened a split within the tribe, and in 1961 the Miccosukees wrote their own constitution and gained recognition. Ironically, these culturally conservative people had supported termination because they wanted as little to do with the federal government as possible in order to preserve their traditional way of life. Consequently, in 1971, they dispensed with a federal agency and began contracting for services.

Three Southern Indian tribes were terminated. In 1953, without congressional sanction, the Bureau of Indian Affairs withdrew federal services, that is, health care and education, from the Coushatta in Louisiana. In 1973 the federal government restored recognition and services to the Coushatta. In 1954 Congress terminated the Alabama-Coushatta in Texas. Their territory became a state reservation until a dispute over hunting regulations in 1981 led the Texas attorney general to assert that no Indian reservations existed in Texas. The Alabama-Coushatta petitioned Congress for restoration, which they received in 1987. In 1959 the Catawbas decided to accept termination. They offered their "New Reservation," the land acquired in 1944, for sale, but they retained the "Old Reservation," the 630 acres they had held since the 1850s. In 1962 their termination was supposedly finalized, but in 1993, as part of the land settlement enacted by Congress, the Catawbas once again became a federally recognized tribe. While these tribes did not experience the disastrous consequences of termination that other peoples, such as the Menominee of Wisconsin, did, they certainly suffered in terms of lost services and economic opportunities.

A second route to recognition employed by very few Southern tribes is Congressional legislation that authorizes the Bureau of Indian Affairs to provide services to them. Before the creation of an administrative process in 1978, this was a way in which communities that had no prior government-to-government relationship with the United States achieved recognition. The most noteworthy congressional action relating to Southern Indians was the Lumbee Bill passed in 1956. The Lumbees had sought recognition since the 1930s. Anthropologist and Commissioner of Indian Affairs John Collier supported their efforts, but political considerations led the secretary of interior, under which the BIA operated, to veto their recognition. Factional strife, which manifested itself in a debate over what name the tribe would take— they had been, at various times, Croatans, Cherokees of Robeson County, and Siouans—also made it difficult for the Lumbees to present their case. Finally, in the early 1950s, they agreed on "Lumbee," for the nearby Lumber River, and Congress extended them recognition. The same legislation, however, prohibited the BIA from providing services to them. That is, the Lumbees were recognized and terminated in the same legislation, and, as of 2000, they have not been able to get Congress to rescind the second provision.

In 1978 the Bureau of Indian Affairs established a procedure for acknowledging the eligibility of tribes for services, an action that constitutes recognition. George Roth of the BIA's Branch of Acknowledgment and Research has summarized the criteria for acknowledgement:

To be federally recognized, a group must demonstrate that it has existed as a distinct community, within which tribal processes have existed, since first sustained contact with non-Indians. The group must have been identified as an Indian group throughout history by entities outside itself, such as the federal government, local governments, other Indian tribes, or scholars. In addition, the membership must be able to demonstrate ancestry from the historic tribe (or tribes that have combined, for example, the Tunica-Biloxi) from which the present tribe is derived.[19]

Under these provisions three Southeastern tribes have been recognized — the Tunica- Biloxi (1981), Poarch Band of Creeks (1984), and the Jena Band of Choctaws (1995). Eight other groups headquartered in the Southeast have been denied recognition, and many groups have notified the BIA of their intent to petition for acknowledgment.[20]

Indian tribes seek federal recognition not only because the BIA provides services, or because "federally recognized" brings a certain cache, but also because recognition conveys sovereignty, the right of Native people to govern themselves. Since the mid-1970s the federal policy of **self-determination** has permitted tribes to provide their own services with funding from the BIA. Federally recognized Indian tribes make and enforce their own laws, although ten major crimes are tried in federal courts, and impose their own taxes, paying federal but not state income taxes. Tribes are also exempt from state regulatory law, a circumstance that has made reservations a target for companies wishing to dispose of toxic waste without state interference.

Tribal sovereignty and exemption from state taxes and regulation have proved a boon for many Southern tribes. The Seminoles have been leaders in expanding the exercise of sovereignty. In the 1970s they began selling cigarettes on Seminole reservations without collecting the state excise tax. Since the tribal tax was far less than the state tax, Floridians flocked to Seminole "smoke shops," which became an immediate financial success. The state tried to stop the practice, but federal courts upheld the Seminoles' right to sell cigarettes without state tax, and in 1979 the Florida legislature passed a bill entering into a lucrative economic agreement with the Seminole Tribe of Florida concerning cigarette sales.

Smoke shops were followed by high-stakes bingo. In 1979 Seminoles began offering bingo at their Hollywood reservation, near Ft. Lauderdale and Miami, with $10,000 jackpots. By the second year the tribe was making more than $5 million annually. Florida law permitted bingo but limited jackpots, and the state challenged the Seminoles in court. The Seminoles contended that their sovereignty exempted them from state regulation, and the courts agreed (see **Billie, James**; *Seminole Tribe* v. *Butterworth*). Other tribes followed the Seminoles' example and opened high-stakes bingo. In 1982 the first night of Cherokee bingo in western North Carolina attracted 4,000 players from as far away as Philadelphia, Miami, and even Canada. Bingo soon metamorphosed into casino gambling, and tribes began using their enormous profits for tribal projects, scholarship funds, and per capita payments. In 1988 Congress passed the Indian Gaming Regulatory Act, which requires tribes to enter into compacts with states if they want to offer slot machines and other forms of gambling designated as Class III gaming, but it also mandates that states negotiate in good faith. If states refuse to come to terms with tribes, tribes can force mediation and the secretary of the interior can impose a solution. In 1996 in *Seminole Tribe of Florida* v. *Florida et al.*, however, the United States Supreme Court ruled that a state could not be compelled by suit to negotiate in good faith, a decision that has resulted in continuing contention over the issue. As of 1999, six Southern tribes—the Choctaw Nation of Oklahoma, the Chitimacha, Coushatta, and Tunica Biloxi tribes of Louisiana, the Mississippi Choctaws, and the Eastern Band of Cherokees—had secured compacts and opened casinos or, in the case of the Oklahoma Choctaws, simulcast horse race wagering. Other tribes operate facilities for Class II gaming, which includes high-stakes bingo, under the oversight of the National Indian Gaming Commission.

Only federally recognized tribes can open casinos, but most tribes in the South do not have federal recognition. Some, like the Mattaponis, whose Virginia reservation dates to colonial times, long rebuffed overtures from the Bureau of Indian Affairs; not until 1995 did they notify the bureau of their intention to seek recognition. According to Mattaponi Chief Curtis Custalow in 1983, they simply did not want the "red tape" that goes with recognition.[21] Many other tribes are more anxious for federal recognition. Tribes that already have recognition, however, are not always supportive of the efforts of other groups to achieve that status. They fear that extending recognition to additional tribes compromises their own identity as Indians, further divides the limited funds available from the Bureau of Indians Affairs, and threatens potential competition for their gaming enterprises. They also question whether such groups are "real Indians." For tribes without federal recognition, their particular situations vary dramatically.

Until the 1970s, states largely abdicated responsibility for Native people to the federal government and did little to include them in policy decisions.

Nevertheless, Indians are citizens of states, and, as such, they are entitled to public education, employment opportunities, and all services that states afford their other citizens. Recognizing the need to address Native people's concerns, Louisiana established the first office of Indian affairs in the South in 1970, and North Carolina followed suit with the establishment of an Indian commission in 1971. Other states that have created offices, councils, or commissions are Florida (1974), Alabama (1975), Virginia (1983), and Georgia (1992). Officially recognized Indian tribes and organizations in North Carolina elect the members of the commission, ensuring that the development of policy and administration of programs remains in Native hands. Elsewhere the governor and/or legislature appoint members. The responsibilities and authority of these bodies vary considerably, and they serve Native communities in a number of different ways. The focus of the Florida Governors Council on Indian Affairs, Inc., a nonprofit corporation chartered by executive order, is on employment and job training, while the Georgia Council on American Indian Concerns deals almost exclusively with protection of Indian graves and repatriation of human remains, and the Virginia Council on Indians conducts research and identifies issues for presentation to the state legislature. Some bodies administer grants from federal agencies, such as the Department of Education and the Department of Housing and Urban Development. These grants are separate from BIA funding, which goes only to federally recognized tribes. Some state commissions offer assistance to tribes in preparing petitions for federal recognition. The Jena Band of Choctaws, for example, credits that tribe's success in gaining recognition in part to technical assistance from the state. Louisiana also has given its Office of Indian Affairs the responsibility for negotiating gaming compacts with its four federally recognized tribes.

Several states have recognized Indian tribes. Most commonly, legislatures have extended recognition. Sometimes recognition has come as a result of intense lobbying by descendant groups, organizations of people who have Native ancestors but few of the other attributes normally recognized as constituting a tribe. Legislatures in other states have carefully followed criteria based on that of the BIA. The Virginia legislature, for example, has recognized eight tribes that, among other criteria, have been identified as indigenous to Virginia, have occupied a specific site, and have compiled substantial documentation concerning their membership and tribal organization. As scrupulous as the process might be, however, the non-Indian legislature has determined which groups meet the criteria. In North Carolina the Commission of Indian Affairs, which is composed of the elected representatives of Indian tribes and urban Native organizations, makes decisions about recognition. The commission has established a strict set of criteria for recognition, including documentation that an Indian tribe with recognized membership, leadership, and institutions (such as schools and churches) has existed over time.

Also living in the South are many people who have Native ancestry but belong to no tribe. In 1996 only 2 percent of Southerners identified themselves racially as "Indian," but 40 percent claimed Native ancestry, considerably more than the 22 percent who claim descent from a Confederate soldier.[22] Most of these people have no desire to affiliate with a tribe, but many who do have been thwarted in their attempts to enroll. The United States Supreme Court has recognized the right of tribes to determine their own membership requirements. This means that having a Cherokee grandmother, no matter how high her cheekbones or straight her hair, will not get a person on the Eastern Band roll unless the applicant can prove the grandmother's legitimate enrollment and adequate blood quantum. Often people find this exclusion troubling. In 1994 a correspondent to the *Cherokee One Feather* complained, "It is unfair that I cannot be recognized as a Cherokee Indian simply because I cannot locate my ancestors' names on the rolls . . . . Those of us who cannot enroll . . . feel the same pride in our hearts of being Cherokee that they do, but we are always on the outside looking in."[23] As poignant as these sentiments may be, Indian tribes have the right to decide who belongs and who does not, and any attempt to compromise this right, however well intended, jeopardizes tribal sovereignty.

Sovereignty is important to Southern Indians because it provides a legal basis for ethnic identity, cultural traditions, and historical experiences. As Native Southerners enter the twenty-first century, however, sovereignty is under siege from many quarters—states want to control smoke shops and gambling, some members of Congress have sought to reduce federal aid to Indians, white entrepreneurs denounce what they consider to be preferential treatment for tribes, and poorly informed non-Indians with claims to Native ancestry demand to participate in tribal economic and cultural revitalization. The issues are enormously complex, but an understanding of the region's Native past is essential to resolving them. Native Southerners are heirs to cultures that evolved in the region over thousands of years. In the last four centuries interactions with the peoples of Europe and Africa have shaped their history. While change is a major element of that history, so is cultural continuity. Sovereignty, which tribes enjoyed when Europeans arrived and retain as an important though limited right today, enables each tribe to

balance continuity and change in ways that make sense for its unique circumstances. Sovereignty also guarantees that the future South will be as
culturally rich and ethnically diverse as the historical South, and perhaps
more equitable, as Native people exercise their sovereign power to maintain
a distinct identity without suffering legal liabilities. No longer merely the
forgotten victims of greed and racism, Native Southerners are an important
force in the region.

Notes

1. James H. Merrell, "The Racial Education of the Catawba Indians," *Journal of
Southern History* 50(1984): 379.

2. Petition of One Hundred Red Men, 6 Dec. 1849; quoted in Ronald N. Satz,
"The Mississippi Choctaw: From the Removal Treaty Onward," in *After Removal:
The Choctaw in Mississippi*, ed. Samuel J. Wells and Roseanna Tubby (Jackson:
University Press of Mississippi, 1986), 16.

3. Treaty with the Creeks, 1832, in *Indian Affairs: Laws and Treaties*, 2 vols., ed.
Charles J. Kappler (Washington, D.C.: Government Printing Office, 1904) 2:343.

4. John R. Finger, *The Eastern Band of Cherokees, 1819–1900* (Knoxville: University of Tennessee Press, 1984), 41.

5. Harry A. Kersey Jr., "Those Left Behind: The Seminole Indians of Florida,"
in *Southeastern Indians Since the Removal Era*, ed. Walter L. Williams (Athens:
University of Georgia Press, 1979), 174.

6. James H. Merrell to Charlie Rose, October 18, 1989, Livermore Library, University of North Carolina at Pembroke.

7. Helen C. Rountree, "The Indians of Virginia: A Third Race in a Biracial State,"
in *Southeastern Indians Since the Removal Era*, ed. Williams, 34.

8. Charles Hudson, *The Catwaba Nation* (Athens: University of Georgia Press,
1970), 87–88.

9. Ruth Underhill to Frank Speck, quoted in Max E. Stanton, "Southern Louisiana Survivors: The Houma Indians," in *Southeastern Indians Since the Removal
Era*, ed. Williams, 101.

10. Gerald M. Sider, *Lumbee Indian Histories: Race, Ethnicity, and Indian Identity
in the Southern United States* (Cambridge: Cambridge University Press, 1993), 142.

11. Quotes are from Karen I. Blu, *The Lumbee Problem: The Making of an American Indian People* (Cambridge: Cambridge University Press, 1980), 54–55.

12. Ibid.

13. W. McKee Evans, "The North Carolina Lumbees: From Assimilation to Revitalization," in *Southeastern Indians Since the Removal Era*, ed. Williams, 52–53.

14. Quoted in Theda Perdue, *Native Carolinians: The Indians of North Carolina*
(Raleigh: Division of Archives and History, 1985), 54–55.

15. Hudson, *The Catawba Nation*, 80.

16. Frank G. Speck's field notes, quoted in Rountree, "The Indians of Virginia," in *Southeastern Indians Since the Removal Era*, ed. Williams, 40.

17. Quoted in Theda Perdue, "Indians in Southern History," in *Indians in American History: An Introduction*, ed. Frederick E. Hoxie and Peter Iverson (2nd ed., Wheeling, Ill.: 1998), 137.

18. Jonathan B. Hook, *The Alabama-Coushatta Indians* (College Station: Texas A&M University Press, 1997), 65.

19. George Roth, "Overview of Southeastern Indian Tribes Today," in *Indians of the Southeastern United States in the Late Twentieth Century*, ed. J. Anthony Paredes (Tuscaloosa: The University of Alabama Press, 1992), 184.

20. The status of petitions can be tracked on the BIA web site at www.doi.gov/bia/bar/indexq.htm

21. Quoted in Helen C. Rountree, *Pocahontas's People: The Powhatan Indians of Virginia Through Four Centuries* (Norman: University of Oklahoma Press, 1990), 253.

22. John Shelton Reed, "The Cherokee Princess in the Family Tree," *Southern Cultures* 3 (1997): 111–13.

23. Sharon Flora to Editor, *Cherokee One Feather*, October 19, 1994.

1. Mississippian temple mound at Etowah.

2. A Pisgah rectilinear complicated stamped jar with a collared rim (c. A.D. 1000-1400) from Haywood County, North Carolina.

3. Stone statues of a man and woman found at Etowah.

4. An artist's conception of Cahokia. Painting by William R. Iseminger.

Timucuas hunting in sixteenth-century Florida.

6. Timucuas farming. Note their Europeanized features.

7. Timucuas greet the French in North Florida.

8. Timucuas engage the French in battle.

9. Timucuan chieftainess.

10. Indian woman and young girl in eastern North Carolina. Painting by John White, 1585.

11. Indian village of Secoton in eastern North Carolina. Painting by John White, 1585.

12. Indians fishing in eastern North Carolina. Painting by John White, 1585.

13. Indian in body paint in eastern North Carolina. Painting by John White, 1585.

14. Engraving of Pocahontas.

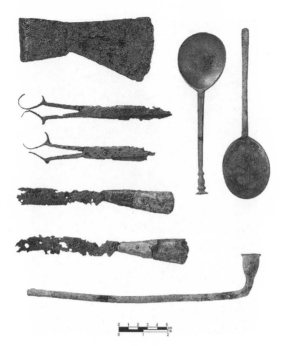

15. European trade goods found at Occaneechi Town (Franklin Site), North Carolina.

16. Seven Cherokees in London, 1730.

17. Tomochichi and his nephew. John Faber engraving (c. 1744) of Willem Verelst painting.

18. Benjamin Hawkins and the Creek Indians. Painting by an unidentified artist, c. 1805.

Louisiana Indians Walking Along a Bayou. Painting by Alfred Boisseau, 1847.

20. Self-portrait by Hilis Hadjo (Josiah Francis).

21. Major Ridge, Cherokee, c. 1830.

22. Opothle Yoholo, Creek, c. 1830.

23. Ball Play of the Choctaw—Ball Up. Painting by George Catlin (1796–1872).

24. A Choctaw Woman. Painting by George Catlin (1796–1872).

25. Dress belonging to Cherokee Rachel Martin Davis, before 1843.

26. Malmaison, Choctaw Chief Greenwood Leflore's residence.

27. Cherokee Chief John Ross's house, Park Hill, c. 1860.

28. Creek Chief Samuel Checote and his family after the Civil War.

Lumbee Henry Berry Lowry and his band.

30. Cherokee Female Seminary, Tahlequah, c. 1890.

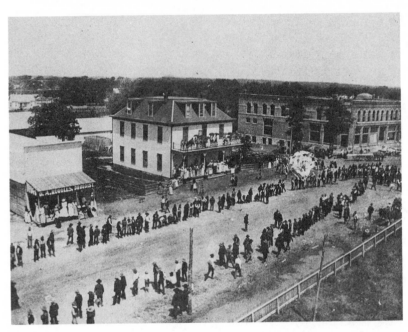

31. Voting in Wewoka, Seminole Nation, late nineteenth century.

32. Cherokee pre-ballgame dance, c. 1890.

33. Seminole family in front of chickee, c. 1921.

34. Wilma Mankiller wearing a traditional "tear dress" and beads and delivering a State of the Nation address during her tenure as principal chief of the Cherokee Nation.

35. Carolina Indian Circle Powwow, 1999, at the University of North Carolina. Left to right: Tonia Jacobs (Waccamaw), Jessica Jacobs (Coharie/Waccamaw), James Stevens (Lumbee), and Christina Morrow (Meherrin/Occaneechi).

Part II

People, Places, and Events, A to Z

Prepared by Karl Davis and Rose Stremlau

agriculture

Native Southerners relied on agriculture for a significant portion of their subsistence. As early as 3,000 years ago Southeast Native Americans cultivated local plants such as lambs quarters, marsh elder, and sunflowers, plants previously relied on in wild form. They soon added squash to their repertoire. By about A.D. 300, Southeastern Indians grew corn as a primary subsistence crop from which as much as 60 percent of their calories came. About A.D. 1000, beans appeared in the Southeast. Native people farmed the rich riverine bottomlands whose enormous productivity gave rise to the **Mississippian tradition**. After contact with Europeans, Native Americans quickly adopted some Old World plants, such as watermelons and peaches, which often spread faster than the Europeans themselves. Corn continued to be a mainstay of Native subsistence, however, and has become a hallmark of Southern cuisine. Corn also was the religious focus of the major ceremony in the Southeast, the **Green Corn Ceremony**. On their arrival, Europeans found Native women performing most of the agricultural work, which contributed to their view that Native people were "savages" who virtually enslaved their own women. Their role as farmers was actually an important component of the high status most Southeastern societies accorded women. The long tradition of agriculture in the Southeast makes the **"civilization" program** introduced by the United States in the 1790s seem ludicrous because it proposed to teach Indians to farm. Policy makers discounted the horticultural practices of women and sought to convert men from hunters to farmers. The program was moderately successful at best, and in some

Southeastern communities well into the twentieth century farming was women's work.

Algonkian languages

Algonkian languages were common on the coastal plain from North Carolina into the Chesapeake and north. The Algonkian-speaking Shawnee occupied the Ohio valley and much of what is now Kentucky, though groups of Shawnee could be found in other parts of the Southeast at various times in history, including the Savannah River in the seventeenth century. Powhatans and Pamlicos of Virginia spoke Algonkian languages, as did the Nanticokes from the northern Chesapeake. Numerous distinct Algonkian groups such as the Pomeiock, Wingadacoa, and Secotan inhabited the North Carolina coast at the time of European contact.

allotment

Allotment refers to the idea of breaking up tribal domains into separate individual farms. Christian reformers active in the period after the **Civil War** aggressively embraced allotment as the final solution to the problem of the persistence of Native American cultures. The idea of allotment grew out of European and Anglo-American frustration with the communal systems of land tenure that characterized all Indian tribes. Americans believed only the private individual ownership of land could stimulate personal ambition and drive society to greatness. Native societies were moribund, critics argued, because their ethic of sharing and communalism stifled personal success and social growth. This rejection of emergent American capitalism was one of the features of Indian cultures that most infuriated reformers and policy makers. As early as the administration of President Thomas Jefferson, Americans pressured Native groups to abandon their community-based culture and embrace privatization. Choctaw and Chickasaw **removal** treaties and, especially, the Creek's **Treaty of Washington** (1832) embodied this principle. In the 1850s government agents inserted provisions for allotment in several treaties, and the 1866 **Reconstruction treaty** with the Choctaws and Chickasaws contained similar language. These provisions were always voluntary, however, because the treaties guaranteed traditional Native land use systems. During the 1870s and 1880s reformers actively pursued the allotment program. They believed that their ultimate goal, wholesale Native culture change and integration into American society, could never succeed as long as tribal communities, which strengthened cultural values of sharing and generosity, survived. Homestead and railroad advocates, who had no interest in Indian culture change, liked allotment because they saw it as a way to acquire vast amounts of Indian-owned land. Both groups were powerful in Congress, but the government could not mandate allotment until the U.S. Supreme Court ruled in the 1886 case of *United States* v. *Kagama* that Congressional law could override treaties. The next year, 1887, Congress enacted the Dawes Severalty or General Allotment Act. Exempting the Five Tribes of Indian Territory because they had clear titles to their lands, the act provided that Indian reservations should be surveyed, tribal censuses taken, and plots distributed to individuals. The separate allotments would be protected from sale or taxation by restrictions that would last for 25 years. At the time each Native person received an allotment, he or she would also receive citizenship in the United States. All lands not allotted would be classified as surplus and sold by the United States to homesteaders, the money received to be deposited into tribal accounts under government control. In 1893 Congress established the **Dawes Commission** to negotiate similar arrangements with the Five Tribes. By the time Congress abandoned this policy, in the 1934 **Indian Reorganization Act**, more than two-thirds of the land owned by tribes in 1887 had been lost.

Anoatubby, Bill (Chickasaw, b. 1945)

Anoatubby was born in Tishomingo, Oklahoma, one of six children raised by his widowed mother. A football star in high school, he received a degree in accounting from East Central Oklahoma University. In 1975, after a career in banking, he began working for the Chickasaw Nation as health care director. In 1979 he was elected the first lieutenant governor of the Chickasaw Nation under the new constitution. In 1987, after the retirement of Overton **James**, he became governor. Anoatubby improved services for the nation by working to increase the number of tribal employees from 30 in 1975 to 1,600 in 1999, and, consequently, he has made the Chickasaws economically successful. Reelected in 1999, Governor Anoatubby planned to continue economic development in the Chickasaw Nation.

Archaic tradition (8000–700 B.C.)

Beginning about 10,000 years ago, as a result of a global warming trend, regional diversification of tools and subsistence patterns began to appear in North America. Indigenous people in the Southeast came to rely heavily on diverse sources of food, including small game and plant products. Groups still ranged widely in small nomadic bands in order to take advantage of seasonal availability of food sources. The development of the *atlatl*, or spear-thrower, improved large-game hunting, especially of the white-tailed deer. Pottery tempered with fiber appeared on the South Carolina coast during the late Archaic period, as did the earliest domestication of indigenous plants (see **agriculture**). By the end of the Archaic period the climate was much as it is today, population growth had forced groups to use smaller territories more efficiently, and the beginnings of sedentism were apparent.

Arpeika (Florida Seminole, c. 1765–1870)

Also known as Sam Jones, Arpeika led the Seminole resistance to removal efforts by the United States. He refused to accept all agreements signed by other chiefs authorizing removal to the West and fought American expansion into Florida in one of the longest and most expensive guerrilla wars in the history of the United States (see **Seminole Wars**). In 1837 Osceola ignored Arpeika's warning not to meet with General Thomas Jesup to discuss terms for peace, and Jesup took **Osceola** and his followers hostage. Because of Arpeika's leadership and prowess as a healer, the Miccosukees elected him principal chief of their band. In late 1837 U.S. troops made a final effort to capture Arpeika and his 400 or so followers. Though badly outnumbered, he selected the battlefield at Cooacoochee near Lake Okeechobee and directed the Miccosukee troops in the war's most difficult battle, which lasted for more than three hours. The Seminoles retreated to continue the resistance, leaving only 10 dead on the battlefield; the Americans lost 26 with 112 wounded. Arpeika refused to turn over African Americans living among the Seminoles, and he and his people fought until the United States declared the war over in 1842 and withdrew from the area. By 1849, nearly 100 years old, he led Seminole resistance to further removal efforts with war leader Billy **Bowlegs** and about 120 warriors. In 1858 he remained in Florida, with 12 warriors, while others were forcibly removed to Indian Territory (Oklahoma).

art

Well-made tools from the earliest occupations of the Southeast suggest pride and artistry. Beginning around 4,000 years ago, **Archaic** peoples made jasper beads, carved stone bowls, and, toward the end of the period, coiled fiber-tempered pots. **Woodland** people produced finely worked copper and mica sheets and stone decorative and display objects including animal effigy pipes and jewelry. **Mississippian** people carved shell and stone, and they cut, shaped, and incised copper for ceremonial purposes. After contact, Southeast groups continued pottery making and basketry, but portions of their material culture were lost or dramatically altered by European goods. Much culture endured, however, through artistic adaptation by many groups. Creek people came to be known for their carefully worked beaded bags, belts, and sashes. Choctaw and Cherokee women crafted split-cane baskets that were strong and flexible, and they continued weaving traditional styles and added new materials, dyes, and designs. The Seminoles developed a style of colorful patchwork sewing, while Creeks incorporated ribbons into their fabric designs. Southeastern Indians have produced a number of accomplished twentieth-century artists, including painters Jerome **Tiger**, Merv Jacobs, and Woody Crumbo, sculptors Willard Stone and John Julius Wilnote, basket weavers Elizabeth John and Rowena Bradley, and potters Bill Glass and Joel Queen.

Attakullakulla (Cherokee, c. 1700–1780)
Attakullakulla appears most frequently in the historical record as a diplomat, but in his youth he was a skilled warrior. The nephew of Old Hop, who later became civil chief of the Overhill Cherokees (in what is today eastern Tennessee), Attakullakulla traveled to London in 1730 in a delegation of Cherokees escorted by Sir Alexander Cuming. In 1738 he became the Cherokees' peace chief. Upon his return he promoted a British alliance. About 1740 he was captured by the Ottawas, who were allies of the French, and he remained with them until 1748. Well-treated by his captors, he developed a more open mind toward European powers that served his people well. He returned to the Cherokee Nation, became the second-ranked chief in the Overhill towns, and embraced play-off diplomacy as a way to free Cherokees from the monopoly South Carolina held on their trade. In 1751 he led a delegation to Virginia to try to open trade routes, and he promoted relations with the French-allied Shawnees and Senecas. Having made it clear to South Carolina authorities that the Cherokees had a choice, he went to war against the French in 1752 and arrived triumphant in Charleston the next year to demand a commission and better terms for trade. In 1756 he negotiated successfully for the construction of Fort Loudoun to offer protection to Overhill towns, and when Fort Loudoun fell in the **Cherokee War**, he ransomed John Stuart, the Southern Indian superintendent, and escorted him to safety. He was the primary Cherokee negotiator of the terms that ended the war. He agreed to land cessions in the 1770s, in particular, the Henderson Purchase of 1775 that challenged the sole authority of the Crown to purchase land from Indians. During the American Revolution he professed loyalty to the Crown and then negotiated an alliance with the United States,

conflicting actions that were nevertheless consistent with his goal to maintain Cherokee independence.

Big Warrior (Creek, d. 1825)

Big Warrior, or Tustanuggee Thlucco, was headman of the largest Upper Creek town, Tuckabatchee. In 1811 Big Warrior hosted Shawnee leader Tecumseh's visit to discuss a possible pan-Indian alliance against the United States. He rejected Tecumseh's proposal and instead chose to protect Creeks who carried out executions of other Creeks accused of killing American homesteaders. Enemies blamed him for the death of popular leader Little Warrior. During the **Creek War** of 1813–14, Redstick insurgents besieged Tuckabatchee and forced Big Warrior to side with the United States and Creek leader William McIntosh. Big Warrior assisted the United States in the defeat of the Redsticks and signed the Treaty of Fort Jackson ending the Creek War. He complained bitterly about the provisions of the treaty, especially those that called for the largest Creek land cession to date, mainly land of Creeks who had supported the United States. Big Warrior opposed further land cessions for the rest of his life and traveled to Washington to argue against the Treaty of Indian Springs, which called for additional cessions. He died in Washington, D.C., during negotiations.

Billie, James (Florida Seminole, b. 1944)

A Vietnam veteran, Billie has served on the Tribal Council of the Florida Seminoles in Big Cypress since the late 1970s, and has since led the way to economic prosperity for the Seminoles through expansion and preservation of their gaming industry. Elected chairman of the Tribal Council in 1979, Billie opened a dialogue with the Oklahoma Seminoles for division of federal funds and aggressively led negotiations with the Florida government to resolve disputes. Florida governor Bob Graham agreed to compensate the Seminoles $7 million for land relinquished in Palm Beach County pending the council's agreement to withdraw opposition to a nearby development and to end their lawsuit against the state. As one of the longest serving chief executives in the Western Hemisphere, Billie also negotiated agreements that provided water rights for the Seminoles and added more than 14,000 acres to Big Cypress. His modernization efforts have put the Florida Seminoles at the forefront of economic development among indigenous groups. His interest in music, blending Seminole components with country and folk music, led to the albums *Alligator Tales* and *Seminole Fire,* for which he was awarded the Living Legend Award by the Native American Music Association.

Boudinot, Elias (Cherokee, c. 1803–1839)

Boudinot, born near present-day Rome, Georgia, was a journalist and signatory of the Cherokees' removal treaty. Originally known as Galagina, or Buck, he attended the Moravian Mission School at Spring Place, and in 1818 he enrolled in the American Board of Commissioners for Foreign Missions School in Cornwall, Connecticut, where he remained until 1822. Upon entering the Foreign Mission School, he took the name Elias Boudinot in honor of a benefactor. His engagement to Harriet Gold, a white woman, sparked outrage in Cornwall and ultimately led to the closing of the school. The couple married in 1826. Boudinot served as clerk of the Cherokee Council from 1825 until 1827. He undertook a lecture tour in 1826 to raise funds for the purchase of a printing press and type in the **Sequoyah** syllabary. He was successful, and in 1828 he became editor of the *Cherokee Phoenix*, a bilingual newspaper. He also collaborated with Samual Austin Worcester on the translation of hymns and the New Testament, and he translated the missionary tract *Poor Sarah; or, The Indian Woman*. He was adamant in his opposition to removal, until it became clear that Georgia would not abide by the U.S. Supreme Court's ruling in **Worcester v. Georgia**. When he sought to open the columns of the *Phoenix*, which the Cherokee nation owned, to debate on the issue in 1832, he was forced to resign. On December 29, 1835, he joined a small unauthorized group of Cherokees in signing the Treaty of New Echota. In 1837, Boudinot, recently widowed and remarried to Delight Sargent, moved to Indian Territory, where he continued his work with Worcester. On June 22, 1839, he was killed for ceding tribal land in violation of Cherokee law.

Boudinot, Elias Cornelius (Cherokee, 1835–1890)

Boudinot was a leader of the Confederate Cherokee and a supporter of assimilation. Following the murder of his father, Elias Boudinot, in 1839, he was raised by his deceased mother's relatives in Manchester, Vermont. He later moved to Fayetteville, Arkansas, to study and practice law. Involved in Democratic politics, Boudinot served as secretary for Arkansas's secession convention, and, following the state's secession in 1861, he helped his uncle, Stand **Watie**, enlist Cherokee soldiers for the Confederacy. During the Civil War, Boudinot rose to the rank of lieutenant colonel and was elected to the Confederate Congress. In 1866 he represented the Confederate Cherokees at treaty negotiations in Washington, D.C. Unlike most Cherokees, Boudinot supported **allotment** in severalty, United States citizenship, railroad construction, economic development, Oklahoma statehood, and the dissolution of tribal government. In 1868 Boudinot was largely responsible for the relocation of an Arkansas tobacco company to the Cherokee Nation in an effort to avoid excise taxes from which the federal government exempted Indians. The resulting U.S. Supreme Court decision in *Cherokee Tobacco Case* (1871) curtailed this right and compromised tribal sovereignty.

Bowlegs, Billy (Seminole, 1810–1859)

Known as the Alligator chief, Bowlegs led the resistance to the removal efforts of the United States during the Third **Seminole War**. His mother was a Miccosukee from a prominent clan. As a child, he witnessed the removal attempts of the U.S. government and the tribe's retreat into the everglades. He earned his reputation as an able military leader in campaigns during the Second Seminole War (1835–42). As Bowlegs rose to power, he maintained diplomatic connections with the Spanish in Cuba. He spoke at least three languages and was an able general and negotiator. When the Armed Occupation Act passed the U.S. Congress in 1842, which encouraged U.S. citizens to move to Florida, Bowlegs launched a guerrilla war resisting U.S. troops and homesteaders. In 1852 he traveled to Washington and met with President Millard Filmore, but he refused to accept the government's insistence on Seminole removal to Oklahoma. In 1857 Bowlegs led the last military resistance of Seminoles in Florida. With his capture in 1858 he was taken to Fort Myers and then to the Seminole reservation in Oklahoma, where he died of smallpox a year later.

Bronson, Ruth Muskrat (Cherokee, 1897–1982)

Bronson, born in the Delaware District of the Cherokee Nation, was a reformer who emphasized education and leadership development. In 1925 she graduated from Mount Holyoke College, and in 1923, at the conference of the Committee of One Hundred, an influential reform organization, Bronson delivered an address emphasizing the importance of educational opportunities for Indians. She accepted a teaching position at the Haskell Indian Boarding School in Lawrence, Kansas. In 1931 she moved to Washington to direct the Bureau of Indian Affairs' scholarship program that enabled Native youth to pursue higher education. In 1944 she published *Indians Are People, Too*, in which she cautioned that romanticizing Native people undermined their achievements. In 1945 she opened the Washington office of the National Conference of American Indians (NCAI). She held a number of positions at NCAI, including executive secretary and editor of its *Washington Bulletin*. From 1957 through 1962, Bronson worked as the Bureau of Indian Affairs' health education specialist on the San Carlos

Apache Reservation, where she established Ee-Cho-Da-Nihi, a club that organized women to improve their lives and communities.

Brown, John F. (Oklahoma Seminole, 1840?–1919)

As an educated, politically savvy leader, Brown represented a departure from his predecessors in the Oklahoma Seminole Nation. He was born in the Cherokee Nation to an army doctor, John F. Brown, and Brown's Seminole wife, Lucy Redbird, daughter of John Jumper. He attended Cherokee schools while his father served as government physician for the Seminoles. Following the Civil War, he accompanied the Confederate Seminole delegation from Indian Territory to negotiate for peace. He witnessed an ineffectual Seminole leadership at the negotiations. He returned to the capital of the Seminole Nation, Wewoka, to pursue business interests, particularly cotton ginning, and was a partner in the Wewoka Trading Company. He negotiated with the Creeks for settlement of land disputes and in 1885 was chosen principal chief after he had already assumed many of his predecessor's duties. In 1893, confronted by the **Dawes Commission**, Brown fought against **allotment**, and he shunned statehood for Oklahoma. Land grabs intensified in the area, putting pressure on Chief Brown's position as leader, but he continued to rely on the courts and insisted on Seminole treaty rights. After intense local and federal pressure, he agreed to a graduated allotment that he thought would protect the Seminoles from losing their land. In 1901 Brown lost his bid for reelection, having to fend off accusations of financial mismanagement and corruption. In 1905, after the death of Brown's successor, the General Council of the Seminole Nation reappointed Brown as principal chief. He profited from Seminole allotment, enriching himself and his family through real estate deals. In 1952, the **Indian Claims Commission** condemned his actions but denied federal responsibility for any corruption.

Caddoan languages

Caddoan speakers lived on the western edge of the Southeast: Caddo, Anadarko, and Nabedache in Texas and western Louisiana, Pawnee and Wichita in Oklahoma and Kansas.

Cahokia (A.D. 900–1250)

At its height, between A.D. 1050 and 1150, Cahokia was the largest and most elaborate of the **Mississippian** sites. The civilization lay in the upper Mississippi near present-day East St. Louis, Illinois. Corn agriculture sustained the large population that reached as many as 10,000 to 20,000 people at a time. More than 100 earthen mounds with flat tops occupied the 5-square-mile site. The 100-foot-high Monk's mound dominated the region and was probably the center of a ceremonial life that emphasized the importance of fertility, the harvest, the seasons, and perhaps competence in warfare. An elite who inherited their status governed the society. They maintained control through economic coercion, threats of violence, and proof of their spiritual power. A vigorous life of ceremonies, trade, craft activities, construction projects, and subsistence activities occupied the lives of the commoners at Cahokia. The site was abandoned by A.D.1400 because the society collapsed, probably because of resource depletion, especially timber and soil nutrients.

Cherokee Nation v. Georgia (1831)

In 1831 the U.S. Supreme Court dismissed this case brought by the Cherokee Nation, contesting Georgia's attempt to extend state laws into the Cherokee Nation. The Court stated that Indian tribes were, in the words of Chief Justice John Marshall, "domestic dependent nations" with no standing before the Court. In essence, the Court recognized the unique position of Indian tribes as both autonomous and under the guardianship of the United States government.

Cherokee Tobacco Case (1871)

In the 1871 *Cherokee Tobacco Case* the U.S. Supreme Court ruled against Cherokees Elias Cornelius **Boudinot** and Stand **Watie**, owners of a company located within the Cherokee Nation that manufactured chewing tobacco. The Watie and Boudinot Tobacco Company significantly undersold their competitors because, according to the Cherokee treaty of 1866, Cherokee manufactures were not subject to federal excise taxes. Acting on complaints from white-owned tobacco companies in neighboring Arkansas, on December 26, 1869, United States marshals seized the factory. The Supreme Court decided that federal tax laws applied within Native nations despite treaty provisions to the contrary unless Congress specifically excluded them. The decision, in conjunction with an unrelated 1871 law ending the treaty system and denying the sovereignty of tribes, began the process of subjecting Native people to federal jurisdiction.

Cherokee War

In 1758 English officers recruited several Cherokee warriors to help fight French and Shawnee enemies in Ohio. While on their return home through western Virginia, the Cherokees killed some cattle belonging to local farmers. The farmers, claiming later that they thought the warriors were enemy Shawnees, ambushed and killed several of the Cherokees. While the relatives of the slain warriors raided the backcountry settlements, 22 Cherokee headmen traveled to Charleston to talk peace. Carolina authorities captured the headmen and held them as hostages against the surrender of the raiding party. To hasten compliance, a South Carolina army marched toward the Cherokee Nation with the hostages in custody. The Carolinians reached Fort Prince George, encountered a smallpox epidemic, incarcerated the hostages in the fort, and fled back to Charleston. A Cherokee force surrounded the fort, killed an officer, and demanded the release of the hostages. Instead, the English slaughtered them. The Cherokees then extended the war into eastern Tennessee by surrounding Fort Loudoun. Another Cherokee force defeated a relief army of English and Native troops headed for Fort Loudoun, causing the garrison of that post to surrender. In 1761 another English army invaded the Cherokee Nation. This time successful, the English avenged earlier losses by devastating much of eastern Cherokee country.

chiefdoms

By A.D. 800 societies in the Southeast came to recognize a distinct class of people, chiefs, who obtained their status through kinship. Chiefs occupied positions of political, economic, and military authority in their communities and often exerted profound influence well beyond a single town. Alliances with neighboring chiefdoms enhanced an individual leader's authority. Surrounding themselves with symbols of their power, chiefs based much of their claims to authority on their spiritual connections, which they claimed enabled their communities to thrive. They sought and displayed exotic goods, material symbols of their spiritual and political power. Chiefly power also rested on the practice of **redistribution**. A chief acquired food from commoners and tributary villages that he stored in public granaries and used to feed visitors as well as subjects who were in need. Chiefdoms are most commonly associated with the **Mississippian** tradition, but non-Mississippian peoples who produced substantial surpluses, like the Calusas of south Florida and the Powhatans of Virginia, also had chiefdoms.

Chitto Harjo (Creek, 1846–1912)

Born in Boley, Creek Nation, he was given the name Wilson Jones. Chitto Harjo, or Crazy Snake, succeeded **Opothle Yoholo** as traditionalist leader opposed to Creek assimilation into American society. He distrusted Creek constitutionalism and wanted to reestablish council government and preserve communal ownership of land, traditional religion, and Creek lifestyle. Bitter opposition to the attempts of the **Dawes Commission** to force **allotment** on the Five Tribes led to his organization of a rival government and eventually a full-scale uprising. He and his followers, called Snakes, attacked white homesteaders and Creeks who favored allotment of land. In 1901 U.S. marshals arrested Chitto Harjo and 66 of his followers. After the court suspended his sentence, he returned to the Creek Nation to pursue a strategy of political action and lobbying against statehood for Oklahoma. Finding little recourse through diplomatic channels, in 1909 he joined the Smoked Meat Rebellion to oppose the exercise of federal law in the Creek Nation. He ended his life a fugitive.

"civilization" program

"Civilization" has always been a central feature of United States Indian policy, but its position on the priority list of American policy goals has risen and fallen since 1790. The main idea of civilization is the transformation of Native people from being culturally Indian to Anglo-American. First articulated in a coherent fashion by President George Washington and his secretary of war, Henry Knox, civilization was the essence of Indian policy until about 1820. Several assumptions underlay the policy. Most important was the idea that Anglo-American culture defined civilization, which meant that Indians were without civilization. They could learn to be civilized, however, and it was the responsibility of the American government to teach them. Once instructed, Native people would understand that Anglo-American culture was superior and be grateful. When they became civilized, they would be integrated into the mainstream of American society as fully equal members. Knox and Washington believed that since there could be no place in the United States for uncivilized people, the cultural transformation of the Indians was their only alternative to extinction. Saving them in this manner was thus the honorable thing to do. At the same time, as they became civilized, Indians would recognize that they had no need for large blocks of hunting lands. They would willingly sell their excess land to support American expansionism, happy to receive money to invest in the improvement of their farms. The view emergent in the 1820s that Indian deficiencies were racial, and thus unchangeable, rather than cultural challenged the civilization policy and led to its replacement by the **removal** policy of the 1830s. Proponents of civilization never entirely abandoned their cause, however,

and in the late nineteenth century they reemerged triumphant in the allotment policy of 1887. During the twentieth century, concepts of cultural
relativism and tribal **self-determination** have muted the forces of civilization, but they nevertheless persist, particularly in the Christian missionary
community.

Civil War

Native Southerners became embroiled in the Civil War. Slave owners politically dominated the Five Tribes in Indian Territory, and once federal
troops withdrew in 1861 leaders of all five tribes signed treaties with the
Confederacy (see **slavery**). The Choctaws and Chickasaws were nearly unanimous in their support of the South, but many Indians were either neutral
or Unionist. Among the Creeks and Cherokees old grievances stemming
from removal surfaced, and they plunged into their own civil wars. Following
the Confederate defeat at Pea Ridge in March 1862, Union forces invaded
Indian Territory. Confederate and Union Indians, organized into military
units, attacked one another's communities. As refugees fled toward Kansas
and Texas, raiders pillaged, burned, and destroyed nearly every improvement
the Creeks and Cherokees had made to their land. Perhaps 10 percent of
the population of the Five Tribes died in the conflict. On July 14, 1865, the
Civil War ended in Indian Territory when the Chickasaws surrendered. Na-
tive people in the Southeast were also drawn into the war. The Thomas
Legion of Eastern Cherokees, the 69th North Carolina Infantry, served primarily as a home guard, but several Cherokees were present at the fall of
Richmond. Mississippi Choctaws and Catawbas also contributed troops to the
Confederate army. The Lumbees, denied the right to vote or bear arms under
North Carolina's 1835 constitution, were nonetheless forcibly conscripted into
Confederate labor battalions to build fortifications and make salt. They resisted
in the Lowry War that outlasted the Civil War by seven years (see **Confederate
treaties; Lowry, Henry Berry; Opothle Yohola; Watie, Stand**)

clothing

Clothing in the Native Southeast served practical functions but was also a
vital source of expression. Men and women distinguished themselves from
each other through what they wore. In the summer months men wore a
simple breechcloth or flap made of deerskin drawn between the legs and
belted around the waist. Women usually wore a knee-length deerskin skirt.
In the deep South woven fiber, including Spanish moss, may have been
substituted by some groups such as the Timucuas. Children usually went

naked until they reached puberty. When traveling, people often wore deerskin moccasins. In winter men wore leggings made of skins, and sashes or robes. They often used woven fiber, feathers, or fur to make large robes or cloaks. Some they decorated with shells. **Powhatan's** deerskin mantle, for example, was decorated with shells that both bordered it and formed the outline of facing bears. With the introduction of European trade Southeast Natives quickly added wool and other fabrics to their wardrobe. Warm, fast-drying wool was particularly attractive as a substitute for the heavy leather flap. Men also adopted cotton shirts and turbans, while women began to wear skirts, blouses, and shawls and make bags, robes, and sashes from cloth. Many groups fashioned unique apparel from an array of sources. Creek women added colorful ribbons to their European-style calico dresses. Each size and color of ribbon conveyed different symbolic meanings. In the late nineteenth century Seminoles developed a distinctive patchwork design. Women stitched small squares of fabric into elaborate designs on hand-cranked sewing machines and then used the colorful patchwork for skirts, shirts, and jackets. Nevertheless, Southeastern Indians have increasingly dressed in ways that are indistinguishable from their Euro-American neighbors.

Colbert, Daugherty (Winchester) (Chickasaw, 1810–1880)

Colbert negotiated with the Choctaws for a distinct Chickasaw land base and a defined boundary between Choctaw and Chickasaw territory. They finally reached an agreement in 1855. In 1856 he helped organize a government and was elected governor in 1858. On the eve of the Civil War, Colbert advocated secession and signed a treaty with the Confederate government. During the Union invasion he fled to Texas with his slaves and followers. He negotiated with the United States government for an armistice and insisted on the independence of the Chickasaw Nation. In 1865 he signed the Treaty of Fort Smith acknowledging peace with the United States and accepting the terms of the Confederate surrender. In 1866 he traveled to Washington to finalize the treaty with the United States that provided for emancipation. Colbert bitterly resisted freeing Chickasaw slaves and even suggested that they be indentured to their former owners following the war to allow for their assimilation into society. In 1866 Cyrus Harris defeated Colbert for the Chickasaw governorship (see **Civil War; Confederate treaties; Reconstruction treaties; slavery**).

Colbert, Levi (Chickasaw, d. 1834)

Levi was one of the many sons of James Logan Colbert, a Scottish trader married into the Chickasaw Nation in 1729. A prominent family, the Colberts came to dominate Chickasaw politics in the early nineteenth century. A council member in 1820, he favored education for Chickasaw youth and encouraged the construction of Charity Hall mission school by Presbyterian missionaries. At the same time, he was a traditional Chickasaw in many ways. He had several wives and advocated common ownership of land. He met Secretary of War John C. Calhoun in 1824, but refused to agree to further land cessions. In 1829 he led efforts for the adoption of a code of written laws, leading some non-Indians to assume that he exercised absolute control of the Chickasaw Nation. When squatters supported by the Mississippi government pressured the Chickasaws for more land, Colbert negotiated a treaty that provided 160 acres of land for each Chickasaw, including women and children. He soon realized that the U.S. government was unwilling to protect his people from the extension of discriminatory state laws, and he agreed to negotiate for removal (see **Treaty of Pontotoc**). In 1832 he led a delegation to Fort Gibson, became ill, and died in the summer of 1834.

Confederate treaties

During the summer and fall of 1861, the Creeks, Choctaws, Chickasaws, Seminoles, and Cherokees signed treaties of alliance with Albert Pike representing the Confederate States of America. The Confederacy agreed to fulfill all former federal financial obligations, defend Indian Territory against Union invasion, and accept Indian delegates to the Confederate Congress. In return the Native nations provided three regiments of troops for the Confederate army. Many members of the Five Tribes opposed the treaties or remained neutral, however. Early in 1863 Union Cherokee soldiers stationed in Kansas crossed the border and held a council in which they repudiated the Confederate treaty, abolished slavery within the Cherokee Nation, censured Confederate Cherokee leaders, and reaffirmed their loyalty to Principal Chief **John Ross** (see **Civil War**; **Opothle Yohola**; **slavery**).

Creek War (1811–1814)

The Creek civil war began in 1811 because factions within the Creek Nation disagreed over how to handle a number of problems, in particular loss of trade, growing debt, frustration with market-oriented leaders, and encroachments on land by American citizens. Several leaders, including William **McIntosh** and **Big Warrior**, sought solutions that appeased the growing Anglo-American presence on their borders, while others, led by a number of charismatic prophets, hated concessions and insisted on resistance to accommodation. When officials from the United States demanded executions of Creeks involved in the deaths of white homesteaders, Big Warrior and his faction complied. Angered by the deaths of popular men, many of whom the prophetic party, called Redsticks, considered heroes, and disgusted with the policies of those who embraced certain Anglo-American values, the Redsticks besieged Big Warrior's town of Tuckabatchee. The situation quickly spun out of control. With the support of Creeks a group of Mississippi militia raided at Burnt Corn Creek a party of Redsticks returning from Pensacola with arms. Though the fight concluded indecisively, the situation became more polarized. Redsticks then attacked a stockade called Fort Mims to punish Creeks involved with the Burnt Corn incident and take revenge against the Mississippi militia. The United States government labeled the attack a "massacre" and took the opportunity to enter the war. The invasion of the Creek Nation in 1813 kept the underequipped Redstick army on the run. Led by Andrew Jackson, the U.S. Army won one victory after another, eventually cornering a large party of Redsticks at Horseshoe Bend in March 1814. Jackson routed the Redsticks, and the survivors either fled to join the Seminoles or surrendered to Jackson. The **Treaty of Fort Jackson** in 1814 officially ended the conflict and resulted in the largest Creek land cession to date. Ironically, most of the ceded land belonged to those who had been willing to accommodate the demands of the United States.

Curtis Act

Named for Charles Curtis, a congressman from Kansas, the Curtis Act of June 28, 1898, expressed the frustration in Congress over the refusal of the Five Tribes to negotiate **allotment** agreements. To go into effect immediately, the act required the **Dawes Commission** to proceed unilaterally with allotment the moment the tribal rolls were completed. The act also abolished all tribal laws, closed tribal courts, and subjected all residents of Indian Territory to federal law. Tribal governments were to close down March 6, 1906, but in denying tribal governments the power to enact and enforce laws, the Curtis Act effectively abolished them immediately. The only authority they retained was to complete the negotiation of allotment agreements. The law also provided for the establishment of town sites and town governments and determined procedures for regulating tribal mineral lands. Congress left a loophole for the tribes, however, by providing that they were free to negotiate better allotment agreements with the Dawes Commission.

Davis, Alice Brown (Seminole, 1852–1935)

Alice Brown Davis was the daughter of Lucy Redbird, a member of the Tiger clan, and John Frippo Brown, a Scottish physician hired by the federal government to attend the medical needs of Seminoles during removal. One of eight children, she was born at Park Hill, Cherokee Nation. Trained in Presbyterian and Baptist mission schools and tutored by her father, she was a highly educated young woman by the time the family moved to the Seminole Nation soon after the Civil War. She nursed for her father when needed and taught at the Mekasukey Academy for Boys at Sasakwa. In 1874 she married George Rollins Davis. After living for several years in the Cherokee Nation, in the mid-1880s the Davis family returned to the Seminole Nation, where they opened a trading post at Arbeka and established a ranch. The mother of eleven children, Davis assumed management of the family businesses when she was widowed in the late 1890s. She also served as superintendent of the Seminole girl's school at Emahaka, a position she held from 1892 until statehood, when she was forced to surrender management of the institution to the Department of the Interior. At the same time, Davis worked as court interpreter from the 1890s until her death, even traveling to Palm Beach in 1905 to interpret in a case involving a Florida Seminole. Between 1903 and 1910 Davis served on at least three delegations of Seminoles sent by the council to Mexico to negotiate fulfillment of a land grant promised Wildcat by the Mexican government. A devout Baptist, she also traveled to Florida several times to establish ties with Seminoles there and convert them to Christianity. In 1922 President Warren Harding appointed Davis Principal Chief of the Seminole Nation. She succeeded her deceased brother, John F. **Brown** Jr., in that position. Davis's tenure as chief was marked by a vigorous and diligent defense of the interests of the nation. For example, when a resurvey of the Seminole-Creek boundary revealed an error that required the Seminoles to surrender land, including several Baptist churches, Chief Davis refused to sign the documents necessary to complete the transfer. Davis died in office, like her brother before her, at the age of 83.

Dawes Commission

Created by Congress on March 3, 1893, as the Commission to the Five Civilized Tribes, the body quickly became known as the Dawes Commission, after its chairman, retired Massachusetts Senator Henry L. Dawes. Because each of the Five Tribes held their lands under an unrestricted, fee simple title, federal property law protected them from **allotment** mandated by Congress. The task of the commission was therefore to negotiate allotment agreements with the governments of the Five Tribes. Rebuffed repeatedly by delegates appointed by the tribal governments, the commission moved to inflame public opinion in the United States by smearing those governments, charging them with corruption, and claiming that the interests of the American intruders were in jeopardy. Congress responded in 1895, with legislation authorizing the commission to begin to survey the nations, and in 1896 with authorization to prepare tribal rolls. Preliminary talks with tribal delegations got underway late in 1897. Following the passage of the **Curtis Act** in 1898, the empowered commission achieved negotiated agreements with all the tribes. The original commission was composed of three men: Dawes, Meredith H. Kidd, and Archibald S. McKennon. In 1895 the Congress enlarged the commission to five and added Thomas B. Cabaniss and Alexander B. Montgomery. While Dawes retained membership until his death in 1903, he became inactive in 1897. In that year Tams Bixby joined the commission with the appointment of acting chairman. Congress dissolved the commission in 1905 and handed its duties over to a commissioner to the Five Civilized Tribes. Bixby held that office until 1907 and then J. George Wright until 1914, when the office of commissioner was abolished

Dial, Adolph (Lumbee, 1922–1995)

A native of Robeson County, North Carolina, Dial attended Pembroke State University and received advanced degrees at Boston University. Following service in World War II for which he was decorated, Dial returned to Robeson County to teach in the segregated Indian high school, earning respect beyond the local community as a Native American educator. The author of *The Lumbee, The Only Land I Know*, and numerous articles, Dial accepted a professorship at his alma mater, where he spent most of his professional career and became Chair of Native American Studies. An advocate of Lumbee federal recognition, he received the H. B. Lowry award and the Jefferson Award for his efforts. Elected to the North Carolina legislature in 1990, Dial continued his work for Native Americans. He served on the U.S. Congress's American Indian Policy Review Commission and was chairman of the Lumbee Regional Development Association. Dial also served on the Lumbee Federal Recognition Committee and on the Constitution Committee. On his retirement, he sat on the Board of Trustees at Pembroke and was a visiting professor at the University of North Carolina at Chapel Hill. Dial was a lifelong member of Prospect United Methodist Church, founded by his grandfather.

disease

Prior to European contact Southeast Native groups suffered few epidemic or endemic diseases, though treponemic diseases such as yaws were common. Problems with malnutrition and poor dental hygiene, the result of a corn-heavy diet, affected the large agricultural societies. With the arrival of Europeans new diseases devastated Native populations. Modern estimations place deaths in some societies as high as 95 percent. Sedentary cultures suffered the most. Epidemics of smallpox recurred in many populations while endemic viruses, such as influenza, caused much suffering and death. The diseases malaria, cholera, and yellow fever took their toll, especially in coastal regions, where many tribes disappeared or retreated inland soon after contact with Europeans. The total population losses in the Southeast from Old World diseases may never be known.

Downing, Lewis (Cherokee, 1823–1872)

Born in the old Cherokee Nation in the East, Downing was the principal chief of the Cherokees following the **Civil War**. As a young man he converted to Christianity, was ordained a Baptist minister, and, on August 3, 1844, was named pastor of Flint Baptist Church. Downing was also active in the Cherokee Temperance Society. In 1845 he was elected to the first of his three terms on the Cherokee National Committee. In the Civil War he served as chaplain in John Drew's regiment, most of which switched from the Confederacy to the Union in 1862, and he became a lieutenant colonel in the Third Indian Home Guards (Union). He also served on the Federal Cherokee Council. Following the Civil War he formed the Downing Party as an alternative to the Ross Party and the Treaty Party, which had their roots in removal politics. He brought together both Unionists and former Confederates in an effort to unify the divided tribe. Elected principal chief in 1867, Downing served until his death.

Etowah (c. A.D. 700–1650)

Members of a **Mississippian chiefdom** in what is now north Georgia, Etowah people farmed the riverine soils, exploited aquatic resources, and hunted turkey and deer. Six large flat-topped temple mounds presided over the site on the Etowah River. Etowahans possessed an elaborate material culture, which they traded with their neighbors. Etowah-style copper carvings have been found as far away as north Florida. They made fine, distinctive pottery, worked marine shell into ceremonial ornaments, and used copper, mica, lead ore, and stone to make art objects. Some European artifacts have been found there, but Etowah collapsed in the century following Hernando de Soto's expedition, perhaps because the introduction of European **disease** decimated the ruling classes and rendered chiefdom political organization difficult.

fishing

Late **Archaic** Southerners began exploiting freshwater shellfish as early as 4,000 years ago. In **Woodland** times coastal resources became more important as people exploited numerous species of fish and shellfish, as seen in the extensive shell middens found along the coast. Harvest of fish became increasingly important as Woodland people came to know their environment more intimately. They may have incorporated seasonal fishing into their subsistence strategy by visiting key fishing areas at peaks times of year to maximize use of resources. Europeans witnessed Native Americans using nets, baskets, elaborate weirs and traps, spears and even poisons made from buckeyes to harvest fish at shoals near the fall lines along the numerous rivers in the Southeast. One observer even claimed to see a lasso used to capture a large sturgeon. People ate fish fresh or preserved their catch by drying and/or smoking it for later use.

Folsom, David (Choctaw, 1791–1847)

Born near the current site of Starkville, Mississippi, Folsom was the son of Nathaniel Folsom and a Choctaw woman from a prominent clan. Along with Peter **Pitchlynn**, Folsom advocated education as a means of improving the Choctaws' ability to deal with the United States. In 1824 he traveled to Washington with **Pushmataha** to prevent land cessions. By 1826 Folsom was the first national leader recognized by all three Choctaw districts in Mississippi. After realizing the bleak prospects of staying in Mississippi under control of the state government, Folsom reluctantly participated in removal negotiations. In 1830 he signed the **Treaty of Dancing Rabbit Creek,** after years of opposition to removal. He settled with his wife, Rhoda Nail, on a farm near Caddo, Choctaw Nation, Indian Territory. He was the first Choctaw chief elected by ballot. A Christian, he encouraged Presbyterian, Methodist, and Baptist missionaries to establish churches in the Choctaw Nation. Reflecting his belief that the Choctaws needed to develop a strong economy in order to maintain their culture and autonomy, he founded and operated a productive salt factory in Indian Territory.

gathering

Part of a woman's economic responsibility in the Southeast was to gather wild plant foods. She learned her methods from the older women in her family and passed on her knowledge to her younger kin. Nuts and seeds of various kinds, including acorns, hickory nuts, and chestnuts, provided an important part of the diet, especially in **Archaic** times. Seasonal harvest of berries, roots, greens, and medicinal plants also supplemented and enriched the diet. Men harvested wild plants for medicinal and ceremonial use, particularly the leaves and bark of the yaupon holly, used to make a strong black tea rich in caffeine. Through **Woodland** and into **Mississippian** times, gathered foods remained an important part of Native life in the Southeast. Gathering continued into the nineteenth century, though a shrinking land base reduced the practicality of gathering for many people. Nuts, fruits, and berries are the most widespread wild foods that Native (and non-Native) people gather. Other foods are specific to particular regions. The Seminoles, for example, gather cootie, a starchy tuber that grows in the everglades, and Eastern Cherokees gather ramps, or onions, and sochan, a wild green, in the Great Smoky Mountains.

government

For more than 9,000 years, from **Paleo-Indian** times into the **Woodland** period, small groups of Native Americans probably governed themselves by consensus under the leadership of proven family members. With the development of settled villages occupied for years at a time, individuals began to exert more influence in society. So-called big men societies, in which individuals used redistribution of food and exotic trade goods to enhance their status in the community, may have developed by the middle Woodland period. With the rise of **Mississippian chiefdoms** an elite developed in some societies that ascribed status to individuals at birth. Some leaders, as shown by retainer executions at **Cahokia**, had the power of life and death over their subjects. Kinship probably remained an important factor in government, and the clans also may have functioned politically in chiefdoms as well. Europeans observed Native governments that had acknowledged leaders and reached decisions through consensus. According to sociologist Duane Champagne, Southeastern Indians did not traditionally differentiate between kinship, religious life, and politics. Cherokees were the first to differentiate and organize a strictly secular republican government that broke with traditional forms. The Creeks, or at least the Creek Tribal Towns, never completely made the shift. All federally recognized tribes by the end of the twentieth century, however, had constitutions or comparable governing documents that provided for representative government.

Green Corn Ceremony

Practiced widely in the eighteenth and nineteenth centuries, the Green Corn Ceremony marked the maturity of the corn crop for Native people in the Southeast, and they considered its observance essential for community harmony and success. Much preparation went into the ceremony, with each clan given specific tasks to perform over a period of several weeks. Several distinct ceremonies and rituals marked the event, including religious dances, a recitation of the town's history, the lighting of a new fire, plunging into a river for purification, and feasting on the new crop. The chief of a town usually conducted the ceremony while the lead healer and town speaker played significant roles. Purification and restoration of harmony was a goal of the ceremony, so fasting and purging as well as ceremonial bathing were important. Rituals emphasized distinctions between men and women and their different contributions to society, and while men conducted many of the public events women presented the new crop in the ceremony's central act. Coming-of-age ceremonies during the Green Corn Ceremony endowed young men and women with adult names. All crimes but murder were forgiven, and unhappy spouses could dissolve their marriages and take new partners. Feasting, including the eating of the first corn of the year, followed the completion of the Green Corn Ceremony. Many traditional communities of Native Southerners continue observance of the Green Corn Ceremony (see **agriculture; music and dance; religion**).

Hagler (Catawba, c.1690–1763)

Also known as King Haigler, this eighteenth-century Catawba chief unified his people and helped them survive expansion by the colony of South Carolina. In 1751, in Albany, New York, he met with New York governor De Witt Clinton to establish a permanent peace and form an alliance to combat attacks from the Cherokees and Shawnees. In 1758, honoring his agreements with the British, Hagler led Catawba troops against Ft. Duquesne. In 1759, he directed a similar campaign against the Cherokee. Having survived an epidemic in 1738, he saw his people suffer more smallpox outbreaks, one of which, in 1760, was particularly devastating. Hagler negotiated a treaty to ensure a 15-square-mile tract of land for the Catawbas, which also provided for a British fort nearby. He vigorously opposed alcohol, and, though he tolerated missionaries, he never converted to Christianity himself. Ambushed and killed in 1763 by a group of Shawnees, Hagler left a legacy of security and autonomy for the Catawba. A weathervane atop the town hall in Camden, South Carolina bears his image.

Harjo, Joy (Creek, b. 1951)

Born in Tulsa, Oklahoma, Harjo is a Creek poet and musician. While she studied painting at the Institute of American Indian Art (IAIA) in Santa Fe,

Harjo began writing. She graduated in 1976 from the University of New Mexico with a degree in creative writing. In 1978 she earned a master's degree at the University of Iowa in fine arts and writing. In 1991 she taught at the IAIA and joined the faculty of the University of New Mexico. In 1975 she published her first book of poetry, *The Last Song*, republished in 1979 with additional work in *What Moon Drove Me This*. Her books also include *She Had Some Horses* (1983), *Secrets from the Center of the World* (1989), the acclaimed *Mad Love and War* (1990), which was a recipient of the William Carlos Williams Award of the Poetry Society of America, and *The Woman Who Fell From the Sky* (1994). She was one of seven writers awarded the 1997 Lila Wallace Readers' Digest Fund Writers' Award. Harjo's band, Poetic Justice, in which she plays saxophone, performs songs based on her poetry (see **music and dance**).

Harjo v. *S. Kleppe* (1976)

Shortly after the 1970 act of Congress that authorized citizens of the Five Tribes to elect their leaders, Allen Harjo and three other traditional Creeks brought suit against the secretary of the interior on the grounds that he had concentrated the power to disburse tribal funds in the hands of the principal chief, Claude Cox. Without regard to the Creek constitution of 1867, which placed primary governmental power in the hands of the National Council, Harjo charged, the secretary and Cox had conspired to make the office of principal chief the sole embodiment of Creek government. Two things were at issue in this case. The constitution had recognized the historic autonomy of the Creek towns and had required that delegates to the council be chosen by and representative of those towns. The second point related to the constitution itself. Had the **Curtis Act** and other congressional legislation of the late nineteenth and early twentieth century terminated the constitution of 1867 and the council government, or had the secretary and Chief Cox illegally subverted it? Following an extraordinarily detailed discussion of Creek political history prior to 1970, the court found that the constitution of 1867 was in force, the council representing the Creek towns was the primary engine of Creek national government, and that Creek sovereignty had never been terminated. In *Muscogee (Creek) Nation v. Hodel* (1988) the court used the Harjo decision to uphold the right of the Creek National Council to create a tribal court system and exercise criminal and civil jurisdiction over tribal citizens.

Hogan, Linda (Chickasaw, b. 1947)

A poet, writer, and educator, Hogan was born in Denver, where her family had been relocated (see **relocation**). While working at various jobs, Hogan began to write. She attended night school in the mid-1970s at the University of Colorado, and, in spite of criticism from her colleagues, she nurtured her interest in her Chickasaw heritage. In 1978 she received a master's degree in English and creative writing. Since 1989 she has been a member of the faculty at the University of Colorado. She has published four books of poetry, all critically acclaimed, and her poems have appeared in numerous volumes. Her novel *Mean Spirit* was published in 1990. She writes fiction, essays, plays, and screenplays and continues to be influenced by her Chickasaw heritage.

Hopewell treaties

Negotiated with the Cherokee, Choctaw, and Chickasaw nations at Hopewell plantation in South Carolina during the winter of 1785–86, the Hopewell treaties opened relations with the tribes and stipulated that the federal government had the sole right to conduct Indian affairs. American commissioners Benjamin Hawkins, Andrew Pickens, Joseph Martin, and Lachlan McIntosh negotiated the treaties. The Cherokee talks were first. In November 1785 the parties signed an agreement that established peace, specified the boundaries of the Cherokee Nation, and established the obligation of Congress to regulate trade. The commissioners then signed similar treaties with the Choctaws and the Chickasaws on January 3 and January 10, 1786, respectively. The Hopewell treaties reinforced the precedent of dealing with Indians as sovereign nations through treaties. Although North Carolina and Georgia challenged federal claims to authority in Indian affairs, the Hopewell treaties strengthened federal control of Indian policy.

housing

The earliest Native people in the Southeast sought shelter in caves or under rock overhangs, while Archaic peoples on their seasonal migrations constructed relatively temporary shelters near their food sources. Woodland peoples favored circular houses built of saplings covered with bark, and Mississippian peoples often lived in rectangular structures. Many Native people distinguished between summer and winter houses. For winter they built circular one-room houses, as much as 30 feet across, sided with wattle and daub, and supported by posts buried in the ground. Dirt piled up against the outside walls served as insulation, and a central hearth kept these winter houses very warm. Roofing materials varied depending on local material and could be planks, woven mats, brush, or palm fronds. A matrilineage, an extended family related through women, might also own an arbor-style house, open on three or four sides, in which they spent much time in summer months. In the early eighteenth century most Native Southerners lived in rectangular bark-covered houses. Women owned the houses and were responsible for their maintenance. Most families also kept a corncrib for storing preserved produce from their farms. Both men and women kept gender-specific sweat lodges that may have belonged to clans. The Florida Seminoles developed the chickee, an open raised structure particularly well suited to swamp living. In pre-European times houses often clustered around a small central square, while a palisade may have surrounded the whole village. After the European arrival villages often became more diffuse, with homes scattered along a river to facilitate agriculture, hunting, and gathering. In the nineteenth century Southeastern Indians quickly adopted European building techniques. Most families lived in log cabins, but those who had become wealthy built substantial clapboard or brick houses with plastered walls, brick or stone chimneys, and glass windows.

hunting

Native people depended on hunting for part of their subsistence. **Paleo-Indians** hunted large migratory animals, like mastodons, which are now extinct, with spears and techniques such as impounds. The demise of these animals led to dependence on smaller animals such as the white-tail deer. **Archaic** people used an atlatl or spear-thrower for hunting, and **Woodland** people developed a bow and arrows. People of these traditions developed an intimate knowledge of the game animals of the Southeast. **Mississippian** people continued to hunt using traps and snares as well as bows and arrows. In addition to deer, they hunted wild turkeys, bears, and a host of smaller game such as rabbits and squirrels. They ate the meat, made clothing, blankets, and bags from the skins, and used bones, antlers, claws, hooves, and teeth for tools and ornaments. Hunting involved religious rituals and purification, and beliefs about hunting mandated an ecological balance (see **religion**). The deerskin **trade**, pursued most vigorously in the South by the English in the eighteenth century, undermined these beliefs, as Indians, enmeshed in a world economic system that rendered them dependent on European goods, killed large number of deer to satisfy their needs. The deerskin trade collapsed at the end of the eighteenth century, and Anglo-Americans turned their economic attention to another Native commodity—land—which cotton, only recently viable commercially, demanded in large quantities. Whereas the deerskin trade had required Indian participants, the cotton boom precipitated Indian **removal**.

Indian Claims Commission

For years tribes had tried to sue the United States in the Court of Claims in order to force payments for lost property and for other purposes. But because the United States has sovereign immunity, each attempt had to be preceded by an order by Congress agreeing to the suit. In 1946, in association with a broader congressional interest to terminate the political relationship between the federal government and the tribes, Congress established the Indian Claims Commission. The idea was that the government could not sever its historic ties to the tribes without a full and complete accounting in which all claims for past misdeeds had been adjudicated. The law limited claims to land transactions, usually cases in which the government had underpaid the tribe, and stipulated that a judgment in favor of the tribe must be compensated by money only, not a grant of land. A three-judge panel was to hear the claims and the commission was allotted five years to complete its job. But the ICC was overwhelmed by claims. Congress increased the number of judges to five and extended the life of the commission to 1978. At that time all pending cases were transferred under blanket authorization to the Court of Claims. According to its final report, the ICC had dismissed 204 claims, awarded 274, and paid out to tribes $818,172,606.64. Of these totals the Cherokees received $20,107,288.22; the Chickasaws $190,934.78; the Chickasaws and Choctaws jointly $3,489,843.58; the Choctaws $250,000; the Creeks $8,462,120.82; and the Seminoles $16,147,733.66.

Indian Removal Act

On May 28, 1830, President Andrew Jackson signed the Indian Removal Act. Heated debates had preoccupied Congress for several weeks following Jackson's first State of the Union address in which he urged legislative action on **removal**. The final vote was 102-97 in the House, reflecting widespread public opposition to the measure outside the South. The margin of victory was somewhat wider in the Senate. The law authorized the president to negotiate removal treaties with Eastern tribes, the result to be an exchange of land for new country in the West. The president was to agree to transport the tribes to the West at government expense, support them for one year upon arrival, and compensate them for any improvements they were forced to leave behind. The law also provided that the president should promise to protect the Indians in the possession of their new land forever against interference from any source. Under the auspices of this act, approximately 100,000 Eastern Indians were relocated west of the Mississippi River during the 1830s.

Indian Reorganization Act
Signed into law June 18, 1934, the Indian Reorganization Act, or Wheeler-Howard Act, represented the culmination of more than a decade of reformist agitation against the federal government's allotment policy. Spearheaded by John Collier, director of the American Indian Defense Association, the IRA came into being largely because President Franklin Roosevelt appointed him commissioner of Indian affairs in 1933. The law was a dramatic revision of Collier's ideal program but it nevertheless constitutes a landmark in the history of U.S. Indian policy. The law brought **allotment** to an end, but, perhaps more important, it sought to rectify much of the damage allotment had done to tribal communities. Provisions include the return to tribal ownership of unsold surplus land on reservations, a loan fund to enable tribes to purchase land, help to organize tribal constitutional governments, authorization to incorporate for economic development projects, and support for revitalizing cultural traditions. The act specifically excluded the Five Tribes of Oklahoma, but many groups in the South benefited from the opportunities offered. In the era of the New Deal the Lumbees responded to the IRA with a concerted attempt to achieve recognition, and the Mississippi Choctaws organized themselves along IRA lines.

Indian Trade and Intercourse Acts
Congress enacted the first Trade and Intercourse Act in 1790 in order to fulfill treaty obligations that regulated commercial relations with Native tribes. The act outlined the rules of **trade** and stipulated that only individuals holding licenses issued by federal officials could legally cross the boundaries into Indian country to trade. Congress also asserted its control over land purchases from tribes, stipulating that no purchases were legal unless concluded by federal officials and tribal leaders in treaty arrangements. Applicable only to American citizens, Congress designed the laws to keep peace on the frontier by prohibiting actions that might elicit a military response by the tribes. As relations with the tribes grew more complex, Congress enacted more comprehensive Trade and Intercourse Acts in 1793, 1796, 1799, 1802, and 1834. The most important body of added regulations applied to the administration of the civilization policy through the distribution of livestock, agricultural implements, and other "civilized" goods (see **"civilization" program**).

Iroquoian languages
Iroquoian speakers lived in the mountains and piedmont between Algonkian and Muskogean speakers. The Cherokees, who probably separated from the

northern Iroquois thousands of years ago, are the best known southern Iroquoian group. The Tuscaroras, whom linguists believe spilt off from the northern group somewhat later than the Cherokees, lived in North Carolina before their migration north to join the Iroquois League. The Meherrins of eastern North Carolina also spoke an Iroquoian language.

James, Overton (Chickasaw, b. 1925)

Born in Bromide, Oklahoma, Overton James graduated from high school in 1942 and enlisted in the U.S. Navy. He attended Southeastern State College in Durant, where he received a B.A. and then an M.A, both in education. In 1963 he was director for Indian Education in Oklahoma. Community leaders recruited James to unseat the appointed governor, Floyd Maytubby, but the federal government would not allow an election until 1971, when James was elected governor of the Chickasaw Nation. James built a government center at Tishomingo, Oklahoma, with donations from local businesses. He brought in capable employees for the Chickasaw government and encouraged economic development for the nation. James served four terms as president of the Inter-Tribal Council of the Five Civilized Tribes.

Jumper, Betty Mae (Florida Seminole, b. 1923)

Born Betty Mae Tiger, Jumper was the first woman chief of the Florida Seminoles. Her mother raised her in a traditional chickee (Seminole house) and insisted on Seminole traditions. Her grandparents discouraged Anglo-American education, but when a comic book piqued her interest, she resisted her grandparent's wishes and went to boarding school in Cherokee, North Carolina. In 1945, as one of the first Florida Seminoles to receive a high school diploma, she continued her education at the Kiowa Indian hospital in Oklahoma. She returned to Florida to help her people improve health care. She married Moses Jumper on her return. When the tribe organized a constitutional government in 1957, she was named to the Tribal Council in the first election. In 1967 she was elected to the position of tribal chief. She worked on improving health care and providing other services, such as education and housing. When Jumper completed her four-year term, she took over as director of Seminole Communications to publish the tribal newspaper. In 1995 she published a collection of tribal stories, *Legends of the Seminoles*, and in 1994 was awarded the Florida State Department's Folklife Heritage Award. She was inducted into the Florida Women's Hall of Fame, and holds an honorary degree from Florida State University.

kinship

Southeastern Native Americans reckoned kinship through their mother's family—children were always members of their mother's clan. Kinship gave an individual his or her identity and thus his or her place in society. All Native Southerners understood the importance of their relatives and knew the obligations involved. Only relatives avenged murder, and only the threat of vengeance offered protection. Therefore, a person without kin was in constant danger of losing his or her life. Kinship determined distribution of food and other goods, often decided community leadership, and established whom one could or could not marry. In many groups members of one's mother's clan would be off limits for marriage, while the clan of one's father's father might be a suitable, if not required, place to look for a mate. Southeast Native Americans also organized their societies through matrilineal clans, large extended kin groups that traced descent from ancient mythical ancestors. Some groups had as few as four clans, others had more than a hundred. In Creek society each clan served specific political and religious functions. Because clans were dispersed in towns throughout a tribe's territory, kinship helped form bonds between communities. Matrilineal kinship was so contrary to the practice of Europeans and their understanding of the Bible that policy makers and missionaries tried to undermine or abolish it in the process of "civilizing" Native people. Furthermore, clans came under attack since they were the mechanism for punishing crime, which reformers thought should rest with the government. While Native Southerners no longer reckon kinship solely through the mother's line, some continue matrilineal clan affiliations.

Leflore, Greenwood (Choctaw, 1800–1865)

Greenwood Leflore was the son of a French trader, Louis Le Fleur, and a Choctaw woman named Rebecca Cravat. Born June 3, 1800, he lived until the age of 12 at his father's trading post, called French Camp, on the Natchez Trace. But in 1812 he went to Nashville to receive an education. He remained in Nashville until 1818 when he returned to the Choctaw Nation with his bride, Rosa Donley, daughter of a leading Nashville family. By the 1820s Leflore was a slave-owning cotton planter and remained such for the rest of his life, eventually accumulating some 15,000 acres of prime cotton land and 400 slaves. In 1822 he was chosen chief of the Western District of the Choctaw Nation; in 1830 he was elected chief of the nation. During his tenure as chief he defended Choctaw sovereignty, encouraged education, and espoused Methodist Christianity. He also was instrumental in various

Choctaw political reforms, particularly the drafting of a written code of laws. In 1830 he signed the Treaty of Dancing Rabbit Creek, which provided for the removal of the Choctaws to the West, but he did not remove with his tribesmen. Rather, he remained in Mississippi, became a leading planter and political figure, served three terms in the Mississippi state legislature, and built and furnished a mansion, "Malmaison," which has become legendary in the annals of Southern plantation architecture. Leflore opposed the secession of Mississippi, refused to support the Confederacy, lost most of his property during the Civil War, and died August 21, 1865. He was buried wrapped in the American flag.

Lowry, Henry Berry (Lumbee, c. 1846–?1872)

The youngest of ten sons, Lowry rose to prominence in Robeson County, North Carolina as a leader of Lumbee resistance to Confederate conscription of labor during the **Civil War**. Following the war he reorganized his band and led raids against wealthy conservatives, especially members of the Ku Klux Klan, many of whom threatened Lumbee rights. Even though he was considered a fugitive, Lowry became a hero to many in the area, particularly Indians but also impoverished whites and blacks. The North Carolina government designated him an outlaw in 1868, and he was arrested repeatedly but always managed to escape. He also led raids against the Lumberton jail to free captured associates. After authorities took his wife Rhoda hostage to attempt to quell his actions, Lowry raided the homes and threatened the lives of local leaders responsible for taking Lumbee hostages, eventually earning his wife's freedom. In 1872 Lowry vanished.

Mankiller, Wilma (Cherokee, b. 1945)

Mankiller was born in Tahlequah, Oklahoma. She lived in a Cherokee community until 1956 when her family relocated to San Francisco as part of the United States policy to assimilate Indians (see **relocation**). As a teenager, Mankiller became deeply involved with the San Francisco Indian Center, where she headed an effort to secure a health clinic for Indians in the Bay area. Mankiller married soon after finishing high school, had two daughters, and enrolled in college courses. The takeover of Alacatraz Island in 1969 by Indian activists led her to become more deeply involved in the struggle for Native American rights. Following her father's death and her divorce in the early 1970s, Mankiller decided to return to Oklahoma. She moved back permanently in 1977. She received a job with the Cherokee Nation as a grant writer and community organizer, completed her degree at the University of Arkansas, and in 1986 married Charlie Soap. Diagnosed in California with serious kidney disease, Mankiller's health was seriously compromised by a car accident and myasthenia gravis after she returned to Oklahoma, but illness did not prevent her from rising to prominence. In 1983 she was elected deputy chief, and in 1985 she succeeded Ross **Swimmer**, who resigned to head the BIA, as principal chief. She was reelected in 1987 and 1991. She has written her autobiography, *Mankiller: A Chief and Her People.*

Martin, Phillip (Mississippi Choctaw, b. 1926)
Martin was born near Philadelphia on the Mississippi Choctaw reservation. He graduated from high school in Cherokee, North Carolina. After serving in the Air Force from 1945–55, he returned to Mississippi to attend Meridian Junior College. He has served as chief of the Mississippi Choctaw repeatedly since 1959. During the periods in which he was not chief he served as a councilman, as director of the housing authority, and as health care director. As a Choctaw leader, Martin presided over the economic development of his nation, helping reduce Choctaw unemployment since 1979 from 50 percent to 20 percent. He sat on the board of Chata Enterprise, which has developed industries in Choctaw, especially one that manufactures wiring harnesses for automobiles. He was also instrumental in developing the Choctaw Greetings Enterprise, which hand finishes cards for American Greetings of Cleveland. He has won numerous civic awards for his work with housing and health care improvements and for his help in improving the Choctaw economy.

McCurtain, Green (Choctaw, 1848–1910)
Born to a prominent family near Skullyville, Choctaw Nation, Indian Territory, McCurtain rose to a leadership position in the Choctaw Nation. He attended local schools in Indian Territory, and as a young man he worked as a merchant. As an adult, he turned his attention to law and politics. In 1872, he served as sheriff of Skullyville County and later served three terms on the National Council. He was also a member of the schoolboard. As tribal treasurer, he reorganized the tribe's finances. He was a member of the delegation appointed to negotiate with the **Dawes Commission**. Viewing **allotment** as inevitable, he sought to negotiate the best deal he could for the Choctaws. In 1896, running under a newly organized party, he won election for tribal chief and was reelected in 1902. In 1906 Oklahoma statehood mandated the dissolution of the Choctaw government, but McCurtain continued to lead the tribe informally until his death in 1910.

McGhee, Calvin (Poarch Creek, 1904–1970)

From a poor rural farming family in southern Alabama, McGhee had only a fifth grade education, but he led the fight to win a settlement from the United States government in the 1940s and dominated Poarch Creek politics until his death. In 1950 he established a formal council to make land claims against the federal government. In 1961 he attended the Chicago Indian Conference to familiarize himself with problems common to Indian groups and to end his tribe's isolation. He met with President John F. Kennedy at the White House and later negotiated with Lyndon B. Johnson, arguing that the Treaty of Fort Jackson of 1814 had been unfairly imposed. McGhee also fought for federal recognition of the Poarch Creeks. In 1970 his tribe gave their first thanksgiving powwow, an expression of Indian identity and tribal unity that has become an annual event. His son, Houston McGhee, and other family members continued McGhee's work after his death, and the Poarch Creeks earned federal recognition in 1984, the first such tribe in Alabama to do so.

McGillivray, Alexander (Creek, c.1750–1793)

Born in Little Tallassee, in modern-day central Alabama, of the prominent Wind clan, McGillivray was a well-known Creek leader who argued for more political cohesion in the Creek Nation to further collective interests. Educated in Charleston at the insistence of his Scottish father, Lachlan McGillivray, Alexander McGillivray found advantages to understanding European politics and culture. He repeatedly fought against encroachments by homesteaders and politicians in Georgia. A loyalist during the Revolutionary War, McGillivray sought a treaty with the Spanish to secure Creek power. He led a delegation to New York to undercut attempts by the Georgia government to deal with the Creeks on their own. The **Treaty of New York** of 1790 allowed land cessions but also established a government-to-government relationship between the Creek Nation and the United States. He had at least two wives and two children, Alexander and Elizabeth. He died in Pensacola, Florida at the home of his economic ally, William Panton, after an extended illness.

McIntosh, Waldo Emerson "Dode" (Oklahoma Creek, 1893–1983)

The son of Albert Gallatin and Mary Boulton McIntosh, of Carthage, Tennessee, McIntosh attended public schools there as a child until joining family in Oklahoma to finish his education in tribal schools. He served in World

War I and, after returning to the Creek Nation, he used his family's wealth and influence to build a lumber and real estate business. He married Lulu Vance; they had five children. McIntosh served as county treasurer and tax assessor and patented "Creek Indian Plaid," a special tartan that recognizes the dual ancestry of many Creeks. He served as chief of the Muskogee Nation 1961–71 as well as member and president of the Inter-Tribal Council of the Five Civilized Tribes.

McIntosh, William (Creek, c. 1775–1825)

Born in Coweta in the Creek Nation, McIntosh rose to a leadership position as a member of the important Wind Clan. His close economic connections to the powerful Indian agent Benjamin Hawkins enhanced McIntosh's power. He assisted the United States in its suppression of the Redstick Creeks in the Creek War and signed the Treaty of Fort Jackson. In the next decade he colluded with David Mitchell, Indian agent to the Creeks, to control tribal finances, develop business interests, and enrich himself. Though he was present at the council meeting at which leaders agreed to execute anyone who promised to give up more Creek land, he signed the **Treaty of Indian Springs** in 1825, ceding the remainder of Creek land in Georgia. Creek leaders subsequently executed McIntosh at his home.

Mississippian tradition

Around A.D. 800 in many areas of the Southeast, the **Woodland tradition** gave way to the Mississippian. Mound building intensified for both religious and political purposes. Flat-topped mounds served as ceremonial centers for a priestly class to exercise its spiritual power for the benefit of the community (see **chiefdoms**). A new emphasis on the agricultural cycle overshadowed the Woodland preoccupation with death. **Religion** focused on fertility, of both humans and the land, on the maintenance of the seasons, and on military prowess. Leaders commissioned the crafting of fine artworks used for ornamentation and ceremonialism, in order to enhance their status, build alliances, and impress neighbors (see **Southeastern Ceremonial Complex**). Mississippian peoples cultivated corn on a large scale, which may have provided 60 percent of their calories, though they supplemented their diets with beans and squash, indigenous crops, wild foods, fish, and game (see **agriculture; fishing; gathering; hunting**) The production of a surplus meant economic security, but it also gave elites enormous power. The Mississippian tradition had declined in many areas by the fourteenth century and gave way to smaller, more egalitarian societies. **Diseases** brought from the Old World may have meant the ultimate demise of the Mississippian Tradition. Europeans saw only a few Mississippian societies, but the hierarchical structure of Natchez, Creek, and other Southeastern governments as well as their farming techniques, religious beliefs, and **kinship** systems probably derived from Mississippian.

Moundville (c. 1150–1450)

A **Mississippian** site in present-day west central Alabama on the Black Warrior River, Moundville dominated the region for nearly 300 years until the eve of European arrival. Twenty mounds mark the site with the largest earthwork reaching 56 feet, suggesting that Moundville was a major ceremonial center in the Southeast. As many as 3,000 people lived at the site at a time, intensely farming corn for subsistence and **redistribution**. Burials suggest elite status for a noble class who may have influenced society through their control of resources, professed spiritual powers, distribution of exotic goods, and threats of violence. From their position at the ceremonial center at Moundville, elites controlled dozens of smaller towns and villages scattered along the rivers of central Alabama.

Musgrove, Mary (Creek, c. 1700–1763)

Born Coosaponakeesa, Musgrove began her life in the Creek town of Coweta. Her mother was probably from the Wind clan, and her uncle Brims was a powerful Creek chief. Her English father arranged for her to live with a family in South Carolina when she was six so that she could learn to speak, read, and write English. In 1716 she married English trader John Musgrove. In 1732 they established a trading post at Yamacraw Bluff on land given Mary by Yamacraw chief Tomochichi. She met Georgia founder James Oglethorpe and, by earning his confidence, secured an alliance between the Creeks and the British. After the death of Musgrove she married Jacob Matthews, who had been her indentured servant. After Matthews died in 1742, her third marriage to Anglican priest Thomas Bosomworth proved more politically beneficial. Through the 1750s, she remained a major figure in the diplomatic relations between Georgia and South Carolina and the Creek Nation. At the same time, she was actively engaged in winning British recognition of her claims to three coastal islands granted her by the Creek council. Paritally successful, she retired to St. Catherines Island on the Georgia coast, where she spent the rest of her life out of Creek politics.

Mushulatubbee (Choctaw, c. 1770–1830)

Mushulatubbee was a prominent chief who governed the northeastern district of the Choctaw Nation in the early nineteenth century. Although he initially resisted efforts by the United States to involve Choctaws in the War of 1812, he eventually acquiesced and allowed troops to fight with Andrew Jackson against insurgent Creek Redsticks in the **Creek War**. In 1820, pressured by Jackson, Mushulatubbee agreed to the Treaty of Doak's Stand because of the growing threat from Anglo-American settlers in Mississippi who tried to impose their laws on the Choctaws. The treaty gave the Choctaws land west of the Mississippi. In 1824 he went with a delegation to Washington, D.C., to prevent further land cessions, but in 1830 he signed the **Treaty of Dancing Rabbit Creek**, ceding the Choctaw's remaining land in Mississippi. Because of his seeming willingness to cede Choctaw land and consider removal, Mushulatubbee lost the election of 1830 to John **Folsom**, who was opposed to further land cessions. Mushulatubbee died of smallpox near the Choctaw Agency on the Arkansas River in the Choctaw Nation.

music and dance

Southeast Indians used music and dance to enhance the effectiveness of their rituals and ceremonies. Songs told stories, clarified ceremonies, and carried messages to the sun or other spiritual forces. Chosen men used numerous percussion instruments, gourd rattles, and various skin drums, including a water drum, to perform for dances. Singers usually chanted in rhythm, although at times the village speaker, one of the chief's main assistants, might lead the singing. The speaker's words often conveyed instructions to the audience or dancers. Ceremonial songs often ended with a shout or exclamation from the crowd, presumably a word of thanks. Sometimes musicians used flutes made of cane, wood, or bone during ceremonies, but usually they played these instruments for entertainment or as a greeting to visitors. Individuals followed careful prescriptions for formal dances, particularly those connected to the important **Green Corn Ceremony**. Men and women usually danced separately, in a rhythmic stomping step, and always danced counterclockwise in a circle around a ceremonial fire. Some Southeastern Native women attached rattles made of turtle shells to their ankles to enhance the message. In modern times cans are sometimes used as a substitute. In modern stomp dances men and women dance together, but in separate circular paths or alternating with each other. Stomp dances are religious observances and are different in form and meaning from powwows, whose dances come from the Plains and Great Lakes and in which some

Southeastern Indians participate. Native people from the Southeast are also making important contributions to contemporary music by incorporating Native traditions, themes, and styles into modern jazz, country and western, gospel, and rock formats. Two particularly significant performers are Joy **Harjo** and James **Billie**.

Muskogean languages

The languages in the Muskogean family were the most common in the Southeast. Chickasaw in northern Mississippi, Choctaw in central and southern Mississippi and western Alabama, Houma in Alabama, Creek in Alabama and Georgia, Apalachee in the Florida panhandle, Alabama-Koasati in southern Alabama, Apalachicola, Calusa, Chiaha, Guale, Mikasuki-Hitichiti, and Seminole make up part of this vast family of languages.

Nanih Waiya

In one of their accounts of their origins, Choctaws explain that their people entered this world from the underworld through a mound of earth called Nanih Waiya. Identified today as a burial mound in Winston County, Mississippi, the sacred location spiritually tied the Choctaw to the land. Choctaw leaders in the nineteenth century drew on the symbolism of the mound when they made changes to Choctaw laws and government. When they arrived in the West after removal from Mississippi, the Choctaws constructed a council house and named it after the mound.

Natchez revolt

In 1729 the Natchez on the lower Mississippi River rebelled against the French for taxing the fur trade and confiscating their land in order to construct Fort Rosalie. After the Natchez attacked the French settlement established near where Natchez, Mississippi now stands, French and Choctaw armies retaliated and destroyed the Natchez villages. While some Natchez refugees fled to the Chickasaws and Creeks, the French enslaved and transported to their Caribbean Island colonies many others (see **slavery**).

Ocmulgee (c. A.D. 900–1100)

Developed around A.D. 900, the **Mississippian** site of Ocmulgee on the Macon Plateau in central Georgia was a large fortified town built on a bluff overlooking the Ocmulgee River. Three typical flat-topped ceremonial mounds mark the site. A large earth-covered council house that resembles a small mound distinguishes this site from others of the Mississippian tradition. Inside the earth lodge is a raised earthen platform in the shape of an eagle, an effigy common to Southeastern ceremonial life (see **Southeastern Ceremonial Complex**).

Oconostota (Cherokee, c. 1712–c. 1782)

Born in present-day eastern Tennessee, Oconostota, the Great Warrior of Chota, was a principal Cherokee war chief. In 1736 he responded to a French visit to Chota by flying French banners atop his house, and in the 1740s he led a delegation to Fort Toulouse. In 1753, however, he led 400 Cherokee warriors against the French-allied Choctaws at the request of South Carolina's government. He vacillated between imperial powers because his first loyalty was to the Cherokees, and he exploited European alliances to further Cherokee interests. In 1759 Oconostota was among the Cherokee headmen held hostage by Governor William Lyttleton for refusing to turn over warriors who had raided white settlements, but **Attakullakulla** managed to secure his release. He led the attack at Fort Prince George that resulted in the slaughter of the hostages, commanded the Cherokee warriors who defeated Colonel Archibald Montgomery's invading army in 1760, and engineered the siege of Fort Loudoun (see **Cherokee War**). In 1768 Oconostota negotiated an alliance with the Iroquois, a traditional enemy. In 1775 he agreed to the Henderson Purchase, in which the Cherokees sold 20 million acres in central Tennessee and Kentucky to a private company, but the next year he repudiated the transaction and joined the British side in the American Revolution. Oconostota died in Chota, where his friend Joseph Martin fulfilled his request to be buried, like a white man, in a coffin facing east. But his eyeglasses, knife, pipes, cup, beads, and vermilion were also interred with him, according to Cherokee custom.

Oklahoma Indian Welfare Act

The Oklahoma Indian Welfare Act, or Thomas-Rogers Act, applied Commissioner of Indian Affairs John Collier's reorganization policy to the Oklahoma tribes. Although Collier wanted to extend all the protections of the **Indian Reorganization Act** to the Oklahoma Indians, Congress instead passed a weaker, less protective law on June 26, 1936. Although the law did not reverse **allotment** policy or protect Indian land holdings, the Oklahoma Indian Welfare Act enabled the Oklahoma tribes to reorganize their governments. In addition, the law enabled the Oklahoma tribes to form corporations through which to utilize government grants, manage their resources, and acquire land. The Creek tribal towns of Thlopthlocco,

Alabama-Quassarte, and Kialegee and the United Keetoowah Band of Cherokees organized under the terms of this legislation.

Opothle Yoholo (Creek, c.1798–1862)
Opothle Yoholo first appears in the documentary record in the 1820s as speaker of the Tuckabatchee and Upper Creek Councils. Closely associated with Tustannuggee Thlucco (**Big Warrior**), head chief of the Upper Creeks, he was in a prestigious leadership position. He opposed the **Treaty of Indian Springs** and agreed to the execution of Creek leader William **McIntosh**. In 1826 he led a delegation to Washington to renegotiate McIntosh's treaty. He signed another treaty in 1832, but he tried to cling to the remaining Creek land and ensure sovereignty by agreeing to allotments. He negotiated with Mexico for a possible Creek homeland away from the expanding United States. Forced to move west, he continued leadership of the traditionalist faction. He opposed the Confederate Creeks at the outset of the **Civil War** and fled with his followers north to avoid the bitter conflict in Indian country. He died in Kansas, a hero to many Creeks.

Osceola (Seminole, 1804–1838)
Also known as Billy Powell and Usse Yahola (Black Drink Singer), Osceola rose to a prominent leadership position in the Second **Seminole War**. His mother came from a leading Creek clan and his great uncle was the Redstick leader Peter McQueen. Osceola worked under the tutelage of Neamathla during the First Seminole War in 1819 and received his adult name at the **Green Corn Ceremony** that year. In 1825 he moved to Big Swamp, where he married two women. In 1832 he was elected war chief, or Tustannuggee. He resisted all **removal** treaties and organized a sustained military resistance to the United State's incursions. His murder of Seminole leader Charlie Emathla for favoring removal was one of the sparks that ignited the Second Seminole War. Osceola contracted malaria in 1836, impairing his ability to make war. He agreed to peace negotiations in 1837 but was betrayed by U.S. general Thomas Jesup, who took Osceola captive and sent him to a St. Augustine prison. Allowed to have his wives and children join him, Osceola was transferred to Ft. Moultrie in Charleston harbor. He died there and was buried headless after an army doctor made off with his head as a trophy.

Paleo-Indian tradition (to 8000 B.C.)
The earliest humans to occupy the southeastern region of North America lived by **hunting** large game animals, including giant sloths, mastodons, and

relatives of the horse. People traveled long distances in small bands in search of game animals, but they probably exploited other plant and animal resources along the way. Southeastern Paleo-Indians carefully crafted spear points in the Clovis tradition similar to those used throughout North America at this time, but they later gave way to a distinct fluted point with greater variation in size and style. As the large game disappeared because of climate changes, overhunting, or both, Paleo-Indians turned their attention to more diverse sources of food, including smaller game and a variety of wild plants, and the **Archaic tradition** emerged about 8,000 years ago.

Piomingo (Chickasaw, d. 1795)

Piomingo, or Hopoi Mingo, led the Chickasaws during the era of the American Revolution. He advocated an alliance with the British, the Chickasaws' traditional trading partner. To oust unscrupulous traders, he negotiated trade regulations with British superintendent John Stuart. Piomingo insisted that the British survey Chickasaw territory so that all would know the boundaries and respect them. After the Revolutionary War he met with officials from Virginia to forge an alliance with the new American government. In an agreement signed in 1783, he agreed to expel European enemies of the United States, and, in exchange, Virginia officials agreed to recognize Chickasaw boundaries and promised to stem the flow of Anglo-American immigrants across Chickasaw territory. In 1786 he signed the Treaty of **Hopewell** giving the United States exclusive rights in dealing with the Chickasaws and promising perpetual peace. He negotiated for trade with officials in Tennessee to provide the Chickasaws with arms and ammunition in order to protect them against their enemies, who were supplied by Spain and British merchants operating in Spanish territory. Piomingo resisted an alliance with the Spanish, but other Chickasaw leaders saw an advantage to such an association. Piomingo allowed American agents access to Chickasaw villages to facilitate trade and remained staunchly pro-American during his political career.

Pitchlynn, Peter (Choctaw, 1806–1881)

The son of interpreter John Pitchlynn and a Choctaw woman, Pitchlynn, also known as Hatchootucknee, was educated at Choctaw Academy in Kentucky and Nashville University. He returned to the Choctaw Nation to head the Lighthorse guard, a national police force, and in 1825 he helped establish a permanent annuity for the Lighthorsemen. He initially resisted **removal** but, seeing no alternative to living under increasingly oppressive Mississippi state laws, he eventually agreed that the Choctaws should go west. Pitchlynn encouraged adoption of a constitution in 1860, argued for neutrality during the **Civil War**, and served as principal chief in 1864–66. He signed the armistice ending the war. Pitchlynn handled distribution of the "net proceeds," annuity payments for land cessions forced on the Choctaws for participation on the Confederate side. He led a delegation to Washington, argued against establishment of a territorial government for Indian Territory, and strongly supported Choctaw rights and sovereignty.

Pocahontas (Powhatan, c. 1596–1617)

Pocahontas was the favorite daughter of the chief **Powhatan**. She may have ritually rescued John Smith to cement an alliance with the English, though Smith misunderstood the event. As relations with the English deteriorated after 1610, Pocahontas stopped visiting Jamestown, and she married a Powhatan warrior, Kocoum. Samuel Argall took her hostage in 1613 to force concessions from her father, but his plan failed when Powhatan declined to redeem her. She lived in Jamestown as a hostage for a year, converted to Christianity, and learned the English language and English customs. In April 1614 she married John Rolfe, a prominent colonist whose experiments growing tobacco ultimately proved the economic salvation of Virginia. She gave birth to a son and traveled to England to promote the Virginia Company's colony. She fascinated the British elite, who dubbed her "the beautiful savage." She died in England of an unknown disease at about 21 years of age. Rolfe left their son with relatives and returned to Virginia, where he died. Her son returned to Virginia as an adult and became the progenitor of a number of prominent Virginians who identified ethnically as white rather than Indian.

Posey, Alexander (Creek, 1873–1908)

Posey was born in Eufaula to a large Creek family. His first language was Creek. Educated in English in Creek schools, he continued his education at Bacone Indian University. A journalist by profession, he was associated with several newspapers in the Creek Nation, most prominently, the *Indian Journal*. He helped prepare a census of the Creek population for the **Dawes Commission** and accepted an allotment himself, but he saw danger in the policy, especially to traditional culture. He wrote the "Fus Fixico" letters in which fictional Creek characters discussed issues of allotment and sovereignty. Rife with skepticism, the letters advocated the preservation of tradition and gradual change. He drowned while attempting to cross the flood-swollen Canadian River near Eufaula.

Poverty Point (c. 1700–700 B.C.)

Poverty Point is a late **Archaic** site in the lower Mississippi valley that is remarkable for its large ceremonial earthworks. The site is marked by six semicircular ridges and has two mounds, one 66 feet high and more than 600 feet long. A center for the exchange of valuable exotic raw materials such as copper, galena, quartz, and jasper, the people at Poverty Point apparently held a **trade** fair seasonally to feast, perform ceremonies, meet old friends and relatives, and exchange goods and knowledge. There is evidence, in particular, of numerous beadmakers who perhaps swapped wares or acquired raw materials. Clumps of fired clay, both decorated and plain, may have served as cooking bricks or to heat sweat lodges. A few signs of cultivation exist, but most of the food there was gathered or hunted seasonally.

Powhatan (Powhatan, c. 1550–1618)

Powhatan was the paramount chief of the chiefdom that occupied the Virginia coastal plain. Called Tsenacommacah, his chiefdom totaled more than 30 tribes when the English settlers established Jamestown in 1607. His plan to incorporate Jamestown into his chiefdom included the ceremonial execution of the colony's leader, John Smith, who failed to understand and thus refused to conform to Powhatan's expectations. Powhatan nevertheless suplied Jamestown with much needed food. Powhatan sought trade and alliance with the Virginians but was unwilling to be bullied by them. Consequently, relations between the two were always tense. In 1617 Powhatan abdicated his office in favor of his brother, Itoyatan, and died the next year.

Powhatan Wars

Opechancanough, chief of the Powhatan chiefdom following the death of his brother Itoyatan in 1618, opposed accommodation to the expansion of English settlement in Virginia. In 1619 relations between the Powhatans and the English settlers grew increasingly strained when colonists established a school to convert Indian children to Christianity. In 1622 the Powhatans attacked English settlements and killed approximately 350 men, women, and children, an estimated third of the English colony's population. Until peace negotiations in 1632, warfare and retaliation persisted intermittently. After the reestablishment of peace, English settlers encroached deeper into Powhatan and allied territory, seizing village sites to accommodate their rapidly growing tobacco economy. Virginians also attempted to enslave Native people (see **slavery**). In 1644 Opecancanough led a second attack. Quickly defeated by Virginia forces, Opecancanough was captured and murdered in prison. In the treaty of 1646 the Powhatans ceded most of their land to the

English and accepted the rule of Virginia law. Within several years the Virginians again seized Powhatan lands and restricted the people to several reservations established in the interior of the colony. By 1669 disease, war, and migration had decimated the Powhatan population.

Pushmataha (Choctaw, c. 1764–1824)

Born in the Six Town division of the Choctaw Nation, Pushmataha rose to prominence as a war chief leading raids against the Osage and Caddo across the Mississippi. In 1804 he chaired a delegation to Washington and agreed to cede land in Alabama and Mississippi to eliminate Choctaw debts, earn annuity payments, and build trading posts in the Choctaw Nation. He persuaded his people to ignore the Shawnee Tecumseh's arguments for a pan-Indian alliance and helped the United States army defeat the Creek Redstick insurgents in 1814 (see **Creek War**). In 1816 Pushmataha signed the Mount Dexter Treaty, providing for Choctaw education. In 1820 he agreed to the Treaty of Doak's Stand, which exchanged a tract of Choctaw land in the East for land west of the Mississippi. When the United States reneged on its treaty obligations, he traveled to Washington, D.C., again, where he died of an unknown illness. The revised treaty for land cessions was signed after his death.

Reconstruction treaties

During the summer of 1865 representatives of the United States government met with delegates of the Five Tribes at Fort Smith, Arkansas, to discuss terms of surrender. The American position was that by signing treaties with the Confederate states, the Five Tribes had severed relations with the United States and could be treated as conquered enemies (see **Civil War**; **Confederate treaties**). The American agenda included confiscating enough land to establish reservations for Plains tribes, erecting a territorial government under federal control, encouraging allotment, permitting the construction of railroads, and enforcing the emancipation of slaves and the adoption of freed people into the tribes as fully equal citizens (see **slavery**). The delegates to the Fort Smith talks did not have authorization to agree to such demands, however, which led to resuming negotiations in Washington early in 1866. Competing Cherokee and Creek delegations representing Union and Confederate sympathizers complicated this second round of discussions. Furthermore, because the "Southern" delegates tended to be better-educated, more entrepreneurial, and more sophisticated in negotiation than the more traditional "Northern" ones, they tended to control the talks. The result was that the treaties ignored loyalism, failed to compensate adequately the losses of the loyalists, and recognized the business interests of the former rebels. All the treaties contained provisions that furthered the federal agenda to some degree. The Creeks surrendered the western half of their country, the Seminoles surrendered all of theirs and were required to purchase a new nation from the Creeks, and the Choctaws and Chickasaws gave up their jointly held Leased District. This freed all of Indian Territory west of the 98th meridian for new reservations. All tribes agreed to free their slaves, but the Choctaws and Chickasaws successfully avoided a requirement to extend citizenship to theirs. All tribes agreed to railroad construction and accepted in principle a scheme for territorialization. Confederate Cherokees failed to win recognition as a distinct tribe but gained a separate district within the nation with a degree of autonomy. In return, the United States agreed to pay compensation for the land cessions and to resume annuity payments suspended during the Civil War.

redistribution
Redistribution refers to the practice by which chiefs gained control of surplus food and exotic foreign goods for the purpose of giving them away. In the giving, chiefs demonstrated generosity, an important social value, rewarded kin and other followers, acquired new supporters, and reaffirmed their spiritual and temporal power. Redistribution was a key means by which **Mississippian** chiefs held power, and in post-Mississippian times it was a central public responsibility of town chiefs.

religion
Carefully planned burials began in late **Archaic** times, around 4,000 years ago, suggesting some form of ritualized spiritual belief. **Woodland** people spent much time and effort on mortuary rituals, constructing burial mounds and acquiring exotic goods for internment with the dead. **Mississippian** people held complex beliefs concerning life, death, and other worlds. Retainer executions or suicides indicate a clear notion of an afterlife, but Mississipian rituals focused on fertility, not death. The sun made the crops grow, and the movement of the sun governed the ceremonial cycle. Mississippians may have built temple mounds in order to elevate the priestly leaders closer to the sun. The sun continued to be a major spiritual force for Southeastern Indians after the arrival of Europeans. Native Southerners did not rigidly separate the sacred and profane in the way that Europeans did. They regarded the fundamental nature of everything—rivers, mountains, crops,

game, and themselves—as spiritual, and every act, however mundane it might seem to outsiders, was fraught with spiritual meaning. Native Southerners dichotomized the world, and they took care to maintain balance and harmony between spiritual opposites. They regarded anomalies, things that did not fit their categories, as particularly powerful, and anything that crossed a categorical boundary was therefore out of place. Blood held profound power, and menstruating women and warriors returning from battle sequestered themselves because of their contact with blood. Public ceremonies focused on restoring harmony and reaffirming categories. Private ceremonies sought to balance spiritual forces. Hunters, for example, asked pardon from the deer they killed in order to avoid retaliation by its spirit. Southeastern Indians considered **disease** to be a spiritual malady and treated it by counteracting the spiritual forces with purification, prayers, decoction of sacred plants, and other rituals. One form of traditional Southeastern religion continues to be practiced at stomp grounds. Most Native people in the Southeast, however, are Christians. While Christianity shares some features of traditional religion—fasting and sharing, for example—there are fundamental differences. Historian William McLoughlin has pointed out that Christianity cannot through its rituals cure the sick or make the corn grow, and it emphasizes individual salvation over community harmony. Furthermore, it is exclusive, that is, Christians must forsake all other religions, whereas Native religions are inclusive, and practitioners can seek new sources of power, including Christianity, within the context of their own religious beliefs. What emerged in many Native congregations in the early nineteenth century was a syncretic Christianity that merged elements of traditional religion with the message of missionaries.

relocation
When veterans and defense workers returned home after World War II, unemployment on the reservations skyrocketed. Relocation was one solution to this problem. Applied initially in 1948 to the Navajos and Hopis, the plan was to encourage people to move to cities. The government would pay the costs of relocation, provide classes to instruct people about urban life, help find housing, and locate jobs in cooperating businesses. Early successes led to a massive expansion of the program and linked it to the emerging sentiment in Congress to terminate all relations between the United States and the tribes. Wholesale relocation came to be seen as a way to empty reservation communities and thus justify ending federal services. But as the numbers of relocatees grew, the support services collapsed and many Native

people found themselves dumped into the strange and hostile urban environment. The families of Wilma **Mankiller**, principal chief of the Cherokee Nation between 1985 and 1995, and Chickasaw writer Linda **Hogan** relocated to San Francisco and Denver respectively. Despite the problems of the federal relocation policy, since World War II large numbers of Native people have sought economic opportunity in America's cities where they have created Indian neighborhoods, built community centers, and participated in a wide variety of political and social movements. According to the 1990 census, nearly 60 percent of Native people live in urban areas.

removal
Removal, the policy of relocating Indian nations living east of the Mississippi to land west of the river, dominated United States Indian policy in the 1820s and 1830s. Rejecting the goal of assimilation that had shaped U.S. policy since Washington's time, Andrew Jackson's administration, in particular, promoted separation and removal (see **Indian Removal Act**). American desire for Indian land motivated Indian removal, but so did racism, which denied the ability of Native people to become "civilized." At the same time, debates over federal versus state jurisdiction and paternalistic humanitarian concerns also motivated removal. Although some Americans opposed removal, particularly following Georgia's extension of state law over Cherokee lands in 1828, Indian people provided the most determined resistance to removal. The Cherokees contested their removal in the U.S. Supreme Court, while the Seminoles resisted removal with warfare (see *Cherokee Nation* v. *Georgia*; *Worcester* v. *Georgia*; **Seminole Wars**). Creeks, Chickasaws, and Choctaws also opposed removal, but in the end, most members of all five nations were forced to surrender their lands in the Southeast and relocate in what is today Oklahoma (see **Treaty of Dancing Rabbit Creek**; **Treaty of New Echota**; **Treaty of Payne's Landing**; **Treaty of Pontotoc**; **Treaty of Washington**).

Ridge, John (Cherokee, 1803–1839)
Born in Oothcaloga, Cherokee Nation, to Major **Ridge** and Susanna Wickett, Ridge was a prominent Cherokee politician and planter. He studied at Spring Place Moravian Mission, Brainerd Mission, an academy in Knoxville, Tennessee, and the American Board of Commissioners for Foreign Missions School in Cornwall, Connecticut. In Cornwall he met Sarah Bird Northrup, a white woman, and their marriage in 1824 caused an uproar in the New England town. He served as interpreter for the Cherokee Council before accepting a position in 1825 as adviser to the Creeks and secretary of their

delegation to Washington. Forced out of the Creek Nation in 1826 by federal officials, Ridge returned home to practice law and operate his plantation and ferry. In 1829 he served as clerk of the Cherokee Council, and from 1830 to 1832 he was a member and president of the Committee, the upper house of the Cherokee legislature. Following the extension of state law over the Cherokee Nation and the government's failure to enforce **Worcester v. Georgia**, Ridge abandoned his opposition to **removal**. His advocacy of a removal treaty led to his impeachment by the council, but he was not convicted. In Washington when his father and cousin Elias **Boudinot** signed the **Treaty of New Echota**, Ridge added his signature as soon as Treaty Party delegates arrived in the capital. In 1837 he moved to Indian Territory, where he settled on Honey Creek and opened a general store. On June 22, 1839, Ridge was killed for signing the Treaty of New Echota.

Ridge, John Rollin (Cherokee, c. 1827–1867)

Born near present-day Rome, Georgia, to John **Ridge** and Sarah Bird Northrup, John Rollin Ridge was a prominent writer. In 1839 he witnessed his father'smurder, and his mother moved the family to Fayetteville, Arkansas. Educated in New England and Arkansas, he was haunted by thoughts of revenge. In 1849 he killed David Kell, a Ross supporter, and fled first to Missouri and then, in 1850, to California. There he succeeded as a journalist, novelist, and poet after he failed as a miner, trapper, and trader. He wrote for, edited, and managed a number of California newspapers, including the *Sacramento Bee*. In 1854 he wrote *The Life and Adventures of Joaquin Murrieta, the Celebrated Bandit, a Reinterpretation of the Robin Hood Tale*. Ridge was also a poet; a volume of his work was published in 1868. Although he never returned to Indian Territory for fear of assassination or criminal prosecution, in 1866 Ridge headed the southern delegation to Washington at the request of his uncle Stand **Watie**. In 1867 Ridge died of "brain fever" in California. His complied articles on Native Americans were published in 1991 as *A Trumpet of Our Own*.

Ridge, Major (Cherokee, c. 1770–1839)

A warrior as a young man, The Ridge became a proponent of Cherokee "civilization" and, ultimately, removal. He participated in the armed resistance against the United States in the late 1780s and early 1790s but then he settled down with his wife, Susanna Wickett, to become a planter in the Oothcaloga Valley in present-day north Georgia. He purchased slaves, operated a ferry, and became a partner in a store. In 1807 he executed Dou-

blehead for ceding land. He served as head of the Lighthorse Guard, am-
bassador to the Creeks, and member of the Committee in the years before
the War of 1812. He fought alongside Andrew Jackson against the Redstick
Creeks at the Battle of Horseshoe Bend, rising to the rank of major, which
he subsequently took as his first name (see **Creek War**). Ridge served the
Cherokee Nation in many positions, including co-chief with John **Ross** in
the interim before the constitution of 1827 took effect in 1828. He served
in the council, on the committee, and on many delegations to Washington.
Convinced after 1832 that **removal** could not be avoided, he signed the
Treaty of New Echota. In 1837 he moved to Indian Territory, and he was
killed two years later for signing the removal treaty.

Rogers, Will (Cherokee, 1879–1935)

Will Rogers was a famous satirist and entertainer. During his childhood in
Oolagah, Cherokee Nation, Rogers learned and perfected trick roping from
Dan Walker, an African American cowboy. From 1901 to 1903 he traveled
widely performing in Wild West shows, and in 1905 he debuted in Madison
Square Garden and New York's vaudeville theaters. Although Rogers worked
steadily, he never headlined until he began narrating his roping routine.
From 1916 to 1924 Rogers' mix of down-home humor and political satire
made him a hit with the Ziegfeld Follies. During the 1920 presidential
campaign, the *Los Angeles Recorder* hired Rogers as a political commentator
and, beginning in 1922, he wrote a syndicated column for the *New York
Times*. His humor targeted government and big business, in particular. He
compiled his articles and letters into several books, the most famous of which
is *The Illiterate Digest*, published in 1924. Beginning in 1929, Rogers appeared in seventeen films, and in 1930 Rogers' weekly radio broadcast pre-
miered. Throughout his career Rogers was a philanthropist, to the point of
threatening his own financial solvency. He died in a plane crash near Point
Barrow, Alaska. Moved by his death, newspapers devoted pages to tributes,
movie theaters darkened, and radio networks broadcast silence. In 1991 the
Broadway musical *Will Rogers' Follies*, based on his work, won a Tony Award.

Ross, John (Cherokee, 1790–1866)

Ross, or Coowescoowe, was the most prominent Cherokee statesman of the
nineteenth century. During the Creek War Ross fought against the Redstick
Creeks alongside Andrew Jackson's forces (see **Creek War**). As a young man
he operated a store and plantation at Rossville on the Tennessee River and
became wealthy supplying government contracts. In 1827 he moved to

"Head of Coosa," where he built a two-story house, cultivated 170 acres with slave labor, and operated a ferry across the Coosa River. His public service began in 1816 as a member of a Cherokee delegation to Washington. He served as president of the constitutional convention in 1827, and the next year the Cherokees elected him principal chief. He vigorously opposed Cherokee **removal** from their homeland in the Southeast, and he devised the strategy of taking the Cherokee cases to the U.S. Supreme Court (see *Cherokee Nation* v. *Georgia*; *Worcester* v. *Georgia*). He tried to discredit the minority that negotiated the **Treaty of New Echota** in 1835 and to convince the United States Senate to deny ratification. Although he failed in the latter, he obtained concessions in 1838 that permitted the Cherokees to wait until winter and to manage their own removal. Accompanying his people west on the Trail of Tears, Ross lost his own wife near Fayetteville, Arkansas. Upon arrival, he struggled to reunite the Cherokee Nation. The deaths of three leaders of the Treaty Party led to a civil war, but in 1846 Ross presided over a truce and became chief of a united Cherokee Nation. In the American **Civil War** he tried to remain neutral, but withdrawal of federal troops and Confederate pressure compelled him to accept a Confederate alliance in the summer of 1861 (see **Confederate treaties**). He was captured or, perhaps more accurately, rescued by United States soldiers in 1862. He spent the remainder of the war in Washington defending the Cherokees' loyalty to the Union. Four sons served in the Union Army; one died. Following the war he thwarted an attempt by Confederate Cherokees to divide the nation (see **Reconstruction treaties**). When Ross died in 1866 in Washington, he left a legacy of Cherokee unity and nationalism.

self-determination

A reversal of the **termination** policy of the 1950s and 1960s, the Indian Self-Determination and Education Assistance Act of January 4, 1975, granted a greater degree of self-rule to Indian tribes than they had enjoyed since the onset of allotment in the late nineteenth century. The act enables tribal governments to contract with the Bureau of Indian Affairs to manage for themselves various services such as schools, health care, housing, and policing. Under the contracts the bureau provides the money and expert advice as needed, the tribes provide the plans and personnel to carry out the programs.

Seminole Tribe v. *Butterworth* (1981)

This 1981 decision of the U.S. Supreme Court overturned an attempt by the state of Florida to close a high-stakes bingo facility on a Seminole reservation. The court ruled that Florida's gaming laws were regulatory rather than prohibitory and thus did not apply to the Seminole Nation. The ruling cited the "retained sovereignty" doctrine of **Worcester v. Georgia** (1832), noting that the Seminoles had never surrendered their sovereign right to regulate their own internal affairs. The Seminoles retained the right to conduct gaming within the territorial limits of their reservation because state law only regulated gambling, it did not prohibit it.

Seminole Wars

The Seminoles fought three wars with the United States. In 1816 the United States Army initiated the First Seminole War by destroying the so-called Negro Fort, a black and Seminole stronghold on the Apalachicola River, while pursuing runaway slaves (see **slavery**). Raids and counterraids followed until General Andrew Jackson initiated a scorched earth campaign against the Seminoles. On April 6, 1818, he captured the Spanish garrison at St. Marks and hanged two Englishmen on charges of inciting and supporting the Seminoles. American forces operating in Florida convinced Spain to agree to sell the colony in 1819. The second war arose from the removal policy. Although leaders signed a **removal** treaty at Payne's Landing in 1832 and affirmed their agreement at Fort Gibson in 1833, the Seminoles refused to relocate or turn over runaway slaves who had integrated into their society (see **Treaty of Payne's Landing**). Conflict began in December 1835 when warriors opposing removal led by **Osceola** killed Charley Emathla, a pro-removal leader, and Wiley Thompson, Seminole agent. Shortly thereafter Seminole warriors attacked and killed Major Francis Dade and approximately 100 troops who were part of a military effort to remove them. The United States spent nearly $40 million over seven years defeating, capturing, and removing most Seminoles to Indian Territory. In 1842 the federal government withdrew, allowing several hundred Seminoles to remain in Florida. The Third Seminole War began in 1855 when Chief Billy **Bowlegs** retaliated against a crew of surveyors who had looted his camp. Following an initially ineffective response, in 1856 Colonel William S. Harney wore down Seminole resistance by continuously patrolling their territory and chasing them. On March 27, 1858, the Seminoles accepted the government's terms of surrender. Some Seminoles were relocated to Indian Territory, but others remained in Florida.

Sequoyah (Cherokee, c. 1770–?1843)

Sequoyah developed a syllabary that enabled Cherokees to read and write their own language. Born at Tuskegee in what is now eastern Tennessee,

Sequoyah fought in late eighteenth-century Cherokee campaigns and against the Redsticks in the **Creek War**. Signatory to an unpopular land cession in 1816, Sequoyah moved to Arkansas. By then he had already been at work for several years on a system for writing Cherokee. Having observed the ways in which Europeans used writing, Sequoyah decided that literacy was a skill, not a magical power, and that he could acquire it. By 1821 he had developed a syllabary consisting of 86 symbols (later reduced to 85) that represented Cherokee syllables. He traveled among the western Cherokee in Arkansas and returned to the Cherokee Nation in the East to teach people how to read and write. Soon thousands were literate; by 1835 more than half of Cherokee households had members who could read and write their own language. The Cherokee Nation awarded Sequoyah a special medal for his achievement. The Cherokee Nation purchased a printing press and type and in 1828 began publishing the *Cherokee Phoenix* as well as trans-lations of Christian hymns, tracts, and the New Testament. His syllabary also made it possible for Cherokee medicine men to record their sacred formulas, many of which are housed at the Smithsonian Institution and Yale University. When the eastern Cherokees arrived in Indian Territory, Sequoyah helped mediate an agreement. Looking for a legendary lost band of Cherokees, Sequoyah traveled to Mexico in 1842, where he died in 1843 or 1845.

Siouan languages
Although these languages are generally associated with the Plains, some Siouan speakers lived in the Southeast. On the northwestern fringe of the region were the Osage, Ponca, Omaha, Quapaw, and Kansa. Other lan-guages in the heart of the Southeast show Siouan traits. These include Catawba and Cheraw in South Carolina, Ocaneechi and Cape Fear in North Carolina, Yuchi in Georgia, and Biloxi, Ofo, and Tutelo on the Gulf Coast.

slavery
When Europeans arrived in the Southeast, they referred to unfree people among some Southern Indians as "slaves," but these individuals brought little economic advantage to their "masters." More likely, they were war captives, held either as hostages or potential adoptees. Very early, however, Europeans provided a market for captives, whom whites enslaved for their labor, and the **trade** in Indian slaves reached its peak in the early eighteenth century. Southern Indians began capturing African American slaves from

their white masters as well as Native people from neighboring tribes. By the end of the eighteenth century some Indians were keeping African Americans as laborers or investments, and in the nineteenth century, under the U.S. **"civilization" program,** plantation slavery became a prominent feature of Cherokee, Chickasaw, Choctaw, and Creek economic life. Southern Indians took slaves west during **removal** — the Chickasaws even invested much of their capital in slaves — and the institution flourished in Indian Territory. But slavery caused friction. Seminoles had incorporated African Americans into their society on more equitable terms than other tribes. While Seminoles feared for the safety of these people, Indian masters resented the influence that virtually free people had on their own slaves. Slavery also exacerbated divisions within the Creek and Cherokee nations, producing widespread defections to the Union in the **Civil War. Reconstruction treaties** required that former slaves be admitted to citizenship in the Indian nations, but the Choctaws managed to delay and the Chickasaws to avoid this provision.

Smith, Nimrod Jarrett (Eastern Cherokee, 1837–1893)
Born near Murphy, North Carolina, Smith served as a sergeant in the Thomas Legion in the **Civil War.** After the war he served as clerk of the council that wrote the first constitution for the Eastern Band of Cherokees in 1868. In 1880 he was elected chief of the Eastern Band, and he served in that position until 1890. During his tenure the Cherokees entered into contract with Quakers from Indiana to provide schools, lost a suit against the western Cherokees for a portion of their annuities, and incorporated under North Carolina law. Incorporation gave the Cherokees legal security for their assets, enabled them to act as a corporate body, and offered protection against involuntary allotment. At the beginning of the twenty-first century the Eastern Band still governs itself according to a modified version of this corporate charter.

Smith, Redbird (Cherokee, 1850–1918)
Smith was a leader of the Cherokee opposition to allotment and statehood. He belonged to the conservative Keetoowah Society, which had opposed the Confederacy in the **Civil War,** and continued to be a force in Cherokee politics after the war. Smith came to believe that the Keetoowahs should be oriented toward religion rather than politics. The Keetoowah Society was open to Christians as well as non-Christians, but at the end of the nineteenth century a cleavage developed between those who favored allotment, mostly Christians, and those who did not, primarily followers of traditional religion.

Opposition to allotment seemed hopeless, and so the opposition increasingly turned to traditional sources of spiritual power to deal with the situation confronting them. Smith had attended the stomp dances of the Creeks and Natchez, and he led a movement within the Keetoowah Society to rekindle sacred fires and organize stomp grounds. He chaired a Keetoowah committee to recover the Cherokees' sacred wampum belts that chronicle the tribe's history, and in 1896 he sponsored a stomp dance in the Illinois District of the Cherokee Nation. In the center of a stomp ground burned sacred fire, reportedly kindled from fire brought west on the Trail of Tears, and the people danced around it with the men singing and the women setting the rhythm with shell shakers attached to their legs. In addition to leading this religious revitalization, Smith participated in the Four Mothers' Society, organized about 1895 to resist allotment, and in 1902 he was arrested and jailed for refusing to register for an allotment. He finally registered and then turned his back on political activism. In 1905 he led the Nighthawk Keetoowahs to split from the more politicized Keetoowah Society and establish sacred fires throughout the nation. Under his leadership the Nighthawk Keetoowahs wrote a constitution defining themselves as a strictly religious organization, recognized the seven Cherokee clans as fundamental to the stomp dance, and reconfigured the stomp ground to reflect the Cherokee clans rather than the Creek and Natchez pattern of four arbors that had been followed previously (see **religion**).

Southeastern Ceremonial Complex

With much of the symbolism well-developed during middle **Woodland** times, the Southeast Ceremonial Complex, or Southern Cult, reached its fullest expression during the **Mississippian tradition**. The complex showed widespread consistent symbolism, stretching from Texas to the Atlantic and from the Ohio valley south through Florida. The expressions included stylized images of mythical and otherworldly animals such as winged serpents, humanoids such as birdlike warriors with the attributes of other animals, and a cross in a circle that perhaps depicted the earth and the cardinal directions. Chiefs adopted elaborate, exotic regalia to emphasize their status, which included ritual axes, carved shell gorgets, elaborate headdresses, and feather cloaks. A vigorous trade in finished crafts helped spread symbols of the complex, and specific chiefdoms gained renown as producers of specific objects. Many chiefs, for example, prized **Etowah** copper carvings. Carved shell from the Atlantic reached as far as **Cahokia**. The Southeast Ceremonial Complex probably related most closely to the power and influence of chiefs and may have been meant to symbolize and enhance their power. The complex died out with the collapse of the **chiefdoms**, though much of the symbolism remained in the beliefs of many groups of the Southeast.

Swimmer, Ross (Cherokee, b. 1943)

Born in Oklahoma City, Swimmer graduated from law school at the University of Oklahoma. In 1972 he became the general counsel for the Cherokee Nation. Beginning in 1975 the Cherokees elected Swimmer to three terms as principal chief. During this time he negotiated for the return of the Cherokee Capitol Building in Tahlequah, provided for construction of the W. W. Hastings Hospital in Tahlequah, and successfully lobbied Congress to pass legislation enabling the Cherokee Nation to sue for the value of resources removed from their land. In 1976 Swimmer guided the nation in drafting a constitution to replace the one of 1839. Throughout his term as principal chief he emphasized prosperity through **self-determination** and asset utilization. Although diagnosed with non-Hodgkins lymphoma in 1981, he won reelection in 1983, with Wilma **Mankiller** as his deputy chief. In 1985 Ronald Reagan appointed Swimmer assistant secretary of the interior for Indian affairs. As the head of the Bureau of Indian Affairs, he continued to emphasize tribal self-government and economic self-sufficiency. Swimmer resigned and returned to Tulsa in 1989 to a private law practice and, in 1992, he became president of Cherokee Nation Industries (see **self-determination**).

termination

Dwight Eisenhower's presidential victory in 1952 put the Republican Party in power for the first time in 20 years. Eager to dismantle as much of the New Deal as they could, Republican congressmen sought ways to reduce the budget and cut the federal bureaucracy. Indians were ideal targets because they lacked national political power, possessed valuable timber and mineral resources, and lived on reservations that could easily be described to an ill-informed citizenry as concentration camps. House Concurrent Resolution 108 (August 1, 1953) expressed the "sense of Congress" that the treaty relations between the tribes and the government should be terminated. Couched in terms of "freeing" the Indians from supervision, Congress hoped to wipe out tribal governments, end the various economic and social services the government provided under the treaties, sell off tribal resources, obliterate the reservations, and forcibly integrate Native people into mainstream society. Several Southern tribes were slated for termination, including the

Eastern Band of Cherokees and the Seminoles, but the Catawbas and the Coushattas were the only ones Congress terminated. Termination was so disastrous and opposition was so fierce, particularly from Native people represented by the National Congress of American Indians, that Democrats John F. Kennedy and Lyndon Johnson drifted away from it. In 1970 President Richard M. Nixon formally renounced termination and committed the federal government to the policy of **self-determination**.

Tiger, Jerome (Creek/Seminole, 1941–1967)

Born in Eufala and raised in Muskogee, Jerome Tiger was shaped from childhood by the same forces of tradition and modernity that influence many Creeks. The West Eufala Baptist Church, led by his minister grandfather, was a rural communal village where Tiger experienced a traditional childhood. When he was ten, his family moved to Muskogee, where his world was largely non-Indian. In the public schools of Muskogee Tiger found his two passions, art and boxing. He served in the navy and attended Cooper School of Art in Cleveland before settling down in Muskogee to a remarkably prolific artistic career. He quickly developed a unique, instantly recognizable style marked by fine lines, vivid color, and a clean uncluttered look. Painting from his Creek soul, he depicted Creek history and culture, both traditional and modern. He also continued boxing, winning the Oklahoma Golden Gloves middleweight championship. On August 13, 1967, he died from an accidental self-inflicted gunshot (see **art**).

Tishomingo (Chickasaw, c. 1736–1838)

Tishomingo was an important district chief who assumed national responsibility as the Great Warrior in 1795 after the death of **Piomingo**. Along with other Chickasaw headmen, he played an active role during the 1820s in leading the nation's resistance to **removal**. After realizing that the federal government was unwilling to protect the Chickasaws from the imposition of Mississippi law and from land-hungry Mississippi homesteaders, Tishomingo agreed to consider arguments for compliance with the United States' demands. In 1832 Tishomingo ordered the seizure of a trader's goods in the Chickasaw Nation, charging that the trader operated the store illegally under Chickasaw law. A Mississippi court ruled against Tishomingo, fined him $500, and threw him in jail. He saw removal differently after this incident and acquiesced to the agreement signed at Pontotoc Creek in 1832 that allowed for the cession of the Chickasaws' remaining land in Mississippi (see **Treaty of Pontotoc**). After removal, he continued to hold a leadership position in one of the four districts of the Chickasaw Nation. The Chickasaws named their capital for him

Tomochichi (Creek/Yamacraw, c.1660–1739)

Born in Apalachicola, Tomochichi quickly rose to a leadership position in the Creek Nation because of his diplomatic skill and clan connections. About 1730 he established a village on Yamacraw Bluff on the Savannah River because of political differences with other Creeks. His village was adjacent to Savannah, founded in 1733 by James Edward Oglethorpe. With Mary Musgrove as his interpreter, he established friendly relations with Oglethorpe and his Georgia colony. In 1734 Oglethorpe took Tomochichi, his wife, nephew, and several other Yamacraw leaders to London to meet King George II at Kensington Palace, cement an alliance, and settle terms for **trade**. Frustrated by encroachments by Savannah settlers, in 1736 he relocated his village some six miles distant, but he retained good relations with Oglethorpe. At his death, Oglethorpe arranged a state funeral and buried Tomochichi in one of Savannah's squares.

Trade

Extensive trade began in middle **Woodland** times, mainly in exotic raw materials that people exchanged over long distances—obsidian from Yellowstone, shell from the Gulf of Mexico and Atlantic Ocean, copper and mica from the Appalachians. **Mississippian** people exchanged goods closer to home and often traded finely worked finished products, such as sheets of copper and shell gorgets. Europeans entered established trade networks and found well-traveled trails throughout the Southeast. European demand for deerskins brought them deep into the Southeast, where they traded guns and ammunition, metal tools and kettles, fabric, and alcohol. Initially, chiefs controlled the trade and colonies imposed regulations. After 1760 this system began to break down, and alcohol became a disruptive force in many Native communities. Warfare intensified in some areas as a result of trade, especially where some groups enjoyed a technological advantage in the form of guns and ammunition and people competed for sparse resources. With the American Revolution the trade slowly diminished in the Southeast as Native people ceded hunting grounds, foraging livestock depleted deer habitats, and transatlantic merchants turned their attention from deerskins to cotton. Native hunters had become well acquainted with the market, however, and so they turned their attention to other enterprises including livestock herding, plantation agriculture, taverns, stores, toll roads, and ferries.

Treaty of Dancing Rabbit Creek
Signed on September 27, 1830, this was the removal treaty of the Choctaw
Nation. Secretary of War John H. Eaton and John Coffee negotiated for the
United States; Greenwood Leflore, **Mushulatubbee**, and Nittakaichee,
chiefs of the three districts, headed the Choctaw delegation. In return for
the cession of all their land in the East and a commitment to move to the
West, the United States affirmed the nation's right to possess forever the tract
located west of Arkansas between the Canadian and Red Rivers. **Removal**
was to occur in three waves, one-third of the nation in each, between 1831
and 1833. The United States agreed to pay the costs of removal and subsistence in the West for one year, compensate for abandoned improvements,
increase the annuity payments by $20,000 for 20 years, and underwrite the
costs of constructing schools, paying teachers, and providing 40 scholarships
a year for 20 years for higher education. Several reserves of up to 2,560 acres
were set aside within the cession for various prominent Choctaw individuals
and others who had already become farmers. Eaton and Coffee regarded
these tracts as bribes because the recipients could sell them, pocket the
money, and accompany the rest of the Choctaws west. One of the most
controversial provisions of the treaty authorized any head of household who
wished to remain in Mississippi as a citizen of the state to apply to William
Ward, the Choctaw agent, for a grant of 640 acres for him or herself plus
additional tracts of 320 acres for unmarried children over 10 years of age
and 160 acres for each child under ten. If the recipients lived on and improved these tracts for five years, they received clear title. Ward made it
extremely difficult to make application for these reserves and only 69 families
ultimately received them. One of those who remained was Greenwood **Leflore**, chief of the Western district.

Treaty of Doaksville
Signed January 17, 1837, this is the agreement concluded between Chickasaw and Choctaw commissioners that provided the Chickasaw Nation with
a home in Indian Territory. The Chickasaw removal treaty, signed October
20, 1832, at Pontotoc Creek, stipulated that removal would occur only when
the Chickasaws found a suitable location in the West. Chickasaw land rangers repeatedly explored Indian Territory but found nothing that did not already belong to another tribe. During the mid-1830s life for the Chickasaws
in Mississippi became increasingly difficult, while both federal and state
pressure on them to remove was continually more intense. Finally, in an act
of desperation, the Chickasaws decided to pursue the idea of moving in with

the Choctaws. This treaty finalized that arrangement. In return for a payment of $530,000, the Choctaw Nation deeded to the Chickasaw Nation a tract of territory that would become the Chickasaw District of the Choctaw Nation. Incorporated within the Choctaw Nation as one of four administrative districts, the Chickasaw Nation surrendered its sovereignty in order to find a home for its people. The terms of the treaty guaranteed a total separation of tribal funds but in other ways provided for "equal rights and privileges" for Chickasaws. They could live anywhere, they had full citizenship rights, and the Chickasaw Nation became a full partner in future negotiations with the United States. This situation prevailed until 1855 when the Chickasaws, at the cost of $150,000, secured Choctaw agreement to the conversion of the Chickasaw District into the sovereign Chickasaw Nation.

Treaty of Fort Jackson
Signed August 9, 1814, by Major General Andrew Jackson and 36 Creek chiefs, this treaty ended the so-called Creek War of 1813–14. Fort Jackson was a temporary military stockade hastily erected at the confluence of the Coosa and Tallapoosa River in present Alabama, the site of the long-abandoned French Fort Toulouse. The Creek War had its origins in a civil conflict between two groups of Creeks, the Redsticks, who were religious revitalizationists and cultural conservatives, and the supporters of the chiefs, most of whom believed that the best hope for the Creek Nation was to preserve a friendly relation with the United States. State and federal military became involved in the Creek civil war at the invitation of the chiefs, who feared that they were about to be overwhelmed by the Redsticks. Jackson replaced General Thomas Pinckney as the negotiator of peace with the Creeks, but not before Pinckney had led the chiefs to believe that a land cession would be taken only from the Redstick towns. Jackson repudiated that idea, however, and demanded a cession of 22 million acres, more than half the territory of the Creek Nation, which required many allied Creek towns to surrender their lands as well. Jackson was motivated, in large part, by a desire to split the Southern tribes into isolated islands of tribal lands surrounded by American territory occupied by settlers. He therefore demanded the cession of the lands on the western and southern border of the Creek Nation, thereby separating the Creeks from the Seminoles to the south and the Choctaws and Chickasaws to the west. Vigorous and unanimous objections by the Creek chiefs failed to move Jackson, who threatened to turn his army against them if they withheld agreement. Thus they signed. They also sent a protest to Washington, along with complaints against Jack-

son drafted by their agent, Benjamin Hawkins. The Senate ratified the treaty, however, and the Creeks lost the land.

Treaty of Indian Springs

On February 12, 1825, William McIntosh and 50 other Creeks signed a treaty negotiated at McIntosh's tavern at Indian Springs with government commissioners Duncan G. Campbell and James Meriwether. The Creek signatories agreed to cede all of the nation's land claimed by Georgia plus two-thirds of their holdings located within the boundaries of Alabama. The United States agreed to grant an equal amount of land west of the Mississippi between the Arkansas and Canadian Rivers and pay $400,000 to cover the costs of removal, subsistence in the West, and improvements abandoned in the East. This arrangement was in opposition to the will of the Creek National Council, and McIntosh was the only high ranking chief who signed it. Despite the fact that the Creek signatories lacked authorization to negotiate a treaty or sell the nation's land, the U.S. Senate ratified and President John Quincy Adams proclaimed the document March 7, 1825. Failing to convince the government that the treaty was illegal, the Creek Council met, cited its law which pronounced a death sentence on anyone who sold national land without council authority, tried McIntosh in absentia, and convicted and sentenced him. The council appointed Menawa, a war leader from Okfuskee, to head a force of specially appointed police to execute McIntosh and two others. They carried out their orders on May 1, 1825. The Georgia state government reacted to the execution of McIntosh by threatening to invade the Creek Nation with its militia. In order to defuse a potentially explosive situation, President Adams invited the Creek Council to send a delegation to Washington to consult about the crisis. The result of the discussions was a new treaty, signed January 24, 1826. This document declared the Treaty of Indian Springs null and void and sold the land desired by Georgia for $217,600 plus a perpetual annuity of $20,000. The United States agreed to acquire land in the West, where the friends and relatives of McIntosh and any other Creeks who might wish to could move, and guaranteed to the Creeks the land claimed by Alabama that had been ceded in the nullified treaty. The United States also agreed to pay various compensations for improvements abandoned, property belonging to McIntosh that had been destroyed, as well as the costs of **removal** plus subsistence in the West for one year.

Treaty of New Echota

When the favorable decision in **Worcester v. Georgia** brought no relief, and as the Georgia lottery continued to give away Cherokee land under the terms of Georgia law, a small group of Cherokees began to argue that **removal** was the only way to safeguard the lives and futures of the Cherokee people. Led by Elias **Boudinot**, former editor of the *Cherokee Phoenix*, his cousin John **Ridge**, and his uncle Major **Ridge**, these people had attempted to generate a public debate on the merits of removal that the government and the people refused to consider. In frustration, late in 1835 they made it clear that they were willing to talk to American commissioners William Carroll and John Schermerhorn on the subject of removal. Meeting in late December in New Echota, the capital of the Cherokee Nation, the two sides agreed to and signed the treaty. In return for the cession of all the Cherokee lands in the East, the American commissioners agreed to pay $5 million, affirmed the earlier grant of land west of the Mississippi, and added the 800,000-acre "Neutral Lands" in what became southeastern Kansas for a payment of $500,000. The American commissioners also agreed that the United States would establish various funds to meet the many social needs of the Cherokees. These funds—$200,000 for government expenses, $50,000 for orphans, $150,000 to augment the school fund, $100,000 for poor relief, and others— were to be invested in public stocks, the interest to be paid annually to the Cherokee government. At government expense, including the promise to include a physician with every detachment, the Cherokee delegates agreed that within two years of ratification of the treaty the Cherokee people would remove. Principal Chief John **Ross** and an official delegation of Cherokees were in Washington when the treaty was presented to the Senate for ratification. Despite their vigorous protests, and with the realization that the Treaty Party was an unofficial and unrepresentative minority group of Cherokee citizens, the Senate ratified the treaty in May 1836. Over the next two years the Ross government worked tirelessly to overturn the treaty. Having failed, in May 1838 federal and Georgia troops arrived in the Cherokee Nation to enforce the removal order. In 1839 unknown assailants killed the two Ridges and Boudinot for having violated Cherokee law by selling national lands without authorization.

Treaty of New York
The Creeks had refused to send delegates to meet Congressional peace commissioners at **Hopewell** because the officials were under orders to demand that the Creek council validate cessions of land made to Georgia in 1783 by a handful of town chiefs acting independently of council authority. Thus, throughout the 1780s, the Creek Nation and the United States remained in a state of war. Indeed, in 1786 Creek warriors attacked and drove off all Georgia settlers who had attempted to occupy the contested tract.

Alexander **McGillivray**, who had emerged during the 1780s as one of the most influential Creek leaders, announced that he would never negotiate with the United States under those circumstances. The establishment of U.S. constitutional government in 1789 changed the balance of power in the Southeast and convinced McGillivray that the Creeks needed to negotiate with the new government. At the same time, President George Washington and Secretary of War Henry Knox accepted McGillivray's argument that the cession of lands to Georgia had been illegal. Under those circumstances, in 1790 McGillivray and a number of Creek leaders journeyed to New York to discuss a treaty. Negotiated largely between McGillivray and Knox, the document was signed August 7. The two nations agreed to peace and an exchange of prisoners. They also defined the eastern and northern boundary of the Creek Nation in such a way as to convey much of the land ceded illegally in 1783 to Georgia. The United States agreed to guarantee all remaining Creek lands, to defend Creek borders, to require all Americans who wished to enter the nation to obtain a passport first, and recognized the right of the Creek government to punish any Americans who entered the nation illegally for whatever reason. Knox authorized the payment of a $1,500 perpetual annuity, the distribution of various trade goods, and promised to donate for the future benefit of the Creek people an unspecified amount of livestock, draft animals, and agricultural implements. This was the first formal expression of the "civilization" policy Knox and Washington had devised. Knox and McGillivray also agreed on two secret articles. One appointed McGillivray to the rank of brigadier general in the U.S. Army at a salary of $1,500 per year, the other permitted the importation of goods duty free through American ports. And finally, the treaty prohibited any treaty relation between the Creek Nation and any state. McGillivray and Knox hoped this provision would protect the Creeks from future aggressions by the state of Georgia.

Treaty of Payne's Landing

In 1823, following the purchase of Florida from Spain and its organization as a territory, the United States and the Seminoles began treaty relations. In return for annuities and permission for a handful of villages to remain in the Florida Panhandle, the Seminoles exchanged their claims to Florida and received a reservation in the peninsula north of Lake Okeechobee. The reservation was not fertile enough to sustain the number of Seminoles located there and many lived off the reservation. Many African Americans claimed as slaves by Georgia and Florida planters lived with the Seminoles (see **slavery**). For both reasons, Floridians welcomed the **removal** policy and agitated for the expulsion of the Seminoles. In May 1832 James Gadsden met at Payne's Landing on the Oklawaha River with a delegation of Seminole leaders to discuss removal. The treaty, signed May 9, stipulated that for $15,400 cash, a $3,000 annuity for 15 years, an extension for 10 years of their $1,000 annuity for a blacksmith, reimbursement for cattle, payment of up to $7,000 to settle the claims of planters for lost or stolen slaves, and a blanket for every man and a frock for every woman the Seminoles surrendered their reservation in Florida and agreed to remove to the West at government expense and unite with the Creeks in their nation. The arrangement was conditional on an excursion to the western Creek country to permit seven named chiefs, accompanied by an interpreter and John Phagan, their agent, to decide that the land was good and the Creeks were willing to have them move in. On March 28, 1833, while in the West, the seven Seminole chiefs signed an agreement at Fort Gibson with three American commissioners, Montfort Stokes, Henry L. Ellsworth, and John F. Schermerhorn, that expressed their satisfaction with the land offered them in the Creek Nation. Although the Seminole council had authorized the chiefs to inspect and report only, the federal government interpreted this document as binding on the nation and insisted that it fulfill its obligation to remove.

Treaty of Pontotoc

The Chickasaws first discussed removal with Secretary of War John Eaton and John Coffee in August 1830 at Eaton's plantation near Franklin, Tennessee. The provisions for removal depended on the ability of Chickasaw land rangers to select a block of land suitable for their nation somewhere south of 36 degrees 30 minutes latitude. But all the land south of that line had already been granted to the Choctaws, Creeks, and Cherokees, leaving nothing for the Chickasaws, and the treaty became null and void. A second negotiation, again with John Coffee, occurred at the Chickasaw council grounds on Pontotoc Creek in October 1832. This treaty and its supplement, plus a second treaty concluded in May 1834 in Washington with Secretary Eaton and its supplement, represent the most elaborate, comprehensive, and complex removal agreement completed between a Native nation and the United States. Removal continued to depend on finding a suitable homeland, no longer limited to the country south of 36-30, but failure no longer voided the arrangement. Indeed, from the beginning the government expected the Chickasaws to move in with the Choctaws, despite the disinclination of either party to such a solution. The basic Pontotoc agreement prevailed throughout. The United States agreed to survey the Chickasaw Nation and offer it for sale at auction under the rules of the General Land Office. The Chickasaws would receive the proceeds of the sale, minus all expenses incurred by the United States, to be invested in stocks as a national fund. The tribe would pay for its own removal. Between the completion of the survey and removal, Chickasaw families were authorized to select reserves, to include their homes, in sizes ranging from one to four sections (a section is one square mile, or 640 acres) depending on their size, with additional sections available to slaveholders (see **slavery**). The government agreed to remove all intruders who entered the nation before removal. Chickasaw negotiators also provided a $100 annuity to **Tishomingo**, nearing 100 years of age, and $50 annually for the aged Queen Pucaunla, mother of the Chickasaw king Ishtehotopa. The supplement affirmed the rights of female heads of families to reserves and set the minimum auction price for improved reserves at $3.00 per acre, far above the minimum government price of $1.25 per acre. The 1834 document made the reserves personal rather than tribal property and created a seven-member commission with the authority to supervise and validate their sales. Under these terms if a Chickasaw head of family was deemed competent by the tribal commission to manage his or her own affairs, that person could negotiate the sale of his or her reserve and pocket the proceeds. If the commission decided that a head of family was not competent, it would supervise the sale and dispose of the income in the name of the holder of the reserve. The system was designed, of course, to assure that every Chickasaw citizen received a fair deal. The commission was empowered to administer reserves for orphans as well. Members of the commission received extra sections in payment for service, as did other especially deserving individuals. Two Mississippi attorneys, for example, shared a section as payment for representation and advice. This document also carefully modified the General Land Office rules in order to maximize the price of reserves and required the United States to give the Chickasaw Nation a complete accounting of the land sales every six months. The supplement to the 1834 treaty provided $3,000 to pay the expenses of "old chiefs" Levi **Colbert** and Isaac Alberson to take the waters at a spa in order to recover their health and earmarked another $3,000 to be spent annually for 15 years to educate young Chickasaw men and women in American colleges. Despite the provisions that required the United States to protect the Chickasaws from intruders and the oppressions of Mississippi law, scoundrels and cheats hounded them mercilessly and the council began to take seriously the prospect of moving into the Choctaw Nation. In January

1837 Chickasaw and Choctaw delegates worked out the terms in the **Treaty of Doaksville. Removal** occurred as soon as possible thereafter.

Treaty of Washington

Unlike the other treaties negotiated in the early 1830s with the Southern tribes, the March 24, 1832, treaty concluded between Secretary of War Lewis Cass and a delegation of Creek leaders was not a removal treaty. The brainchild of **Opothle Yohola**, speaker of the Creek National Council, this was an allotment treaty designed to permit the Creeks to remain in the East in autonomous town clusters. The treaty called for a cession of all the Creek land, its speedy survey, and the allotment of half sections (320 acres) to every head of family. Ninety reserves of one section each were for chiefs. The allotments were to be selected so that those belonging to the members of each town would adjoin, creating blocks of privately owned land that together would preserve the social and political integrity of the towns. Twenty half sections were earmarked for the support of orphans and 29 sections were held aside as a tribal fund. In return, the United States agreed to pay $100,000 to cover national debts and relief for the indigent, an annuity of $12,000 for five years to be followed by $10,000 for 15 years, and $3,000 per year for 20 years to support the costs of educating Creek youth. In addition, Cass agreed to compensations for ferries and bridges, legal judgments against chiefs, various damages sustained by the Creeks, and pensions for several elderly chiefs. In hopes that the Creeks would choose to remove rather than remain in the East, the government permitted the allottees to sell their reserves under supervision and agreed to pay the costs of transport and subsistence for one year, provide each warrior with a rifle and ammunition and each family with a blanket. The government agreed to protect the Creeks from intruders while the surveys and selection of allotments were underway.

Tuscarora War (1711–13)

The Tuscarora War resulted from a combination of trade abuses and the establishment of European settlements that encroached on Tuscarora lands. Although they initially prospered as middlemen between European traders and other Southeastern tribes, by the early 1700s the Tuscaroras had lost their ability to control the trade satisfactorily. Indebted to the traders, Tuscarora hunters returned to their villages to find them looted by Carolinians claiming their women and children in payment for goods already consumed. In the midst of this growing tension, in 1711 Baron Christoph von Graffenried founded the Swiss colony of New Bern on Tuscarora land without payment. In retaliation, Tuscarora warriors attacked and killed some 200 settlers. Carolina troops retaliated in two invasions in 1712 and 1713 against the Tuscarora villages. Aided by several hundred Indian allies, many of them Yamasee allies of the Charles Town traders, the armies smashed a Tuscarora fort, captured many prisoners who were sold into slavery, and shattered the Tuscarora Nation (see **slavery**). Most of the survivors fled north and in 1722 joined the Iroquois Confederacy, becoming the Sixth Nation, but some may have remained in Carolina hidden away in isolated places.

Ward, Nancy (Cherokee, c. 1738–c. 1822)

Nancy Ward, or Nanye-hi, was born in Chota, near present-day Knoxville, Tennessee. She married a warrior, Kingfisher, and bore two children, Fivekiller and Catherine. In 1755, when Kingfisher was mortally wounded fighting the Creeks during the Battle of Taliwa, Ward continued fighting. The Cherokees won, and she was honored with the title War Woman. As a War Woman, she had the power to determine the fate of captives and to dance with warriors. After menopause, her title became Beloved Woman. She married a white trader, Brian Ward, and, during the Revolutionary War, Ward urged the Cherokees not to fight against the American colonists. When Cherokee warriors planned to raid white settlements in 1776 and 1780, Nancy Ward warned the white communities. Following the 1776 raid along the Holston River, she freed Mrs. William Bean, a white captive, who supposedly taught Ward how to make butter. In 1781 she helped free traders whom the Cherokee had captured. Ward spoke at treaty conferences with the United States in 1781 and 1785. In 1817 she sent a message to the Cherokee Council urging them not to cede land. The nation ceded Chota in 1819. Ward moved to the Ocoee River in eastern Tennessee, where she opened an inn.

warfare

Small populations inhibited warfare until middle **Woodland** times, when competition for resources led to violence. The scale of violence increased with the rise of **Mississippian** culture, as seen in the frequent use of wooden palisades to protect villages and the martial motifs common in the **Southeastern Ceremonial Complex**. Chiefs often conquered their neighbors and demanded tribute, and De Soto met several chiefs who tried to use the Spaniards to achieve their own military goals (see **chiefdoms**). By the time of the eighteenth century Southeastern men practiced warfare on a smaller scale, sometimes to protect resources, but usually to restore social and spiritual balance through clan vengeance. European wars involved numerous Native American groups who found advantage in siding with one or another European power for political or economic reasons. **Kinship** continued to play an important part in warfare well into the American period, but other issues increasingly embroiled Native people in armed conflicts. The **Creek War** (1811–14) inadvertently drew the Creeks into the War of 1812, and the Five Tribes in Indian Territory, as well as some tribes in the Southeast, participated in the American **Civil War**. Southern Indians also fought in all the wars of the twentieth century, often in numbers disproportionately high for their populations, and modern powwows usually include a dance honoring warriors/veterans.

Watie, Stand (Cherokee, 1806–1871)

Watie was a leader of the Confederate Cherokees. Born near present-day Rome, Georgia, Watie studied at the Spring Place Moravian Mission. In addition to farming, he operated a ferry, was temporary editor of the *Cherokee Phoenix* in 1832, and served as the clerk of the Cherokee Supreme Court from 1823 to 1830. In 1835 he signed the **Treaty of New Echota**, and two years later he moved to Honey Creek in Indian Territory. In 1839 he escaped execution for signing the removal treaty, and he became the leader of the Treaty Party. In September 1842 he married Sarah Caroline Bell, his fourth wife. He was a principal signatory of the Treaty of 1846 that ended the chaos that had raged since removal. In the years before the Civil War he served the Cherokee Nation as an interpreter, clerk of the Supreme Court, and member and speaker of the council. In 1861, before the Cherokee Nation officially joined the Confederacy, Watie began enlisting soldiers, and during the **Civil War** he rose to the rank of brigadier-general, participating in battles at Wilson's Creek (1861), Chustenahlah (1861), and Pea Ridge (1862). Once the Cherokee Nation divided, Watie became principal chief of the Southern Party. After the war he represented the Confederate Cherokees at the Fort Smith conference (see **Reconstruction treaties**). He ultimately moved to Webbers Falls, practiced law, farmed, and engaged in milling and tobacco manufacturing. In 1870 he was a delegate to the General Council of Indian Territory.

Woodland tradition (1000 b.c.–a.d. 1600)

Beginning about 3,000 years ago, people in the Southeast began to use developments of the late **Archaic** more extensively, namely, pottery, plant cultivation, and mortuary rituals. Pottery and **agriculture** became widespread in the Southeast, bringing a more sedentary lifestyle and a greater connection to place than earlier peoples had. They also began burying their dead in mounds. Middle Woodland peoples added large earthworks to their cultures, often with elaborate designs and symbolic meanings. Woodland people exchanged raw materials great distances, especially obsidian, copper, and mica. The trade fairs at **Poverty Point** are an example of this far-flung **trade**. By A.D. 400, the Middle Woodland gave way to a more dispersed, tribal people who built no large earthworks but developed a more defined and consistent pottery tradition. Ethnic differences between people may have developed, as did a stronger reliance on clans to solve political problems. **Mississippian** began to replace many of the Woodland cultures by A.D. 800, but some Woodland peoples still lived in the Southeast at European contact.

Worcester v. *Georgia* (1832)

This U.S. Supreme Court decision of March 1832, delivered by Chief Justice John Marshall, reinforced the status of Indian nations as sovereign. The case was brought on behalf of Samuel Worcester, a missionary to the Cherokees who was imprisoned by the state of Georgia for his failure to take an oath of allegiance to the state. The Court ruled that state law could not extend into the Cherokee Nation and instructed Georgia to free Worcester. Marshall's decision affirmed that the Cherokees were self-governing because "a weaker power does not surrender its independence — its right to self-government, by associating with a stronger, and taking its protection." This argument has become the doctrine of "retained sovereignty" and is a cornerstone of federal Indian law. The Georgia government refused to act, however, and Worcester remained in jail until freed by a gubernatorial pardon.

Yamassee War (1715–17)

Beginning as a punitive military campaign against British **trade** policies, the Yamassee War ultimately involved colonists and Native groups throughout much of Georgia and South Carolina. Named for the principal organizers of the insurgency movement, the Yamassees allied with the Creeks and protested growing Indian debt, English slaving raids against Indian villages, and unfair treatment in trade. Actions first began against traders working in Indian towns—between 60 and 80 were killed in the first three days—and then moved toward Charleston. With the city besieged, the

English responded with their military supported by Cherokee allies. They soon crushed the Yamassee resistance, most of whom fled south and fell under the protection of their Spanish allies. In peace negotiations with the Creeks the English agreed to define boundaries, regulate trade, and end dealing in Indian slaves (see **slavery**). The British Crown took control of the colonies and revoked the trade monopoly of the Carolina proprietors to ensure peace.

Part III

Chronology

75,000–45,000 B.C.	First exposure of Bering land bridge makes human migration from Asia possible.
23,000–12,000 B.C.	Second exposure of Bering land bridge provides the opportunity for an extended period of human migration.
8000 B.C.	Paleo-Indian tradition, the culture of early Native people in the Americas that was characterized by hunting of big-game animals, ends.
8000–700 B.C.	Archaic tradition, in which specific regional variations began to emerge, results in the appearance of pottery, atlatls, and domesticated plants in the South.
3000 B.C.	Agriculture emerges in the Southeast. Pottery first appears in the region.
700 B.C.–A.D. 1600	Woodland tradition, characterized by burial mounds and the cultivation of corn, squash, and beans, is widespread in the South.
A.D. 300	Corn, which originated in Central America, appears in the Southeast.
800–1600	Mississippian tradition, characterized by chiefdoms, temple mounds, and intensive agriculture, dominates the South.
1000	Beans are first cultivated in the Southeast.
1492	Columbus arrives in the Caribbean
1493	Papal Donation recognizes Spain's claims to America and requires the Christianization of the Native people.

1512	Laws of Burgos forbid enslavement of Indians and establish the *encomienda*.
1513	Ponce de Leon explores Florida.
1519–21	Spanish conquer Aztecs in Mexico.
c. 1520	European disease appears in Southeast
1526	Lucas Vásquez de Allyón attempts to plant colony on Georgia coast.
1528	Pánfilo de Narváez attempts to establish a colony of 400 people on the coast of the Gulf of Mexico in present-day Florida.
1533	Pizarro conquers Inca empire in Peru.
1539–43	Hernando de Soto conducts an expedition across the interior Southeast.
1542	New Laws of the Indies require Catholic Church to expand its activities in order to prepare Native people for integration into Spanish American society.
1559–61	Tristán de Luna y Arellano expedition attempts and fails to establish two colonies, one at Ochuse on Pensacola Bay and one in the interior at Coosa.
1565	Pedro Menéndez de Avilés founds Santa Elena and St. Augustine.
	Jesuits begin ministry to the Guales.
1566–68	Juan Pardo conducts two expeditions from Santa Elena into the interior Southeast.
1573	Pacification Ordinance forbids military conquest of Native people.
	Franciscans replace Jesuits in La Florida.
1585	Walter Raleigh founds English colony on Roanoke Island in present-day North Carolina.
1587	Franciscans establish Timucua missions.
	Raleigh's "Lost Colony" settles Roanoke.
	John White explores Carolina coast and draws pictures of Indians.
1597	Guales revolt against the Spanish.
1605	The Spanish reopen the Guale missions.
1607	The English colony of Jamestown is founded.
1618	Tobacco becomes a major crop in Virginia and makes Native land more valuable than Native trade.
1622–34	War between the Powhatans and Virginia over English encroachments.

1633	Franciscans establish Apalachee missions.
1634	Maryland founded.
1644–46	War between the Powhatans and Virginia, in which the Powhatans are decisively defeated.
1647	Apalachees revolt against the Spanish.
1656	Timucuas revolt against the Spanish.
1670	The English found Carolina.
1676	Bacon's Rebellion in Virginia is precipitated in part by demands for Indian land.
1680	The Savannahs, armed with guns from Carolina, wipe out the Westoes.
1683	The Spanish close their Guale missions.
1684	La Salle constructs French colony near present-day Galveston, Texas, which lasts until Indians destroy it three years later.
1689–97	King William's War between France and England engages Indian allies and initiates nearly a century of intermittent wars for empire in North America.
1699	French build a fort at Biloxi Bay.
1702	French found Mobile.
1702–08	English destroy Spanish missions in north Florida.
1702–13	England and France fight Queen Anne's War.
1711–13	Traders' abuse of Indian people, the enslavement of Indians, and land encroachment provoke the Tuscarora War, in which the Tuscaroras are defeated.
1715	A confederation of Southern Indians punish traders for abuse in the Yamassee War and kill almost all English traders except those in the Cherokee Nation.
1717	French construct Fort Toulouse near present-day Montgomery, Alabama.
1718	French found New Orleans.
1722	Main body of the Tuscaroras joins Iroquois Confederacy.
1729	The Natchez revolt against the French and their destruction of Fort Rosalie provokes a French and Choctaw invasion that defeated the Natchez and dispersed them among other tribes.
1732	Beginning of a sustained French effort to destroy the Chickasaws, who were trading partners and military allies of the English.

1733	Georgia founded.
1738	Smallpox devastates Cherokees.
1744–48	King George's War erupts between England and France and their Indian allies.
1756–63	French and Indian War (Seven Years War) results in the French loss of Canada and Louisiana and the end of French involvement with Southern Indians.
1758	English build Ft. Loudoun and Fort Prince George in the Cherokee nation ostensibly to offer protection to villages while warriors fought the French to the north but in actuality to monitor and manipulate the Cherokees.
1759–61	Cherokee War breaks out when the English kill allied warriors and then murder prominent chiefs held as hostages. Devastating invasion follows the fall of Fort Loudoun, and the Cherokees ultimately surrender.
1763	Royal Proclamation prohibits English settlement west of the Appalachians.
	British grant Catawbas 144,000-acre reservation.
1764	Alabamas and Coushattas leave villages in the Creek Nation and settle further west.
c. 1775	A group of Cherokees settle on St. Francis River in Arkansas.
1776–83	American Revolution
1783	Peace of Paris ends the American Revolution and conveys title to all land previously claimed by the English king east of the Mississippi between the Great Lakes and Florida without reference to the Indians.
	Treaty of Augusta, negotiated with the state of Georgia, recognizes Creek responsibility for property lost by Georgians in the revolution and agrees to a land cession as compensation.
1784	Creeks, Choctaws, and Chickasaws sign treaties with the Spanish that recognize their land claims and promise trade and military aid. These treaties provide an example of the play-off diplomacy that enabled Indians to retain autonomy and resist the demands of the United States.
1785	Treaty of Galphinton between an unauthorized and unrepresentative group of Creeks and the state of Georgia confirms the Treaty of Augusta and increases the size of the cession.

1785–86	Treaties of Hopewell with the Cherokees, Chickasaws, and Choctaws open formal relations between these tribes and the United States and reaffirm the British practice of negotiating treaties with Indians.
1789	Constitution of the United States conveys the authority to conduct Indian relations to the federal government.
1790	Treaty of New York, the first treaty between the Creek Nation and the United States, establishes peace, provides for a land cession, and initiates the government's "civilization" program among the Creeks by providing tools and instruction.
	First Trade and Intercourse Act establishes rules to regulate trade, prohibits unauthorized persons from entering tribal lands, and outlines relations between the United States and the tribes.
1791	Treaty of Holston with the Cherokees promises them instruction in and assistance with "civilization," a program intended to make it possible to assimilate Indians into American society.
1794	Chickamaugas, Cherokees who had continued to wage war after the end of the American Revolution, make peace with the United States.
1796	Congress establishes government trading factories. Tennessee enters the Union.
1796–1816	Benjamin Hawkins serves as chief federal agent to southern Indians.
1798	Congress creates Mississippi Territory, which is home to Cherokees, Chickasaws, Choctaws, and Creeks and later becomes the states of Mississippi and Alabama. Moravians request permission to open school among Cherokees.
1799	A Presbyterian missionary arrives among Chickasaws.
1803	Louisiana Purchase from France roughly doubles the size of the United States and prompts Thomas Jefferson to consider the possibility of relocating eastern Indians to the vast region.
1808	Cherokees begin recording laws, reorder inheritance patterns to provide for patrilineal descent, and establish a national police force.

1810	Cherokee migration to Arkansas follows cession of territory in the Southeast.
1813	Virginia allots Gingaskin reservation.
1811–14	Creek Civil War pits Creeks against each other and provides an opportunity for the United States to intervene.
1814	Treaty of Fort Jackson ends the Creek War and requires an enormous cession of Creek land, much of it home to Creeks who actually allied with the United States.
1815	Treaty of Ghent ends War of 1812.
1817	Alabama Territory organized.
	Mississippi admitted to Union.
	Cherokees enact their Articles of Government, a formal structure for political decision-making, centralized authority, and delegated power.
1816–18	First Seminole War is caused by the United States invasion of Spanish Florida to destroy the "Negro Fort" and Seminole towns engaged in raids across the border. The U.S. capture of St. Marks and hanging of two Englishmen encourages Spain to sell Florida to the United States.
1817–19	Cherokees migrate to Arkansas following land cessions in the southeast.
1818	Creeks begin recording their laws.
	Quapaws relinquish territory south of Arkansas River.
	Osage cede land in Oklahoma.
1819	Alabama admitted as a state.
	Panic of 1819 ends the boom that followed the War of 1812 and leaves many Southerners in quest of economic opportunity, including that promised by the acquisition of Indian land.
	United States purchases Florida from Spain.
	Sixty Cherokee families in North Carolina take private reservations and become the nucleus of the Eastern Band of Cherokees.
1820	Treaty of Doak's Stand provides for the exchange of 5 million acres of Choctaw land in the East for 13 million acres west of the Mississippi.
1821	Sequoyah invents the Cherokee syllabary.

1823	Virginia allots Nottoway reservation. Treaty of Moultrie Creek, the first treaty between the United States and the Seminoles, provides for peace, the sale of a tract of Seminole land in northern Florida, and the tribe's relocation to a reservation in the central part of the peninsula.
1824	Bureau of Indian Affairs established in the U.S. War Department.
1825	Treaty of Indian Springs, illegally negotiated with Creek chiefs who had been bribed, surrenders all Creek land in Georgia and two-thirds of their holdings in Alabama. Creeks execute William McIntosh and two others for signing the Treaty of Indian Springs. Osage cede land in Oklahoma.
1826	Treaty of Washington, at President John Quincy Adams's insistence, replaces the illegal Treaty of Indian Springs but accomplishes essentially the same things. Choctaws adopt a constitution.
1827	Cherokees write a republican constitution patterned after those of the Southern states that describes the specific territory over which the Cherokee Nation is asserting sovereignty.
1827–32	Alabama extends laws over Creeks.
1828	Arkansas Cherokees exchange their land for territory in northeastern Oklahoma.
1828–30	Georgia extends law over Cherokee Nation, abolishes Cherokee government, and makes provisions for a lottery to distribute Cherokee land to state citizens.
1828–34	*Cherokee Phoenix* published in the Sequoyah syllabary and in English.
1829	Chickasaws begin recording laws.
1830	Indian Removal Act authorizes the president to negotiate removal of eastern Indians west of the Mississippi and appropriates $500,000 for that purpose. Treaty of Dancing Rabbit Creek provides for Choctaw removal.
1831–33	Choctaw Nation moves west of the Mississippi.

1831	*Cherokee Nation* v. *Georgia* defines the Cherokees as a "domestic dependent nation" and declines to hear their appeal.
1832	Treaty of Pontotoc commits the Chickasaws to removal. Treaty of Payne's Landing provides for Seminole removal. *Worcester* v. *Georgia* recognizes Cherokee sovereignty, but Georgia ignores the decision. Treaty of Washington provides for allotment of Creek land in the East and removal of those who choose to sell out and go west.
1835	Treaty of New Echota, negotiated with an unauthorized minority, commits the Cherokee Nation to removal.
1835–42	Second Seminole War erupts when the United States army tries to remove the Seminoles by force. The conflict results in the relocation of most Seminoles into the Creek Nation west of the Mississippi.
1836	Congress awards land to several Creeks in Alabama, including Lynn McGhee, and enables them to remain in the East.
1836–37	Creeks are removed as a military action when they resist white encroachments on their allotments.
1837	Treaty of Doaksville permits the Chickasaws to settle in the Choctaw Nation. Chickasaws remove.
1836	Creeks expel Christian missionaries.
1838	Choctaws write constitution in West.
1838–39	Cherokees remove.
1839	The Cherokees execute Treaty Party leaders, Major Ridge, John Ridge, and Elias Boudinot. Cherokees write new constitution in the West.
1840	Cherokee Act of Union brings the Old Settlers and Ross party together. Creeks establish national Council in the West. Catawbas sign treaty with South Carolina ceding their reservation.
1841	Creeks permit Presbyterians to open school.
1844	Tunicas lose most of their land. *Cherokee Advoate* begins publication.

1845	Creeks permit Seminoles to establish separate towns.
1846	Treaty between Cherokee National Party and Treaty Party brings period of civil war to an end.
1849	Bureau of Indian Affairs moves from the War Department to the Department of Interior.
c. 1850	South Carolina returns 630 acres to the Catawbas.
1851	Cherokees open male and female seminaries in the West.
1854	Alabamas receive 1,280 acres in Texas; some Coushattas join them.
1855	Chickasaws purchase land from the Choctaws and establish their own nation.
1856	Chickasaws write constitution.
1855–58	Third Seminole War erupts in Florida over encroachments on land occupied by the Seminoles who had avoided removal and taken refuge in the Everglades.
1856	Seminoles who were removed establish a nation in the West separate from the Creek Nation.
1859	Creeks reject a constitution.
1861–65	Civil War in the United States engulfs Southern Indians, who spilt between the Confederacy and the Union.
1861	Cherokee, Chickasaw, Choctaw, Creek, and Seminole Nations in Indian Territory sign Confederate treaties. Opothle Yoholo and followers, who oppose the Creeks' Confederate alliance, flee to Union Kansas with Confederate Creeks and Cherokees in pursuit.
1862	Union troops invade Cherokee Nation and rescue Unionist Chief John Ross.
1864–72	Lowry War begins as Lumbee resistance to the conscription of labor by the Confderacy and, after becoming a struggle for economic and political justice in Robeson County, North Carolina, forces the state to acknowledge the Native ethnicity of the Lumbees.
1866	Reconstruction treaties reestablish United States relations with the Cherokees, Chickasaws, Choctaws, Creeks, and Seminoles after the Civil War and pave the way for economic development of Indian Territory.
1867	Creek Nation writes a constitution.

1869	United States recognizes the Eastern Band of Cherokees as a distinct tribe.
	Congress creates advisory Board of Indian Commissioners.
1870	Alabamas and Coushattas in Texas come under U.S. military jurisdiction, which, in essence, conveys federal recognition.
	Missiouri, Kansas, and Texas Railroad enters Cherokee Nation.
1870–76	Five Tribes meet annually in General Council of Indian Territory to address common problems with economic development, intruders, and conflicts of sovereignty.
1871	Congress ends treaty making with tribes, who subsequently become the object of legislation rather than participants in negotiation.
	Atlantic and Pacific (St. Louis and San Francisco) Railroad enters the Cherokee Nation.
	Cherokee Tobacco Case extends federal tax law to the Indian nations, a major step in subjecting them to federal authority.
1872	Chickasaw Oil and Gas Company founded to drill for oil on land used by Choctaws and Chickasaws.
1874	United States establishes the Union Agency in Muskogee to administer federal relations with all five southern tribes.
1883	Catholic mission to Mississippi Choctaws opens.
1883	Mormons baptize first Catawbas.
1885	Major Crimes Act makes it a federal crime for Indians to commit murder, manslaughter, rape, assault, larceny, and arson against other Indians in their own nations.
	North Carolina legislature provides schools for the Indians of Robeson County that are separate from those provided for blacks and whites.
1886	*United States* v. *Kagama*, originally a California case, brings a ruling by the U.S. Supreme Court upholding the Major Crimes Act of 1885.
1887	General Allotment (Dawes) Act, which exempts the Five Tribes, provides for the allotment of tribal land to individuals.

	North Carolina opens a normal school to train Indian teachers for segregated Indian schools.
1889	Unassigned lands in Indian Territory opened to white homesteaders.
	Eastern Band of Cherokees incorporate under North Carolina law.
1890	Western half of Indian Territory organized as Oklahoma Territory.
1891	Women's National Indian Association buys land for Florida Seminoles.
	Cherokee Oil and Gas Company founded by 36 Cherokees under the authority of the Cherokee Nation to search for oil.
1893	Cherokee Outlet opened to white homesteaders.
	Dawes Commission established to negotiate allotment agreements with the Five Tribes.
	Dawes Commission begins survey of the tribal lands of Southern Indians in Indian Territory.
	Creek Oil and Gas Company founded to explore for oil.
1896	Dawes Commission begins drawing up tribal rolls in preparation for the assignment of allotments.
1897–1902	Five Tribes negotiate allotment agreements with Dawes Commission.
1898	Curtis Act mandates allotment of the lands of Southern Indians in Indian Territory.
1901	Congress grants United States citizenship to members of the Five Tribes.
1903	In *Lone Wolf* v. *Hitchcock* the U.S. Supreme Court rules that Congress can abrogate treaties with Indians.
1904	Congress lifts restrictions on allotments of the former slaves of the Cherokees, Choctaws, Creeks, and Seminoles who received allotments.
1905	Glenn Oil Pool discovered in the Creek Nation.
1906	National governments of the Five Tribes dissolved.
1907	Oklahoma, a combination of Oklahoma Territory and Indian Territory, enters Union.
1908	Congress lifts restrictions on the allotments of people enrolled as less than "half-blood."

	Congress establishes competency commissions to determine whether or not to lift restrictions on the allotments of people who still retain them.
1911	Federal reservation established for Seminoles at Big Cyprus in south Florida.
	Society of American Indians established to work for the reform of Indian policy.
1919	Chitimacha land in Louisiana placed in trust.
1923	Virginia passes a Racial Integrity Law that redefines many of the state's Indians as "Negro."
	American Indian Defense Association organized.
1924	Congress grants citizenship to those Native people not already granted citizenship through allotment.
1926	Hollywood Reservation for Florida Seminoles opens near Fort Lauderdale.
1928	Meriam Report criticizes allotment and decries conditions in Native communities.
1930	Eastern Band Cherokees receive the right to vote.
1934	Congress passes the Indian Reorganization, or Wheeler-Howard, Act that ends allotment and enables tribes to reorganize themselves but exempts Oklahoma Indians.
1936	Oklahoma Indian Welfare Act extends some of the provisions of the Indian Reorganization Act to Oklahoma.
1939	Thlopthlocco and Alabama-Quassarte Creek tribal towns incorporate under the Oklahoma Indian Welfare Act as political entities separate from the Muskogee Creek Nation.
	Segregated public school for Poarch Creeks opens in Alabama.
1940	Kialegee Creek tribal town incorporates under the Oklahoma Indian Welfare Act.
1943	Catawbas come under the administration of the Bureau of Indian Affairs.
1943	Mississippi Choctaws write IRA constitution.
1944	Segregated public school for the Houmas opens in Louisiana.
	South Carolina purchases land for the Catawbas.

1946	Indian Claims Commission established to recommend settlement of claims of Indian tribes against the federal government.
	United Keetoowah Band of Cherokees recognized by the BIA.
1953	Congress calls for termination of federal recognition of and services to Indian tribes.
	Coushatta in Lousiana terminated.
1954	Alabama-Coushatta terminated.
1956	Relocation Act provides for the resettlement of rural Indians in urban areas.
	Congress recognizes and then terminates Lumbees.
1957	Seminole Tribe of Florida writes constitution under the provisions of the IRA.
1958	Lumbees disrupt Ku Klux Klan rally in Robeson County.
1962	Miccosukee Tribe of Indians writes constitution and receives federal recognition.
	Congress terminates the Catawbas.
1964	The U.S. Civil Rights Act prohibits segregated facilities for Native Americans as well as African Americans.
1968	Indian Civil Rights Act extends the Bill of Rights and Fourteenth Amendment to Indians in dealing with their tribal governments, but it also limits the authority of the states over tribal land.
	American Indian Movement, which militantly demands justice for Native people, is founded in Minneapolis.
1970	Louisiana Office of Indian Affairs established.
	United States permits Five Tribes to elect chiefs for the first time since Oklahoma statehood.
1971	Native American Rights Fund, which challenges injustice in the courts, is founded.
	North Carolina Commission of Indian Affairs is established.
1973	Siege at Wounded Knee, South Dakota, brings Native militancy to the fore.
1974	Florida Governors Council on Indian Affairs, Inc., is established.

1975	Indian Self-Determination and Educational Assistance Act grants Indians self-rule and the right to contract for federal services.
	Alabama Indian Affairs Commission is established.
1976	In *Harjo* v. *Kleppe* the U.S. Supreme Court rules that Creek sovereignty had never been terminated and that the constitution of 1867 was still in force.
	Cherokee Nation of Oklahoma writes a new constitution.
1978	Indian Child Welfare Act makes tribes, rather than external agencies, ultimately responsible for their children.
	BIA establishes regulations for the acknowledgment and recognition of tribes that do not have a government-to-government relationship with the United States.
1979	Seminoles open high-stakes bingo in Florida.
	Muskogee (Creek) Nation of Oklahoma writes constitution.
1981	In *Seminole Tribe of Florida* v. *Butterworth* the U.S. Supreme Court rules that Florida does not have the right to close Seminole high-stakes bingo because the state's laws permit bingo and only regulate its operation. The "retained sovereignty" of Indian tribes frees them from state regulation.
1981	Tunica-Biloxi in Louisiana are federally recognized.
1983	Virginia Council on Indians established.
	Chickasaw Nation of Oklahoma writes constitution.
1984	Poarch Band of Creeks is federally recognized.
	Choctaw Nation of Oklahoma writes a constitution.
1987	Congress restores federal recognition to the Alabama-Coushatta, who had been terminated.
1988	Congress passes the Indian Gaming Regulatory Act to provide federal oversight of tribal gaming operations.
1990	Congress passes the Native American Grave Protection and Repatriation Act, which requires museums and other institutions to inventory their human remains and funerary objects, notify the tribes to whom they belong, and facilitate repatriation.

1992	Georgia Council on American Indian Concerns is founded.
1993	Congress settles Catawba claims and restores their federal recognition.
1995	Jena Band of Choctaws in Louisiana is federally recognized.
1996	*Seminole Tribe of Florida* v. *Florida* denies the right of tribes to bring suit against states to force negotiation of gaming compacts.

Part IV

Resources

Compiled with the assistance of Joe Anoatubby, Karl Davis, and Rose Stremlau

1. Indian Tribes

Agencies that administer Indian affairs and the tribes themselves can be sources of a wealth of information about history, government, and current events.

Administration of Indian Affairs

Bureau of Indian Affairs
1849 C Street, NW
Washington, DC 20240-0001

Alabama Indian Affairs Commission
One Court Square, Suite 106
Montgomery, AL 36130

Florida Governors Council on Indian Affairs, Inc.
1341 Cross Creek Circle
Tallahassee, FL 32301

Georgia Council on American Indian Concerns
205 Butler Street, Suite 1352 E
Atlanta, GA 30334

Louisiana Office of Indian Affairs
365 N. Fourth Street
Baton Rouge, LA 70802

North Carolina Commission of Indian Affairs
217 W. Jones Street
Mail Service Center 1317
Raleigh, NC 27699-1317

Virginia Council on Indians
P.O. Box 1475
Richmond, VA 23218

Federally Recognized Tribes

Federally recognized tribes have a government-to-government relationship
with the United States, receive services administered by the Bureau of Indian
Affairs, and enjoy limited sovereignty on their tribal land that is held in trust
by the federal government.

ALABAMA

Creek Nation East of the Mississippi (Poarch Band of Creeks)
HCR69A, Box 85-B
Atmore, AL 36502

FLORIDA

Seminole Tribe of Florida
6300 Stirling Road
Hollywood, FL 33024

Miccosukee Tribe
Box 440021, Tamiami Station
Miami, FL 33144

LOUISIANA

Chitimacha Tribe
P.O. Box 661
Charenton, LA 70523

Coushatta Tribe
Box 818
Elton, LA 70532

Jena Band of Choctaws
P.O. Box 14
Jena, LA 71342-0014

Tunica-Biloxi Indian Tribe
P.O. Box 331
Marksville, LA 71351

MISSISSIPPI

Mississippi Band of Choctaw Indians
P.O. Box 6010, Choctaw Branch
Philadelphia, MS 39350

NORTH CAROLINA

Eastern Band of Cherokee Indians
P.O. Box 455
Cherokee, NC 28719

OKLAHOMA

Alabama-Quassarte Tribal Town
P.O. Box 537
Henryetta, OK 74437

Cherokee Nation of Oklahoma
P.O. Box 948
Tahlequah, OK 74465

Chickasaw Nation of Oklahoma
P.O. Box 1548
Ada, OK 74820

Choctaw Nation of Oklahoma
P.O. Drawer 1210
16th and Locust Streets
Durant, OK 74701

Kialegee Tribal Town
318 Washila, Box 332
Wetumka, OK 74883

Muskogee Nation of Oklahoma
P.O. Box 580
Okmulgee, OK 74447

Seminole Nation of Oklahoma
P.O. Box 1498
Wewoka, OK 74884

Thlopthlocco Tribal Town
P.O. Box 706
Okemah, OK 74859

United Keetoowah Band of Cherokee Indians
2450 Muskogee Ave.
P.O. Box 746
Tahlequah, OK 74465

SOUTH CAROLINA

Catawba Tribe of South Carolina
P.O. Box 11106
Rock Hill, SC 29713

TEXAS

Alabama and Coushatta Tribes of Texas
Route 3, Box 659
Livingston, TX 77351

State-Recognized Tribes

Some Southern states extend recognition to Indian tribes. The criteria and process for recognition varies substantially from state to state. The following list does not include tribes that have also been recognized by the federal government.

Alabama

Cherokees of Southeast Alabama
2212 50th Street
Valley, AL 36854

Cherokee Tribe of Northeast Alabama
53 Buckworth Circle
Trafford, AL 35172

Echota Cherokee Tribe of Alabama
59 Highway 487
Vandiver, AL 35176

Machis Lower Creek Indian Tribe
708 South John Street
New Brockton, AL 36351

Mowa Band of Choctaw Indians
1080 Red Fox Road
Mount Vernon, AL 36560

Star Clan of Muskogee Creeks
P.O. Box 126
Goshen, AL 36035

Georgia

Cherokee Tribal Council of Georgia
P.O. Box 227
St. George, GA 31646

Georgia Tribe of Eastern Cherokees
420 Walmart Way, Suite B
Box 152
Dahlonega, GA 30533

Lower Muskogee Creek Tribe—East of the Mississippi, Inc.
Route 2, Box 370
Whigham, GA 31797

NORTH CAROLINA

Coharie Intra-Tribal Council
7531 N. U.S. Highway 421
Clinton, NC 28328

Cumberland County Association for Indian People
200 Indian Drive
Fayetteville, NC 28301

Guilford Native American Association
P.O. Box 5623
Greensboro, NC 27403

Haliwa-Saponi Tribe, Inc.
P.O. Box 99
Hollister, NC 27844

Indians of Person County
846 Epps-Martin Road
Roxboro, NC 27573

Lumbee Regional Development Association
P.O. Box 68
Pembroke, NC 28372

Meherrin Indian Tribe
P.O. Box 508
Winton, NC 27986

Metrolina Native American Association
1200 W. Tyvola Road
Charlotte, NC 28217

Triangle Native American Society
P.O. Box 26841
Raleigh, NC 27611

Waccamaw Siouan Development Association
P.O. Box 221
Bolton, NC 28423

VIRGINIA

Chickahominy, Eastern Division
Providence Forge, VA 23140

Chickahominy Indian Tribe
8200 Lott Cary Road
Providence Forge, VA 23140

Mattaponi Indian Reservation
Route 2, Box 240
West Point, VA 23181

Monacan Indian Tribe
P.O. Box 1136
Madison Heights, VA 24572

Nansemond Indian Tribal Association
P.O. Box 2095
Portsmouth, VA 23702-2095

Pamunkey Nation
Route 1, Box 2220
King William, VA 23086

United Rappahannock Tribe
HCR 1, Box 2
Indian Neck, VA 23148

Upper Mattaponi
P.O. Box 183
King William, VA 23086

Other Tribes in the Southeast

The following tribes have petitioned the Bureau of Indian Affairs for federal recognition or they have notified the bureau of their intent to petition as of April 2000. This list by no means includes all Southeastern tribes, but since tribes change names, divide, unite, organize, and disband, a complete list is virtually impossible to compile. Addresses, which shift frequently for some groups as their leadership changes, have been omitted, but these usually can be obtained from the BIA. The following information can be found on the BIA Web site, as can petition numbers and the status of petitions. The categories are those used by the BIA. Tribes marked with an asterisk (*) are state recognized.

PETITIONERS AWAITING AMENDED PROPOSED FINDING

Biloxi, Chitimacha Confederation of Muskogees, Inc., La.
United Houma Nation, Inc., La.

WAITING FOR ACTIVE CONSIDERATION

Meherrin Tribe, N.C.*

DENIED ACKNOWLEDGMENT

Lower Muskogee Creek Tribe-East of the Mississippi, Ga.*
Creeks East of the Mississippi, Fla.
Principal Creek Indian Nation, Ala.
Southeastern Indian Confederacy (SECC), Ga.
Red Clay Inter-tribal Indian Band, SECC, Tenn.
MaChis Lower Alabama Creek Tribe, Ala.*
MOWA Band of Choctaw, Ala.*
Yuchi Tribal Organization, Okla.

PETITION WITHDRAWN (MERGED WITH ANOTHER PETITION)

Cane Break Band of Eastern Cherokees, Ga.

PETITION WITHDRAWN AT PETITIONERS' REQUEST

Tuscola United Cherokee Tribe of Florida and Alabama, Inc., Fla.
Tuscarora Indian Tribe, Drowning Creek Reservation, N.C.

REGISTER OF INCOMPLETE PETITIONERS

Four Hole Indian Organization/Edisto Tribe, S.C.

Cherokee Indians of Georgia, Inc., Ga.

Clifton Choctaw, La.

Florida Tribe of Eastern Creek Indians, Fla.

Choctaw-Apache Community of Ebarb, La.

Georgia Tribe of Eastern Cherokees, Inc. (aka Dahlonega, Cane Creek Band), Ga.

Haliwa-Saponi, N.C.*

Seminole Nation of Florida (aka Traditional Seminole), Fla.

Indians of Person County (formerly Cherokee-Powhatan Indian Association), N.C.*

Oklewaha Band of Yamassee Seminole Indians, Fla.

Caddo Adais Indians, Inc., La.

Langley Band of the Chickamogee Cherokee Indians of the Southeastern U.S., Ala.

Occaneechi Band of Saponi Nation, N.C.

PeeDee Indian Association, Inc., S.C.

Apalachee Indians of Louisiana, La.

LETTERS OF INTENT TO PETITION

Apalachicola Band of Creek Indians, Fla.

Coree (aka Faircloth) Indians, N.C.

Hattadare Indian Nation, N.C.

Santee Indian Organization (formerly White Oak Indian Community), S.C.

Upper Rappahannock Tribe, Inc., Va.

Upper Mattaponi Tribe, Inc., Va.*

Coharie Intra-Tribal Council, Inc., N.C.*

Cherokees of Jackson County, Alabama, Inc., Ala.

Waccamaw Siouan Development Association, Inc., N.C.*

Northern Cherokee Tribe of Indians, Mo.

Sac River and White River Bands of the Chickamauga Cherokee Indian Nation of Arkansas and Missouri

Northern Cherokee Nation of Old Louisiana Territory, Mo.

Meherrin Indian Tribe, N.C.*

Waccamaw-Siouan Indian Association, S.C.

Chicora Indian Tribe of South Carolina (formerly Chicora-Siouan Indian People), S.C.

Chicora-Waccamaw Indian People, S.C.
Ani-Stohini/Unami Nation, Va.
Amonsoquath Tribe of Cherokee, Mo.
Mattaponi Tribe (Mattaponi Indian Reservation), Va.*
Monacan Indian Tribe, Inc., Va.*
Apalachee Indian Tribe, La.
Chickahominy Indian Tribe, Va.*
Eno-Occaneechi Tribe of Indians, N.C.
Beaver Creek Band of Pee Dee Indians, S.C.
Western Arkansas Cherokee Tribe, Ark.
Western Cherokee Nation of Arkansas and Missouri, Ark.
Cherokee Nation West—Southern Band of the Eastern Cherokee Indians
    of Missouri and Arkansas, Mo.
Piedmont American Indian Association, S.C.
Mississippi Band of Chickasaw Indians, Miss.
Lost Cherokee of Arkansas and Missouri, Ark.
Cherokee Nation of Alabama, Ala.
Yamassee Native American Moors of the Creek Nation, Ga.
Pee Dee Indian Nation of Beaver Creek, S.C.
The Old Settler Cherokee Nation of Arkansas, Ark.
Ozark Mountain Cherokee Tribe of Arkansas and Missouri, Mo.
Creek-Euchee Band of Indians of Florida, Fla.
Saponi Nation of Missouri, Mo.

GROUPS THAT AT ONE TIME FILED A LETTER OF INTENT TO PETITION,
BUT ARE NO LONGER IN CONTACT WITH THE BIA

Etowah Cherokee Nation, Tenn.
Waccamaw-Siouan Indian Association, S.C.
The Langley Band of Chickamogee Cherokee Indians of the Southeastern
    United States, Ala.

CASES REQUIRING LEGISLATION TO PERMIT PROCESSING

Lumbee Regional Development Association (LRDA/Lumbee), N.C.*
Hatteras Tuscarora Indians, N.C.
Cherokee Indians of Robeson and Adjoining Counties, N.C.
Cherokee Indians of Hoke County, Inc., N.C.
Tuscarora Nation of North Carolina, Inc., N.C.
Tuscarora Nation East of the Mountains, N.C.

2. Bibliographies and Finding Aids

Anderson, William L., and James A. Lewis, eds. *A Guide to Cherokee Documents in Foreign Archives.* Metuchen, N.J.: Scarecrow, 1983.

Calloway, Colin G., ed. *New Directions in American Indian History.* Norman: University of Oklahoma Press, 1988.

Chepesiuk, Ron, and Arnold Shankman, eds. *American Indian Archival Material: A Guide to Holdings in the Southeast.* Westport, Conn.: Greenwood, 1982.

Danky, James P., and Maureen E. Hady, eds. *Native American Periodicals and Newspapers, 1828–1982: Bibliography, Publishing Record, and Holdings.* Westport, Conn.: Greenwood, 1984.

DeWitt, Donald L. *American Indian Resource Materials in the Western History Collections, University of Oklahoma.* Norman: University of Oklahoma Press, 1990.

Fogelson, Raymond D. *The Cherokees: A Critical Bibliography.* Bloomington: Indiana University Press for the Newberry Library, 1978.

Green, Michael D. *The Creeks: A Critical Bibliography.* Bloomington: Indiana University Press for the Newberry Library, 1980.

Hill, Edward E., comp. *Guide to Records in the National Archives of the United States Relating to American Indians.* Washington, D.C.: National Archives and Records Service, 1981.

Johnson, Steven L. *Guide to American Indian Documents in the Congressional Serial Set: 1817–1899.* New York: Clearwater, 1977.

Kersey, Harry A., Jr. *The Seminole and Miccosukee Tribes: A Critical Bibliography.* Bloomington: Indiana University Press for the Newberry Library, 1987.

Kidwell, Clara Sue, and Charles Roberts. *The Choctaws: A Critical Bibliography.* Bloomington: Indiana University Press for the Newberry Library, 1980.

Miller, Jay, Colin G. Calloway, and Richard A. Sattler, comps. *Writings in Indian History, 1985–1990.* Norman: University of Oklahoma Press, 1995.

Murdock George P., and Timothy J. O'Leary. *Ethnographic Bibliography of North America.* 5 vols. 4th ed. New Haven: Human Relations Area Files, 1975.

O'Donnell, James H., III. *Southeastern Frontiers: Europeans, Africans, and American Indians, 1513–1840.* Bloomington: Indiana University Press for the Newberry Library, 1982.

Pilling, James Constantine. *Bibliography of Muskhogean Languages.* Bureau of American Ethnology Bulletin No. 9. Washington, D.C.: Government Printing Office, 1889. Reprint, New York: AMS, 1973.

Prucha, Francis Paul. *A Bibliographical Guide to the History of Indian-White Relations in the United States.* Chicago: University of Chicago Press, 1977.

————. *Indian-White Relations in the United States: A Bibliography of Works Published, 1975–1980.* Lincoln: University of Nebraska Press, 1982.

Swagerty, William R., ed. *Scholars and the Indian Experience: Critical Reviews of Recent Writing in the Social Sciences.* Bloomington: Indiana University Press for the Newberry Library, 1984.

3. Published Primary Sources

Adair, James. *The History of the American Indians: Particularly Those Adjoining to the Mississippi, East and West Florida, Georgia, South and North Carolina and Virginia.* London: E. C. Dilly, 1775. Reprint, Johnson City, Tenn.: Watauga, 1930.

Observations of a trader who spent forty years among Southern Indians. Despite Adair's desire to prove that the Indians were descended from the Ten Lost Tribes of Israel, a belief common in the eighteenth century, his observations represent the best early account of Southern Native culture.

Baird, W. David, ed. *A Creek Warrior for the Confederacy: The Autobiography of Chief G. W. Grayson.* Norman: University of Oklahoma Press, 1988.

Memoir of Creek Civil War soldier and postwar tribal political figure. Grayson's discussion of late nineteenth-century Creek politics and government are important both as an insider's view and as one of the very few extended descriptions of tribal affairs in the period before and during allotment.

Bernard-Bossu, Jean. *Travels in the Interior of North America, 1751–1762.* Translated and edited by Seymour Feiler. Norman: University of Oklahoma Press, 1962.

Observations of Indian life primarily on the lower Mississippi River, but Bossu also traveled into the interior South and commented on the Creeks and Chickasaws as well.

Carter, Clarence. *The Territorial Papers of the United States*. 26 vols. Washington, D.C.: Government Printing Office, 1934–62.

In the volumes on the Southwest Territory and on Mississippi, Alabama, and Orleans territories, the official correspondence printed in this set regarding Southern Indians in the late eighteenth and early nineteenth centuries is significant and easily used.

Caughey, John W. *McGillivray of the Creeks*. Norman: University of Oklahoma Press, 1938.

Gleaned mostly from Spanish archives and translated back into English, this collection of McGillivray's correspondence from the 1780s and early 1790s, plus Caughey's elaborate introduction, is the key source for McGillivray and Creek history in the period.

Cherokee Nation. *Laws of the Cherokee Nation: Adopted by the Council at Various Periods* [1808–1835]. Printed for the benefit of the Nation. Wilmington, Del.: Scholarly Resources, 1973.

This is the earliest of several editions of Cherokee laws reprinted, along with the laws of other tribes, by Scholarly Resources in a multivolume collection.

Chickasaw Nation. *Constitution and Laws of the Chickasaw Nation: Together with the Treaties of 1832, 1833, 1834, 1837, 1852, and 1866/ Published by Authority of the Chickasaw Legislature by Davis A. Homer*. Wilmington, Del.: Scholarly Resources, 1973.

One of several volumes of Chickasaw laws in the publisher's reprint series. Other volumes are not listed here.

Choctaw Nation. *The Choctaw Laws: Passed at the Special Sessions in January, 1894 and April, 1894 and the Regular Session, October 1894*. Wilmington, Del.: Scholarly Resources, 1975.

Clayton, Lawrence, Vernon J. Knight, and Edward C. Moore, eds. *The De Soto Chronicles: The Expedition of Hernando de Soto to North America in 1539–1543*. 3 vols. Tuscaloosa: University of Alabama Press, 1993.

The definitive edition of the narratives of the De Soto exploration.

Creek Nation. *Constitution and Laws of the Muskogee Nation / as Compiled by L. C. Perryman, March 1st, 1890*. Wilmington, Del.: Scholarly Resources, 1975.

Current-Garcia, Eugene, ed., with Dorothy B. Hatfield. *Shem, Ham and Japheth: The Papers of W. O. Tuggle Comprising His Indian Diary, Sketches and Observations, Myths and Washington Journal in the Territory and at the Capital.* Athens: University of Georgia Press, 1973.

Observations of an attorney who represented the Creeks in the 1870s. In addition to his discussion of contemporary Creek affairs, Tuggle collected many myths that form a part of Creek oral literature.

Dale, Edward Everett, and Gaston Litton. *Cherokee Cavaliers: Forty Years of Cherokee History as Told in the Correspondence of the Ridge-Watie-Boudinot Family.* Norman: University of Oklahoma Press, 1939.

Correspondence between members of one of the major Cherokee families in the middle decades of the nineteenth century.

DeBraham, William G. *Report of the General Survey in the Southern District of North America.* Edited by Louis DeVorsey. Columbia: University of South Carolina Press, 1971.

Observations of British surveyor in late eighteenth century South, including much about Southern Indians and their environment.

Foreman, Grant, ed. *A Traveler in Indian Territory: The Journal of Ethan Allen Hitchcock, Late Major-General in the United States Army.* Cedar Rapids: Torch, 1930. Reprint, with foreword by Michael D. Green. Norman: University of Oklahoma Press, 1996.

Diary of a special investigator who traveled throughout Indian Territory in the early 1840s looking into charges of fraud during the removals. Hitchcock's journal includes much valuable information about life in Indian Territory in the years immediately following removal.

Grant, C. L., ed. *Letters, Journals and Writings of Benjamin Hawkins.* 2 vols. Savannah: Beehive, 1980.

Correspondence of U.S. Indian Agent to the Creeks, 1796–1816.

Hudson, Charles. *The Juan Pardo Expeditions: Exploration of the Carolinas and Tennessee, 1566–68.* Washington, D.C.: Smithsonian Institution Press, 1990.

Spanish explorer in South who reported on conditions after De Soto.

Jacobs, Wilbur R. *Indians of the Southern Colonial Frontier: The Edmond Atkin Report and Plan of 1755*. Columbia: University of South Carolina Press, 1955.

  Description of trade and political relations between Native nations and British citizens in the South.

Hann, John H., ed. and trans. *Missions to the Calusa*. Gainesville: University of Florida Press, 1991.

  Translated Spanish letters and reports about the Calusas in the late sixteenth, seventeenth, and early eighteenth centuries.

Kappler, Charles J. *Indian Affairs, Laws and Treaties*. 5 vols. Washington, D.C.: Government Printing Office, 1903–41. Vol. 2., *Treaties*. Reprint, New York: Interland, 1972.

  Contains all the treaties negotiated between the United States and Southern tribes.

Kinnaird, Lawrence, ed. *Spain in the Mississippi Valley, 1765–1794*. 2 vols. Annual Report of the American Historical Association, 1945.

  Spanish correspondence regarding Indian policy in Louisiana. The letters often contain detailed descriptions of the Native tribes of Louisiana Territory.

Lawson, John. *A New Voyage to Carolina*. Edited by Hugh T. Lefler. Chapel Hill: University of North Carolina Press, 1967.

  Exploration of North Carolina in early eighteenth century. One of the earliest accounts of Carolina Indians.

Littlefield, Daniel F., Jr. and Carol A. Petty Hunter, eds. *The Fus Fixico Letters of Alexander Posey*. Lincoln: University of Nebraska Press, 1993.

  Posey's column, published in Indian Territory newspapers, of satirical commentary on Creek relations with the United States and the Dawes Commission in 1890s.

Louis-Philippe, King of France, 1830–1848. *Diary of My Travels in America*. Translated by Stephen Becker. New York: Delacorte, 1977.

  Description of visit among the Cherokees.

Lumpkin, Wilson. *The Removal of the Cherokee Indians from Georgia, 1827–1841*. 2 vols. New York: Dodd, Mead, 1907. Reprint, New York: Augustus M. Kelley, 1971.

Memoir of the Georgia politician who led the campaign to remove the Cherokees.

McDowell, William L., ed. *Journals of the Commissioners of the Indian Trade, September 20, 1710–August 29, 1718*. Columbia: South Carolina Archives Department, 1955.

These records document the colonial government's monopoly of the Indian trade before the collapse of proprietary government. They also reveal the ways in which Native people manipulated the trade in this period and forced concessions.

————, ed. *Documents Relating to Indian Affairs, May 21, 1750–August 7, 1754*. Columbia: South Carolina Archives Department, 1958.

The records and correspondence of the South Carolina Committee on Indian Trade constitute the major primary source for economic and political relations between Southern Indians and Carolina. They have been published in this volume and the one cited below.

————, ed. *Documents Relating to Indian Affairs, 1754–1765*. Columbia: South Carolina Archives Department, 1970.

McWilliams, Richebourg Gaillard, ed. and trans. *Iberville's Gulf Journals*. University: University of Alabama Press, 1981.

Journals of French governor of Louisiana and relations with Indians.

McWilliams, Richebourg Gaillard, ed. and trans. *Fleur de Lys and Calumet, Being the Penicault Narrative of French Adventure in Louisiana*. Baton Rouge: Louisiana State University Press, 1953.

French-Indian relations in eighteenth-century Louisiana.

Milfort, Louis LeClerc. *Memoirs: or, A Cursory Glance at My Different Travels and My Sojourn in the Creek Nation*. Edited by John Francis McDermott. Chicago: Donnelly, 1956. Revised edition, edited by Ben C. McCary. Savannah: Beehive, 1972.

Memoir of life among the Creeks in the late eighteenth century.

Moulton, Gary, ed. *The Papers of Chief John Ross*. 2 vols. Norman: University of Oklahoma Press, 1984.

Official correspondence of Cherokee principal chief, 1820s–1860s.

Nairne, Thomas. *Nairne's Muskhogean Journals: The 1708 Expedition to the Mississippi River*. Edited by Alexander Moore. Jackson: University of Mississippi Press, 1988.

One of the earliest journals of a Carolina diplomat sent to the Creeks and Chickasaws.

Norton, John. *The Journal of Major John Norton*. Edited by Carl F. Klinck and James J. Talman. Toronto: Champlain Society, 1970.

A Mohawk officer from Canada visits the Cherokees in the early nineteenth century and describes Cherokee culture and public affairs.

Perdue, Theda. *Nations Remembered: An Oral History of the Five Civilized Tribes, 1865–1907*. Westport, Conn.: Greenwood, 1980.

Personal recollections selected from the Oklahoma Indian-Pioneer Papers, a massive New Deal project to interview people who lived in Oklahoma before statehood. The collection includes hundreds of interviews with Indians, some of which are reprinted here.

———, ed. *Cherokee Editor: The Writings of Elias Boudinot*. Knoxville: University of Tennessee Press, 1983.

Selected editorials from *Cherokee Phoenix* (1820s and 30s) and other writings. The particular focus is on Boudinot's interpretation of the removal crisis among the Cherokees.

Perdue, Theda, and Michael D. Green, eds. *The Cherokee Removal: A Brief History with Documents*. Boston: Bedford, 1995.

Documents important to the history of Cherokee removal.

Phillips, Joyce B., and Paul Gary Phillips. *The Brainerd Journal: A Mission to the Cherokees, 1817–1823*. Lincoln: University of Nebraska Press, 1998.

Journals kept by missionaries with the American Board of Commissioners for Foreign Missions.

Quinn, David B. ed. *The Roanoke Voyages, 1585–1590*. Cambridge, Mass.: Hakluyt Society, 1955.

Documents relating to Sir Walter Ralegh's efforts to establish a colony on the Carolina coast.

Romans, Bernard. *A Concise Natural History of East and West Florida: Containing an Account of the Natural Produce of All the Southern Part of British America. 1775*. Florida Facsimile and Reprint series. Gainesville: University of Florida Press, 1962. Edited, and with introduction, by Kathryn E. Holland Braund. Tuscaloosa: University of Alabama Press, 1999.

Observations of a naturalist in the South in mid-eighteenth century, including much about Southern Indians.

Rowland, Dunbar. *Mississippi Territorial Archives, 1798–1803*. Nashville: Press of Brandon, 1905.

———, ed. *Mississippi Provincial Archives, 1763–66: English Dominion*. Nashville: Press of Brandon, 1911.

Official correspondence relating to Mississippi and West Florida. Because Indians were important to government policy, the reports and correspondence in this and the following volumes in the Mississippi Territorial and Provincial series include much on Southern Indians.

Rowland, Dunbar, and Albert Godfrey Sanders, eds. and trans. *Mississippi Provincial Archives: French Dominion*. 3 vols. Jackson: Mississippi Department of Archives and History, 1927–32.

Rowland, Dunbar, Albert Godfrey Sanders, and Patricia Galloway, eds. and trans. *Mississippi Provincial Archives: French Dominion*. 2 vols. Jackson: Mississippi Department of Archives and History, 1984.

Strachey, William. *The Historie of Travell into Virginia Britania*. 1612. Reprint, edited by Louis B. Wright and Virginia Freund. London: Hakluyt Society, 1953.

The first detailed account of Jamestown and relations with the Powhatans.

Stiggins, George. *Creek Indian History: A Historical Narrative of the Genealogy, Traditions and Downfall of the Ispocoga or Creek Indian Tribe of Indians*. Edited by Virginia Pounds Brown. Birmingham: Birmingham Public Library Press, 1989.

Reminiscences of a Creek man about the period of the Creek Civil War, 1811–14, including much on Creek culture.

Waring, Antonio. *Laws of the Creek Nation.* Athens: University of Georgia Libraries Miscellaneous Publications, 1960.

This little volume prints the written laws of the Creek Nation compiled in the 1820s.

Waselkov, Gregory A., and Kathryn E. Holland Braund, eds. *William Bartram on the Southeastern Indians.* Lincoln: University of Nebraska Press, 1995.

Descriptions of Southern Indians by a naturalist in 1770s.

Williams, Samuel Cole, ed. *Lieut. Henry Timberlake's Memoirs, 1756–1765.* Johnson City, Tenn.: Watauga Press, 1927.

Memoirs of an English officer stationed in Cherokee Nation.

4. Oral Traditions

The following volumes contain much of the printed versions of the oral literature of the Southern Indians. Their importance lies in the ways in which Natives interpreted the important events in their histories, ordered their physical and spiritual worlds, and sought to influence the course of events. Titles or subtitles indicate the scope of these works.

Duncan, Barbara R. *Living Stories of the Cherokee.* Chapel Hill: University of North Carolina Press, 1998.
Kilpatrick, Alan. *The Night Has a Naked Soul: Witchcraft and Sorcery among the Western Cherokee.* Syracuse: Syracuse University Press, 1997.
Kilpatrick, Jack Frederick, and Anna Gritts Kilpatrick. *Friends of Thunder: Folktales of the Oklahoma Cherokees.* Dallas: Southern Methodist University Press, 1964.
———. *Walk in Your Soul: Love Incantations of the Oklahoma Cherokees.* Dallas: Southern Methodist University Press, 1965.
———. *Run Toward the Nightland: Magic of the Oklahoma Cherokees.* Dallas: Southern Methodist University Press, 1967.

Lankford, George E., ed. *Native American Legends: Southeastern Legends: Tales from the Natchez, Caddo, Biloxi, Chickasaw, and Other Nations.* Little Rock: August House, 1987.

Mooney, James. "Myths of the Cherokee." *Nineteenth Annual Report of the Bureau of American Ethnology.* Washington, D.C.: Government Printing Office, 1900. Reprint, New York: Johnson, 1970.

———. "Sacred Formulas of the Cherokees." *Seventh Annual Report of the Bureau of American Ethnology.* Washington, D.C.: Government Printing Office, 1891. Reprint, Nashville: Charles and Randy Elder–Booksellers, 1982.

Swanton, John R. *Myths and Tales of the Southeastern Indians.* Bureau of American Ethnology Bulletin No. 88. Washington, D.C.: Government Printing Office, 1929. Rerprint, with introduction by George E. Lankford. Norman: University of Oklahoma Press, 1995.

5. Archaeological Studies

The volumes in this section represent a selection of the best and most recent interpretations of the archaeological record for Southern Indians. Much of it focuses on the Mississippian period, and together the following entries demonstrate the vitality and dynamism of Southern Indian history prior to the invasion of Europeans. Most titles indicate the subject of the book.

Anderson, David G. *The Savannah River Chiefdoms: Political Change in the Late Prehistoric Southeast.* Tuscaloosa: University of Alabama Press, 1994.

Barker, Alex, and Timothy Pauketat, eds. *Lords of the Southeast: Social Inequality and the Native Elites of Southeastern North America.* Washington, D.C.: American Anthropological Association, 1992.

Blakely, Robert, and Bettina Detweiler-Blakely. "The Impact of European Diseases in the Sixteenth Century Southeast: A Case Study." *Midcontinental Journal of Archaeology* 14 (1989): 62–89.

Blitz, John H. *An Archaeological Study of the Mississippi Choctaw Indians.* Jackson: Mississippi Department of Archives and History, 1985.

Brain, Jeffrey P. *Tunica Archaeology.* Cambridge, Mass.: Peabody Museum of Archaeology, 1988.

Davis, Dave D. *Perspectives on Gulf Coast Prehistory.* Gainesville: University Press of Florida, 1984.

DePratter, Chester B. *Late Prehistoric and Early Historic Chiefdoms in the Southeastern United States.* New York: Garland, 1991.

Dickens, Roy S. *Cherokee Prehistory.* Knoxville: University of Tennessee Press, 1976.

Dye, David H., and Cheryl Anne Cox, eds. *Towns and Temples along the Mississippi.* Tuscaloosa: University of Alabama Press, 1990.

Dye, David H., and Ronald C. Brister, eds. *The Protohistoric Period in the Mid-South, 1500–1700.* Jackson: Mississippi Department of Archives and History, 1986.

Emerson, Thomas E. *Cahokia and the Archaeology of Power.* Tuscaloosa: University of Alabama Press, 1997.

Galloway, Patricia, ed. *The Southeastern Ceremonial Complex: Artifacts and Analysis.* Lincoln: University of Nebraska Press, 1989.

Keel, Bennie C. *Cherokee Archaeology: A Study of the Appalachian Summit.* Knoxville: University of Tennessee Press, 1976.

Knight, Vernon James, Jr. *Tukabatchee: Archaeological Investigations at an Historic Creek Town, 1984.* Moundville: University of Alabama Office of Archaeological Research, 1985.

Knight, Vernon James, Jr., and Vincas P. Steponaitis, eds. *Archaeology of the Moundville Chiefdom.* Washington, D.C.: Smithsonian Institution Press, 1998.

Larson, Lewis H. *Aboriginal Subsistence Technology on the Southeastern Coastal Plain During the Late Prehistoric Period.* Gainesville: University Presses of Florida, 1980.

Lewis, R. Barry, and Charles Stout, eds. *Mississippian Towns and Sacred Places: Searching for an Architectural Grammar.* Tuscaloosa: University of Alabama Press, 1998.

Morgan, William N. *Precolumbian Architecture in Eastern North America.* Gainesville: University Presses of Florida, 1999.

Morse, Dan F., and Phyllis A. Morse. *Archaeology of the Central Mississippi Valley.* New York: Academic, 1983.

Pauketat, Timothy R. *The Ascent of Chiefs: Cahokia and Mississippian Politics in Native North America.* Tuscaloosa: University of Alabama Press, 1994.

Pauketat, Timothy R., and Thomas E. Emerson, eds. *Cahokia: Domination and Ideology in the Mississippian World.* Lincoln: University of Nebraska Press, 1997.

Rogers, J. Daniel, and Bruce D. Smith, eds. *Mississippian Communities and Households.* Tuscaloosa: University of Alabama Press, 1995.

Scarry, C. Margaret, ed. *Foraging and Farming in the Eastern Woodlands.* Gainesville: University Presses of Florida, 1993.

Scarry, John E., ed. *Political Structure and Change in the Prehistoric Southeastern United States.* Gainesville: University Presses of Florida, 1996.

Smith, Bruce D. *Mississippian Settlement Patterns.* New York: Academic, 1978.

———, ed. *Mississippian Emergence: The Evolution of Ranked Agricultural Societies in Eastern North America.* Washington, D.C.: Smithsonian Institution Press, 1990.

Smith, Marvin T. *Archaeology of Aboriginal Culture Change in the Interior Southeast.* Gainesville: University of Florida Press, 1987.
    Focuses on Coosa, particularly its collapse.

Steponaitis, Vincas P. "Prehistoric Archaeology in the Southeastern United States, 1970–1985." *Annual Review of Anthropology* 15 (1986): 363–404.

Walthall, John A. *Moundville: An Introduction to the Archaeology of a Mississippian Chiefdom.* Tuscaloosa: Alabama Museum of Natural History, 1977.

———. *Prehistoric Indians of the Southeast: Archaeology of Alabama and the Middle South.* Tuscaloosa: University of Alabama Press, 1980.

Weisman, Brent. *Excavations on the Franciscan Frontier: Archaeology at the Fig Springs Mission.* Gainesville: University of Florida Press, 1992.

Welch, Paul D. *Moundville's Economy.* Tuscaloosa: University of Alabama Press, 1990.

Widmer, Randolph J. *The Evolution of the Calusa: A Nonagricultural Chiefdom on the Southwest Florida Coast.* Tuscaloosa: University of Alabama Press, 1988.

Williams, Mark, and Gary Shapiro, eds. *Lamar Archaeology: Mississippian Chiefdoms in the Deep South.* Tuscaloosa: University of Alabama Press, 1990.

6. General Works

Abel, Annie Heloise. *The Slaveholding Indians.* 3 vols. Cleveland: Arthur H. Clark, 1915–25. Reprint, with introduction by Theda Perdue and Michael D. Green. Lincoln: University of Nebraska Press, 1992–93.

    Detailed history of the Five Tribes in the U.S. Civil War. Despite a number of racist assumptions by the author, these volumes are useful because Able included complete transcriptions of many letters and reports otherwise hard to find.

Axtell, James. *The Indians' New South: Cultural Change in the Colonial Southeast.* Baton Rouge: Louisiana State University Press, 1997.

Overview of relations between Southern Indians and Europeans before U.S. independence.

Bailey, Minnie Elizabeth Thomas. *Reconstruction in Indian Territory: A Story of Avarice, Discrimination and Opportunism.* Port Washington, N.Y.: Kennikat, 1972.

Provides an introductory overview as well as separate detailed descriptions of the negotiation of the Five Tribes' Reconstruction treaties, their provisions, and their implementations.

Baird, W. David. "Are There Real Indians in Oklahoma?" *Chronicles of Oklahoma* 68 (Spring 1990): 4–23.

Discussion of how the histories of the Five Tribes differ from the histories of other Indians and shape modern Indian identity in Oklahoma.

Burton, Jeffrey. *Indian Territory and the United States, 1866–1906.* Norman: University of Oklahoma Press, 1995.

Detailed history of how Congress asserted legal control in Indian Territory through the establishment of a federal court system.

Champagne, Duane. *Social Order and Political Change: Constitutional Governments among the Cherokee, the Choctaw, the Chickasaw, and the Creek.* Stanford: Stanford University Press, 1992.

Important comparative analysis of the political systems of the Five Tribes before 1907 and a compelling explanation of their differences.

Coker, William A., and Thomas Watson. *Indian Traders of the Southeastern Spanish Borderlands: Panton, Leslie and Company, 1783–1847.* Pensacola: University of West Florida Press, 1986.

Company history of the biggest European trading firm in the South. Especially good on trade relations with the Creeks.

Cotterill, Robert S. *The Southern Indians: The Story of the Civilized Tribes Before Removal.* Norman: University of Oklahoma Press, 1954.

In many ways outdated, this remains the only general interpretation of the histories of the Southern nations before removal.

Crane, Verner W. *The Southern Frontier, 1670–1732*. Durham: Duke University Press, 1929. Reprint, with preface by Peter H. Wood. New York: Norton, 1981.

Important early history of relations between Carolina and the Indians, particularly the Creeks. Crane was the first historian to understand the importance of the Indian trade to early South Carolina history.

Crawford, James. *The Mobilian Trade Language*. Knoxville: University of Tennessee Press, 1978.

Linguistic and historical study of the major Southern trade language and its largely Choctaw roots.

Crawford, James M., ed. *Studies in Southeastern Indian Languages*. Athens: University of Georgia Press, 1975.

Linguistic essays on the Yuchi, Cherokee, Choctaw, Chickasaw, and Mobilian languages.

Cumming, William P. *The Southeast in Early Maps*. 3rd ed. Chapel Hill: University of North Carolina Press, 1998.

Depiction and historical and geographical discussion of early maps of the South.

Debo, Angie. *And Still the Waters Run: The Betrayal of the Five Civilized Tribes*. Princeton: Princeton University Press, 1972 [1940].

Description of frauds perpetrated on members of Five Tribes after allotment.

———. *The Five Civilized Tribes of Oklahoma: Report on Social and Economic Conditions*. Philadelphia: Indian Rights Association, 1951.

DeVorsey, Louis, Jr. *The Indian Boundary in the Southern Colonies, 1763–1775*. Chapel Hill: University of North Carolina Press, 1966.

Geographical history of the Southern Indians including a careful analysis of the survey of the boundaries between the Southern colonies and the Cherokees and Creeks.

Dobyns, Henry F. *Their Number Become Thinned: Native American Population Dynamics in Eastern North America*. Knoxville: University of Tennessee Press, 1983.

Population history of Southeast in which Dobyns tests his theory about the human carrying capacity of the South and offers an estimate of pre-Columbian population.

Doran, Michael F. "Population Statistics of Nineteenth Century Indian Territory." *Chronicles of Oklahoma* 53 (1975): 492–515.

———. "Antebellum Cattle Herding in the Indian Territory." *Geographical Review* 66 (1976): 48–58.

Fite, Gilbert C. "Development of the Cotton Industry by the Five Civilized Tribes in Indian Territory." *Journal of Southern History* 15 (1949): 342–53.

Foreman, Grant. *Indian Removal: The Emigration of the Five Civilized Tribes of Indians.* Norman: University of Oklahoma Press, 1932.

The only detailed histories of the removal of the Five Tribes. Quotes heavily from records in the National Archives and newspapers.

———. *The Five Civilized Tribes: Cherokee, Chickasaw, Choctaw, Creek, Seminole.* Norman: University of Oklahoma Press, 1934.

Histories of the Five Tribes in Indian Territory between removal and the U.S. Civil War.

Franks, Kenny A. "Confederate Treaties with the Five Civilized Tribes." *Chronicles of Oklahoma* 50 (Winter 1972–73): 458–74.

———. "The Implementation of the Confederate Treaties with the Five Civilized Tribes." *Chronicles of Oklahoma* 51 (Spring 1973): 21–33.

Fundaburk, Emma Lila, ed. *Southeastern Indians—Life Portraits: A Catalogue of Pictures, 1564–1860.* Tallahassee: Rose, 1992.

Collection of all known paintings depicting Southern Indians.

Galloway, Patricia, ed. *The Hernando de Soto Expedition: History, Historiography, and "Discovery" in the Southeast.* Lincoln: University of Nebraska Press, 1997.

Essays that focus on the problem of the accuracy of the De Soto journals and the scholarship that has used them.

Gibson, Arrell M., ed. *America's Exiles: Indian Colonization in Oklahoma.* Oklahoma City: Oklahoma Historical Society, 1976.

Essays on the removal of the Five Tribes. Factual but not very interpretive.

Graebner, Norman. "Pioneer Indian Agriculture in Oklahoma." *Chronicles of Oklahoma* 23 (1945): 232–48.

———. "The Public Land Policy of the Five Civilized Tribes." *Chronicles of Oklahoma* 23 (1945): 107–18.

Hoffman, Paul E. *A New Andalucia and a Way to the Orient: The American Southeast During the Sixteenth Century.* Baton Rouge: Louisiana State University Press, 1990.

History of Spanish policy toward Florida and its Indian residents and the Spanish explorations of the Southeast.

Hudson, Charles. *The Southeastern Indians.* Knoxville: University of Tennessee Press, 1976.

The main ethnography of Southern Indians. Summarizes archaeology and history and addresses in detail topics such as belief system, subsistence, and social organization.

———. *Knights of Spain, Warriors of the Sun: Hernando de Soto and the South's Ancient Chiefdoms.* Athens: University of Georgia Press, 1997.

History of the expedition of De Soto through the South and its impact on Southern Indians. Attempts to connect archaeological sites to the places De Soto visited and proto-historic tribes with modern Indians.

Hudson, Charles, and Carmen Chaves Tesser, eds. *The Forgotten Centuries: Indians and Europeans in the American South, 1521–1704.* Athens: University of Georgia Press, 1994.

Historical essays on Southern Indians and Europeans.

Hudson, Charles M., ed. *Black Drink: A Native American Tea.* Athens: University of Georgia Press, 1979.

Essays by several authors on the role of Yaupon holly in the cultures of Southern Indians.

Hulton, Paul. *America 1585: The Complete Drawings of John White.* Chapel Hill: University of North Carolina Press, 1984.

Hulton, Paul, and David B. Quinn. *The American Drawings of John White, 1577–1590.* London: Trustees of the British Museum, 1964.

White's drawings and paintings of the Indians of coastal Carolina represent the earliest depiction of those people and, along with his commentary, constitute the earliest insight into Southern Indian life.

Kwachka, Patricia B., ed. *Perspectives on the Southeast: Linguistics, Archaeology, and Ethnohistory.* Athens: University of Georgia Press, 1994.

Essays on language, culture, and history among Southern Indians.

McEwan, Bonnie G., ed. *Indians of the Greater Southeast: Historical Archaeology and Ethnohistory.* Gainesville: University Presses of Florida, 2000.

Archaeologists connect their research to historic tribes.

McKenney, Thomas L., and James T. Hall. *History of the Indian Tribes of North America, with Biographical Sketches and Anecdotes of the Principal Chiefs, Embellished with One Hundred and Twenty Portraits from the Indian Gallery in the Department of War, at Washington.* 3 vols. Philadelphia: Frederick W. Greenough, 1838–44. Revised edition. Edinburgh: J. Grant, 1933–34.

The government official responsible for administering U.S. Indian policy in the 1820s and 1830s, McKinney began the practice of commissioning portraits of Indian leaders who visited Washington. This set prints those portraits, accompanied by McKenney's discussions of the people represented and something of the histories of their tribes. While it covers many tribes, the portraits of Southern Indians contained here are the only depictions of many of the important Southern Indian leaders.

Milling, Chapman J. *Red Carolinians.* Chapel Hill: University of North Carolina Press, 1940.

Brief histories of the Indians of North and South Carolina in the seventeenth and eighteenth centuries, including chapters on the Tuscarora and Yamassee Wars.

Miner, H. Craig. *The Corporation and the Indian: Tribal Sovereignty and Industrial Civilization in Indian Territory, 1865–1907.* Columbia: University of Missouri Press, 1976.

Excellent history of railroad, mining, and other American companies in Indian Territory and their impact on the Five Tribes.

Mooney, James. *The Siouan Tribes of the East.* Washington, D.C.: Smithsonian Institution Press, 1894.

Linguistic and cultural studies of the groups in eastern Carolina that scholars believe spoke Siouan languages.

Morris, John W., Charles R. Goins, and Edwin C. McReynolds. *Historical Atlas of Oklahoma*. 3d ed. Norman: University of Oklahoma Press, 1986.

This historical atlas includes much information on the tribes relocated to Indian Territory.

O'Donnell, James H., III. *The Southern Indians in the American Revolution*. Knoxville: University of Tennessee Press, 1973.

Focuses on Indian-white relations and military history.

Paredes, Anthony J., ed. *Indians of the Southeastern United States in the Late Twentieth Century*. Tuscaloosa: University of Alabama Press, 1992.

Essays on many of the Native groups living in the South today.

Perdue, Theda. *Native Carolinians: The Indians of North Carolina*. Raleigh: Division of Archives and History, 1985.

Overview of histories of North Carolina Indians.

Prucha, Francis Paul. *The Great Father: The United States Government and the American Indians*. 2 vols. Lincoln: University of Nebraska Press, 1984.

The most comprehensive history of U.S. Indian policy.

Quinn, David B. *Set Fair for Roanoke: Voyages and Colonies, 1584–1606*. Chapel Hill: University of North Carolina Press, 1985.

History of the Lost Colony of Roanoke.

Rogin, Michael P. *Fathers and Children: Andrew Jackson and the Subjugation of the American Indian*. New York: Knopf, 1975.

Psychohistory of Andrew Jackson's attitudes toward Indians and how they influenced his Indian policy.

Royce, Charles C., comp. *Indian Land Cessions in the United States*. Eighteenth Annual Report of the Bureau of American Ethnology. Washington, D.C.: Government Printing Office, 1899.

Collection of maps showing every land cession ever made by a tribe. An enormously important source.

Satz, Ronald N. *American Indian Policy in the Jacksonian Era*. Lincoln: University of Nebraska Press, 1975.

Detailed history of the development and implementation of removal policy.

———. *Tennessee's Indian Peoples: From White Contact to Removal, 1540– 1840.* Knoxville: University of Tennessee Press, 1979.

For general audiences.

Spoehr, Alexander. "Changing Kinship Systems: A Study in the Accultura- tion of the Creeks, Cherokee, and Choctaw." *Field Museum of Natural History Anthropological Series* 33 (1947): 153–235.

Traces persistence and change in the matrilineal kinship systems of the Southern Indians.

Strickland, Rennard. *The Indians in Oklahoma.* Norman: University of Okla- homa Press, 1980.

Overview of Oklahoma Indian history.

Swanton, John R. *Indian Tribes of the Lower Mississippi Valley and Adjacent Coast of the Gulf of Mexico.* Bureau of American Ethnology Bulletin No. 43. Washington, D.C.: Government Printing Office, 1921.

Early ethnography of the Natchez and several other small lower Mis- sissippi River tribes.

———. *The Indians of the Southeastern United States.* Bureau of American Ethnology Bulletin No. 137. Washington, D.C.: Government Printing Office, 1946. Reprint. Washington, D.C.: Smithsonian Institution Press, 1979.

Classic ethnographical overview of Southern Indians contains extensive excerpts of a number of primary sources.

Usner, Daniel H., Jr. *Indians, Settlers, and Slaves in a Frontier Exchange Economy: The Lower Mississippi Valley Before 1783.* Chapel Hill: Uni- versity of North Carolina Press, 1992.

Important study of the French in Louisiana and relations with Choc- taws and other Native people.

———. *American Indians in the Lower Mississippi Valley: Social and Eco- nomic Histories.* Lincoln: University of Nebraska Press, 1998.

Essays on Natchez and Choctaw history and Indians in nineteenth-century Louisiana.

Wallace, Anthony F. C. *The Long, Bitter Trail: Andrew Jackson and the Indians*. New York: Hill and Wang, 1993.

History of removal.

Williams, Walter L., ed. *Southeastern Indians since the Removal Era*. Athens: University of Georgia Press, 1979.

Essays on Southern Indians who did not remove.

Wood, Peter H., Gregory A. Waselkov, and M. Thomas Hatley eds. *Powhatan's Mantle: Indians in the Colonial Southeast*. Lincoln: University of Nebraska Press, 1989.

Essays on Southern Indians, including Wood's important population history.

Wright, J. Leitch, Jr. *The Only Land They Knew: The Tragic Story of the Indians in the Old South*. New York: Free Press, 1981.

An insightful overview of Southern Indian history. The chapter on interactions between Native Americans and African Americans is particularly good.

Wright, Muriel H. *A Guide to the Indian Tribes of Oklahoma*. Norman: University of Oklahoma Press, 1951.

Brief essays on all the tribes removed to Indian Territory.

Young, Mary Elizabeth. *Redskins, Ruffleshirts, and Rednecks: Indian Allotments in Alabama and Mississippi, 1830–1860*. Norman: University of Oklahoma Press, 1961.

History of the land frauds suffered by Creeks and Chickasaws before removal.

7. Alabama-Coushattas, Caddoes, and Chitimachas

Carter, Cecile Elkins. *Caddo Indians: Where We Come From*. Norman: University of Oklahoma Press, 1995.

Caddo history written by a Caddo scholar.

Hook, Jonathan B. *The Alabama-Coushatta Indians*. College Station: Texas A & M Press, 1997.

Places Alabama-Coushatta history in the broader context of U.S. Indian policy.

Hoover, Herbert T. *The Chitimacha People*. Phoenix: Indian Tribal Series, 1975.

For nonscholarly readers.

LeVere, David. *The Caddo Chiefdoms: Caddo Economics and Politics, 700–1835*. Lincoln: University of Nebraska Press, 1998.

The best history of the Caddos.

Pertulla, Timothy K. *The Caddo Nation: Archaeological and Ethnohistoric Perspectives*. Austin: University of Texas Press, 1992.

Sophisticated history that weaves archaeological and documentary evidence into an ethnohistorical interpretation of the Caddos.

Smith, F. Todd. *The Caddo Indians: Tribes at the Convergence of Empires, 1542–1854*. College Station: Texas A&M Press, 1995.

8. Apalachees, Timucuas, and Calusas

Gannon, Michael V. *The Cross in the Sand: The Early Catholic Church in Florida, 1513–1870*. Gainesville: University Presses of Florida, 1965.

Classic interpretation of the role of the Catholic Church in Florida history, with a special focus on missions to the Indians.

Hann, John H. *Apalachee: The Land Between the Rivers*. Gainesville: University Presses of Florida, 1988.

Comprehensive history of the Apalachees written largely from Spanish sources.

———. *A History of the Timucua Indians and Missions*. Gainesville: University Press of Florida, 1996.

The most complete history of Spanish missions among the Timucuas.

———, ed. and trans. *Missions to the Calusa*.

See under Published Primary Sources.

Hann, John H., and Bonnie G. McEwan. *The Apalachee Indians and Mission San Luis*. Gainesville: University Presses of Florida, 1998.

History of the main Spanish mission among the Apalachees

Milanich, Jerald T. *Florida Indians and the Invasion from Europe*. Gainesville: University Press of Florida, 1995.

Summary history of the impact of the invasion of Europeans on Florida's Indians.

———. *The Timucua*. Cambridge: Blackwell, 1996.

———. *Florida's Indians from Ancient Times to the Present*. Gainesville: University Press of Florida, 1998.

An overview of Florida's Indian people.

Milanich, Jerald T., and Charles Hudson. *Hernando de Soto and the Indians of Florida*. Gainesville: University Press of Florida, 1993.

Valuable partnership of Milanich, the foremost student of Florida Indians, and Hudson, the leading scholar on De Soto's entrada into the Southeast.

Milanich, Jerald T., and Samuel Proctor, eds. *Tacachale: Essays on the Indians of Florida and Southeastern Georgia during the Historic Period*. Gainesville: University Presses of Florida, 1978.

Wickman, Patricia Riles. *The Tree That Bends: Discourse, Power, and the Survival of the Maskoki People*.

See under Seminoles and Miccosukees.

Widmer, Randolph J. *The Evolution of the Calusa: A Nonagricultural Chiefdom on the Southwest Florida Coast*. Tuscaloosa: University of Alabama Press, 1988.

The leading work on the Calusas of south Florida, a rare example of a chiefdom that was not built on an agricultural foundation.

Worth, John E. *Timucuan Chiefdoms of Spanish Florida*. 2 vols. Gainesville: University Press of Florida, 1998.

The standard ethnohistorical study of the Timucuas.

9. Catawbas

Hudson, Charles. *The Catawba Nation*. Athens: University of Georgia Press, 1970.

> The classic ethnographic account of the Catawbaws.

Merrell, James. *The Catawbas*. New York: Chelsea House, 1989.

> For young readers or nonspecialists.

———. *The Indians' New World: Catawbas and Their Neighbors from European Contact Through the Era of Removal*. Chapel Hill: University of North Carolina Press, 1989.

> Explains how the European invasion disrupted the tribes of the Carolina Piedmont region and led to the creation of the Catawba Nation, a new tribe.

10. Cherokees

Anderson, William L., ed. *Cherokee Removal: Before and After*. Athens: University of Georgia Press, 1991.

> Collection of essays by leading scholars on the history of the removal of the Cherokee Nation.

Anderson, William L., and James A. Lewis, eds. *A Guide to Cherokee Documents in Foreign Archives*.

> See under Bibliographies and Finding Aids.

Andrew, John A., III. *From Revivals to Removal: Jeremiah Evarts, the Cherokee Nation, and the Search for the Soul of America*. Athens: University of Georgia Press, 1992.

> Under the pseudonym "William Penn," Evarts led the defense of Cherokee rights during the public debates on removal. This important biography puts Evarts into the context of the politics of Indian removal.

Corkran, David. *The Cherokee Frontier: Conflict and Survival, 1740–1762*. Norman: University of Oklahoma Press, 1962.

> Old-fashioned Indian-white relations.

Dickens, Roy S. *Cherokee Prehistory.*

See under Archaeological Studies.

Duncan, Barbara R. *Living Stories of the Cherokee.*

See under Oral Traditions.

Everett, Dianna. *The Texas Cherokees: A People Between Two Fires, 1819–1840.* Norman: University of Oklahoma Press, 1990.

The history of Cherokees who settled in Texas before the mass removal west in the 1830s.

Finger, John R. *The Eastern Band of Cherokees, 1819–1900.* Knoxville: University of Tennessee Press, 1984.

Finger's two volumes on the Eastern Band of Cherokees (the second is listed below) combine to form the best work on that group.

———. *Cherokee Americans: The Eastern Band of Cherokees in the Twentieth Century.* Lincoln: University of Nebraska Press, 1991.

Fogelson, Raymond D. *The Cherokees: A Critical Bibliography.*

See under Bibliographies and Finding Aids.

———. "Who Were the Ani Kutani? An Excursion into Cherokee Historical Thought." *Ethnohistory* 31 (1984): 255–63.

Superb account of how the Cherokees interpreted historical change.

Foreman, Grant. *Sequoyah.* Norman: University of Oklahoma Press, 1938.

Biography of the man who developed the Cherokee syllabary and enabled the Cherokees to become the first Native nation in North America to possess a written language.

Franks, Kenny A. *Stand Watie and the Agony of the Cherokee Nation.* Memphis: Memphis State University Press, 1979.

Biased but interesting biography of an important Cherokee political figure who rose to the rank of general in the Confederate army during the U.S. Civil War.

Gabriel, Ralph Henry. *Elias Boudinot, Cherokee, and His America.* Norman: University of Oklahoma Press, 1941.

Biography of the man who edited the Cherokee national newspaper, the *Cherokee Phoenix.* and led the movement within the nation that accepted removal as inevitable.

Gaines, W. Craig. *The Confederate Cherokees: John Drew's Regiment of Mounted Rifles.* Baton Rouge: Louisiana State University Press, 1989.

Account of Cherokee regiment that largely deserted the Confederate cause.

Gearing, Fred. *Priests and Warriors: Social Structures for Cherokee Politics in the Eighteenth Century.* Memoir 93. Washington, D.C.: American Anthropological Association, 1962.

Classic but dated ethnohistorical study of Cherokee political systems.

Godbold, E. Stanly, Jr., and Mattie U. Russell. *Confederate Colonel and Cherokee Chief: The Life of William Holland Thomas.* Knoxville: University of Tennessee Press, 1990.

Biography of Thomas, the man who represented the interests of the Eastern Band of Cherokees to state and federal governments from the 1830s through the Civil War.

Goodwin, Gary. *Cherokees in Transition: A Study of Changing Culture and Environment Prior to 1775.* Chicago: University of Chicago Press, 1977.

Focuses on land use and subsistence.

Gulick, John. *Cherokees at the Crossroads.* Chapel Hill: Institute for Research in Social Science, University of North Carolina, 1960.

Ethnographic interpretation of the Eastern Band of Cherokees based on extensive fieldwork conducted in the 1950s.

Halliburton, R., Jr. *Red Over Black: Black Slavery Among the Cherokee Indians.* Westport, Conn.: Greenwood, 1976.

Focuses on slavery after removal. Appendices include WPA interviews with former slaves and a census of Cherokee slaveholders in 1835.

Hatley, Tom. *The Dividing Paths: Cherokees and South Carolinians Through the Era of Revolution.* New York: Oxford University Press, 1993.

Best single study of eighteenth-century Cherokees and the breakdown of their reciprocal relationship with South Carolina.

Hendrix, Janey B. *Redbird Smith and the Nighthawk Keetoowahs.* Park Hill, Okla.: Cross-Cultural Education Center, 1983.

Detailed study of the emergence and history of the Keetoowahs in the western Cherokee Nation during the late nineteenth and early twentieth centuries.

Hill, Sarah H. *Weaving New Worlds: Southeastern Cherokee Women and Their Basketry.* Chapel Hill: University of North Carolina Press, 1997.

An imaginative study of Cherokee history through an analysis of baskets and basket making.

Journal of Cherokee Studies. Museum of the Cherokee Indian (1976–).

Keel, Bennie C. *Cherokee Archaeology.*

See Archaeological Studies.

Kilpatrick, Alan. *The Night Has a Naked Soul.*

See under Oral Traditions.

Kilpatrick, Jack Frederick, and Anna Gritts Kilpatrick. *Friends of Thunder.*

See under Oral Traditions.

———. *Run Toward the Nightland.*

See under Oral Traditions.

———. *Walk in Your Soul.*

See under Oral Traditions.

King, Duane H., ed. *The Cherokee Indian Nation: A Troubled History.* Knoxville: University of Tennessee Press, 1979.

A collection of essays by several authors.

Littlefield, Daniel F., Jr. *The Cherokee Freedmen: From Emancipation to American Citizenship.* Westport, Conn.: Greenwood, 1978.

One in a series of books by Littlefield on the struggle by former slaves of Southern Indians to gain the rights and privileges of citizenship.

Lumpkin, Wilson. *Removal of the Cherokee Indians.*

See under Published Primary Sources.

McLoughlin, William G. *Cherokees and Missionaries, 1789–1839.* New Haven: Yale University Press, 1984.

Uses the missionary experience among the Cherokees to explore the tensions between religion and politics.

———. *Cherokee Renascence in the New Republic.* Princeton: Princeton University Press, 1986.

Cherokee history from the late eighteenth century to removal placed in the context of romantic nationalism.

———. *Champions of the Cherokees: Evan and John B. Jones.* Princeton: Princeton University Press, 1990.

Biographies of two Baptist missionaries, father and son, to the Cherokees. A landmark interpretation of the impact of Christianity on a Southern tribe.

———. *After the Trail of Tears: The Cherokees' Struggle for Sovereignty, 1839–1880.* Chapel Hill: University of North Carolina Press, 1993.

History of the Cherokee Nation in Indian Territory after removal.

———. *The Cherokees and Christianity, 1794–1870: Essays on Acculturation and Cultural Persistence.* Edited by Walter H. Conser Jr. Athens: University of Georgia Press, 1994.

Published after McLoughlin's death, this collection includes a particularly fine analysis of the differences between traditional Cherokee religion and Christianity.

———, ed. *The Cherokee Ghost Dance: Essays on the Southeastern Indians, 1789–1861.* Macon: Mercer University Press, 1984.

Collection of previously published essays.

Malone, Henry T. *Cherokees of the Old South: A People in Transition.* Athens: University of Georgia Press, 1956.

Dated but still very readable account of the Cherokees' cultural transformation in the early nineteenth century.

Mankiller, Wilma, and Michael Wallis. *Mankiller: A Chief and Her People*. New York: St. Martin's, 1993.

Autobiography of the principal chief of the Cherokee Nation of Oklahoma, 1985–95.

Mihesuah, Devon A. *Cultivating the Rosebuds: The Education of Women at the Cherokee Female Seminary, 1851–1909*. Urbana: University of Illinois Press, 1993.

Study of this pioneering institution of higher education pays attention to issues of race and class as well as gender.

Mooney, James. "Myths of the Cherokees."

See under Oral Traditions.

———. "Sacred Formulas of the Cherokees."

See under Oral Traditions.

Moulton, Gary E. *John Ross: Cherokee Chief*. Athens: University of Georgia Press, 1978.

Balanced biography of the Cherokees' longest serving chief, 1828–1866.

———. *The Papers of Chief John Ross*.

See under Published Primary Sources.

Neely, Sharlotte. *Snowbird Cherokees: People of Persistence*. Athens: University of Georgia Press, 1991.

Ethnographic study of an eastern Cherokee community and the issues that both unite and divide it.

Norgren, Jill. *The Cherokee Cases: The Confrontation of Law and Politics*. New York: McGraw-Hill, 1996.

Study by a legal scholar of the cases brought to the U.S. Supreme Court by the Cherokees during the removal crisis.

Perdue, Theda. *Slavery and the Evolution of Cherokee Society, 1540–1866*. Knoxville: University of Tennessee Press, 1979.

Analysis of culture change among the Cherokees.

———. *The Cherokee*. New York: Chelsea House, 1989.

For general readers.

———. *Cherokee Women: Gender and Culture Change, 1700–1835*. Lincoln: University of Nebraska Press, 1998.

Important new interpretation of Cherokee history before removal that focuses on gender issues.

Perdue, Theda, ed. *Cherokee Editor: The Writings of Elias Boudinot*. See under Published Primary Sources.

Perdue, Theda, and Michael D. Green, eds. *The Cherokee Removal: A Brief History with Documents*. See under Published Primary Sources.

Phillips, Joyce B., and Paul Gary Phillips, eds. *The Brainerd Journal*. See under Published Primary Sources.

Reid, John P. *A Better Kind of Hatchet: Law, Trade, and Diplomacy in the Cherokee Nation During the Early Years of European Contact*. University Park: Penn State University Press, 1976.

Demonstrates the accommodations that the English made in their early eighteenth-century dealings with the Cherokees.

Reid, John P. *A Law of Blood: The Primitive Law of the Cherokee People*. New York: New York University Press, 1970.

Study of tribal law that links kinship and politics.

Royce, Charles C. *The Cherokee Nation of Indians*. Chicago: Aldine, 1975.

A reprint of an old but still useful general history of the Cherokees. Particularly good for its discussion of land cessions.

Starkey, Marion. *The Cherokee Nation*. New York: Knopf, 1946.

Strickland, Rennard. *Fire and the Spirits: Cherokee Law from Clan to Court*. Norman: University of Oklahoma Press, 1975.

Uses law to explore both change and persistence.

Thornton, Russell. *The Cherokees: A Population History*. Lincoln: University of Nebraska Press, 1990.

A comprehensive demographic analysis of the Cherokees over time.

Walker, Robert Sparks. *Torchlights to the Cherokees: The Brainerd Mission*. New York: Macmillan, 1931.

Account of the work of the American Board of Commissioners of Foreign Missions missionaries among the Cherokees.

Wardell, Morris L. A *Political History of the Cherokee Nation, 1838–1907*. Norman: University of Oklahoma Press, 1938.

Long on facts, short on analysis. Useful.

Wilkins, Thurman. *Cherokee Tragedy: The Story of the Ridge Family and the Decimation of a People*. New York: Macmillan, 1970. 2nd edition. Norman: University of Oklahoma Press, 1981.

Cherokee history that focuses on the removal crisis among the Cherokees and the role of the Ridge family.

Williams, Samuel Cole, ed. *Lieut. Timberlake's Memoirs*.

See under Published Primary Sources.

Woodward, Grace. *The Cherokees*. Norman: University of Oklahoma Press, 1963.

Dated.

Young, Mary. "Racism in Red and Black: Indians and Other Free People of Color in Georgia Law, Politics, and Removal Policy." *Georgia Historical Quarterly* 73 (1989): 492–518.

———. "The Exercise of Sovereignty in Cherokee Georgia." *Journal of the Early Republic* 10 (1990): 43–63.

11. Chickasaws

Baird, W. David. *The Chickasaw People*. Phoenix: Indian Tribal Series, 1974.

Part of a series of books intended for a general audience.

Gibson, Arrell M. *The Chickasaws*. Norman: University of Oklahoma Press, 1971.

Dated but useful study frames Chickasaw history in terms of "full-bloods" versus "mixed bloods."

Hale, Duane K., and Arrell M. Gibson. *The Chickasaw*. New York: Chelsea House, 1991.

Written for a nonscholarly audience.

Journal of Chickasaw History. Chickasaw Historical Society (1995–).

Littlefield, Daniel F., Jr. *The Chickasaw Freedmen: A People Without a Country.* Westport, Conn.: Greenwood, 1980.

The best of Littlefield's books on Native Southerners and African Americans, this work chronicles the unsuccessful attempt of freedmen to gain citizenship in the Chickasaw Nation.

Nairne, Thomas. *Nairne's Muskhogean Journals.*

See under Published Primary Sources.

Swanton, John R. "Social and Religious Beliefs and Usages of the Chickasaw Indians." *Forty-Fourth Annual Report of the Bureau of American Ethnology.* Washington, D.C.: Government Printing Office, 1928.

Classic account of Chickasaw culture.

12. Choctaws

Baird, W. David. *The Choctaw People.* Phoenix: Indian Tribal Series, 1973.

Written for a general audience.

Baird, W. David. *Peter Pitchlynn: Chief of the Choctaws.* Norman: University of Oklahoma Press, 1972.

Biography of a Choctaw political leader in the early nineteenth century.

Blanchard, Kendall. *The Mississippi Choctaws at Play: The Serious Side of Leisure.* Urbana: University of Illinois Press, 1981.

Documents persistence in the cultural values associated with sports ranging from traditional stickball to modern basketball and football.

Blitz, John H. *An Archaeological Study of the Mississippi Choctaw Indians.*

See under Archaeological Studies.

Byington, Cyrus. *A Dictionary of the Choctaw Language.* Edited by John R. Swanton and H. S. Halbert. Bureau of American Ethnology Bulletin No. 46. Washington, D.C.: Government Printing Office, 1915.

Carson, James Taylor. *Searching for the Bright Path: The Mississippi Choctaws from Prehistory to Removal.* Lincoln: University of Nebraska Press, 1999.

Excellent recent ethnohistorical study links nineteenth-century Choctaw life and Mississippian antecedents.

Debo, Angie. *The Rise and Fall of the Choctaw Republic*. Norman: University of Oklahoma Press, 1934.

The classic book on Choctaw history in Indian Territory.

Densmore, Frances. *Choctaw Music*. Bureau of American Ethnology Bulletin No. 136. Washington, D.C.: Government Printing Office, 1943.

DeRosier, Arthur H., Jr. *The Removal of the Choctaw Indians*. Knoxville: University of Tennessee Press, 1970.

Factual but not ethnohistorical.

Faiman-Silva, Sandra. *Choctaws at the Crossroads: The Political Economy of Class and Culture in the Oklahoma Timber Region*. Lincoln: University of Nebraska Press, 1997.

Ethnographic study of Choctaw timber industry workers in contemporary Oklahoma.

Ferrara, Peter J. *The Choctaw Revolution: Lessons for Federal Indian Policy*. Washington, D.C.: Americans for Tax Reform Foundation, 1998.

Details the recent "economic miracle" of the Mississippi Choctaws under the leadership of Chief Phillip Martin.

Galloway, Patricia. *Choctaw Genesis, 1500–1700*. Lincoln: University of Nebraska Press, 1995.

Important interpretation of the origins of the Choctaw tribe.

Gregory, Hiram F. "Jena Band of Louisiana Choctaw." *American Indian Journal* 3 (1977): 2–16.

Kidwell, Clara Sue. *Choctaws and Missionaries in Mississippi, 1818–1918*. Norman: University of Oklahoma Press, 1995.

Chronicles the role of missionaries in the political and cultural life of the Choctaws.

Kidwell, Clara Sue, and Charles Roberts. *The Choctaws: A Critical Bibliography*.

See under Bibliographies and Finding Aids.

McKee, Jesse O. *The Choctaw*. New York: Chelsea House, 1989.

For a nonscholarly audience.

McKee, Jesse O., and Jon A. Schlenker. *The Choctaws: Cultural Evolution of a Native American Tribe*. Jackson: University Press of Mississippi, 1980.

Standard ethnography of the Mississippi Choctaws.

Reeves, Carolyn Keller, ed. *The Choctaw Before Removal*. Jackson: University Press of Mississippi, 1985.

Collection of uneven essays.

Smith, Allene DeShazo. *Greenwood LeFlore and the Choctaw Indians of the Mississippi Valley*. Memphis: Davis, 1951.

Dated but entertaining biography of a colorful figure in Choctaw and Mississippi politics.

Swanton, John R. *Source Material for the Social and Ceremonial Life of the Choctaw Indians*. Bureau of American Ethnology Bulletin No. 103. Washington, D.C.: Government Printing Office, 1931.

Classic early Choctaw ethnography.

Wells, Samuel J., and Roseanna Tubby, eds. *After Removal: The Choctaw in Mississippi*. Jackson: University Press of Mississippi, 1986.

The essay by Ronald Satz in this collection is the best summary of postremoval Mississippi Choctaw history.

White, Richard. *The Roots of Dependency: Subsistence, Environment, and Social Change Among the Choctaws, Pawnees, and Navajos*. Lincoln: University of Nebraska Press, 1983.

Interesting application of world systems theory to Native American tribes. The Choctaw section covers the period to removal.

13. Creeks

Baird, W. David, ed. *A Creek Warrior for the Confederacy*.

See under Published Primary Sources.

Braund, Kathryn E. Holland. *Deerskins and Duffels: Creek Indian Trade with Anglo-America, 1685–1815*. Lincoln: University of Nebraska Press, 1993.

Study of Creek involvement in trade with South Carolina and Georgia. Pays considerable attention to the cultural impact of the trade on the Creeks.

Buckner, Henry Frieland. *A Grammar of the Maskwke or Creek Language*. Marion, Ala.: Domestic and Indian Mission Board of the Southern Baptist Convention, 1860.

Caughey, John W. *McGillivray of the Creeks*.

See under Published Primary Sources.

Corkran, David. *The Creek Frontier, 1540–1783*. Norman: University of Oklahoma Press, 1967.

Traditional history of Indian-white relations.

Current-Garcia, Eugene, ed., with Dorothy B. Hatfield. *Shem, Ham and Japheth*.

See under Published Primary Sources.

Debo, Angie. *The Road to Disappearance*. Norman: University of Oklahoma Press, 1941.

The standard history of the Creeks, with an emphasis on the period from removal to Oklahoma statehood.

Doster, James F. *The Creek Indians and their Florida Lands, 1740–1823*. 2 vols. New York: Garland, 1974.

Gatschet, Albert S. *A Migration Legend of the Creek Indians, with a Linguistic, History, and Ethnographic Introduction*. Philadelphia: Brinton's Library of Aboriginal American Literature, 1884.

This and the following study by Gatschet are among the earliest attempts by a scholar to link linguistic and historical study of the Creeks.

———. "Tchikilli's Kasi'hta Legend in the Creek and Hitchiti Languages with a Critical Commentary and Full Glossaries to Both Texts." *Transactions of the Academy of Science of St. Louis* 5 (1888): 33–239.

Grant, C. L., ed. *Letters, Journals and Writings of Benjamin Hawkins*.

See under Published Primary Sources.

Green, Donald E. *The Creek People*. Phoenix: Indian Tribal Series, 1973.
Written for a general audience.

Green, Michael D. *The Creeks: A Critical Bibliography*.
See under Bibliographies and Finding Aids.

————. *The Politics of Indian Removal: Creek Government and Society in Crisis*. Lincoln: University of Nebraska Press, 1982.
Creek political history during the removal crisis, 1815–1836.

————. *The Creeks*. New York: Chelsea House, 1990.
For young readers or a nonacademic audience.

Griffith, Benjamin W., Jr. *McIntosh and Weatherford, Creek Indian Leaders*. Tuscaloosa: University of Alabama Press, 1988.
Combined biography of two important early nineteenth-century Creek leaders.

Halbert, H. S., and T. H. Ball. *The Creek War of 1813 and 1814*. Chicago: Donohue and Henneberry, 1895. Reprint, with introduction by Frank L. Owsley Jr. Birmingham: University of Alabama Press, 1969.
The classic early history of the Creek civil war.

Henri, Florette. *The Southern Indians and Benjamin Hawkins, 1796–1816*. Norman: University of Oklahoma Press, 1986.
Study of the agent most responsible for the cultural transformation of Southern Indians.

Knight, Vernon James, Jr. *Tukabatchee*.
See under Archaeological Studies.

Kosmider, Alexia. *Tricky Tribal Discourse: The Poetry, Short Stories, and Fus Fixico Letters of Creek Writer Alex Posey*. Moscow: University of Idaho Press, 1998.
Literary analysis of Posey's work that links it to the Creek oral literary tradition.

Littlefield, Daniel F., Jr. *Africans and Creeks: From the Colonial Period to the Civil War*. Westport, Conn.: Greenwood, 1979.

Study of African Americans, primarily slaves but also free people, among the Creeks and the tensions that their presence created.

———. *Alex Posey: Creek Poet, Journalist, and Humorist*. Lincoln: University of Nebraska Press, 1992.

Biography of Alexander Posey, author of the "Fus Fixico" letters. Published in the late nineteenth and early twentieth century in Indian Territory newspapers, the letters offered satirical commentary on contemporary political conditions, especially the allotment of Creek lands and the breakup of the Creek Nation.

Littlefield, Daniel F. Jr., and Carol A. Petty Hunter, eds. *The Fus Fixico Letters of Alexander Posey*.

See under Published Primary Sources.

Lomawaima, K. Tsianina. *They Called It Prairie Light: The Story of the Chilocco Indian School*. Lincoln: University of Nebraska Press, 1994.

History of an important boarding school, written by a Creek scholar and based on interviews with former students.

Loughridge, Robert M., and David M. Hodge. *English and Muskogee Dictionary*. St. Louis: J. T. Smith, 1890.

Martin, Joel W. *Sacred Revolt: The Muskogees' Struggle for a New World*. Boston: Beacon, 1991.

Discussion of the religious causes of the Redstick Movement and the Creek civil war.

Milfort, Louis LeClerc. *Memoirs: or, A Cursory Glance at My Different Travels and My Sojourn in the Creek Nation*.

See under Published Primary Sources.

Nairne, Thomas. *Nairne's Muskhogean Journals*.

See under Published Primary Sources.

Owsley, Frank Lawrence, Jr. *Struggle for the Gulf Borderlands: The Creek War and the Battle of New Orleans, 1812–1815*. Gainesville: University Presses of Florida, 1981.

Places the Creek War in the context of the War of 1812.

Posey, Alexander. *Poems of Alexander Posey, Creek Indian Bard*. Muskogee: Hoffman, 1969 [1910].

Pound, Merritt. *Benjamin Hawkins, Indian Agent*. Athens: University of Georgia Press, 1951.

Old-fashioned biography that is not nearly as interesting as its subject.

Saunt, Claudio. *A New Order of Things: Property, Power, and the Transformation of the Creek Indians, 1733–1816*. Cambridge: Cambridge University Press, 1999.

Examines the role of the growing inequity of wealth among Creeks in culture change.

Stiggins, George. *Creek Indian History*.

See under Published Primary Sources.

Sturtevant, William C. "Creek into Seminole." *North American Indians in Historical Perspective*. Edited by Eleanor Leacock and Nancy O. Lurie. New York: Random House, 1971.

Important discussion of the cultural similarities and differences between the Creeks and Seminoles.

Swanton, John R. *Early History of the Creek Indians and their Neighbors*. Bureau of American Ethnology Bulletin No. 73. Washington, D.C.: Government Printing Office, 1922.

Histories of each of the Creek towns.

———. "Religious Beliefs and Medical Practices of the Creek Indians." *Forty-Second Annual Report of the Bureau of American Ethnology*. Washington, D.C.: Government Printing Office, 1928.

Scholarly discussion of the Creek belief system.

———. "Social Organization and Social Usages of the Creek Confederacy." *Forty-Second Annual Report of the Bureau of American Ethnology*. Washington, D.C.: Government Printing Office, 1928.

Ethnography of Creek social and political culture.

Warde, Mary Jane. *George Washington Grayson and the Creek Nation, 1843–1920*. Norman: University of Oklahoma Press, 1999.

Biography of an important Creek public figure is the best history of the Creek Nation in the second half of the nineteenth century currently in print.

Waring, Antonio. *Laws of the Creek Nation*.

See under Published Primary Sources.

Womack, Craig S. *Red on Red: Native American Literary Separatism*. Minneapolis: University of Minnesota Press, 1999.

An important study of Creek literature by a Creek literary scholar who develops the linkage between a people's literature and their national identity.

Wright, J. Leitch, Jr. *Creeks and Seminoles: The Destruction and Regeneration of the Muscogulge People*. Lincoln: University of Nebraska Press, 1986.

Argues that ethnic differences divided the Creek Nation. Problematic thesis.

14. Lumbees

Blu, Karen I. *The Lumbee Problem: The Making of an American Indian People*. Cambridge: Cambridge University Press, 1980.

Calls into question traditional markers of Indian identity. The "problem" is not the Lumbees but the difficulties scholars encounter in trying to make this tribe fit interpretive models.

Dial, Adolph L. *The Lumbee*. New York: Chelsea House, 1993.

Written for a general audience by a distinguished tribal member.

Dial, Adolph L., and David K. Eliades. *The Only Land I Know: A History of the Lumbee Indians*. San Francisco: Indian Historian Press, 1975.

Based on oral tradition as well as documentary evidence.

Evans, W. McKee. *To Die Game: The Story of the Lowry Band, Indian Guerrillas of Reconsruction*. Baton Rouge: Louisiana State University Press, 1971.

Wonderful study of this conflict and its role in Reconstruction racial politics.

Sider, Gerald M. *Lumbee Indian Histories: Race, Ethnicity, and Indian Identity in the Southern United States*. Cambridge: Cambridge University Press, 1993.

A fascinating and frustrating reverse chronology that examines the issues that divide Lumbee people.

15. Powhatans

Barbour, Philip L. *Pocahontas and Her World*. Boston: Houghton Mifflin, 1970.

Biography of Pocahontas written within the context of the early seventeenth-century history of relations between the Powhatans and the Virginians.

Gleach, Frederic W. *Powhatan's World and Colonial Virginia: A Conflict of Cultures*. Lincoln: University of Nebraska Press, 1997.

Good recent ethnohistorical interpretation of the Powhatan chiefdom and its relations with early Virginia.

Potter, Stephen R. *Commoners, Tribute, and Chiefs: The Development of Algonquian Culture in the Potomac Valley*. Charlottesville: University Press of Virginia, 1993.

Ethnohistorical study of the development of chiefdoms in the Potomac River valley written largely from the archaeological record.

Rountree, Helen C. *The Powhatan Indians of Virginia: Their Traditional Culture*. Norman: University of Oklahoma Press, 1989.

Comprehensive ethnographic study of Powhatan culture.

——. *Pocahontas's People: The Powhatan Indians of Virginia Through Four Centuries*. Norman: University of Oklahoma Press, 1990.

Excellent history of the Powhatans from that carries their story to the present. The chapters on the early twentieth century are particularly strong.

Rountree, Helen C., ed. *Powhatan Foreign Relations, 1500–1722*. Charlottesville: University Press of Virginia, 1993.

Sheehan, Bernard. *Savagism and Civility: Indians and Englishmen in Colonial Virginia*. London: Cambridge University Press, 1980.

Looks at both the conflict of cultures and the assumptions Englishmen made about Native people.

Strachey, William. *The Historie of Travell Into Virginia Britania*.

See under Published Primary Sources.

Woodward, Grace Steele. *Pocahontas*. Norman: University of Oklahoma Press, 1969.

Factual account with little cultural context.

16. Seminoles and Miccosukees

Covington, James W. *The Seminoles of Florida*. Gainesville: University Press of Florida, 1993.

Rather pedestrian survey of Seminole history in Florida.

Garbarino, Merwyn S. *The Seminole*. New York: Chelsea House, 1989.

For a general audience.

Howard, James H. *Oklahoma Seminoles: Medicines, Magic, and Religion*. Norman: University of Oklahoma Press, 1984.

Ethnographic description and analysis of Oklahoma Seminole religious culture.

Kersey, Harry A., Jr. *Pelts, Plumes, and Hides: White Traders Among the Seminole Indians, 1870–1930*. Gainesville: University Presses of Florida, 1975.

Examines the ways in which the Seminoles entered the late nineteenth-century international market economy and fell victim to its vicissitudes.

———. *The Seminole and Miccosukee Tribes: A Critical Bibliography*.

See under Bibliographies and Finding Aids.

———. *The Florida Seminoles and the New Deal, 1933–1942*. Boca Raton: Florida Atlantic University Press, 1989.

Case study of the conflict generated by the Indian Reorganization Act within the Indian community.

————. *An Assumption of Sovereignty: Social and Political Transformation Among the Florida Seminoles, 1953–1979*. Lincoln: University of Nebraska Press, 1996.

Explores the remarkable creativity of the Seminoles in expanding sovereignty and asserting their rights.

Lancaster, Jane F. *Removal Aftershock: The Seminoles' Struggle to Survive in the West, 1836–1866*. Knoxville: University of Tennessee Press, 1994.

Littlefield, Daniel F., Jr. *Africans and Seminoles: From Removal to Emancipation*. Westport, Conn.: Greenwood, 1977.

————. *Seminole Burning: A Story of Racial Vengeance*. Jackson: University Press of Mississippi, 1996.

Account of the lynching of two young Seminole men accused of murder in late nineteenth-century Indian Territory. Explores racial tensions on the eve of Oklahoma statehood.

McReynolds, Edwin C. *The Seminoles*. Norman: University of Oklahoma Press, 1957.

The standard history of the Seminoles.

Mahon, John K. *History of the Second Seminole War: 1835–1842*. Gainesville: University Presses of Florida, 1967.

A conventional, well-documented history of this conflict.

Schultz, Jack M. *The Seminole Baptist Churches of Oklahoma: Maintaining a Traditional Community*. Norman: University of Oklahoma Press, 1999.

A fascinating ethnographic study of how Seminole Baptist Churches help their members preserve and maintain community and identity.

Sturtevant, William C. "Creek Into Seminole."

See under Creeks.

Weisman, Brent Richards. *Like Beads on a String: A Culture History of the Seminole Indians in North Peninsular Florida*. Tuscaloosa: University of Alabama Press, 1989.

————. *Unconquered People: Florida's Seminole and Miccosukee Indians.*
Gainesville: University Press of Florida, 1999.

Disappointing summary: too technical for non-archaeologists, too cursory for scholars.

West, Patsy. *The Enduring Seminoles: From Alligator Wrestling to Ecotour-
ism.* Gainseville: University Press of Florida, 1998.

Demonstrates that tourism made a traditional Seminole lifestyle feasi-
ble for some Seminole bands. Great photos poorly reproduced.

Wickman, Patricia Riles. *Osceola's Legacy.* Tuscaloosa: University of Alabama Press, 1991.

Fascinating study of the legend and personal effects of Osceola and the
attraction they hold for non-Indians.

————. *The Tree That Bends: Discourse, Power, and the Survival of the Maskoki People.* Tuscaloosa: University of Alabama Press, 1999.

A cultural history of the Native peoples of Florida in the sixteenth to
the eighteenth centuries.

Wright, J. Leitch, Jr. *Creeks and Seminoles.*

See under Creeks.

17. Selected Fiction

Bell, Betty Louise (Cherokee). *Faces in the Moon.* Norman: University of
Oklahoma Press, 1994.

The story of a contemporary Cherokee woman and the community of
women in which she grew up.

Carter, Forrest. *The Education of Little Tree.* New York: Delacorte, 1976.

Extraordinarily sensitive account of a young Cherokee boy growing up
in east Tennessee. Falsely represented as a memoir when first published,
this work was later exposed as a fictional account written by a white
man renowned for his racist attitudes toward African Americans. Un-
fortunately, these circumstances seriously detract from a really good
book.

Conley, Robert J. (Cherokee). *The Witch of Going Snake and Other Stories*. Norman: University of Oklahoma Press, 1988.

Cherokee oral tradition plays a major role in these short stories.

———. *Mountain Wind Song: A Novel of the Trail of Tears*. Norman: University of Oklahoma Press, 1992.

Glancy, Diane (Cherokee). *Pushing the Bear: A Novel of the Trail of Tears*. New York: Harcourt, Brace, 1996.

Howe, LeAnne (Choctaw). "Indians Never Say Goodbye." *Reinventing the Enemy's Language: Contemporary Native Women Writings of North America*. Edited by Joy Harjo and Gloria Bird. New York: Norton, 1997.

Hudson, Joyce Rockwood. *Apalachee*. Athens: University of Georgia Press, 2000.

Focuses on the experiences of an Apalachee woman in the early eighteenth century when Creek slave raiders and English colonists invaded north Florida.

Humphreys, Josephine. *Nowhere Else on Earth*. New York: Viking, 2000.

Fictionalized account of Rhoda, the wife of Lumbee guerrilla leader Henry Berry Lowrie.

Littlefield, Daniel F. Jr. (Cherokee), and James W. Parins, eds. *Native American Writing in the Southeast: An Anthology, 1875–1935*. Jackson: University Press of Mississippi, 1995.

McMurtry, Larry, and Diana Ossana. *Zeke and Ned*. New York: Pocket Books, 1997.

Set in post-Civil War Indian Territory.

Posey, Alexander (Creek). *Poems*.

See under Creeks.

Rockwood, Joyce. *Long Man's Song*. New York: Holt, Rinehart and Winston, 1975.

Matrilineal kinship forms the cultural backdrop of this precontact coming-of-age story.

———. *To Spoil the Sun*. New York: Holt, Rinehart and Winston, 1976.

The impact of European disease on the Cherokees is the historical context of this novel.

18. Films

Documentaries

The American Indian Speaks (1973). Encyclopedia Brittanica Educational
   Corporation.

  A Muskogee Creek remembers the Trail of Tears.

Black Warriors of the Seminole (1990). Public Broadcasting System.

  This Emmy Award-winning PBS documentary focuses on the alliance
  between the Seminole Indians of Florida and African Americans.

Broken Journey (1989). Creek Nation Communications.

  Targeted at Native American youth, the film takes a serious look at the
  problem of alcoholism among Indian people.

Cherokee (1976). British Broadcasting Corporation.

  Concise history of the Cherokees and removal; profiles Eastern Cherokee "Unto These Hills" outdoor drama.

Cherokee Artist Series. Shenandoah Film Productions.

  Series has episodes on Jerome Tiger, Willard Stone, Bill Rabbit, Wood-
  row Haney, and Charkes Banks.

Cherokee History Series. Shenandoah Film Productions.

  Series of five films, four of them available in adult or elementary versions, chronicle Cherokee history to 1880.

Civilized Tribes (1976). British Broadcasting Corporation.

  Profiles of Hollywood, Florida Seminoles and Mississippi Choctaws.

Concerns of Native American Women (1977). Public Broadcasting System.

  Dr. Connie Uri, Cherokee physician and law student, is profiled.

The Corn Lady (1991). Betty Mae Jumper.

  Former tribal chairman Betty Mae Jumper tells Seminole stories.

500 Nations (1995). Kevin Costner.

  Overview includes the Southeast.

Four Corners of Earth (1985). WFSU-TV.

Explores culture and lives of Seminole women.

How the West Was Lost:
Unconquered, The Trail of Tears, and *As Long as the Grass Shall Grow*
(1995). The Discovery Channel and 9K*USA.

Three episodes in this series deal with early contact, the removal era, and the allotment period.

Indians, Outlaws, and Angie Debo (1988). WGBH-TV.

Chronicles the professional career of historian Angie Debo, whose research revealed a state conspiracy to rob Indians of land in Oklahoma.

Journey to the Sky: A History of the Alabama Coushatta Indians (1982). Paul Yeager.

Through the use of a folktale, the film chronicles the Alabama Coushatta struggle to preserve their lifeways after contact with the Europeans.

Joy Harjo, Creek Poet (1989). Lannan Foundation.

Focuses on the most prominent twentieth-century Southeastern Native poet.

The Keetoowahs Come Home (1997). Larry Foley.

Follows the United Keetoowah Band's attempt to relocate from Oklahoma to Arkansas.

Land of the Eagles: The Great Encounter (1992). PBS Video.

Lost in Time and *The First Frontier* (1983). Auburn Television.

Traces history of Alabama's first inhabitants.

Make My People Live: The Crisis in Indian Health Care (1984). WGBH-TV.

Health care issues facing four tribes, including the Creeks.

Music of the Creek and Cherokee Indians in Religion and Government.

Music of the Sacred Fire: The Stomp Dance of the Oklahoma Cherokee.

Nations Within a Nation (1988). Oklahoma State University Department of Sociology.

Examines historical, legal, and social background of Native American tribal sovereignty, including the Creek Nation.

Native American Myths (1977). Encyclopedia Brittanica Education Corporation.

Cherokee "First Strawberry" myth is included.

The Native Americans: The Southeast (1994). Turner Broadcasting System.

Part of a series on Native Americans.

A Native Presence. The Kentucky Network.

Explores the influence of Native culture and the contributions of contemporary Native people in Kentucky.

On the Path to Self-Reliance (1982). Peter J. Barton.

Documentary of the Seminole Tribe of Florida provides an overview of tribal history and current economic development.

Real Indian (1996). Malinda Maynor.

Focusing on her own experiences growing up Lumbee, Maynor explores what it means to be a "real Indian."

The Way (1975). Brigham Young University Native American Studies.

Discussion of Native American religion; set in Cherokee Nation, Oklahoma.

The Way West:
Westward, The Course of Europe Makes Its Way and *The Approach of Civilization* (1995). PBS.

Series has two episodes that touch on the Southeast.

The West:
The People and *Empire Upon the Trails* (1996). PBS.

Two episodes in the series deal with Southeastern Indians.

Wilma P. Mankiller: Woman of Power (1992). Mary Scott.

An interview with Wilma Mankiller during her tenure as principal chief of the Cherokee Nation of Oklahoma.

Hollywood Depictions

> Perhaps because they do not fit American stereotypes of Native people, filmmakers have not been very interested in dramatizing the history of Southeastern Indians. The following feature films do include depictions of Native Southerners.

Cimarron (1931)

> The Best Picture of 1931 chronicles one family's experiences in the restless days of settling the American West. Adapted from Edna Ferber's sweeping novel, the story tracks the growth of an Oklahoma town and the homesteaders who came there from the 1890s through the 1920s.

Distant Drums (1951)

> A small but daring group of men ventures into the Florida Everglades to battle the hostile Seminole Indians during their rebellion of 1840 in this tepid adventure movie.

Davy Crockett and the River Pirates (1954)

> The legendary career of Davy Crockett is presented with humor and excitement. He encounters Chickasaws in this film.

Davy Crockett, King of the Wild Frontier (1955)

> Fess Parker plays the famous Indian scout with Buddy Ebsen as his pal George Russel, whose adventures take them from Washington, D.C., to the Alamo. He encounters Southern Indians along the way. Originally filmed as three episodes of the television series.

Naked in the Sun (1955)

> Slave traders, who usually capture and sell Africans, begin doing the same thing with Seminole Indians. Soon, the Native Americans lead a bloody revolt.

Daniel Boone, Trail Blazer (1956)

> Set in 1775, Daniel Boone takes his family far west to build Fort Boone despite the danger of Indian attack, which, of course, materializes. The following are lesser known films:

Fate's Chessboard (1916)
Diane of the Green Van (1917)

The Conquerer (1917)
The Frontiersman (1927)
Drums of Destiny (1937)
Man of Conquest (1939)
Tap Roots (1948)
Ranger of Cherokee Strip (1949)
Cherokee Uprising (1949)
Rose of Cimarron (1949)
Seminole (1951)
Seminole Uprising (1954)
Oklahoma Territory (1960)

Sources on films:
Alan Gevinson, ed. *Within Our Gates: Ethnicity in America, Feature Films, 1911–1960*. Berkeley: University of California Press, 1997.
Elizabeth Weatherford, ed. *Native Americans on Film and Video*. New York: Museum of the American Indian, 1981.
http://www.lib.berkeley.edu/MRC/imagesnatives.html

19. Museums and Sites

National

The following museums and archaeological sites are located outside the South. The museums are of national importance and contain Southeastern artifacts. The sites relate to cultural developments in the Southeast.

Angel Mounds State Memorial (Mississippian), near Evansville, Ind.
Cahokia (Mississippian), East St. Louis, Ill.
Field Museum, Chicago, Ill.
Mound City Group National Monument (Woodland), near Chillocothe, Ohio
Peabody Museum, Harvard University, Andover, Mass.
Serpent Mound State Memorial (Adena: early Woodland), near Locust Grove, Ohio
Smithsonian Institution, Washington, D.C.:
National Museum of American History
National Museum of the American Indian (under construction in 2001)
National Museum of Natural History

ALABAMA

Alabama Museum of Natural History, University of Alabama, Tuscaloosa
Fort Toulouse State Park, near Montgomery
Horseshoe Bend National Military Park, near Danville
Indian Mound (Mississippian), Florence
Mound State Monument (Mississippian), near Tuscaloosa
Russell Cave Monument (Paleo-Indian), near Mt. Carmel

ARKANSAS

Arkansas State University Museum, Jonesboro
Hampson Museum, Wilson
Henderson State College Museum, Arkadelphia
Museum of Science and Natural History, Little Rock
Toltec Mounds State Park (aka Knapp Mounds, Woodland), near Little Rock
University of Arkansas Museum, Fayetteville

FLORIDA

Castillo de San Marcos, National Monument (built on Native site), St. Augustine
Crystal River State Archaeological Site (Woodland), Crystal River
Florida State Museum, University of Florida, Gainesville
Fort Caroline National Memorial (Timucuan artifacts), Jacksonville
Fort Matanzas National Monument (Woodland through historic), near St. Augustine
Gulf Shores Islands National Seashore (Santa Rosa-Swift Creek Culture), Gulf Breeze
Historical Museum of Southern Florida, Miami
Jacksonville Museum of Arts and Sciences
Lake Jackson Mounds, State Archaeological Site (Mississippian), near Tallahassee
Madira Bickel Mound, State Archaeological Site (Woodland and Mississippian), near Bradenton
Safety Harbor Site (late prehistoric–Timucuan), Safety Harbor
South Florida Museum and Planetarium, Bradenton
Temple Mound Museum (several cultures represented), Fort Walton Beach
Turtle Mound, (shell midden- several cultures), New Smyrna Beach
University of Miami, Library, Archives and Special Collections

GEORGIA

Atlanta History Center
Chieftans Museum (Major Ridge's House), Rome

Columbus Museum of Arts and Sciences
Etowah Mounds, (Mississippian), near Cartersville
Kolomoki Mounds State Park (Mississippian), near Blakely
McInstosh's Indian Springs Tavern (belonged to William McIntosh), near
    Jackson
New Echota State Historic Site (Cherokee capitol), near Cartersville
Ocmulgee National Monument (Mississippian), near Macon
Rock Eagle Effigy Mound (Mississippian), near Eatonton
Track Rock Archaeological Area, Chattahoochee National Forest (Archaic),
    near Blairsville
Vann House (Cherokee Joseph Vann's mansion), Chatsworth

KENTUCKY
Adena Park (Woodland), near Lexington
Ancient Buried City (aka Kings Mounds, Mississippian), near Wickliffe
Behringer Museum of Natural History (Adena materials), Covington
Blue Licks Museum (Fort Ancient), Blue Licks Springs
Kentucky Historical Society, Frankfort
Mammoth Cave National Park (Archaic), near Cave City

LOUISIANA
The Historic New Orleans Collection
Louisiana State Exhibit Museum, Shreveport
Marksville State Commemorative Area (Archaic), Marksville
Northwestern State University, Williamson Museum, Natchitoches
Poverty Point State Commemorative Area (Archaic), near Epps

MISSISSIPPI
Bear Creek Mounds (from Paleo-Indian), off Natchez Trace Parkway
Boyd Mounds (several cultures), off Natchez Trace Parkway
Bynum Mounds (Woodland), off Natchez Trace Parkway
Chickasaw Village Site, off Natchez Trace Parkway
Choctaw Agency, Bureau of Indian Affairs, Philadelphia
Emerald Mound (Mississippian), off Natchez Trace Parkway
Grand Village of the Natchez Indians (Mississippian), Natchez
Mangum Mound (several cultures), off Natchez Trace Parkway
Nanih Waiya Historic Site, near Louisville
Owl Creek Indian Mounds, Tombigbee National Forest (Mississippian),
    near Old Houlka

Pharr Mounds (Woodland), off Natchez Trace Parkway
State Historical Museum, Jackson
Tupelo Visitor Center, Natchez Trace Parkway, near Tupelo
Winterville Mounds State Park (Mississippian), near Greenville

MISSOURI
Line Creek Museum (Hopewell and Mississippian artifacts), Line Creek
    Park
Missouri State Museum, Jefferson City
Museum of Science and Natural History, St. Louis
School of the Ozarks, Ralph Foster Museum, Point Lookout
Southeast Missouri State University Museum, Cape Girardeau
Thousand Hills State Park (Woodland and Mississippian), near Kirksville
Towosahgy State park (Mississippian), near East Prairie
University of Missouri, Museum of Man, Art and Archaeology, Columbia
Washington State Park (Mississippian), near DeSoto

NORTH CAROLINA
Charlotte Nature Museum, Inc.
Greensboro Historical Museum
Guilford Native American Center, Greensboro
Morrow Mountain State Park Natural History Museum, near Albemarle
Museum of the Cherokee Indian, Cherokee
Museum of Man, Wake Forest University, Winston Salem
North Carolina Museum of History, Raleigh
Oconaluftee Indian Village, Cherokee
Roanoke Indian Village, Roanoke Island
Schiele Museum of Natural History, Gastonia
Town Creek Indian Mound, State Historic Site (Mississippian), near Mount
    Gilead

OKLAHOMA
Arrowhead Museum, Tishomingo
Cherokee Capital, Tahlequah
Cherokee Cultural Center, Park Hill
Choctaw Trail of Tears Museum, Eagletown
Creek Indian Museum, Okmulgee
Cultural Center Museum, Ponca City
East Central College Museum, Ada

Five Tribes Museum, Muskogee
Indian City U.S.A., near Anadarko
Kerr Museum, near Poteau
Memorial Indian Museum, Broken Bow
Murrell Home, Park Hill
Museum of the Red River, Idabel
Northern Oklahoma State University Museum, Alfa
Oklahoma Historical Society Archives, Oklahoma City
Seminole Museum, Wewoka
Spiro Mounds State Archaeological Site (Mississippian), near Spiro
Stovall Museum, University of Oklahoma, Norman
Thomas Gilcrease Institute, Tulsa
Washita Valley Museum, Pauls Valley
Woolaroc Museum, near Bartlesville

SOUTH CAROLINA
Santee Indian Mound (aka Scott's Lake Site, Mississippian), near Santee
Sewee Mound Archaeological Area, Francis Marion National Forest (shell
        midden, several cultures), near Charleston
South Carolina State Museum, Columbia
University of South Carolina Museum, Columbia

TENNESSEE
Chucalissa Indian Town and Museum (late Woodland), Memphis
Cumberland Gap National Historic Park (several cultures), near Harrogate
Cumberland Museum and Science Center, Nashville
Lookout Mountain Museum, near Chattanooga
McClung Museum, University of Tennessee, Knoxville
Old Stone Fort State Park (Woodland), near Manchester
Pinson Mounds State Archaeological Area (Woodland), near Jackson
Shiloh Mounds, Shiloh National Military Park (Mississippian), near Savannah
Travelers' Rest Historic House, near Nashville

TEXAS
Alabama-Coushatta Indian Museum, near Livingston on Alabama-Coushatta
        Reservation
Caddoan Mounds State Historical Site (Mississippian), near Alto
Texas Memorial Museum, University of Texas, Austin
Washington Square Mound Site (Mississippian), Nacogdoches

VIRGINIA
Colonial National Historical Park, Jamestown Visitor Center
Historic Crab Orchard Museum (Woodland), Tazewell
Pamunkey Indian Museum, King William
Thunderbird Museum and Archaeological Park (several cultures), Front
    Royal

20. Internet Resources

Bureau of Indian Affairs
    www.doi.gov.bureau-indian-affairs.html

    The Bureau of Indian Affairs provides information on federally recog-
    nized tribes, maps of Indian land holdings, and a guide to tracing Native
    American ancestry.

Index of Native American Resources on the Internet
    http://hanksville.phasts.umass.edu/misc/Naresources.html

    This site provides links to hundreds of other sites, including many on
    the Southeast.

NativeWeb
    www.nativeweb.org

    Contains historical and cultural information as well as notices of cur-
    rent issues and events.

Many tribes in the Southeast maintain Web pages. Some of those addresses
are listed below:

Alabama and Coushatta Tribes of Texas
    www.livingston.net/chamber/actribe
Catawba Tribe of South Carolina
    www.southcarolina-info.com/hist/indians/catawba
Cherokee Nation of Oklahoma
    www.cherokee.org
Cherokee Tribe of Northeast Alabama
    www.tsalagi.org
Chickahominy Eastern Division
    www.vmnh.org/tribes.htm

Chickahominy Indian Tribe
   www.vmnh.org/tribes.htm
Chickasaw Nation of Oklahoma
   www.chickasaw.net
Choctaw Nation of Oklahoma
   www.choctawnation.com
Eastern Band of Cherokees
   www.cherokee-nc.com
Echota Cherokee Tribe of Alabama
   http://echota-cherokee.hypermart.net/
Florida Governor's Council on Indian Affairs, Inc.
   www.fgcia.com
Georgia Council of Native American Concerns
   www.ganet.org/indcouncil
Louisiana Office of Indian Affairs
   www.indianaffairs.com
Lumbee Regional Development Association
   www.lumbee-tribe.org
Mattaponi Indian Reservation
   www.baylink.org/Mattaponi
Meherrin Indian Tribe
   www.charweb.org/neighbors/na/meherrin.htm
Mississippi Band of Choctaws
   www.choctaw.org
Monacan Indian Tribe
   mnation538@aol.com
Muskogee Nation of Oklahoma
   www.ocevnet.org/creek.html
Nansemond Indian Tribal Association
   www.nasemond.nativeland.com
North Carolina Commission of Indian Affairs
   www.doa.state.nc.us/doa/cia/indian.htm
Pamunkey Nation
   www.vmnh.org/tribes.htm
Poarch Band of Creeks
   www.oneida-nation.net/useet/Poarch
Seminole Nation of Oklahoma
   www.cowboy.net/native/seminole/index.html

Seminole Tribe of Florida
    www.seminoletribe.com
United Keetoowah Band of Cherokees
    www.uark.edu/depts/comminfo/IKB/welcome.html
United Rappahanock Tribe
    www.indians.vipnet.org/rapph.htm
Upper Mattaponi Tribe
    www.vmnh.org/tribes.htm
Virginia Council on Indians
    www.indians.vipnet.org/who.htm

Index

Page numbers in **boldface type** indicate articles in Part II, "People, Places, and Events, A to Z."

acculturation, 14–15
Acolapissas, 132
Adams, John Quincy, 86, 89, 210, 229
African Americans, 87, 136–41, 156, 212–13
Agricultural Adjustment Act, 135
agriculture, 3, 4, 45, 76, 100, **153–54**; cleared-field, 28; emergence of, **153–54**, 156, 223; in Missisippian period, 161–62, 185; Old World plants and, 153; plantation, 57; in Woodland period, 217–18; *see also individual crops*
AIM. *See* American Indian Movement
Alabama statehood, 228
Alabama-Coushattas, 141, 142; recognition of, 232; recognition restored, 236; termination of, 143, 235
"Alabama Fever," 80

Alabamas, 133, 226, 231; federal recognition of, 232
Alabama Territory, 228
Alberson, Isaac, 214
Alcatraz Island takeover, 182
alcohol. *See* liquor
Algonkian languages, **154**
Alligator Tales, 158
allotment, 111, 114–23, **154–55**, 161, 164, 189, 194; among Alabaman Creeks, 93–94; "civilization" and, 165; Creek, 230; for Eastern Creeks, 127; end of, 121, 179, 234; negotiations for, 183, 190; oil and, 119; opposition to, 168, 203–204; preparations for, 233; protection against, 169; results of, 121; sales of, 119–20; support for, 159; swindles and, 11, 119–20; Treaty of Washington and, **215**; types of,

Cherokees *(continued)*
government declared illegal,
88αrrassment of, 94–95; Hopewell
treaties with, 73, 74, **176**; invasion
by Union, 231; Iroquois alliance
with, 189; land cession by, 63, 228;
law code of, 15; migration of, 228;
mission schools and, 77;
nationalism of, 83–84; post–Civil
War government and, 112;
relations with Osages, 101;
remaining in East, 126, 127–28;
removal of, 94–97, 211, 230; role
in American Revolution, 68;
second defeat of, 69; slavery
abolition and, 167; suicide among,
42; system of jurisprudence of, 15;
"Trail of Tears" and, 97, 102, 200,
204; treaties with Virginia and, 73;
Treaty of Holston and, 75, 227;
Treaty of New Echota and, 230;
voluntary relocation of, 86–87; *see
also* Cherokee War
Cherokees, United Keetoowah Band,
of, 122, 235
Cherokee Supreme Court, 217
Cherokee syllabary, 84, 159, 228, 229
Cherokee Temperance Society, 171
Cherokee Tobacco Case, 115, 160, **162,**
232
Cherokee War, 66–67, 157, **162–63,**
189, 226
Chicago, Rock Island, and Pacific,
railroad, 109
Chicago Indian Conference, 184
Chichimec Wars, 51
Chickahominy, 139
Chickamaugas, 74, 227
Chickasaw District of the Choctaw,
Nation, 209
Chickasaw Oil and Gas Company,
119, 232

Chickasaws, 101, 154, 225; American
Civil War and, **165**; Carolina trade
alliance with, 64; Choctaws and,
103; constitution of 1856 and, 231;
constitution of 1983 and, 236;
control of Mississippi River by, 63;
government centralization of, 85;
Hopewell treaties and, 73, **176,**
191; land purchase by, 231;
mission schools and, 77; post–Civil
War government and, 112;
recording of laws by, 229; reject
intertribal constitution, 115;
removal of, 91–92, **197,** 208–209,
213–15, 230; as slave traders, 60,
63, 64; Treaty of Doaksville and,
230; Treaty of Pontotoc and, 91,
167, 206, **213–14,** 230; and wars
with French, 65
chickee (Seminole house), 177, 180
chiefdoms, 26–32, 28, **163,** 173, 185,
216, 223; collapse of, 43, 205;
origins of, 29; ranking of, 31
"chiefing," 130
chiefs, tribal: appointed by U.S.
president, 120
Chitimachas, 132–33, 141
Chitto Harjo, **163–64**
Choctaw, Oklahoma, and Gulf,
Railroad, 109
Choctaw Greetings Enterprise, 183
Choctaw Indians, Mississippi Band of,
127, 138–39, 141, 142, 179;
constitution of 1943 and, 234
Choctaws, 43, 63, 101, 154; and
alliance with French, 64; American
Civil War and, **165**; Chickasaws
and, 213; constitution of 1826 and,
84, 229; constitution of 1838 and,
230; constitution of 1860, 192;
constitution of 1984 and, 236;
education and, 194; educational